Contingent States

BORDERLINES

A BOOK SERIES CONCERNED WITH REVISIONING GLOBAL POLITICS
Edited by David Campbell and Michael J. Shapiro

For more books in the series, see p. vi.

Contingent States

Greater China and Transnational Relations

WILLIAM A. CALLAHAN

BORDERLINES, VOLUME 22

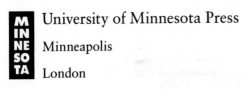

University of Minnesota Press

Minneapolis

London

"Lovers on Aran," from *Poems, 1965–1975*, by Seamus Heaney (New York: Farrar, Straus and Giroux, 1980). Copyright 1980 by Seamus Heaney. Reprinted by permission of Faber and Faber Ltd. and Farrar, Straus and Giroux, LLC.

A version of chapter 4 was originally published as "Negotiating Cultural Boundaries: Confucianism and Trans/national Identity in Korea," *Cultural Values* 3, no. 3 (1999): 329–64. Reprinted with permission.

Published by the University of Minnesota Press
111 Third Avenue South, Suite 290
Minneapolis, MN 55401-2520
http://www.upress.umn.edu

Library of Congress Cataloging-in-Publication Data

Callahan, William A.
  Contingent states : greater China and transnational relations / William A. Callahan.
      p.   cm. — (Borderlines ; 22)
  Includes bibliographical references and index.
  ISBN 0-8166-4399-7 (alk. paper) — ISBN 0-8166-4400-4 (pbk. : alk. paper)
  1. China—Civilization—1976– 2. China—Foreign relations—1976–
3. China—Politics and government—1976– I. Title. II. Borderlines (Minneapolis, Minn.) ; 22
  DS779.23.C36 2004
  951.05—dc22

2004003551

Printed in the United States of America on acid-free paper

The University of Minnesota is an equal-opportunity educator and employer.

12 11 10 09 08 07 06 05 04   10 9 8 7 6 5 4 3 2 1

To Sumalee

BORDERLINES

LOVERS ON ARAN

The timeless waves, bright sifting, broken glass,
Came dazzling around, into the rocks,
Came glinting, sifting from the Americas

To possess Aran. Or did Aran rush
To throw wide arms of rock around a tide
That yielded with an ebb, with a soft crash?

Did sea define the land or land the sea?
Each drew new meaning from the waves' collision.
Sea broke on land to full identity.

SEAMUS HEANEY

Contents

Acknowledgments

Generous and timely support for this research was supplied by the Korea Foundation Research Fellowship Program, the University of Durham Special Research Project Fund, the Universities' China Committee in London, the British Academy (South East Asia Committee), the Stanley Foundation, the University of Durham's Centre for Contemporary Chinese Studies, the University of Chicago's Globalization Project, and the University of Durham Staff Travel Fund. A British Academy fellowship at Harvard University in 2002–3 allowed me to track down elusive sources for the final version.

I would especially like to thank Michael J. Shapiro and Arif Dirlik for their critically helpful comments on this project over the years. For their hospitality during fieldwork, I would also like to thank Han Sang-Jin (Seoul National University) and Song Xinning (Renmin University, Beijing). The two reviewers for the University of Minnesota Press, Roland Bleiker and Christopher R. Hughes, helped shape this book through their constructive criticism.

David Armstrong, David Blaney, Shaun Breslin, Sumalee Bumroongsook, Sukanya Bumroongsook, David Campbell, Chaiwat Satha-Anand, Chen Zhimin, Bruce Cumings, Deng Yong, Anna Dickson, Mick Dillon, Sherry Gray, Liu Hong, Han Do-Hyun, Han Sang-Jin, Jia Qingguo, Jiang Nan, Alastair Iain Johnston, Craig Mulling, Liselotte Odgaard, Somchai Phatharathananund, Suwanna Satha-Anand, Elizabeth Sinn, Song Xinning, Thavesilp Subwattana,

James T. H. Tang, Marie Thorsten, R. B. J. Walker, Stephen Welch, Wei Zhong, Geoffrey White, Bob Williams, and Wu Yong have all added to this book with their incisive comments. Able research assistance was supplied by Koo Chong-wu, Sohn Hee-Jeong, Jung Jung-A, Park Hun-Bong (in South Korea), Mai Qiulin, Yang Min (in China), and Sumalee Bumroongsook (in Thailand). I have also benefited greatly from the guidance of Carrie Mullen and Jason Weidemann at the University of Minnesota Press.

I would also like to thank all the people who gave their time for interviews. Because we talked about sensitive topics, some interviewees in China and Thailand asked that I maintain their anonymity. In the text, they are listed only by time and place. Throughout the book I use the Hanyu pinyin romanization of Chinese, except for some names, such as Lee Teng-hui and Chiang Kai-shek, which are known in English by different romanizations. Unless otherwise noted, the translations from classical and modern Chinese are my own.

Periodical Abbreviations

BBC/SWB	British Broadcasting Corporation, Summary of World Broadcasts
BR	Beijing Review
CD	China Daily
CND	China News Digest (www.cnd.org)
FBIS	Foreign Broadcast Information Service
FEER	Far Eastern Economic Review
FT	Financial Times
IHT	International Herald Tribune
RMRB	Renmin ribao (People's Daily)
SCMP	South China Morning Post, Hong Kong
WP	Washington Post

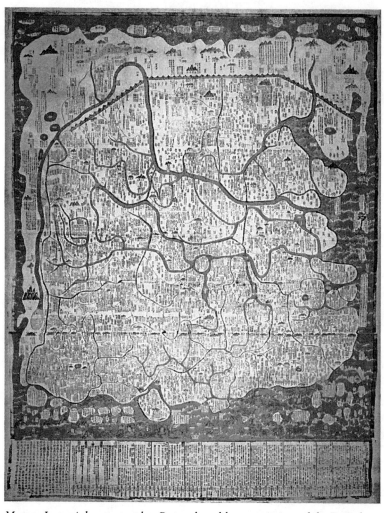

Map 1. Imperial cartography. Reproduced by permission of the British Library; Map 15406.a.28.

Introduction
Contingent Theory and East Asia

Asia is a source of fantasy for Euro-Americans, the site of dream lands such as Thomas More's *Utopia* at the dawn of the Enlightenment, as well as the Pacific Century's capitalist utopia of the East Asian economic miracle. The capitalist dystopia of the East Asian financial crisis, which in July 1997 turned the miracle into a curse, only served to reinforce the logic of Asia as the site of dream production. Although the September 11 attack on New York and Washington, D.C., provoked many to reconsider their understandings of global politics, it merely reinforced this utopian/dystopian image of Asia—and the power of images in international relations.

The contingency of power/knowledge relationships in Asia can be seen in the film *M. Butterfly*, which introduces such stereotypes and playfully subverts them before reasserting them in a reversed form (Cronenberg 1993; Hwang 1988, 94–100). The plot is loosely based on the true story of a French diplomat stationed in Beijing in the 1960s. In the film, the lead character René Gallimard falls in love with Song Liling, a Beijing Opera singer. But as the story develops, we see that he has not fallen in love with a real woman but with an image, a fantasy, the stereotype of the beautiful submissive Oriental woman. In this way, the film toys with Puccini's *Madame Butterfly*, the archetypal East-West Romance, giving it a postcolonial twist. Such stereotypes are not just Euro-American fantasies; Asians increasingly forge their own dreams and nightmares, exchanging fantasies in a complex symbolic economy.

Once René starts his affair, he is promoted from his boring accountancy position to be in charge of the French embassy's intelligence operations. He gets this promotion through his understanding of the "Oriental mind" via Song's Oriental body. The plot is thus propelled by a wonderful combination of imperialist and Cold War anxieties, both obsessed with the problem of *understanding* the East.

But the film is not simply about an Occidental man dominating an Oriental woman: Song (who turns out to be a man) is himself a spy who uses the Oriental stereotype (culled from Hollywood magazines) to his advantage. The Orientalist images, and knowledge/power relations, are thus reversed, transforming like a butterfly. By the end of the film, René has come under the complete power of Song. The Oriental is no longer a defenseless woman, but a conniving man, another popular character in the Orientalist menagerie (see Ling 2002; Said 1978). René eventually commits suicide, like the archetypal jilted Oriental woman in *Madame Butterfly,* thus making the reversal complete. With its juxtaposition of diplomacy, espionage, and Beijing Opera, M. *Butterfly* graphically underlines the performative nature of foreign affairs—if not in a theater state, then in a Beijing Opera state (see Geertz 1980).

SOCIAL SCIENCE FANTASIES

China has been the focus of post–Cold War fantasies in Euro-American social science as well. On the one hand, the enduring dream of the "China market" has morphed into the fabulous economic opportunities provided by Confucian capitalism. On the other, China is seen as a rising threat, the next superpower that will challenge the New World Order in a clash of civilizations. Such discussion is not limited to Sinologists; leading scholars as diverse as Samuel Huntington, Manuel Castells, and André Gunder Frank see understanding "China" as the key for understanding the twenty-first century (Huntington 1996; Castells 2000; Frank 1998). The moral valence of China thus varies erratically from negative to positive and back; at one and the same time (or in quick succession), China has been both an opportunity and a threat (Cumings 1999, 1, 16–18; also see Knight and Nakano 1999, 64–67).

As in *M. Butterfly*, East Asia is seen as ontologically unstable because "China has not been a nation for Americans, but a metaphor" (Cumings 1999, 151). The knowledge/power relationship in Chinese texts is no more stable. The United States is a metaphor for many Chinese intellectuals, caught in a love-hate relationship with the American dream (see Song Qiang 1996, 3–6; Interviews 1999). On the one hand, America is seen as the solution to China's problems with modernity (Chen, Xiaomei 1995; Su and Wang 1991). But on the other hand, according to Chinese scholars, the threat to world peace comes not from the rise of the Chinese empire but from an already existing American empire (Yan Xuetong et al. 1998; Zheng, Yongnian 1999).

And it is not just East and West that fantasize about each other. Conflicts between the People's Republic of China (PRC) and Taiwan also mirror those of René and Song. China has a very romanticized view of Taiwan as the key to its desires for respect and status; reuniting with this "renegade province" has been declared one of the three "sacred missions" of the twenty-first century. The election of the separatist Chen Shui-bian as Taiwanese president in 2000 burst the bubble of this nationalist romance. Beijing reacted to Chen's election by demanding that he acknowledge Beijing's "One China Principle" and accept its teleology of unification (see Zhu Rongji in BBC/SWB 15 March 2000). But the Taiwanese prefer to be ambiguous; their leaders are often coy, saying neither yes nor no. President Chen, for example, told the mainland that he did not necessarily disagree with the One China Principle; he merely needed Beijing to clarify what "One China" meant. Chen himself is known as a chameleon who dexterously reflects his audience's desires. Like Song in *M. Butterfly*, he is famous for his political performances, cross-dressing as Superman, a street vendor, Michael Jackson, and a tricycle coolie in various political campaigns (Hwang 2001, 4).

One of *M. Butterfly*'s messages is that things are not always what they seem; international affairs demand careful scrutiny. Rather than strip away Song's clothes to see the "real China," René made the mistake of believing in his Oriental fantasy. The PRC is actually more interested in its own fantasy of "One China" than in wooing the belovéd, Taiwan. In the afterword to *M. Butterfly*'s original script, Hwang concludes with

> a plea to all sides to cut through our respective layers of cultural
> and sexual misperception to deal with one another truthfully for
> our mutual good, from the common and equal ground we share as
> human beings. For the myths of the East, the myths of the West, the
> myths of men, and the myths of women—these have so saturated
> our consciousness that truthful contact between nations and lovers
> can only be the result of heroic effort. (Hwang 1988, 100)

It is only by cutting through the distorting representations that we
can come to a true understanding of both ourselves and the Other
in this erotic international relations.

Western foreign affairs experts on both the left and the right
agree. Like Hwang, they feel it necessary to dispel the cloud of rhetoric to get to the truth: "China is a second-rank middle power that
has mastered the art of diplomatic theater: it has us willingly sus-
pending our disbelief in its strength." Segal's solution is to "get out
of the theater and see China for what it is" (Segal 1999, 24; Nathan
and Ross 1997). To overcome the limits of metaphorical politics,
Cumings likewise suggests, "both peoples [need to] rediscover the
core of their own, different, civilizations. Then 'China' will finally
become, for Americans, simply China" (Cumings 1999, 170).

Yet this move toward mutual understanding, which seeks to
erase borders toward a common humanity, actually serves to reaffirm national, sexual, and cultural boundaries. By looking for
the truth about China and America, Hwang, Segal, and Cumings
each solidifies the coherence and separateness of such categories.
Each thus reinscribes the border between East and West, female and
male. But these foreign affairs also show how international politics
occurs not solely between evil empires and virtuous nation-states.
Like Heaney's "Lovers on Aran" (this volume's epigraph), politics
involves relating the land to the sea, the domestic to the foreign, the
inside to the outside, constructing an Other to reaffirm the self. The
issue is not just knowing better where the borders between East and
West are drawn so as to erase them; the politics is in the very drawing and erasure of such distinctions, the production of space and
the managing of frontiers (Shapiro and Alker 1996; Connolly 1991,
36–63; Walker 1993).

"Greater China" is the prominent site where the borders between
East and West, nation and state, self and Other are continually
drawn, erased, and reasserted. Further, Greater China is an opti-

mum site for an exploration of boundary production, because it does not exist as a legal or an institutional body. It is recognized neither in the international system nor in international society. There is no seat for Greater China in the United Nations; its existence is not inscribed in international treaties. It is a fantasy, a dream and a nightmare, created through symbolic exchange both between East and West and within East Asia. Indeed, Greater China's contingent state highlights the contingency of its component states: the PRC, Taiwan, and Hong Kong.

Like most globalization literature, the analysis of Greater China generally begins by focusing on increased international economic exchange. The concept of Greater China arose in the 1980s to explain economic flows that traversed the political and ideological barriers of the PRC, Taiwan, and Hong Kong (Bolt 2000; Zhao Wenlie 1995; MacFarquhar 1980). Since the early 1990s, business and government thus have spoken less of the PRC and more of Greater China to describe this network of economic, cultural, and political relations in East Asia and among overseas Chinese communities around the world. These relations are not merely state-to-state diplomacy or patterns of international trade and investment, but involve less formal people-to-people relations, flows, and disjunctures in a transnational political economy.

On the other hand, some fear that this economic integration will lead to military and political expansion, and thus move beyond the PRC as a growing superpower to the creation of a new Chinese empire. The PRC is hence commonly seen as an emerging superpower that threatens Euro-American economic and political hegemony (Deng and Wang 1999; Mearsheimer 2001; Gertz 2000; Yan Xuetong 1998). According to a survey of American public opinion in 1999, China had replaced both the Soviet Union/Russia as the main military threat to the United States, and Japan as the main economic threat (Watts 1999). Although al-Qaeda became viewed as the main security threat in 2001, Beijing is still a major political and economic concern.

Much of the research on Chinese foreign policy since the end of the Cold War has looked to Chinese identity to discover this new superpower's "true intentions." Both Chinese and Euro-American scholars have been involved in a search for the core values that define Chinese nationalism. With the passing of Marxism-Leninism as the guiding ideology, and the marketization of popular media, Chinese culture has weathered a series of identity crises in the past few decades. To address these "spiritual" problems, many scholars and officials in China see nationalism as the most suitable meta-narrative to guide China. The concept of Chinese civilization is thus used to understand Chinese national identity, national interest, and national security (Yan Xuetong 2001; Zhao Suisheng 2000; Zheng, Yongnian 1999; He and Guo 2000; Deng and Wang 1999; Anagnost 1997; Yan Xuetong 1995; Whiting 1995; Dittmer and Kim 1993; Pye 1990; Unger 1996).

Yet rather than taking "nationalism" or "national identity" as an answer to strategic questions of war and peace, this book will problematize "identity" and "Chineseness." Instead of trying to nail down Chinese national identity, or lamenting the ontological and epistemological instability of "China," in this book I will argue that "Greater China" is useful just because it is the unstable product of contingent relations. It is interesting just because it exemplifies the theater of transnational politics. Rather than seeing "Beijing Opera," "theater," or "metaphor" as presenting methodological problems that need to be solved, this book will use a cultural analysis of Greater China to examine the regulatory logic and grammar of boundary production in national, regional, and transnational space.

The purpose of the book therefore is not to be either pro–Greater China or anti–Greater China, but to show how contingent states like Greater China take shape as a set of official and informal practices on the center and the periphery (see Campbell 1998b, ix–xi). This effort to deal with Greater China in its ambiguity and multiplicity is analogous to Benedict Anderson's plea for social scientists to decapitalize "Nationalism-with-a-big N," and thus remove it from our list of ideologies: "It would, I think, make things easier if one treated [nationalism] as if it belonged with 'kinship' and 'religion,' rather than with 'liberalism' or 'fascism'" (Anderson 1991, 5). As I argue more specifically for Confucianism in chapter 5, I think it is more profitable for us to view Greater China as a set of "lower case" day-to-day practices than as a hegemonic meta-narrative for utopia or dystopia. The aim of this book is to demonstrate how critical international relations theory helps us understand Greater China, and how Greater China helps us understand critical international relations theory in new ways.

PRODUCING THEORY IN GREATER CHINA

If Greater China is the product of a contingent network of relations in local, national, regional, global, and transnational space, then a sophisticated examination of this discourse in both Chinese- and English-language sources can tell us about broad themes of globalization and identity, as well as about Chinese foreign affairs. The articulation of Greater China is helpful for understanding the relations between nation and state, culture and ethnicity, state sovereignty and popular sovereignty.

The discursive economy of Greater China thus leads us in different directions than mainstream international relations, globalization, and regionalization. Rather than searching international relations theory for a set of rules of engagement between nation-states or a logic of a global political economy, the volume will argue that Greater China employs a different set of concepts, in a transnational grammar of power and influence: civilization *(wenming, huaxia)*, crisis *(weiji)*, empire *(tianxia)*, Confucianism, harmony *(he)*, "one country, two systems," national humiliation *(guochi)*, friendship *(you)*, and Cultural China *(wenhua Zhongguo)*. Using a critical notion of Chinese civilization, this book reworks some of the traditional themes from area studies literature in relation to contemporary claims about overlapping jurisdictions, rearticulation of boundaries, and the impact of globalizing economic and cultural forms. These decentered practices can help us question the hegemonic concepts of world politics, and allow for the ironic openings that we see in such Euro-American concepts as heterotopia, governmentality, diaspora, cosmopolitics, recognition, outlaws, and so on. Hence these pages will not simply replace Euro-American theory with an "authentically Chinese theory" (Zheng, Yongnian 1999, 9–10), but use Chinese concepts and critical international relations theory to examine how Greater China and globalization are produced. In this way, the volume uses Greater China and East Asia to explore broader issues of sovereignty, network politics, empire, and globalization.

This examination of Greater China joins the move in international relations theory away from state-centric inter/national relations to examine trans/national flows of people, capital, products, and knowledge; it is part of the more general post–Cold War phenomenon of the return of culture and identity to international relations theory (Lapid and Kratochwil 1996; Katzenstein 1996b; Campbell 1998a; Shapiro and Alker 1996; Shapiro 1997). Indeed, one of my aims is to see how concepts like history and civilization take different forms in transnational politics as they perform in nonlinear modes. This book thus takes contingency as the starting point of transnational politics; it therefore questions the logic of explanation that relies on "narra-tivizing historiography where things have a self-evident quality that allows them to speak for themselves," using, rather, a "logic of inter-pretation that acknowledges the improbability of cataloguing, cal-culating, and specifying the 'real causes' and concerns itself instead with considering the manifest political consequences of adopting one mode of representation over another" (Campbell 1998a, 4). And so I do not search for the truth about Greater China so much as trace the discursive economies of the truth claims that employ and produce the analytical category "Greater China" (see Foucault 1972).

To trace these discursive practices, I will look to the thick descrip-tions of ethnography and to Foucault's concept of governmentality. In other words, the positivist/postpositivist debate is not exhausted by the sociological turn of constructivism. Other scholars of critical international relations are looking to anthropology's ethnographic methods to show how borders of territory and identity are negoti-ated in the social relations of identity and difference.

Before exploring critical international relations theory, it is help-ful to recall the emergence of sociological constructivism. Rational-ist theories are generally suspicious of cultural arguments; they claim that "identities and norms are either derivative of material capabilities or are deployed by autonomous actors for instrumental reasons" (Katzenstein 1996a, 5). Hence, culture and norms only enter the fray of international politics as variables in the rational calculation of strategic culture (see Weldes et al. 1999, 3). This severely limits the impact of culture on our understanding of inter-national relations. As Weber argues for "gender," treating culture as a variable contains it within hegemonic discourse as an add-on that does not disturb the hegemonic structures of rationality. Weber, by seeing gender "not as something that can be placed, but instead as something that helps us place things," encourages us likewise to use culture as a way of reconceptualizing world politics (Weber 2001, 89). Rather than looking at culture and identity as stable "things," sociological constructivism urges us to see identity as the product of negotiated relations. Barnett makes this point to explain diplomacy in the Middle East: "identity as a relational construct emerges out of the international and domestic discourse and interactions, imprints security politics and helps us to understand the dynamics of alliance formation" (Barnett 1996, 447).

The first generation of sociological constructivist texts— exemplified by Katzenstein's *The Culture of National Security*— thus broadened the notion of national security to see how norms, identity, and culture guide state policy, as part of a dialogue with rationalist international relations theory (Katzenstein 1996a, 5; also see Wendt 1999). More recently, sociological constructivists have broadened the agenda from national security and national interest to nonstate actors and nonmilitary issues. *Restructuring World Politics,* for example, expands the arena of international norms beyond the "society of states" to analyze how norms work in "nonstate actors of various kinds" (Khagram, Riker, and Sikkink 2002a, 14). In particular, it charts how transnational networks, co-alitions, nongovernmental organizations, and social movements are "makers and managers of meaning" in guiding the norms of world politics (Khagram, Riker, and Sikkink 2002a, 11; also see Sikkink 2002, 302).

This extension of sociological constructivism to address trans-national social movements is helpful for the analysis of contingent states and Greater China. But the focus on the construction of iden-tity through norms only covers half the relations that produce iden-tity. Sikkink points out that if we accept that norms are not merely epiphenomena produced by hegemonic states, we "need to know how these new international norm structures of social purpose are constructed, maintained, and transformed" (Sikkink 2002, 302). To answer this question, it is necessary to understand how iden-tity depends not just on shared norms but also on the exclusion of difference.

These concerns are nicely addressed by a volume that provides an alternative approach to many of the same issues: *Cultures of In-security* (Weldes et al. 1999). While *The Culture of National Security* uses culture to fill the analytic gaps left by rationalist international relations theories, *Cultures of Insecurity* uses the cracks in dominant approaches to question our understanding of international politics.

Whereas the sociological approach tends to search for "norms" as positive inclusive values, "the fabric that holds pluralistic societies together," an anthropological approach foregrounds how communities are formed by excluding difference: security depends upon insecurities (Kowert and Legro 1996, 454; Weldes et al. 1999; also see Lapid and Kratochwil 1996; Krause and Williams, 1997). Instead of discovering a coherent national culture that could easily be essentialized by rationalists as a discrete "substance," a variable that affects state policy, an anthropological approach highlights how identity and difference mutually constitute each other (Weldes et al. 1999, 19; Appadurai 1996, 12). Rather than looking to culture as a substance that has content, such an approach clarifies how culture takes shape in context-sensitive relations between identity and difference.

Some sociological constructivists are leaning in this direction. Sikkink acknowledges the mutual construction of self and Other when she notes "Many norms have both empowering and exclusionary effects" (Sikkink 2002, 310). Barnett more directly looks at how "identity emerges as a consequence of taking into consideration a relevant 'other'" (Barnett 1996, 408). But Campbell argues that there are important theoretical differences between the approaches that I am calling sociological and ethnographic international relations; these differences cannot be bridged, because the two approaches rely on radically different epistemologies and ontologies (Campbell 1998, 212–25). Rather than using otherness in the search for norms, Weldes et al. foreground how culture is multiple and "composed of potentially contested codes and representations, as designating a field on which are fought battles over meaning" (Weldes et al. 1999, 2). Negotiations between identity and difference thus are not simply clashes between these specific norms of national identities; insecurities also come from conceptual differences such as essential/contingent, sovereignty/intervention, domestic/foreign, and national/transnational.

Whereas sociological constructivists chart a progressive widening of security concerns (to women, the environment, and the non-Western world) and a broadening in the participation of norm production (to nonstate bodies and global civil society), Shapiro argues that historically the range of possibility has been narrowing. He thus uses ethnographic international relations not only to deconstruct state representations but to allow openings for nonstate practices of security and identity that have been obscured not just by states but by modernity. Shapiro argues that while

> strategic approaches to warfare tend to be explanatory in emphasis [looking for clarity and depth] . . . , an ethnographic focus is more concerned with the interpretive practices that sustain the antagonistic predicates of war. . . . Rather than naturalizing the boundaries by which states maintain their control over the representations of global issues, the focus involves both criticism and recovery. It is aimed first at disclosing how representations of alterity (dangerous Others) reproduce the identities and spaces that give nation-states and nations in general their coherence, and second at disclosing other forms of affiliation uncoded in state-oriented interpretations. (Shapiro 1997, 31)

To trace the cartography of violence in the present, Shapiro achieves critical distance through an ethnography of the colonial encounters between Europeans and Native Americans. His strategy of criticism and recovery does not search for enduring norms; the juxtaposition of other forms of affiliation "are meant to provide a reverse ethnology which problematizes the present and the self" (Shapiro 1997, 35). Hence national security, national culture, and their norms change from being objects discovered in scholarly research as solutions to security problems, into problems themselves: data that must be deconstructed to allow space for different expressions of identity and security.

With his sophisticated analysis of the politics of boundaries, R. B. J. Walker also helps us to question that logic of international relations that relies on essential states and national norms. By arguing that politics depends upon a "sharp delineation of here from there," Walker interrogates not only how nation-states come to be coherent but how the concepts that we use to understand international relations become coherent (Walker 1993, ix, 1). He encourages us not to take the division between inside and outside, national and international for granted as common sense. Rather we must examine the "historically constituted character of the categories that we use" (nationalism, sovereignty, and so on) "to see how they emerged in response to specific historical conjunctions and contradictions" in Europe (Walker 1993, 91–92).

But, as Foucault affirms, concepts do not arise simply out of

events such as battles or treaties, but out of "the reversal of a relationship of forces, the usurpation of power, the appropriation of a
vocabulary turned against those who had once used it" (Foucault
1984, 88; also see Cumings 1999, 21). Nation-states and sovereignty emerged in East Asia as part of the reversals of imperialism from
Chinese empire to Euro-American-Japanese empire. Theory did
not emerge solely out of administrative imperialism: the spread of
"civilization," the conceptual cultural imperialism of "diplomacy,"
the "family of nations," and now the "international community"
(see Gong 1984; Keene 2001). Thus both Shapiro and Walker not
only deconstruct the state but push us to see how contingent states
such as Greater China have emerged in relation to specific historical
contradictions and reversals.

This critical view of international politics is aided by Foucault's
concept of "governmentality," which expands the notion of power
from juridical concepts of power that restrict action, to productive
notions of power that are generated by social relationships. Rather
than being state-centric and concerned with sovereignty, power in
the "art of government" is more "pastoral" and multiple (Foucault
1982, 215). This contingent power grows out of informal relations. Comparing it with the unified power of Machiavelli's prince,
Foucault argues that

> the practices of government are, on the one hand, multifarious and
> concern many kinds of people: the head of a family, the superior of a
> convent, the teacher or tutor of a child or pupil; so that there are sev-
> eral forms of government among which the prince's relation to his
> state is only one particular mode; while on the other hand, all these
> other kinds of government are internal to the state or society. . . .
> Thus we find at once a plurality of forms of government and their
> immanence to the state; the multiplicity and immanence of these ac-
> tivities distinguishes them radically from the transcendent singulari-
> ty of Machiavelli's prince. (1991, 91)

Rather than state and civil society being distinct, autonomous,
and in opposition, the various forms of government interweave the
state, economy, and society in patterns of power both isomorphic
and holographic. Whereas juridical sovereignty is discontinuous in
that it tries to draw a line between the power of the prince and any
other form of power, the task of the art of government is to establish

a continuity from governing the individual through governing the family to governing the state (Foucault 1991, 91–92).

Thus, though it is common to frame "Communist China" and illiberal Southeast Asian regimes in terms of human rights violations, this book will argue that power also works in productive and multiple ways in Greater China, and will show how the state, the family, and the market work through regimes of power/knowledge. Cultural governance and biopower regulate not just the individual but other spaces: kinship networks, public and private schools, the capitalist workplace, the nation-state, and transnational networks (see Ong 1999).

CONTENTS

Although much analysis frames China as either a conservative nation-state or an aggressive empire, this book uses critical international relations theory to examine the contingent transnational politics of "civilization" in Greater China. Following the logic of criticism and recovery, each chapter is broadly organized into three main parts. The first two parts deconstruct the dualistic debate that frames mainstream understandings of each issue: Greater China as Confucian capitalism or as the threat of China, military force in the South China Sea or diplomacy there, Confucian national identity or transnational Confucian capitalism in South Korea, Britain or China in Hong Kong, and unification or independence in Taiwan. The third part then uses an ethnographic approach to recover an alternative way of understanding each of these problems, and thus possible solutions. This method is not dialectic; there is no synthesis in this third part. Rather than positing the correct answer, the conclusion of each chapter and the book as a whole aim to recover "other forms of affiliation" that still leave space for differences (see Campbell and Shapiro 1998). Thus the chapters do not present alternatives in the sense of answering the same questions in a different way; the alternatives seek to raise a different set of questions, which lead to a different set of solutions.

Hence, while many critical texts deconstruct the nation to highlight the problems that borders and frontiers entail, this book also explores the possibilities that transnationalism affords. By revaluing the traditional Chinese vocabulary of civilization, Confucianism, harmony, and friendship beyond its imperial articulation, I examine not only how people resist power but also how they build different identities and communities on different political terrains. Hence, Greater China challenges not just Euro-American political-economic supremacy, but hegemonic understandings of international relations theory and practice.

Most considerations of self/Other relations in East Asia look to the stark differences between China and the West (see Ling 2002). When applied to international relations, such analysis often results in Orientalist and Cold War inspired understandings of China as part of a clash of civilizations. To avoid such a conceptual trap, this book focuses on Chinese encounters with Otherness on its own territorial and conceptual frontiers. Rather than taking Sino-American relations to represent Chinese foreign policy and/or East Asian international relations (Deng and Gray 2001; Bernstein and Munro 1998; Nathan and Ross 1997), I examine how China deals with identity and difference in East Asia. In this way, I can show how Greater China is produced in relation to its Others; I show how transnational relations take shape along the margins in Southeast Asia, the South China Sea, Korea, Hong Kong, Taiwan—and the underclass in Beijing. This localization of analysis is not just for conceptual reasons. The PRC is large in terms of territory and population, and is influential as a permanent member of the U.N. Security Council. But in terms of military, economic, and cultural influence, it is still a regional power (Pumphrey 2002; Yee and Storey 2002).

Much of the critical research on Greater China focuses on either the center in Beijing or the periphery in Hong Kong, Singapore, or Southeast Asia (Ong 1999; Dutton 1998; Anagnost 1997; Ong and Nonini 1997; Chirot and Reid 1997; Hamilton 1999). This book will examine how the center and the periphery produce each other in Greater China. Though the bulk of the book examines territorial bodies—the South China Sea, South Korea, Hong Kong, and Taiwan—boundaries are examined not to reify them as barriers but to highlight how they are involved in contingent inside/outside relations, and how they function as dynamic spaces of exchange not only of capital but of knowledge practices.

The book thus is not organized like most "surveys" of East Asian international relations or international relations theory. It is suspicious of research that treats the region in terms of autonomous nation-states, and international theory in terms of discrete schools (see Cumings 1999; Campbell 1998b, 124; Appadurai 1996, 167). The four spaces—the South China Sea, South Korea, Hong Kong, and Taiwan—have been chosen because they present empirical problems to Chinese stateliness and territoriality. In the past fifty years, China has fought military battles over the Korean Peninsula, the South China Sea islets, Taiwan—and long ago it fought over Hong Kong. More important, each of these spaces also frames how China negotiates its cultural borders; the concept of Greater China emerged as a conceptual solution to these problems.

Because the South China Sea, Hong Kong, and Taiwan have presented vexing sovereignty problems, they have yielded interesting conceptual innovations. For example, to facilitate unification with Hong Kong, Macao, and Taiwan, the PRC twisted its sacred category of "absolute sovereignty" into the "one country, two systems" formula. Most interestingly, this peculiar solution is now part of international vocabulary: "one country, two systems" was written into international law with the Sino-British Joint Declaration (1984) and is promoted by China as a model for international problem-solving (see Deng Xiaoping 1994, 59–60).

These four spaces thus were chosen as case studies not for geopolitical reasons—because they constitute "East Asia"—but because they graphically show the interrelation between practice and theory. The spaces were problems that provoked theoretical innovation. Therefore, although Japan is very important to regional economics and is crucial to a geopolitical understanding of East Asia, it is not included here, since Japan is peripheral to the transnational relations and theoretical challenges of Greater China. Although South Korea is less important economically and politically than Japan, it provides a fascinating case study of the relations among ethnicity, culture, and territoriality; it therefore is an exemplary case of how the logic of Greater China and Confucian capitalism is used in other non-Chinese spaces including Japan, Vietnam, and Euro-America (see Elman et al. 2002).

Before analyzing these empirical problems and conceptual opportunities, it is necessary to deconstruct the Euro-American discourse of "Greater China." Chapter 1 shows how Greater China has been framed as a "crisis" that has produced both economic opportunities (Confucian capitalism) and dangers (the China threat). It argues that most discussions of Greater China take the coherence and unity of "Chinese civilization" for granted, and reproduce the geopolitical calculus of international relations: Greater China as the next superpower. The chapter concludes by using the concept of heterotopia to decenter analysis of Greater China. Chapter 1 argues that the logic of heterotopia as a multiple and ironic space helps us resist the temptation of coherent and singular definitions of civilization as a "thing." The chapter suggests that civilization and barbarism are best understood as a relation: each continually produces the other.

This contingent notion of Greater China allows us to trace out the discursive economies of self/Other relations in Chinese civilization. Chapter 2 considers how the dividing line between "civilization" and "barbarian" constructs Chinese foreign policy. The chapter examines four historical trajectories that rely on the civilization/barbarian distinction: nativism, conquest, conversion, and diaspora. These themes are used to analyze contemporary texts in Chinese official, academic, and popular culture to highlight the different dynamics of civilization and barbarism, different drawings of boundaries, different modes of inclusion and exclusion, and different relations of self and Other among the trajectories. Each of the narratives employs a specific rhetoric and logic: discovery, entitlement, synthesis, and flexibility. Although many essentialist views of China speak of a coherent China threat, this narrative approach provides a more complex view of how the nativism and conquest narratives guide Chinese foreign policy. Likewise, rather than simply thinking in terms of the economic opportunities of Confucian capitalism, the conversion and diaspora narratives show how economics, culture, and politics are linked in informal as well as formal ways in Chinese texts. The conclusion of the chapter is not that one narrative is truer or better than the others; rather, all four are involved in the contingent relations that produce Greater China in its various forms.

Chapter 2 uses the example of the Chinese diaspora in Thailand to shift analysis from "territorial sovereignty" to "popular sovereignty," in the sense that power and influence are measured in terms of populations rather than of geopolitics. In this way, the chapter examines how the Euro-American concepts of cosmopolitics and governmentality are helpful for explaining transnational relations. The chapter thus provides a conceptual map that guides the next four chapters, which examine the case studies of contemporary "problems" in terms of historical and cultural practices.

The South China Sea disputes present a serious problem of spatiality to the PRC. The region does not contain the guiding referents for sovereignty: territory, population, and authority. Thus the South China Sea disputes provide an exemplary case of how nation-states have to deliberately write their security. Chapter 3 will examine how the Chinese state uses the vocabulary of "civilization" in military and diplomatic performances to include the South China Sea in its nation while excluding rival claimants. Since chapter 2 moves from the logic of empire through nation-state to diaspora, in chapter 3 it is helpful to return to an examination of the tension between nation-state and empire in Greater China. The chapter follows Shapiro and Walker to unmap modernity to examine the imperial Chinese aesthetic of space to show how it figures politics in terms of shared sovereignty. This thick description of traditional Chinese cartography provides a context for rethinking the South China Sea disputes as well as the relation between security and subjectivity. Since conflicts between the exclusive nation-state sovereignties of China, Vietnam, and the Philippines are the problem in this region, the chapter argues that traditional Chinese concepts of space are useful for both explaining and legitimating a transnational subjectivity allowing for overlapping boundaries in a regional commons. Chapter 3 thus problematizes the borderless notion of Greater China introduced in chapters 1 and 2.

To gain critical distance from Confucianism, most texts compare it with liberal democracy. To avoid such an East-West analysis of comparative utopias, chapter 4 goes to South Korea to gain critical purchase on Confucianism as an ideology and knowledge practice. Many call Korea the most Confucian country in the world, yet the discourse of Confucianism in South Korea is far from clear or stable. Here the frontier is not between civilization and barbarian, as in chapters 2 and 3, but between alternate concepts of Confucian civilization. The South Korean case is interesting because it problematizes the standard notions of Greater China as a transnational ethnic Chinese community, the notion used in the earlier chapters. In South Korea identity is based on shared Confucian culture rather than on a common ethnic Chinese ancestry. The chapter uses the Korean example to show how, in East Asia, Confucianism works within temporal and spatial contexts as part of class, national, regional, international, and transnational identity. For example, some

Korean elites try to wean Confucianism away from China to form a "Greater Korea" along much the same economic and cultural logic as Greater China. Confucianism is also used beyond Sino-Korean relations to promote specific political projects: patriarchy, reunification, peace, and even democracy. Thus Confucianism is not a core value of Korean culture or Chinese ethnicity but rather a discourse used in various ways to construct communities. As mentioned above, South Korean Confucianism stands as an exemplary case to explain similar movements in Japan and Vietnam. By showing the slippery relation between ethnicity and culture, nation and state, chapter 4 provides a more critical view of the struggles over the PRC's unironic "One China policy" for reunification with Hong Kong and Taiwan.

Economic ties among Hong Kong, Taiwan, and the mainland produced the concept of Greater China; political unification with Hong Kong and Taiwan remain major issues for the PRC. Chapter 5 examines how the frontier between Hong Kong and mainland China is not just territorial but administrative and cultural. After deconstructing the dominant images of Hong Kong in the British and Chinese imaginaries, the chapter examines competing notions of Chineseness in Beijing and Hong Kong. The chapter uses the conceptual opportunity of the Hong Kong formula "one country, two systems" to critically explore the problems of Westphalia's "one system, many states." In particular, it examines how "one country, two systems" has resonance with the ancient Confucian concept "harmony with difference." This traditional concept of world order is not just ancient exotica; harmony is making a comeback in mainland Chinese international relations theory to explain Chinese foreign policy and world order. Chapter 5 shows how the harmonious negotiation of cultural boundaries in South Korea highlighted in chapter 4 is part of administrative governmentality in Hong Kong.

The first five chapters demonstrate that neither Greater China nor Confucianism has a stable definition. Rather, both are sites of discursive and thus political contention in the negotiation of the frontiers of civilization. Chapter 6 returns to the issues raised in chapter 2, "Questioning Civilization," to examine "popular sovereignty" not just in terms of a population-based sovereignty but as democratic sovereignty of, by, and for the people. The problem here is not just one of geopolitics, of China trying to woo back its Cold War rival in

Taiwan, but of the meaning and practice of Chineseness and democracy. In other words, the chapter shows how the PRC deals with the conceptual frontier of "democracy" via the ideological and territorial frontier of the Taiwan Strait.

Chapter 6 thus examines the interplay among identity, democracy, and violence in cross-straits relations. Using the concepts "recognition" and "Confucian friendship," the chapter reframes the analysis away from East/West analyses of Confucianism versus liberal democracy to differentiate between two different practices of democracy: institutional electoralism and a democratic ethos. Since the mid-1980s, Taiwan has experienced fundamental political reforms that have produced elected leaders; this chapter looks beyond these top-down institutional changes to examine vibrant social movements as examples of a democratic ethos in Greater China.

The book's conclusion draws together the political peculiarities of previous chapters to question the norms of international society. Although Greater China does not fit into the language of international law and diplomacy, most of its component states have been struggling over the past few decades to achieve "normalcy." But the conclusion shows that these states desire a particular form of normalcy: diplomatic recognition and military power. Hence, this final chapter examines how international norms are invested with violence, particularly state-centric violence. To question these contingent states, the chapter looks to contingent peoples: the diaspora abroad and China's massive floating population of wanderers and vagrants at home. Transnational relations do not simply cross territorial boundaries; this chapter uses China's first independent film, *Beijing Bastards,* to recover alternative affiliations among the underclass of the capital. The film is interesting because it highlights inclusion and exclusion not just across the Strait of Taiwan but in the heart of Beijing. Diaspora and hooligans show how identity and power are not performed through the normal channels of sovereignty and citizenship, for both diaspora and hooligans are excluded from the state and civil society. Like Greater China more generally, the diaspora and hooligans' identity and influence emerge through economic, social, and cultural activities; sometimes they are heroic yuppies, other times petty criminals. Finally, the conclusion expands from the micropolitics of the diaspora/hooligans to the macropolitics of Taiwan, to argue that both are outlaws in that they are excluded from (domestic/international) society. But these outlaws engage in a fascinating biopolitics of resistance, a kind of popular sovereignty that recalls the situation of many people in the age of neoliberal globalization. This chapter concludes that we are all diasporic outlaws.

Hence, this book concludes that the struggles that produce Greater China are not between states such as the PRC and Taiwan. They are actually between institutional structures and popular movements, between state sovereignty and popular sovereignty, and between differing productions of Chineseness along the Taiwan Strait, the Shenzhen River, and the South China Sea, and among overseas Chinese, Korean Confucians, and hooligans in China's floating population.

The purpose of the book is to underline how Greater China and Confucianism, nation and state, the foreign and the domestic, sovereignty and diaspora are each dynamic and ambiguous. Although the PRC has been described as the "high church of realpolitick in the post-Cold War world" (Christensen 1996, 37), analysis of foreign policy performances will show it is an exemplary theater state (Geertz 1980). The meaning of Greater China and Confucianism depends upon the circumstances of their articulation and interpretation. Although there has been much critical research on sovereignty and the construction of the nation-state, this book argues that transnational regions are also produced by relations of identity and difference. The four historical trajectories introduced in chapter 2 allow us to conduct a more nuanced analysis of Chinese foreign policy in particular and of transnational governance more generally. We see how the contingent states—the PRC, Thailand, South Korea, Hong Kong, and Taiwan—use nativist, conquest, and conversion notions of civilization to construct and discipline subjects; in this way, they use the transnational tools of Greater China as part of a regulatory logic of capitalism and the nation-state. But popular movements in each of these spaces resist such a top-down management of knowledge practices by pointing to the hazy, ambiguous, multiple, overlapping, and often transnational practices of identity. Curiously, they often do this through the optic of Greater China. As a result, we cannot categorically code Greater China or Confucianism as progressive or conservative, democratic or authoritarian as a stable model for others to follow or a reminder of past mistakes to avoid. The most interesting politics is neither pro-China nor anti-China, is about neither empires nor nation-states, but is produced in the tension between essential nativism and flexible diaspora, between state sovereignty and popular sovereignty.

The importance of East Asian politics goes far beyond the region; in 1997 we saw how East Asia affected the world economically, and with the Taiwan crises of 1996 and 2000 we saw how China affects the world militarily. This study shows how Greater China can also influence the international system politically and theoretically. By problematizing the standard notions of sovereignty, identity, borders, and the nation-state, Greater China provides an example of the shift from international relations to transnational relations, and from state policy to governmentality. Indeed, the book examines how Chinese engagements with globalization and civilization are instructive not just for "dealing with China," but for addressing questions of identity and security in other spaces as well.

1

Defining Greater China:
Civilization as the Answer

Since the end of the Cold War, the world has been reorganizing it-self, moving away from global issues to other forms of international politics. There has been a shift in the study of world politics as well; more attention has been paid to political communities that exist be-tween the global and the nation-state. This shift has led to increased academic attention to regionalism. Certainly, this renewed interest has been prompted by events: the founding of the North American Free Trade Area in 1993 and, especially, the wider and deeper inte-gration of the European Union (E.U.) since 1992 as it moved from a common market to a common currency and potentially to a ro-bust common foreign and security policy for twenty-five nations in 2004. Others have pointed to the return to the normal international politics warped by Cold War superpower rivalry: nations and states have returned to world politics with a vengeance. In Europe this is seen as a contradiction; instead of states further integrating into the European Union, there has been a decay of multinational states into smaller, national units: the disbanding of the Soviet Union in 1991 and of Czechoslovakia in 1993, and the devolution of power to Britain's Celtic fringe in Scotland, Wales, and Northern Ireland in 1999. After over a decade of strife, secession, and war, the multi-national federation of Yugoslavia legally ceased to exist in 2003. This trend toward a politics of national security, legitimate versus rogue states, and asymmetric warfare was boldly reinforced by the developments in world politics after the terrorist attack on New York and Washington, D.C., in 2001.

Where does Asia fit into this schema? On the one hand, it is common to compare the success of regionalism in Europe with its failure in Asia, where there are no comparable institutions to the European Union (E.U.). The main achievement of the Association of Southeast Asian Nations (ASEAN) is that it still exists after three decades. APEC—Asia-Pacific Cooperation—does not even have the stature and stability required to be a noun; it is an adjective for a missing institution. On the other hand, some have suggested that regionalism works in a different way in Asia, through markets and culture rather than institutions. Rather than the formal suprastate politics of the E.U., there is the informal transnational politics of Greater China (see Katzenstein 1997; Ong 1999). Even so, the "rise of Chinese nationalism" discourse in both China and the West is emblematic of the trend toward the national security state. While this concern over the rise of China is usually seen as part of a Sino-American rivalry, the utility of the nation-state also has been reasserted with China's cooperation in the war on terrorism. The deployment of U.S. troops in Central Asia certainly can be seen in China as a threat, as part of an American containment policy. But conflict on its Central Asian frontier actually helps China to firm up the political and territorial boundaries of its Muslim north-western region. Hence the relation of Greater China's regionalism and China's nationalism is not necessarily a contradiction. National security works with transnational political economics in a complex dynamic that reinforces both national and transnational trends. The frontiers of nationalism and transnationalism, politics and economics, inside and outside, are continually shifting in Greater China.

This chapter seeks to add to the consideration of Chinese foreign policy as it relates to Chinese identity, by questioning the standard definitions of Chinese nationalism and Greater China (Zhao Suisheng 2000; Dittmer and Kim 1993; Whiting 1995). As Campbell argues for the United States, foreign policy in its most basic sense is an engaging with the Other, and in so doing a constructing of the self (Campbell 1998a).

There is a long tradition of understanding Chinese foreign policy in terms of cultural and moral categories, such as the traditional Chinese world order (Fairbank 1968b; Shih, Chih-yu 1993; Zhang,

Yongjin 2001). For example, Johnston argues that both Chinese and Western scholars assume that "Chinese political behavior cannot be understood without reference to historical or cultural precedent" (Johnston 1995, xii, 22–23; Johnston 1996, 218; Deng, Yong 1999, 60). Likewise, Bøckman notes that China is a key example of how culture and politics are interwoven (Bøckman 1998, 320). Most famously, Lucian Pye declares that China is not a nation at all but merely "a civilization pretending to be a state" (Pye 1990, 58).

But these culturalist understandings often lead to essentialized views of Chinese identity and practice. It is not a coincidence that one of the central theorists of the political culture school, Lucian Pye, is also a key Sinologist who writes about the "spirit of Chinese politics" (Pye 1992; Pye and Verba 1965). In more recent scholarship, some merely add the culture of Chineseness as a variable into neorealist calculations of war and peace, fragmentation and reunification (Bessho 1999; Huntington 1996; Waldron 1990; Johnston 1995). They thus "expand the old register of hazards to incorporate what are perceived as the newly emergent dangers" (Campbell 1998a, ix). The new danger here is called "Greater China" and "Chinese nationalism."

Certainly, in the past decade there have been interesting studies which have addressed Chinese identity in complex ways. Many look to multiple definitions of Chinese nationalism: affirmative, assertive, aggressive; nativist, antitraditional, pragmatic. But this multiplicity does not endure; rather, the will to conclude pushes authors to settle on the single best definition of Chinese nationalism: assertive, pragmatic, defensive, confident, normal (Whiting 1995, 316; Zhao Suisheng 2000, 16, 28–32; Callahan 2004b).

To avoid this reductive practice, this chapter and chapter 2 will use the tools of critical international relations theory to problematize singular coherent notions of both Chinese nationalism and Greater Chinese transnationalism. Following recent attention to cultural nationalism, I will loosen the concept of Chineseness to see how Chinese civilization constructs identity and difference, self and Other in particular ways: national, regional, global, and transnational. In this manner, I will also go beyond much current critical research that deconstructs "national interest" (Campbell 1998a; Weber 1995; Weldes et al. 1999), to see how Chinese identity works in transnational ways. Shifting from a search for norms of national

identity to an examination of the discursive economy of "civilization and barbarism," shows how Chinese identity and Chinese foreign policy are produced in contingent and transnational forms.

Although the preceding may sound overly theoretical, foreign
policy elites in both China and the United States are increasingly
using these categories to explain both how China is a threat and how
China is fundamentally peaceful. For example, before he became
the U.S. ambassador to Beijing in 1999, Admiral Joseph Prueher
(ret.) made sure to read the Chinese classics to understand Chinese
strategy (Halloran 1999). On the other hand, Chinese think-tanks
argue that China is not a threat because of the "Peaceful Orientation
of Chinese Civilization" (Li Shaojun 2002, 526–34). Each of these
arguments is backed up by in-depth scholarly studies that look to
cultural realism on the one hand (Johnston 1995; Johnston 1996),
and Oriental pacifism (also called *Pax Sinica*) on the other (Zhang,
Yongjin 2001; Yan Xuetong 2001; Yan Xuetong 1995; Liu Zhiguang
1992: 212–32; Zhang, Tiejun 2002; Wang, Qingxin 2001).

But rather than take "civilization" as an answer to political
questions—take Chinese culture, that is, as either a threat to peace
or the key to peace—this chapter and the next will problematize
the category of civilization. In the present chapter, I will critically
examine how China and Greater China are characteristically understood in terms of political culture approaches that seek to define
stable core values (Pye 1985; Pye 1990; Rozman 1991a).

THE CRISIS OF GREATER CHINA

"Greater China" became a common phrase in the 1990s, as a model
for post–Cold War global politics, in academic discourse and the
business plans of globalization (see Shambaugh 1991). Two reports on Greater China were written for the National Committee
on United States–China Relations, while another was written for
the European Commission (Harding 1994; Lampton et al. 1992;
Machetzki 1998; also see Metzger and Myers 1996). As part of
the commercial diplomacy of the Clinton administration, in 1994
the Secretary of Commerce defined the Chinese Economic Area
of mainland China, Taiwan, and Hong Kong as a "Big Emerging
Market" (Hughes 1997a, 148–49; Tsang Shu-ki 1996, 38). In the
United Kingdom, Greater China has in recent years been the topic
of reports in areas as diverse as the Foreign Office, the Department

of Trade and Industry, and the Higher Education Funding Council of England (see HEFCE 1999).

Although there is disagreement among scholars about the borders of Greater China, most see it as including the southeastern provinces of the People's Republic of China (PRC), Taiwan, and Hong Kong. Often the rest of the PRC, Macao, Singapore, and overseas Chinese communities in Southeast Asia are also included (Bolt 2000; Shambaugh 1995a; Harding 1995; Zha Daojiong 1995; Chang, Maria 1995; Uhalley 1994; Kao, Charng 1992; Kao, John 1993; Hughes 1997a; Shambaugh 1991).

Like these different mappings, the phrase "Greater China" has no stable meaning in discourse. "Greater China" is, on the one hand, employed in different ways spatially—from the perspectives of Beijing, Taipei, Hong Kong, Singapore, or Washington and New York. This often leads to a conjunction of geographical and discursive boundaries, which in turn typically reproduce East/West discourse in both its Orientalist and Cold War forms. But, more importantly, "Greater China" is mobilized topically by two general groups of writers, the business press and security studies experts, in each of the localities listed above (Uhalley 1994; Zha Daojiong 1995, 173). As a discourse, "Greater China" produces different meanings in different contexts; hence, some have cautioned against the "unquestioned acceptance of a concept that had yet to be scientifically defined" (Uhalley 1994, 275; Bolt 2000, 9; Harding 1995, 8; Harding 1994, 29). Rather, however, than search for a stable definition and assert truth claims about Greater China, this chapter will examine the contingent logic of "Greater China" as a discourse that enables certain forms of speech and action while restricting others. In other words, Greater China is fascinating just because of—not in spite of—its ambiguity and instability (Zhao Wenlie 1995; see Campbell 1998a).

"Greater China" has been deployed to address a crisis, whether of geopolitics, global capitalism, or identity. In this way "Greater China" is part of the discursive grammar of *weiji. Weiji* is one of the Chinese words that has entered the English language. In Chinese, it means "crisis," and in the 1980s Euro-American business writers turned this phrase into a cliché, underlining how "crisis" in Chinese is not wholly bad. Crisis contains both the characters for *wei*—danger, and for *ji*—opportunity; hence each danger contains possibilities (see Wang Yizhou 1999, 75–84). Every situation is ironic, multicoded, and multilayered, containing both problems and possibilities that cannot be easily separated, discarded, or synthesized into a new unity or a coherent truth.

This ironic understanding of Greater China is borne out in mainstream views found in books like *Greater China: The Next Superpower?* which highlight how Greater China is part of a post–Cold War reconfiguration of international relations that contains various actors, dimensions, and processes. Most important, Shambaugh contrasts the "problem" of de jure political reunification with the "opportunity" of de facto growth in economic and cultural links (Shambaugh 1995a, 1). Traditionally, "Greater China" has been used in the past century to define China geographically as an empire (Uhalley 1994, 276–79). Map 2 shows a map called "Greater China" that includes both "China proper" and "Outer China"—Tibet, Mongolia, and Xinjiang. This map is not simply a Euro-American view (as the product of American intelligence in 1944), for it parallels Chinese maps of the period (OSS 1944; Harding 1995).

The concept of *Greater China* regained currency in Chinese texts at the end of the 1970s when Deng Xiaoping's economic reforms opened up China to foreign investment and trade, initially via Hong Kong (Interview 2002; Uhalley 1994, 283). Ties with Taiwan expanded once Taipei loosened travel, trade, and investment restrictions in 1987. The upshot of this thaw, as is well known, was a dramatic quantitative growth, first in the cultural ties of millions of Taiwanese tourists visiting the mainland, and then equally dramatically in trade and investment across the straits. Economic reforms in China and a loosening of restrictions in Taiwan both helped to "resurrect a wide range of natural economic and cultural relationships that were long restricted by [artificial] political obstacles" (Harding 1995, 8; also see Taiwan Affairs Office 2000, 1; Hughes 1997a, 109–11).

Although the phrase "Greater China" seems to concern only the PRC and its neighbors, the discourse is tied to global debates.[1] It appeared at the end of the Cold War as part of discussions about both "globalization" and Chinese domestic politics. For example, on the one hand, "Greater China" is intimately related to the regionalization of the world economy, exemplified by the creation of the European Union in 1992 and the North American Free Trade Area (NAFTA) in 1993. And on the other, "Greater China" as a violent threat was de-

Map 2. *Greater China in the 1940s. Courtesy of Harvard University.*

ployed as part of the reaction by Euro-Americans and East Asians to the Tian'anmen Square massacre in 1989 (see Zha Daojiong 1995, 178–91; Uhalley 1994, 279–80).

Much like the "Asian values" debate, which arose between 1992 and 1994, the concept of Greater China was produced because East Asians were afraid of being excluded by Fortress Europe and NAFTA. Taiwanese intellectuals surmised that East Asia needed its own economic bloc, and started proposing various versions of a "Greater Chinese Common Market" (Zhao Wenlie 1995; Uhalley 1994, 283–85; Hughes 1997a, 109–11; Bolt 2000). The PRC had already felt the problems of exclusion due to Euro-American sanctions placed on it in the wake of the Tian'anmen Square massacre. At that time, China needed to redirect its attention from Euro-America to regional neighbors. From 1990 to 1992 the PRC normalized relations with Indonesia, South Korea, Singapore, and many other regional states (Lee Lai To 1999, 16–17). The lucrative investments that Taiwan, Japan, South Korea, and the overseas Chinese in Southeast Asia negotiated with China at this time involved more than common cultural roots—they took advantage of the lack of competition from Euro-American business that accompanied the diplomatic isolation of the PRC.

The discourse of "Greater China" is therefore quite complex, and emerged in relation to historical events. Harding profitably divides his analysis into three related areas—economics, culture, and politics—each of which has its own logic, boundaries, center, and organizational form:

> Economically, Greater China involves the expanding commercial interactions among mainland China, Taiwan and Hong Kong. Culturally, it refers to the restoration of personal, scientific, intellectual and artistic contacts among people of Chinese descent around the world. Politically, it refers to the possibility of the re-establishment of a single Chinese state, reuniting a political entity that was disintegrated by more than a century of foreign pressure and civil war. To a degree, the three themes are interrelated: a common cultural identity provides a catalyst for economic ties, and economic interdependence may lay the foundation for political unification. (Harding 1995, 32)

This passage is instructive because it takes for granted the unity of Chinese ethnicity. "Culture" is taken as the foundation necessary to promote the main focus of Greater China discourse: the opportunities of economic exchange. Indeed, as in most globalization literature, analysis of Greater China generally begins by noting an explosion in transnational economic exchange; the Higher Education Funding Council of England's report is indicative in stating that Greater China is an economic opportunity on "a scale beyond anything currently experienced in relation to other countries" (HEFCE 1999). Greater China thus is seen as a utopia for the twenty-first century.

ECONOMIC OPPORTUNITY: CONFUCIAN CAPITALISM

Economic growth is the "opportunity" part of the crisis, an opportunity not just for East Asia but for global capitalism. In this way, Greater China has been seen as the new utopia for transnational capital, the opportunity arising out of a capitalist crisis in the West. This vein of Greater China discourse has been accompanied by the corollary production of "Confucian capitalism." Western capitalism was in trouble due to the stagflation that characterized the 1970s. It was challenged not just by socialism in Eastern Europe, but by a different form of capitalism in East Asia. Starting in 1979, Japan was hailed as a new model of rapid economic growth; in the 1980s the Four Dragons—Taiwan, South Korea, Hong Kong, and Singapore—were added to the list of miracle economies (Vogel 1991; MacFarquhar 1980; Hofheinz and Calder 1982).

Because economic calculations alone could not adequately describe East Asian prosperity, "culture" was mobilized as a way of distinguishing robust Confucian capitalism from lethargic Euro-American capitalism (Berger 1987, 5; Redding 1993, 14; Clegg, Higgins, and Spybey 1990, 37). Yet this Confucian revival began not in China or even East Asia. Rather it appeared in the West, starting with Roderick MacFarquhar's *Economist* article "The Post-Confucian Challenge," which deftly laid out the discourse of the East Asian challenge, Asian values, and Greater China even before they had these names (MacFarquhar 1980). It was followed by publications that elaborated on the Confucian capitalist utopia, by futurologists, sociologists, political economists, philosophers, and so on (Dirlik 1995, 237).

Using the notion of political culture developed by Almond, Verba, and Pye, Peter Berger suggested the notion "economic culture" to describe economic development in Asia (Berger 1987, 7; Pye and Verba 1965; Almond and Verba 1963).[2] He argued that East Asia provides a distinct Second Case of industrial capitalism that was bad news for socialists and laissez-faire capitalists alike (Berger 1987, 157; Tai Hung-chao 1989). Here the core values of civilization are figured as a "comparative advantage" (Berger 1987, 166). In what is now a seminal work, *In Search of an East Asian Development Model*, Berger and his colleagues elaborated the economic culture theme, specifically the comparative advantage of "Sinic [Chinese] civilization" (Berger 1988, 11; Hsiao 1988, 19). This led to an explosion in publications about East Asian capitalism; throughout the discourse "Sinic civilization" was equated with "Confucianism" as a way to generalize about Japan and the Four Tigers. While Max Weber and modernization theory had framed Confucianism as a "traditional" problem that needed to be overcome for development, now Confucianism was seen as the key to rapid economic growth. The comparative advantage of Sinic civilization was the "Cash Value of Confucian Values" (Harris and Hofstede 1990). Much like the image of China itself, Confucianism here radically changed in value.

The core values of the Confucian work ethic are commonly listed as "a positive attitude toward the affairs of the world, a sustained lifestyle of discipline and self cultivation, respect for authority, frugality, and an overriding concern for stable family life" (Berger 1988, 7–8; Bolt 2000). Indeed, the last value, family life, is characteristically taken as the model for the Confucian lifestyle. In the past, the emperor was the Son of Heaven and the Father of his subjects. In the present, the modern word for nation-state in Chinese *(guojia)* translates to "country-family," and the key to Chinese capitalist success has been the family business (Redding 1996; Bolt 2000; Hamilton 1996; Redding 1993; Clegg, Redding, and Cartner 1990; Tai Hung-chao 1989)

The discourse of the East Asian Economic Miracle thus shifted in the 1990s from being based on a Japanese model (Taylor 1996; Chan, Steve 1993), to examine overseas Chinese capitalism. Indeed, the World Bank report *The East Asian Miracle* is part of this migration: although it focuses on a Japanese model, it shows the traces of Greater China discourse (World Bank 1993). Although the report did not consider the PRC, its writers were fascinated with the culture of Chinese capitalism exemplified by overseas Chinese—including those in Hong Kong and Taiwan, but this was edited out because it was difficult to obtain solid "evidence" of the link between culture and economic growth, and there were worries that such linkage was "racist" (Wade 1996, 20).

Other analysts, especially in the business press, were not so shy. Popular business books like John Naisbitt's *Megatrends Asia* argued that the Japanese era had passed and the future lay with the overseas Chinese in their capitalist utopia (Naisbitt 1996). Books with titles using "Japan, Inc.," were popular in the 1980s; in the 1990s they were displaced by titles like *China, Hong Kong, Taiwan, Inc.* (van Kemenade 1998). The hyperbole of a cover story in *Forbes* is typical: "Overseas China: the Giant Economy That Knows No Borders" (Tanzer 1994).

Thus, as the discourse of Confucian capitalism developed in the 1990s, it switched focus from Japan and its regional client states—South Korea, Taiwan, Hong Kong, and Singapore—to overseas Chinese business and Greater China (Bolt 2000; Ong 1999, 7; Rowley and Lewis 1996).[3] Much was made about the differences between Chinese capitalism and Japanese capitalism (Hamilton

1996; Redding 1996; Clegg, Redding, and Cartner 1990). The formal institutions of the developmental state in Japan, the authors argue, are quite different from the informal network capitalism of overseas Chinese (Bolt 2000; Hamilton 1999; Katzenstein 1997). The main debate concerns the role of the state: is it a helpful developmental state or a hindrance to network capitalism; are the policies neomercantilist or neoliberal? In a fascinating essay, Hamilton argues that most of the writing about East Asian capitalism is wrong, because it focuses on developmental state action, whereas "Chinese capitalism cannot be understood apart from the dynamics of the global economy because . . . Chinese capitalism is not a domestic capitalism (i.e., the product of indigenous economic growth), but rather is integral to world capitalism itself" (Hamilton 1996, 331).

Confucian capitalism thus is a different form of capitalism in the world, a "cosmopolitan capitalism" of diasporic Chinese (Hamilton 1999). Because it is not tied to the state as in Japan, Confucian capitalism is not regulated by formal laws or state policy. Rather it is regulated by the informal governmentality of the "connections" of *guanxi* capitalism that tie small Chinese business into global capitalism through a series of subcontracting networks (Ong 1999, 116–17). Overseas Chinese investment in China has been huge, making the country the second most popular host for foreign direct investment after the United States. By April 1999, there were over 330,000 overseas Chinese funded firms in the PRC, with $580 billion in contractual investment and paid-in capital of $270 billion (Bolt 2000, 1). Indeed, some call this network of overseas Chinese capital a new superpower, "the Invisible Empire of the Overseas Chinese" (Seagrave 1995).

Certainly, the discursive shift from Japanophilia to Sinophilia was backed up by economic performance: since the Japanese economic bubble burst in the late 1980s, the Japanese economy was outperformed by the other Asian Tigers—who were renamed Greater China. This was graphically shown in the *Forbes* 1996 listing of the top ten richest individuals in the world. For the first time, half were East Asian—but, surprisingly, only one was Japanese. The other four were ethnic Chinese in Hong Kong, Taiwan, and the Philippines (Higgins 1996). The most comical artifact of danger/opportunity in "Greater China" discourse is a full-page advertisement in the *Financial Times* (and other business newspapers) to announce the launch of *Forbes Global* to potential advertisers (FT 15 January 1998, 7). Appealing to a mixture of capitalist and Maoist utopia, the advertisement is laid out like Cultural Revolution propaganda (showing a dawn with rays of yellow and red sunlight), to declare (in its own celebration of the 150th anniversary of the Communist Manifesto) "Capitalists of the World Unite!" and "All hail the final victory of capitalism." The masses are led in celebration by a young-looking Mao dressed in tie and suspenders, waving a red flag displaying the Japanese Yen symbol. Other characters include a Red Guard who waves a little red book in one hand and carries a briefcase in the other, Fidel Castro cheering, a Vietnamese woman in traditional clothes with a briefcase, and another man waving a mobile phone. The irony of this ad is that it was placed opposite a special report on South Korea's economic crisis. The dreams of a Greater China market persisted in the face of post-1997 economic nightmares.

As Higgins's *Guardian* article, various *Forbes* publications, and *Megatrends Asia* show, this overseas Chinese capitalism is not just a "threat" to Japanese supremacy. Like the Japanese challenge before it, Greater China was figured as a threat to Western identity: "Their [Chinese] identity marks a critical shift in the balance of economic power and underlies a parallel shift in the focus of western phobias" (Higgins 1996, 1). "Greater China" discourse thus arose at the apex of East Asian economic dynamism. Parallel to the "Asian values" discourse, "Greater China" looked to exotic culture to explain capitalist success. The nexus of danger/opportunity for Euro-America shifted from Japan, Inc. to Greater China.

This shift can explain the rapid and vitriolic response to the 1997 Asian economic crisis, which occurred while the U.S. economy was in its longest era of peacetime expansion. Asian values were no longer lionized; Confucian capitalism was commonly refigured as a corrupt "crony capitalism" that was a "trademark of overseas Chinese" (Long 1998, 60; Wade 1998; Robison et al. 2000).

DANGER: CHINA THREAT

In "Greater China" discourse, politics is characteristically framed as a problem to be overcome for economic opportunities: "Taipei and Peking [need] to cast aside political factors and promote economic exchanges" (Kao, Charng 1992, 62). As we saw above, politics is figured as an obstacle to "natural" relations between Chinese compatriots, who had been divided by British imperialism in Hong Kong and by the Cold War in Taiwan (Harding 1995; Harding 1994, 1–2; Kao, Charng 1992; Tsang Shu-ki 1996, 28ff). Both Taipei and Beijing use economic integration for their own version of political reunification. Under the Kuomintang (KMT) regime, Taipei wished to use "the Taiwan experience" to convert the PRC and join Taiwan in the formation of a "democratic, free, equitably prosperous China" (in Zha Daojiong 1995, 181; Uhalley 1994, 283–85; Hughes 1997a); Beijing, on the other hand, wishes to use the Hong Kong formula "one country, two systems" to integrate Taiwan into a Greater China under its control (Taiwan Affairs Office 2000; Hughes 1997a), but if Taiwan strays toward independence, Beijing reserves its right to use force to unify China. Since the leader of the pro-independence Democratic Progressive Party (DPP) was elected president of Taiwan in March 2000, these issues have taken on even more salience (see Christensen 2002). Thus the economic opportunities can lead to political dangers. As the crises accompanying the 1996 and 2000 Taiwanese presidential elections have shown, "reunification" of the PRC and Taiwan is figured as the main threat of violence in Chinese foreign policy (*White Paper on China's National Defense* 2002; Whiting 1998, 289; Nathan and Ross 1997).

This shift from opportunity to danger entails a shift from business texts to security studies texts, with some arguing that military and strategic dimensions need to be added to the cultural-economic-political formula of "Greater China" (Shambaugh 1995a, 2). Huntington provides a good example of such shifts: he uses the language of the Japanese Empire to describe Greater China—e.g., "Greater China and its Co-prosperity Sphere" (Huntington 1996, 168ff). He argues that the PRC as the core state of Greater China will use economic and cultural ties to reassert its "traditional hegemony" in a new form of empire: "China is resuming its place as regional hegemon, and the East is coming into its own" (Huntington 1996, 238).

The capitalist utopia of economic cooperation in Greater China thus gives way to the security dystopia of an irridentist Chinese empire (Chang, Maria 2001). Attention here is shifted from the business activity of overseas Chinese on the periphery back to the political-military activity of the PRC state at the center (Bernstein and Munro 1998, xii–xvii; Huntington 1996, 169; Gertz 2000). The importance of this argument was underlined on the cover of

Foreign Affairs—the headline read "The China Threat"—and on its table of contents, where a picture of a Chinese soldier aiming a rifle at the reader was placed above "China will be the United States' next major adversary" (*Foreign Affairs* 1997, 17; *Foreign Affairs* 2002).[4] This was part of a vigorous debate in the United States about whether to engage or contain China (Pumphrey 2002; Yee and Storey 2002; Roy 1996; Shambaugh 1996). This debate did not just take place among academics and pundits, but characterized policy debate in Washington. A group of conservative members of Congress, their aides, and think-tank fellows calling themselves the "Blue Team" felt that President Bill Clinton's policy of "strategic engagement" was selling out American interests to the growing China threat (Gertz 2000; WP 22 February 2000, A1).

In this argument, much note is made of the modernization of the People's Liberation Army (PLA). China's expanding military is not due solely to economic and military espionage, or to taking advantage of the cut-rate Russian arms bazaar (Cox 1999; Bernstein and Munro 1998, 144, 68); in the 1980s, the People's Liberation Army (PLA) started to engage in business to accumulate capital and acquire dual-use technology (Bernstein and Munro 1998, 141, 130–48; Cox 1999). Using traditional realist calculations of military as well as economic strength, Mearsheimer concludes that even a democratic and prosperous China would be a threat as it challenged the existing balance of power (Mearsheimer 2001, 396–402). The discourse thus moves from Japan, Inc., to Greater China, Inc., to PLA, Inc. (Bickford 1993). Indeed, in *The Coming Conflict with China,* Bernstein and Munro argue that China's military modernization is being paid for by the U.S. consumer and encouraged by a New China Lobby of American big business (Bernstein and Munro 1998, 80, 105–29, 146; also see Gertz 2000). Even though the PLA's entrepreneurial activities were restricted in the late 1990s, the argument continued. Any "trade war" with China, security studies experts have told us, would be different from trade problems with Japan; trade conflict could lead to military conflict because China is not a U.S. ally like Japan (Bernstein and Munro 1998, 148).

China is a threat, according to such security studies texts, because the PRC will convert its economic power into political-military power; this is to be expected as part of a macro international history of the rise and fall of great empires (Kennedy 1989; Huntington 1996, 229;

Christensen 1996, 37, 52; Swaine and Tellis 2000, 218–28; Deng and Yong 1999a; Bernstein and Munro 1998, 52). These experts like to point to militant nationalist texts in the PRC, such as *China Can Say No,* that use such an aggressive expansionist vocabulary. One of the authors of *China Can Say No* posits a "Greater Chinese Economic-Cultural Sphere" to link the Confucian countries of East Asia—including the great traditional enemy Japan. This is more than the Confucian capitalism of the previous section: the ambition is to "develop a pattern of world order" (Song Qiang 1996, 29–30). Thus "the Rise of China"' will challenge not just the status of Taiwan, but the existing world order.

Security studies analyses characteristically end with scenarios that argue how China could be either cooperative or aggressive as a great power (Swaine and Tellis 2000, 187–229; Gertz 2000, 171–98; Bernstein and Munro 1998, 186–202). The "democratic Peace" theory is mobilized to show how a cooperative China needs to be more democratic in a "triumph of reason" (Swaine and Tellis 2000, 187–97; Bachman 2000; McCormick 2000; Friedman 2000; He and Guo 2000). In other words, China would need to become more like "us" in Euro-America: "rationality" is defined as liberal and democratic (Swaine and Tellis 2000, 188; Bernstein and Munro 1998, 95, 101; Nathan and Ross 1997).

"China threat" discourse involves a conceptual shift from Confucian capitalism. While Confucian capitalism relied on the core values of economic culture, "China threat" returns to the essentials of *political* culture to define a single and coherent Chinese state and culture (Swaine and Tellis 2000, 40; Pye 1990; Huntington 1996, 28, 45). Ignoring the evidence of growing democracy at the village level in the PRC and throughout Taiwan (Oi and Rozelle 2000, Chao and Myers 2000; Pei, Minxin 2000; Shi, Tianjian 2000), security studies texts argue that democracy is "contrary to Chinese political culture" (Bernstein and Munro 1998, 15; Huntington 1996, 238). For Huntington, "Confucian democracy" is an oxymoron (Huntington 1991, 300). The "cooperative China" argument is thus easily discarded since those who trumpet such a "total Westernization" of China are (repeatedly) dismissed as naïve (Bernstein and Munro 1998, 201, 204, 206; Christensen 1999, 242). China is taken to be aggressive, not for positive reasons or evidence; rather, China is aggressive because, it is argued, of a lack, because of

Otherness (Swaine and Tellis 2000, 198, 216). Chinese are uncooperative simply because they are different. Thus security studies texts see the exotic nature of Chinese civilization as a threat. Culturalism leads to containment (Su and Sullivan 2000, 285).

Thus, while Confucian capitalism appeals to positive entrepreneurial values, strategic studies texts remind us of China's coercive strategic culture. It is remarkable that, while security studies scholars typically appeal to the universal iron laws of international relations, those who explore Chinese foreign policy in recent texts often appeal to history—at length (Johnston 1995; Swaine and Tellis 2000, 21–96; Bernstein and Munro 1998, 53–56). It used to be common, however, to appeal to a *break* in Chinese history in the twentieth century when the empire entered the modern world of nation-states (Kim, Samuel 1998b; Zhao Suisheng 1998a). Chinese foreign policy texts typically recounted the tributary relations of the imperial era in their first chapter; this linear narrative of diplomatic history would move on to examine the transition in modern history from empire to nation-state. This is much like international relations theory in Euro-America, where history is characteristically deployed to reify, rather than question, the present (Walker 1993, 88). Medieval history is used to show how the past is meaningful as part of a progressive narrative leading to modernity, rather than to recover alternatives to the present (Armstrong 1993, 12–41; Holsti 1995, 1–22). Chinese civilization thus is traditionally considered primarily as the background for studies of the foreign policy of the Chinese nation-state (Zhao Suisheng 1998a; Nathan and Ross 1997, 19–34; Lee Chae-jin 1996; Tu Weiming 1994a).

But recent Chinese foreign policy texts—including one from RAND, written for the U.S. Air Force—have argued for a continuity between imperial and modern Chinese strategy (Swaine and Tellis 2000, x, 7, 97; Johnston 1996, 217). This trend entails an expansion of security studies to include China's unique history and culture (Swaine and Tellis 2000, 2; Bernstein and Munro 1998, 4, 53).

Johnston's "Cultural Realism" is the most sophisticated example of the strategic culture argument (Johnston 1995; Johnston 1996; also see Booth and Trood 1999). As we saw above, it is widely cited even by those policy makers who are more interested in its realism than its culture (Swaine and Tellis 2000, 46–49; Osius 2001; Glaser 2001). Although China has a strong self-image as a peaceful empire that exerted the "soft power" of Confucian civilization, Johnston tells us it also has an enduring tradition of employing the hard power of military coercion. In other words, there are two strategic cultures in China: Confucian-Mencian, which is "Idealist," and Legalist, which is "Realist." Johnston explores both imperial and Maoist history to argue that, when push came to shove, Chinese strategic culture has been *parabellum*. While Western realpolitik says, "if you want peace, prepare for war," Johnston quotes the Chinese classics, "thinking about danger and threat, while residing in conditions of peace" (Johnston 1995, 107).

Thus, in China, he argues, war was a constant occurrence, in a zero-sum game that employed both pure violence and absolute flexibility (Johnston 1995, 61–108; Johnston 1996, 219–20); since one of the main continuities between the revolutionary goals of Mao and the reformist policies of Deng Xiaoping is strategic culture, this can be expected to continue (Johnston 1996, 221). Many security studies texts therefore state that "China Rising" means an expansion of the PRC as a historical necessity (Chang, Maria 2001, 243; Christensen 1999, 240; Huntington 1996, 229): the rise of great-power China is seen as the emergence of a new "evil empire."

Criticisms of China as irredeemably evil were most vociferous from the conservative Blue Team in the late 1990s. Hence it is surprising that the PRC was not included in President George W. Bush's "axis of evil" in 2002. The quick explanation is that the "China Threat" was generated in part by party politics; once Bush was in the White House and Donald Rumsfeld in the Pentagon, the Blue Team was not so concerned about Washington "selling out" to Beijing. But, more important, since 2001 there has been a growing cooperation between Beijing and Washington. China has cooperated with the United States in the "war on terrorism"—even though the military in Beijing is suspicious that the U.S. military deployment in Central Asia is using the "war on terrorism" as an opportunity to encircle China (Shambaugh 2002, 244, 249; *White Paper on China's National Defense* 2002). In 2003, relations between China and the United States were the most stable since 1989.

Actually, cooperation began before September 11, with Colin Powell's visit to Beijing in July 2001. After the EP-3 surveillance plane incident in April, the Bush administration sought to improve relations with China—and, in this regard, it was quicker than previous administrations in changing from the harsh anti-Chinese rhetoric of the presidential campaign to pragmatic diplomacy (Shambaugh 2002, 244; Interview 2003). Hence, China is now seen as a partner in the "war on terrorism" rather than as a "strategic competitor" that is part of an axis of evil. But Christensen warns that the bilateral relationship is not on solid ground, and is determined more by the Taiwan factor than by common concerns over terrorism: "there is a direct relationship between PRC confidence levels on Taiwan and PRC attitudes about the role of the United States and its allies in the region"; when Beijing was confident about political trends in Taiwan in 2001 it cooperated with the United States, but when it became concerned about the success of separatist parties in the December 2001 Taiwanese parliamentary elections, it renewed its criticism of the United States and the "war on terrorism" (Christensen 2002, 7, 8; Shambaugh 2002, 247–49).

It is not strange, then, that the scenarios at the end of security studies texts commonly frame the "China threat" in relation to Taiwan (see Bernstein and Munro 1998, 149–65, 186–202; Gertz 2000, 171–98). While Confucian capitalist discourse examines how Taiwan is an opportunity in Greater China, the "China threat" discourse sees Taiwan as a security danger. The problem is seen as not just for the 23 million residents of the island, but for the United States as well. Again, "management-speak" is employed: U.S. policy needs to manage Taiwan between independence and reunification. The two main crises surrounding Taiwan in 1995–96 and 1999–2000 revolved around the presidential elections and Beijing's desire to guide the result away from independence, and to separate democracy and independence (Christensen 1996, 49). According to security studies texts, it is in the interest of U.S. national security to defend Taiwan because Taiwan is democratic, but this democracy cannot be encouraged if it leads to independence, and thus to international conflict with the PRC (see Taiwan Security Enhancement Act 2000). In other words, the United States not only has to manage Taiwan between popular sovereignty and state sovereignty; it also has to manage China. As the title of a popular book puts it, *Engaging China: the Management of an Emerging Power* (Johnston and Ross 1999).

While Huntington tells us to accept Greater China as a new sphere of influence in détente with the West—or risk "civilizational war"—most security studies texts tell us not to "kowtow" to Chinese culture and "appease" the PRC (Gertz 2000; Segal 1999: 36; Swaine and Tellis 2000; Bernstein and Munro 1998; Christensen 1999, 252; Nathan and Ross 1997, 237). Just as the United States has to manage Taiwan between popular and state sovereignty, it has to manage the "Rise of China" (Swaine and Tellis 2000, 1; Nathan and Ross 1997, xvi).

Even those who say that China is actually not a threat do not question the historical trajectory of China's rise. They merely question the inflated statistics of Greater China: it is growing, but not yet grown (Nathan and Ross 1997, xi–xii; 228ff; Cumings 1999, 151–70; Swaine and Tellis 2000, 237; Pumphrey 2002; Yee and Storey 2002). Segal is most adamant when he argues that China is "overrated as a market, a power, and a source of ideas" and merely a "second-rank middle power" (Segal 1999, 24). According to a broad range of commentators (as we saw in the introduction), the key to a rational policy is, then, to dispel the cloud of rhetoric that surrounds China and look at the facts. (Segal 1999, 24, 36; Cumings 1999, 170; Nathan and Ross 1997; *Foreign Affairs* 2002).

Although many texts, especially in China, assume that "China threat" discourse is a Western production, this discourse also has echoes in Southeast Asia and Northeast Asia (Callahan 2003a; Bolt 2000, 12; Lee Lai To 1999, 59). Not only are there fears of a "mainland China threat" in Taiwan and Hong Kong; China has had a rocky relationship with Southeast Asian countries in terms of both interethnic and international relations; for example, a *Bangkok Post* editorial worried about "China's alarming military growth" (*Bangkok Post*, 27 August 2000). Hence, Chinese officials in the mid-1990s stressed that they were not a threat to Southeast Asian nations either in terms of a renewed Chinese empire or of cultural chauvinism among ethnic Chinese in Southeast Asian countries (Hicks and Mackie 1994). Southeast Asian states do not only fear a reassertion of Imperial China, but have more recent memories of communist insurgencies organized by ethnic Chinese and funded by the PRC. Thus, by 1995, "the term Greater China ha[d] virtually disappeared from the official PRC political discourse" because Beijing saw it as problematic (Zha Daojiong 1995, 184–85; Bolt 2000, 11; Interview in Xiamen 2002); today the phrase only appears in the official English-language newspaper *China Daily*, as part of the name of multinational corporations: Compaq Greater

China, Gemplus Greater China, and Visa International's "Greater China Region and Philippines" section.

Although the term may have passed from official discourse, which now looks to the standard vocabulary of "overseas Chinese" *[Nanyang]* and "Asia-Pacific" *[Ya-Tai]*, the Greater China concept continues in various forms: Greater Chinese economic sphere *(Da Zhonghua jingji quan)*, Chinese economic region *(Zhonghua jingji qu)*, Chinese economic sphere *(Zhonghua jingji quan)*, Greater Chinese economic-cultural sphere *(Da zhonghua jingji wenhua quan)*, Cultural China *(Wenhua Zhongguo)*, civilization-state, empire-state, invisible empire, and ungrounded empire. But the subtlety of these Chinese and English terms is missing from mainstream discussions of Greater China. Geopolitics organizes Shambaugh's *Greater China*, where most chapters are country studies of the component parts of "Greater China": China, Taiwan, Hong Kong, and Macao (Lin, Chong-pin 1995; Leng and Lin 1995; Hook 1995; Baker 1995; Edmonds 1995; Lampton et al. 1992). Likewise, Zhao, Uhalley, and Zha organize their critical view of the discourse around territorial perspectives: "from the PRC," "from Hong Kong," "from Taiwan," "from the United States," and "from Southeast Asia" (Zhao Wenlie 1995; Uhalley 1994; Zha Daojiong 1995). However, this focus on the territorial states, and thus on the unity, coherence, and singularity of the component parts of "Greater China," leads us away from the blurring of boundaries to a standard listing of the facts and figures of these territories.

The cover of Shambaugh's *Greater China*—a commonsense collage of photographs of Deng Xiaoping, Chris Patten, and Lee Teng-hui—speaks to this problem: Greater China is not so much about leaders who represent states, as about the anonymous social and economic forces of the millions of people who are pushing and pulling at the region. Analysts are still dealing with a medieval notion of sovereignty where power is concentrated in the person of the Sovereign (now the State). Radical political action is framed in terms of what to do with the Sovereign/State: either depose the king (in "China threat") or crown a new king (in Confucian capitalism). Foucault suggests that to contest power we need to reconceptualize it away from its close focus on the state: "We need to cut off the King's head: in political theory that has still to be done" (Foucault 1980b, 121). Thus anti-state oppositional discourse tends to reproduce the state even as it resists it: "the struggle in this limited political space has permitted the state to survive, even as we are questioning it" (Foucault 1991, 103).

Hence the discourses of Greater China, Confucian capitalism, and/or "China threat" are unable to address these transnational ambiguities because the key concepts of civilization, security, and sovereignty are not critically examined. Culture is mobilized simply to state that China is naturally capitalist and/or undemocratic; history is uncritically deployed to inform realist security calculations. Indeed, as we saw above, the mainstream discourse that produces Greater China has shifting foundations; it moves from political culture to economic culture and back again. A more fundamental critique of such a normative politics and civilization is necessary.

GREATER CHINA AS A HETEROTOPIA

Rather than merely question the accuracy of the statistics of Greater China's growth, we must interrogate how we frame the relation "China and the world." Instead of trying to correct all the mistakes and misunderstandings, in order to get Confucius and Chinese civilization right, Greater China discourse is an opportunity to refigure political space. In this way, we can begin to write a new social grammar, rather than simply add a new vocabulary of *guanxi* and *weiji* to the state-centric language of international relations (see Dirlik 1998a, 5). Foucault's notion of "heterotopia" is useful here for problematizing the unified notions of civilization and power that mainstream Greater China discourse asserts. Heterotopia carves out a useful space for difference. Political space, for Foucault, is not a question of dangers or opportunities, voids or norms, the real world or utopia/dystopia, but of heterotopia. In his short essay "Of Other Spaces," Foucault discusses the concept of heterotopia—literally, another space—by juxtaposing it with utopia to undermine any notion of "the real world." Utopias "represent society itself in a perfected form, or else society turned upside down, but in any case these utopias are fundamentally unreal spaces" (Foucault 1986, 24). The capitalist utopia/dystopia, opportunity/danger of "Greater China" are good examples of such unreal spaces.

Heterotopias, on the other hand, are "a kind of effectively enacted utopia in which real sites, all other real sites that can be found within the culture, are simultaneously represented, contested, and inverted" (Foucault 1986, 24). Foucault writes that prisons are heterotopia, as are gardens, colonies, cemeteries, boats, and brothels. Hence, heterotopia are not like the clean or pure norms of the social constructivists; they are multiple, and thus involved in struggle and politics. The *Forbes* advertisement's mixed Maoist and capitalist utopia is a case in point. Foucault overstates his case by talking in terms of the ubiquity of heterotopia in every culture. There is little need to universalize heterotopia and list its principles, as he does in the essay. Rather, it is helpful to suggest some conditions and characteristics of heterotopia: real spaces that question what they represent. These are "capable of juxtaposing in a single real place several spaces, several sites that are in themselves incompatible" (Foucault 1986, 25). They are ironic spaces that have their own system of contending codes and power networks.

Greater China, then, is better understood as a heterotopia than as a geopolitical entity. Rather than territorial units, it is composed of highly mobile populations, involved in contradictions and contestations about identity, community, and civilization.

The story of Dao Zhi, the (in)famous Robber Zhi, from the classical Chinese text the *Zhuangzi,* resonates with heterotopia and problematizes simple civilization/barbarian relations. In this story, Confucius is perplexed when he hears that Dao Zhi is a notorious bandit, because Zhi is the younger brother of Liu'xia Ji, a famous government official. Confucius criticizes Liu'xia for not fulfilling the filial duty of properly instructing his younger brother Zhi in the rites, as civilization demands. After receiving an unsatisfying answer from Liu'xia—actually a warning to keep away from Dao Zhi—Confucius sets out to bring this criminal back into the fold of "civilization." The proper way for Confucius to do this is to instruct Dao Zhi in the key Chinese concepts *ren, sheng, yi, zhi, yong*—humanity, sageliness, justice, wisdom, and courage; in short, Confucius ventures out into the wilderness to rescue Dao Zhi from a cultural void of barbarism and to baptize him into civilized society.

The distinction between civilization and barbarism at first seems to be territorial: Zhi's lair is off in the woods. But Confucius soon sees that the distinction is in fact conceptual, a matter of identity practices. Upon meeting, Zhi quickly takes control of the conversation and lectures Confucius about the same concepts of civilization. Zhi tells Confucius that he is not caught in a barbarous void of meaning, a dystopia of vice, but a heterotopia of robbers. Zhi is well aware of the borders of civilization, but he has a much more flexible relation to them than has Confucius. In short, Zhi is not a robber, but an outlaw—outside and alongside the hegemonic code of civilization. The outlaws have the same "five virtues" of humanity, sageliness, justice, wisdom, and courage resident in their real site. Yet Dao Zhi traces out their discursive economies (much as Nietzsche does in *The Genealogy of Morals*) to show how the meaning of these terms is contingent and not essential. The terms have different meanings in his heterotopia. For example, wisdom is knowing whether or not one can pull off the heist, and humanity is acted out in how the loot is divided up—he's no Robin Hood. In this heterotopia, Dao Zhi is involved in a productive construction of civilization.

This reframing and multiplicity confuses Confucius, who is still operating in an exclusive inside/outside binary mode of civilization/barbarism that values ontological stability. At the end of the story, Confucius scurries back to his followers to confront these issues. Or to put it another way, Confucius scurries back to his text. For here I am not recounting the Confucian *Analects* or other sources of orthodox Confucian lore, but the radical retextualization of Confucius from another classical text, the *Zhuangzi*, in order to loosen up the canonical meaning of "Chinese civilization."[5]

This is a heterotopic act in that the *Zhuangzi* takes liberties with historical personages—just as I have with the extant text of the *Zhuangzi* in reading chapters 10 and 29 into one hybrid story—to make points in an oblique way (*Zhuangzi* 1985; also see Graham 1981: 207–10, 233–42). Confucius is out of his cultural universe when he journeys to see Dao Zhi, through *Zhuangzi's* text. Dao Zhi presents a different code, a not altogether new (and thus utopian) code, but a twist on the extant "civilization." In so doing, this illusory civilization makes one question other codes of civilization. Foucault encourages us to do this when he talks of heterotopia "creat[ing] a space of illusion that exposes every real space, all the sites inside of which human life is partitioned, as still more illusory" (Foucault 1986, 27).

Following from this classical notion of multiple Confuciuses in heterotopia I can likewise turn civilization from an answer—a force and source of stability—into a question, and thus a critical opportunity. In other words, with heterotopia we can turn *weiji* from a cliché of international business back into a critical practice. Rather than discuss Greater China via a simple reassertion of "tradition" in Orientalist terms of Chinese uniqueness, we need to examine the complexity of the politics of culture. Some note that culture is the least studied aspect of Greater China (Harding 1995, 21). The next chapter will consider in more detail how Chinese civilization works, through a critical examination of how the border between civilization and barbarism has been negotiated. For this, I must shift from cultural economics and security studies to consider Greater China in terms of popular culture and recycled traditions. Once again, I will use "civilization" not to provide an answer to political questions but to shift the debate to a new problematique. In this way politics can be reinserted into the study of East Asia in a way that still recognizes the importance of cultural forms of modernity.

2

Questioning Civilization: Self/Other Relations in Chinese Foreign Policy

In the previous chapter, I argued that the vigorous debate over Chinese foreign policy in both academic and policy circles increasingly goes beyond diplomacy and political economy to consider the nature of Chinese civilization. Indeed, chapter 1 noted that much of the discussion about "Greater China" is involved in the ironic practice of *weiji*, the Chinese word for a "crisis" that combines the elements of danger *(wei)* and opportunity *(ji)*. In this case, the danger is of Greater China leading to a political reunification that has imperial ambitions of territorial expansion. The opportunity entails an economic reading of Greater China as the newest version of capitalist utopia. Hence, I argue, most discussion of Greater China takes shared culture for granted, and thus is not critical of how "civilization" takes on many different meanings in Chinese practice. The recurrent crisis of Chinese identity (Barmé 1999) underlines how such a critical view of "civilization" is necessary to produce the dangers and opportunities of civilization.

The current chapter will argue that taking *civilization* as an answer to political questions is misleading. Rather than taking civilization as an answer to such questions—Chinese culture as either a threat of war or the key to peace—I problematize "civilization" by framing it as a question, a problem, an interrogation (Walker 1993, 37). While mainstream international relations theory takes for granted that culture is conservative (Pye 1990; Huntington 1996; Katzenstein 1996b), my analysis will show how civilization is not an obvious or coherent *thing*. Civilization is neither idealistic nor Orientalist, progressive nor conservative. Civilization is a multicoded *relationship* in Chinese discourse, involving both dangers and opportunities, problems and possibilities (see Dirlik 1997, 108). Thus rather than "thinking through Chinese civilization" (Hall and Ames 1987) to find a stable answer, I propose to think with and against civilization, and thereby to "use references to a tradition not as a legitimation of reification and closure, but as a source of critical opportunity" (Walker 1993, 43, 31). In other words, "civilization" does not answer the political questions about Greater China or international studies; it shifts the terms of debate on to a different terrain, a new problematique that highlights the transnational character of politics in East Asia and beyond.

To understand peace/war relations and other sites of violence we need to consider how the relations of civilization/barbarian, self/Other, and inside/outside are negotiated. Although such divisions may seem obvious, the struggle over "One China" shows that such distinctions are not clear in China (Yates 1997). In *Writing Security*, Campbell shows how encounters with Otherness have defined "dangers" in United States foreign policy. In this way he opens up a new terrain for study: "Foreign policy shifts from a concern of relations between states that take place across ahistorical, frozen, pregiven boundaries, to a concern with the establishment of boundaries that constitute, at one and the same time, the 'state' and 'the international system'" (Campbell 1998a, 61). Thus, he argues that there are two senses of "foreign policy." On the one hand, foreign policy refers to all practices of differentiation between self and Other; this practice of foreign policy is divorced from the state and applies to encounters with Otherness in sociologicial sites such as ethnicity, race, class, gender, region, and sexuality. On the other hand, foreign policy (in the second sense, which Campbell capitalizes as Foreign Policy) is a performance by the state that serves to reproduce the construction of identity made possible by the first mode of foreign policy (Campbell 1998a, 68–70). Foreign Policy's job, then, is to guard the borders inscribed by foreign policy. Foreign policy, in both senses, is about frontiers of identity and territory.

Chinese foreign policy is also organized around frontiers. While American identity and foreign policy have been shaped by the West and encounters with the different political economy of the Native

Americans, China has been involved in a similar struggle with horse nomads in its own northwest. In America, "The frontier is central to identity because it is not only an open space beckoning those who seek success, but also the (ever-shifting) boundary between 'barbarism' and 'civilization,' chaos and order, the 'feminine' and the 'masculine'" (Campbell 1998a, 146). As John Hay's *Boundaries in China* (1994b) shows, Chinese frontiers likewise are not simply territorial, or civilizational, but based on distinctions of ritual, temporality, class, and gender. Although it is often taken for granted that "civilization" is simply an excuse for Euro-American imperialism, an assumption that no doubt was and continues to be true (see Gong 1984; Keene 2001), "civilization" was also a code for the Chinese empire. As we will see, this code reentered Chinese international relations texts in the 1990s; hence civilizing the natives is not simply the "white man's burden" but a recurrent theme in Chinese foreign policy.

This chapter will thus shift away from the "political culture" approaches of chapter 2 to ethnographic analyses of the politics of culture/the culture of politics. The argument will explore two interrelated points: first, it will shift from considering power in terms of territorial sovereignty to sovereignty conceived in terms of populations, or popular sovereignty. Second, it will shift measurement of power in international relations from quantity—more territory, stronger weapons, faster economic growth—to quality, the ethical questions of addressing Otherness.

The discourse of "Greater China" provides a convenient entry into this dynamic, because the two Chinese terms contain relevant ambiguities. Greater *(da)* can be read either as quantity ("big") or as quality ("great" as in *good*). "China" can be written either territorially (*Zhongguo*, Central States or Middle Kingdom) or in terms of human populations (*Zhonghua*, the "Chineseness" of ethnicity or culture). The shift from territory to population also includes the shift from quantity to quality: *hua* for Chineseness literally means "magnificent" and "flourishing (civilization)," and is a homonym for "transformation."

Using the logic of heterotopia, I am able to resist the temptation of coherent and singular definitions of civilization as a substance, to suggest that civilization and barbarism are best understood as a contingent relation: each continually produces the other. While

Greater China is best conceived as a heterotopia, Hay reminds us that heterochronia—the concept of other times—is also active in China. In addition to linear historical narratives of progress, and cyclical historical narratives of return to a golden age, Chinese memory employs "heterochronicity in which several pasts could be contemporary with the present" (Hay 1994a, 4). Temporality and spatiality are intimately related in the practices of civilization.

This chapter will show how the concept of civilization has been used in Chinese texts in four ways: nativism, conquest, conversion, and diaspora.[1] None of these narratives is ultimately true or false. Together, in a heterotopia/heterochronia of Chinese civilization, these four constitute a repertoire of foreign policy narratives, thus different ways of addressing alterity. Therefore we are not searching for four "things," but examining four sets of relationships.

NATIVISM: GREATER CHINA AS *ZHONGGUO*

The first narrative of civilization is the most familiar to international relations scholars. It defines Chineseness in terms of *guo*-territorial state: *Zhongguo*. Thus it is similar to realism and nationalism, which look to the nation-state as the primary unit of analysis; here, the state is in perpetual conflict with other nation-states (see Zheng, Yongnian 1999). But this is a particular kind of realism, an inward-looking and defensive nationalism best described as nativism.

The nativist school sees civilization as restrictive and taming, as exemplified in an oft-quoted passage from the Confucian *Analects*: "If there is a preponderance of basic stuff over civilization, then there will be barbarism" (Confucius 1979, 6/18, 12/8);[2] civilization is the thing that holds one back from the wilder, more barbaric influences. Indeed, the nativist concept of civilization looks to the Great Wall as a guiding metaphor for Greater China: civilization is seen as complete and perfect, and is involved in dual containment. The Great Wall is not just to keep the barbarians out, but to keep the Chinese in (Waldron 1990, 30; Lattimore 1951). Indeed, rather than simply arguing against Western containment of a "China threat," many Chinese texts push for a self-containment of China (Zheng, Yongnian 1999, 145). In this way, civilization corrals difference into "barbarism." As Connolly pointed out more generally, "Identity requires difference in order to be, and it converts difference into otherness in order to secure its own self-certainty" (Connolly 1991, 64).

Thus, Great Wall strategies involve policing Chinese identity as well as guarding Chinese territory. In nativism, culture is examined to find a set of core values that guide national identity—disregarding forms of self/Other relations such as ethnicity, age, gender, religion, region, and so on. Examples are books like the hypernationalist *China Can Say No* that direct their remonstrations as much at fellow Chinese as against America and Japan. The section titles are not "Yankee Go Home," but "Chinese People: Emotional and Political Choices for the Post Cold-War Era" and "I Spurn *That Kind* of Chinese Person" (Zhang Zangzang 1996, 55–156; Hughes 1997b, 119). Rather than being expansionist or imperialist, the authors of *China Can Say No* feel that isolationism is the best policy:

> America cannot lead any [other] country, it can only lead itself.
> Japan cannot lead any country, and sometimes is unable
>   to lead itself.
> China does not want to lead any country, and only wants
>   to lead itself.
> (He Beilin 1996, 3)

This declaration was seen as important enough to be put in the blurb on the back of the book. Indeed, the nativist argument fits in with an important trend in Chinese international relations theory: realism with Chinese characteristics, and "IR theory with Chinese characteristics" (Liang Shoude 1996; Liang Shoude 1997; Liang and Hong 2000; Chen, Gerald 1999).

The key to "IR theory with Chinese characteristics," though, is not Chinese culture. Rather, it is a spin-off from Deng Xiaoping's call to "build socialism with Chinese characteristics" (Deng Xiaoping 1987). After noting that China has a unique historical experience, and warning Chinese scholars not to "blindly follow Western achievements," leading international relations theorist Liang Shoude looks to three interrelated themes to define his "IR theory with Chinese characteristics": states rights rather than human rights, the interrelation of economics and politics, and "reform and development" as the key to world peace (Liang Shoude 1996, 298, 301–5). State sovereignty is central to all three themes. Ni Shixiong, Jin Yingzhong, and Feng Shaolei argue that Chinese characteristics are defined by another three points: (1) standing on the side of peace-loving people in the world, (2) promoting the "Five Principles of Peaceful Co-Existence," and (3) using a Chinese style of language, expression, and thought (in Song Xinning 2001, 68).

But as these themes attest, it has never been quite clear what is "Chinese" about these characteristics. Zhang Mingqian, a high-ranking official, gives an oppositional and tautological account of international relations theory with Chinese characteristics.

> It is not the Soviet Theory, nor is it the American theory, nor even the theory that could be accepted by the whole world. It must be Chinese opinions of international affairs and the culmination of Chinese understandings of the laws of the development of the international community. (in Song Xinning 2001, 67; Liang and Hong 2000)

Basically, the theory must come from "us" (Chinese), not "them" (foreigners), without examining just what these self/Other relations entail. Although it often begs the question of what is "China" and what is the "West," this nativism is often used by Chinese scholars writing in the West as part of a neorealist position (Deng and Wang 1999). Liang argues that "to emphasize 'Chinese characteristics' is to liberate our minds," but others state that the theory shackles academic research because it comes from Dengist politicized language (Liang Shoude 1996, 298, 294). Song Xinning, for example, deconstructs "IR theory with Chinese characteristics" to show how it is restricted by ideology, deployed as a tool of governance, and thus made useful only to a very narrow concept of politics, national identity, and international relations (Song Xinning 2001).

To see how nativism works, we need to go beyond mainstream international relations theory to examine two groups of scholars in China who have been writing about traditional culture in national and international terms. While a key researcher at a military think-tank, Yan Xuetong expanded his understanding of national interest from military, political, economic, and social factors to include culture. In the recent past, Chinese international relations scholars have disregarded the importance of culture, dismissing it as merely superstructure (Yan Xuetong 1995, 223–27; also see Wang Jisi 1995), but in *An Analysis of China's National Interest,* Yan argues that cultural interest is an important part of comprehensive national strength and power. Although recognizing both the positive and the negative aspects of Chinese civilization, and the necessity of cultural exchange with the West, Yan concludes that for China to be strong it needs to actively promote its traditional culture to "enhance the vitality of [modern] Chinese culture" (Yan Xuetong 1995, 232–35, 249–52). In the strategic proposals offered at the end of his book, Yan recommends that "the government should implement a cultural policy to support the research of Guoxue-national studies" to show how peaceful Chinese civilization is (Yan Xuetong 1995, 296).

Indeed, it is not just the cadre of realist and neorealist foreign policy experts who have taken Yan's advice. The Chinese Defense Ministry has been convinced of the value of a cultural strategy; it included some of Yan's proposals in its 1998 National Defense White Paper (Interviews 1999):

> The defensive nature of China's national defense policy also springs from the country's historical and cultural traditions. China is a country with 5000 years of civilization, and a peace-loving tradition. Ancient Chinese thinkers advocated "associating with benevolent gentlemen and befriending good neighbors," which shows that throughout history the Chinese people have longed for peace in the world and for relations of friendship with the people of other countries.
>
> In military affairs, this maxim means solving disputes by non-military means, being wary of war and strategically gaining mastery by striking only after the enemy has struck. During the course of several thousand years, loving peace, stressing defense, seeking unification, promoting national unity, and jointly resisting foreign aggression have always been the main ideas of China's defense concept. The defense policy of New China has carried forward and developed such excellent Chinese historical and cultural traditions. (White Paper on China's National Defense 1998)

The Peoples Liberation Army thus uses a Confucian vocabulary— "associating with benevolent gentlemen and befriending good neighbors"—and other "excellent cultural traditions" to prove its peaceful intentions (also see Yan Xuetong 2001).

Yan's strategic recommendations lead us to the other area where nativism flourishes in Chinese academia, and also has influence on national policies: Guoxue–national studies. Guoxue is an abbreviation of Zhongguo zhi xue—the study of China—and is concerned with the particularities of Chinese traditional culture rather than with general issues of nationalism (see Wang Jisi 1995). Thus it is often translated as "traditional Chinese studies" and refers to the systematic study of the Chinese tradition that grew up in the nineteenth century as China was embarking on its perilous road from empire to nation-state. In the 1920s, Guoxue was critical of Chinese tradition; this can be seen in the writings of Lu Xun, Hu Shi, and Liang Qichao (Chen Lai 1998, 39–41; Cheng and Cao 1998, 304–5). This group of Guoxue scholars can be seen as using traditional Chinese culture to move "from Westernization to Modernization" (Luo Rongqu 1990).

Since it reappeared in the 1990s, Guoxue takes a less critical view of Chinese tradition (see Xie Qian 1998). Largely reacting to the threat of cultural homogenization, Westernization, and Americanization that are said to accompany globalization, many young intellectuals in China now look for authentically Chinese ways of addressing the challenges of modernity: localism or nativism (Deng Xiaojun 1998, 20; Cheng and Cao 1998, 304; Wang Ning 1998, 2–3; Zhao Suisheng 1997; Zhao Suisheng 1998b). This search was in part a reaction to China's love affair with the West in the 1980s.[3] Since the beginning of the 1990s, Guoxue scholars have looked to Chinese tradition for answers, and either disregard or are hostile to what they perceive as foreign and thus barbaric.[4] They therefore move not "from Westernization to Modernization," but "from modernity to Chineseness" (Xu, Ben 1998; Dirlik and Zhang 2000). Starting in the 1990s, Guoxue's style of nativism has involved a logic of rediscovery of the past, using the language of renaissance, more than a critical analysis of Chinese history (Cheng and Cao 1998; Wang Yuechan 1997). Chinese civilization has been obscured in the past century by incursions not just of foreign armies but of foreign culture. Still, the nativist narrative tells us that the core of Chinese civilization remains whole and merely waiting for (re)discovery (Xu, Ben 1998).

The Confucian renaissance is part of this "Guoxue fever." Surprisingly, it uses military metaphors. As one scholar writes, with the 1980s "Open Door Policy, the ideology of money-worship has accompanied the importation of foreign countries' goods . . . Confucianism, then, is our strongest weapon to defeat the ideology of money-worship [that comes from abroad]" (Zhao Guanglan 1996, 121). The argument thus comes full circle: Guoxue is not just about studying traditional culture; it is also about guarding national security. While mainstream international relations sees security in terms of military, political, and economic strength, this group of texts sees *guarding identity* as the key to security. Such studies are popular with the Chinese government, although some Chinese scholars say that they are not as influential in the academy (Deng Xiaojun 1998, 23; Chen Shaoming 1998, 65).

In the South China Sea disputes (examined in detail in the next chapter), the Chinese government and military use such a logic of discovery. Rather than relying on legal and scientific discourse to bolster claims to the Spratly Islands, official texts appeal to Chinese history to prove the islands' discovery as evidence of a Chinese presence "since ancient times" (Chinese Ministry of Foreign Affairs 1980). Further, Chinese images of the South China Sea also employ the Great Wall as a metaphor. China is defended on its Southern flank by a figurative great wall that consists of: militias of fisherfolk, as in the 1976 film "Great Wall of the South China Sea" *(Nanhai changcheng)*; the best ships the navy has to offer, as in a 1999 national exhibition's "Great Wall on the Seas" *(Haishang changcheng)*;[5] or island groups that themselves are "shaped like a bow that constitutes a Great Wall defending the China mainland" (Li and Hao 1976; Chinese Ministry of Foreign Affairs 1980, 21).[6] The South China Sea claims follow the nativist narrative of civilization because there is no population. Indeed, there is no territory either, but the discursive mechanisms work hard to turn water into territory that needs to be measured, delineated, and defended (Ni and Song 1997, 401–48). Since there are rival claims, the Spratly Islands disputes exist along the ambiguous line dividing inside and outside in China, and thus lead us into the conquest narrative of civilization.

In general, the nativist view of civilization is about territory and quantity: national security is securing the shape of China, both materially and spiritually. The texts we have examined define China in terms of *guo*-territorial state: *Zhongguo*. The barbarians are those who are outside the borders of China. They need to be excluded, be they the horse nomads of imperial times or American fast-food restaurants of today. This view appeals to a defensive, inward-looking Chineseness and foreign policy.

CONQUEST: GREATER CHINA AS *DA ZHONGGUO*

The second narrative of civilization in China also has similarities with mainstream international relations theory—specifically, realism. But rather than being an inward-looking study of nativist self/ Other relations, it uses the metaphor of conquest. To guard identity against foreign threats, it is not enough simply to build a Great Wall; rather, the state needs to attack and expand to conquer (or reconquer) adjacent territories. Rather than guarding the nation-state, as in nativism, civilization here works to reestablish China as an empire-state (Bøckman 1998). In the conquest narrative, civilization is complete but it is also expansive. As is often quoted from the ancient *Book of Songs (Shijing),* "All under heaven is civilized—*Tianxia wenming.*" Thus rather than civilization being attached to the nation-state as in nativism, civilization knits together East Asia: the PRC, South and North Korea, Taiwan, and Japan. This emerging field of regionalism is neither global nor national: "we can determine what constitutes the common regional heritage as distinct from the specific national traditions" (Rozman 1991a, vii; also see Elman et al. 2002).

Historically, regionalism went by another name: *tianxia* also means "empire." Civilization was linked to empire, and to the necessity of conquering barbarians. As Mencius said in a passage that became a precedent for an expansive foreign policy in imperial China, "I have heard of the Chinese converting barbarians, but not of their being converted by barbarians" (Mencius 1970, 3A/4; Dikötter 1992, 18). According to *Civilization and Barbarism,* an ethical handbook for Chinese youth published in 1998, this struggle is part of an unending war between civilization and barbarians:

> In order to fight for land, housing and cattle, in order to fight for women and slaves, in order to satisfy insatiable greed, in order to realize dominance over other people there is unceasing tribal war, race war, national war, state war, flames of war in the four quarters . . . Civilization and barbarism have been tearing and biting at each other in the same way from the beginnings of time until today. (Zhang Guolong 1998, 7)

This unending war between civilization and barbarism on all fronts describes struggles against Mongols on the steppes in imperial China as well as battles with Western barbarians for a reconquest in the modern era.

Thus Chinese civilization, as expressed both in imperial times and in the People's Republic, is not as pacific as tradition tells us. Rather (as we saw in the last chapter), there is a *parabellum* strategic culture in international relations: cultural realism (Johnston

1995; Johnston 1996). Johnston's argument is not just compelling to other scholars. His research is now often cited by policy makers who worry that as an emerging power China constitutes a threat to the world system (see Osius 2001). This argument also tallies with Huntington's notion of Confucian civilization—that it is simply an extension of the borders of the Chinese nation-state; the PRC is the core state of Confucian civilization, and the PLA is the main guarantor of its power (Huntington 1996, 168ff, 238).

There has been a robust reaction to both Johnston and Huntington in Chinese scholarship. Many of the comments are similar to American reactions that question the relevance of culture to international relations and foreign policy: international struggles are more political and economic than cultural (Wang Jisi 1995). Johnston is commonly criticized for telling only the violent part of the story of Chinese civilization; he disregards both the long history of civilian control of the military, and the enduring influence of Confucian pacifism in, e.g., nativism (Interviews 1999). The reaction to Huntington is more complex. In addition to predictable criticisms based on Marxist-Leninist and realist analysis, some Chinese scholars are intrigued by the possibility of a civilizational politics, especially one that recognizes Confucian civilization as dominant in East Asia (Wang Jisi 1995, 23–25; Hughes 1997b, 110). Although many disagree with Johnston's and Huntington's conclusions, they often take the civilizational discourse for granted; the world is organized into pure and coherent "enclaves" of identity (Shapiro 1997, 30–32). Some Chinese scholars therefore agree with the notion of Confucian civilization as a transnational force, but simply change its moral valence from negative to positive (see He Degong et al. 1997).

This positive moral argument for the benefits of Confucian civilization can be seen in both philosophical and international relations texts. In the international relations texts, there has been a return to nineteenth-century notions of world politics as struggle among "great powers" *(daguo, lieqiang)*. A rising China, therefore, will not be limited to its own territory, but will assume the regional and global responsibilities of a "great power" alongside the other, greater powers: the United States, the European Union, Japan, and Russia (Yu Zhengliang et al. 1998). China's rise to prominence is seen as natural and inevitable (Yan Xuetong 2001; Yan Xuetong et al. 1998; He Xin 1996). Thus, while nativism tends toward isolationism, in the conquest narrative China sees itself as one of the five great powers that regulate the world. This argument has loud echoes of the discourse of "great powers" that regulated Europe, and through European imperialism most of the world, during the nineteenth century. Rather than being antihegemonic, great power diplomacy according to the Concert of Europe relied on a "shared aristocratic outlook"—in a word, "imperialism"—to manage the world in a hierarchy of states (Watson 1992, 250). China's role as a permanent member of the U.N. Security Council is an example of this concept of Greater China as a Great Power: Roosevelt included Republican China as the reliable "policeman" of Asia (see Rozman 1999).

Indeed, texts tell us that it is imperative for China to rise in order to check the "new interventionism" of the West that has characterized the post–Cold War era. This era is often called the new Cold War in Chinese texts because of Western urgings to contain China (He Degong et al. 1997; Deng and Yong 1999a; *White Paper on China's National Defense in 2000*). The argument for a peaceful Chinese civilization is articulated in direct response to the Western-inspired "China threat" discourse (Yan Xuetong 2001; Zheng, Yongnian 1999). Li Shaojun's title is "The Peaceful Orientation of Chinese Civilization," but his subtitle is "a response to 'China threat' theory" (Li Shaojun 1999). China therefore needs to extend its power in order to reestablish a balance of power (Interviews 1999).

In this sense, the Chinese texts reverse the arguments of "China threat" discourse. Such discourse is based on the assumption of the benevolence of American hegemony in East Asia, and sees the rise of China as destabilizing the existing balance of power. On the other hand, Chinese texts state that the PRC needs to rise to check the imbalance of American hegemony in East Asia and the world (Deng and Wang 1999; Zheng, Yongnian 1999; Yan Xuetong et al. 1998; He Degong et al. 1997; He Xin 1996).

On a more positive note, Yan expands on the use of traditional Chinese civilization for security studies by exploring strategic culture in terms of the Confucian concepts of benevolence *(ren)* and virtue *(de)* (Yan Xuetong et al. 1999, 49–53). The strategic value of culture is confirmed in other texts that stress the peaceful nature of Chinese civilization. While the West is assumed to be naturally violent and expansionist, China is taken to be fundamentally peaceful (Zheng, Yongnian 1999, 80–82). "Confucian peace studies" consists of benevolent governance *(wangdao)* rather than hegemonic governance *(badao)* (Tian Guangqing 1998, 293–302; Yan Xuetong 2001; Kim Dae Jung 1994, 191); hence the rise of China will not only make the Asia-Pacific more peaceful, but the world more civilized (Yan Xuetong 2001; Xia Liping 2001).

The rise of China to the status of a great power is backed up philosophically by the concept of *Datong*, Great Harmony. Like the nativists, who returned to Chinese civilization for an analytic and descriptive vocabulary, many scholars and officials are reexamining the imperial vocabulary of governance: for example, benevolent governance is actually the "kingly way" (Cao Deben 1998; Yan Xuetong 2001; He Degong et al. 1997, 65–131; Callahan 2003b; Bøckman 1998, 312). *Datong* refers to a utopia described in a famous passage in the ancient *Book of Rites [Liji]*; it involves bringing unity and order to the empire (*Liji jijie* 1998, 581–83; de Bary 1960, 176). Thus the quest for unity that we see in the "One China Principle" goes beyond the borders of the PRC to embrace the empire/world: "Once the nation-states are established, we can pursue the Great Way of 'the Empire held in common,' then there will be a peaceful world" (Tian Guangqing 1998, 276; Liu Zhiguang 1992; Cao Deben 1998, 169; Zhao Guanglan 1996,125). Thus we have an alternative Chinese ideology for world hegemony: rather than an American "democratic peace," we have a Chinese "Great Harmony."

The rise of China as a great power is not limited to peace studies; it has territorial dimensions as well. This is not the first time that China has risen, and in some texts it seems that China is seeking to reestablish the empire at its height in the Qing dynasty. Rather than legitimating a nation-state, as in nativism, civilization works to reestablish China as an empire-state (Bøckman 1998). This is where the imperial vocabulary gets fleshed out in territorial space. In modern Chinese texts, the discourse of the "Century of National Humiliation" guides the conquest-and-reconquest narrative of civilization. These texts characteristically begin by stating the glories of Chinese civilization and its five-thousand-year history. The written texts are characteristically prefaced by maps that show the Chinese empire extending far into Siberia, Central Asia, and Southeast Asia (*Jindai Zhongguo* 1997, 2; Liu Zhen 1974, xii; Cao and Huang 1932, iii). The discourse then recounts how, at the hands of foreign invaders and corrupt Chinese regimes, sovereignty was lost, territory dismembered, and the Chinese people humiliated (Zhongguo geming bowuguan 1997; *Jindai Zhongguo* 1997; He Yu 1997; Callahan 2004a; Cohen 2002). The long-term aim of the conquest narrative is both political and cultural: first to unite these "lost territories" under Beijing's leadership, and second to avenge the humiliation. Both of these projects push for a unified Chineseness. Such images of expansive civilization could be seen with the celebration of the fiftieth anniversary of the founding of the PRC in 1999, which linked military prowess with five thousand years of Chinese civilization in an assertion of "great power" status.

While the nativist narrative of civilization employs a rhetoric of discovery, the conquest narrative, especially in its Century of National Humiliation mode, appeals to a logic of entitlement. It is seen as natural, rather than historical, that China is a great power; territories such as Hong Kong and Taiwan are figured as "naturally" Chinese, only pried away through foreign imperialist meddling and inept governance. It is not seen as necessary to figure power in terms of popular sovereignty, and thus consult the affected populations about their fate. Still, though identity and sovereignty are certainly related, they do not necessarily overlap—territorial sovereignty and popular sovereignty can go in different directions. As chapters 5 and 6 show, self/Other relations can be generated from within Chinese civilization as well as in foreign encounters.

The narrative of conquest again figures civilization in terms of quantity and territory—Greater China as *Da Zhongguo* in an assertion of great-power *(daguo)* status via the Great Harmony *(Datong)*. It is not surprising that such texts often rely heavily on maps; *The Map of the Century of National Humiliation* is the title of maps published in both 1997 and 1927 (*Jindai Zhongguo* 1997; in Jiang Gongsheng 1927). These maps are often used to expand the imagination for expanded territory. While the nativist narrative is anti-imperialistic and antihegemonic, the conquest narrative sees China joining the imperialist club of the Concert of Europe. Still, the conquest narrative contains the seeds of a shift to quality and populations. The overlap can be seen in Chinese texts where military metaphors are used for economic relations, "trade wars." Thus Sunzi's ancient classic, *The Art of War,* is refigured from military strategy to business strategy: *Sunzi's Art of War and Trade Wars* (Yuan Qishan 1999; also see Campbell 1992, 223–43).

To address politics in terms of popular sovereignty, we must examine the next narrative of civilization: conversion.

CONVERSION: GREATER CHINESE AS *DA ZHONGHUA*

The most common way to talk about Chinese civilization is in terms of ethnicity and culture, *Da Zhonghua* (Greater Chinese), rather than of *Da Zhongguo* (Greater China). "Greater Chinese" refers not to territory but to political-economic exchange in the East Asian region. As Katzenstein argues, regionalism in East Asia does not work according to formal state and suprastate institutions as in Europe. Rather, regionalism looks to the informal mechanisms of markets. Rather than being regulated by laws and rules, East Asian regionalism works according to networks of cultural relations (Katzenstein 1997); that overseas Chinese entrepreneurs provide 80 percent of the PRC's foreign direct investment is a celebrated case study of the phenomenon.

This political-economic argument feeds into the third narrative of civilization and barbarism, which works according to a logic of conversion. Here civilization is expansive but not complete, and thus is open to engagement. This view makes a decisive shift to seeing power in terms of populations and quality rather than in terms of territory and quantity: one conquers amounts of territory, but one converts the ideas of people. An oft-cited passage from the Confucian *Analects* illustrates this relation between civilization and barbarians: "Confucius wanted to go and live with the nine barbaric tribes of Yi. Someone said, 'They are uncultured, how can you do this?' Confucius answered, 'If a gentlemen dwells among them, how can they be uncultured?'" (Confucius 1979, 9/13). This quotation underlines how identity is not a matter of essential categories but of performances—in this case, ritual performances. Chineseness, then, is open to whoever will practice it.

By far the most dominant policy in traditional Chinese foreign relations looked to the notion of conversion (Fairbank 1968b; Zhao Suisheng 1998a; Howland 1996). Although idealized views suggest that influence only goes one way, relations between civilization and barbarism, center and periphery, are more complex. Such conversion was not necessarily to a simple Confucian orthodoxy—what we today would call cultural imperialism—but could also be to a constructive notion of Chineseness more characteristic of a heterotopia than were the core values of Guoxue.

Historically, the key to peace was engagement with barbarians via trade and diplomacy that crossed the Great Wall (Jagchid and Simons 1989). For example, one of the emperors of the Tang dynasty, commonly known as the high point of Chinese civilization, declared, "Since Antiquity all have honored the *Hua* [Chinese/civilization] and despised the *Yi* and *Di* [barbarians]; only I have loved both Civilization and barbarians, held together as father and mother" (in Waldron 1990, 47–48). This quotation also underlines how "barbarian" in premodern Chinese language was not a singular term. There were the Yi, Di, Rong, Man, and others. Chinese relations with these different sorts of "barbarians" also differed. Indeed, the Great Wall actually existed more as an image in discourse than as an engineering feat: there was no clear boundary between China and the horse nomads (Waldron 1990, 5, 24).

The Great Wall, then, is not an enduring structure that divided China from the barbarian hordes for millennia. There was no single-line frontier demarcated by a single wall representing a single policy (Waldron 1990, 171). Thus foreign policy debates continually involved Chinese defining themselves with and against the barbarians:

> At root they were about how culturally exclusive China must be in order to remain Chinese; about the nature and authority of the Chinese ruler; about where—and whether—to draw a line between the [barbarian] steppe and China proper. They were, in other words, arguments in which fundamentally different images of the polity collided. . . . [I]n fact the problem facing successive dynasties has not been conquering "China," or recovering it, or even ruling it. The first problem has always been defining it, and that is as true today as it ever was. (Waldron 1990, 190)

Many Chinese scholars reinscribe this narrative when they state that, even when the Han Chinese were conquered by the Mongols and Manchus, the Han Chinese were able to convert these barbarians into the proper Confucian Yuan and Qing dynasties.

This open and expansionist view of civilization is highlighted in the New Confucian renaissance. The leader of the Confucian revival in both the United States and East Asia is Harvard University's Tu

Weiming, who has worked not just as a writer but also as a speaker, organizer, and editor. Using the logic and vocabulary of "Greater China," Tu posited the idea of a "Cultural China" (Tu Weiming 1990; Tu Weiming 1994a; Wang Gungwu 1991). Cultural China includes the PRC, but is neither limited to it nor led by it. Tu's manifesto urges reconceptualization of Chineseness, reversing the center-periphery relations: since the Confucian capitalists on the periphery are successful, they should convert the center in Beijing back to their brand of Chineseness and thus recivilize mainland China via the mechanisms of what Tu calls the "civilization-state."

Here Tu is reversing the logic of Confucian capitalism that we examined in the previous chapter. Rather than taking "culture" for granted and celebrating the ever-expanding "economic" ties as Greater China discourse typically does, Tu rehearses the economic success story as the context for cultural issues. He appeals to a complex notion of identity that works against any "narrow-minded nationalism and racism." Like Greater China, Cultural China is not a place so much as a concept:

> It is true that Cultural China has implications of territory, nationality, race and language, but its essential defining characteristic is that it exceeds the particularities of territory, nationality, race and language. What it signifies is the construction of universal values of global significance. (Tu Weiming 1990, 60)

While Confucian capitalism uses the common cultural core of Confucianism to import capitalism into China, Tu's Cultural China uses the economic enticements of capitalism to export Confucianism (back) into China.

This combination of Confucianism and capitalism has had a measure of success. A huge "New Confucian Studies" project at the Chinese Academy of Social Sciences resulted in dozens of conferences and over one thousand publications by the early 1990s (Dirlik 1995, 238; Lin Tongqi et al. 1995). The opening ceremony of the First International Confucian Studies Association Conference (1994) was held in Beijing's Great Hall of the People. It was opened by Jiang Zemin, while the second conference (1999) was opened by a former vice-premier (RMRB 8 October 1994, 1; CD 8 October 1999). Chinese President Jiang Zemin's stress on the importance of building "spiritual civilization" alongside the material civilization of economic development shows the influence of Confucian values in the service of "building socialism with Chinese characteristics." Jiang goes out of his way to stress the need to "raise the quality" of both the Han and the national minority populations (Jiang Zemin 1999, 8, 10, 12). Thus in addition to bringing up images of high culture, civilization is deployed as a microtechnology of power: it "refers to international standards of labor discipline and orderly behavior in public places" (Anagnost 1997, 11, 75).[7]

Each of these projects is not simply seeking to reestablish Chinese tradition or Confucianism (Li Hongyan 1997, 19–21). Rather, each is involved in the mixing/constructing of harmonious civilization: the politics is shifted from conflicts between East and West, liberalism and Confucianism, Marxism and capitalism, to negotiating the correct mix. They often appeal to the *ti-yong* grammar of nineteenth-century Chinese modernizers who wished to use Western science and technology as a way of preserving Chinese civilization. This vocabulary, however, is updated by a call for a fusion of Eastern and Western civilizations in a pluralistic environment (Wang Jisi 1995). Civilization and barbarism are synthesized into a greater Chineseness *(Da Zhonghua)*, often leading to the use of a modern term for Chinese identity that integrates the overseas Chinese, the mainland Han Chinese, and national minorities into a new "race," *Zhonghua minzu*—the Zhonghua race (Dikötter 1992, 108; Zhao Suisheng 2000, 4; Bøckman 1998, 324; Chun 1996, 132).

Thus the rhetoric of conversion is synthesis of East and West, tradition and modernity, and so on, as well as a blurring of categories of culture, ethnicity, and race. Hong Kong, because of its peculiar history as a British colony and gateway to mainland China, figures prominently as a site of conversion and synthesis, "The Centaur of the East" (Cheung, Dung Kai 1998b, 202–4). Or, as Hong Kong's chief executive said in his 2000 policy address, Hong Kong people need to "enrich our culture in the new era by building on the foundation of an integration of the best of Chinese and foreign cultures" (Tung Chee Hwa 2000, 80).

This Chineseness is not just for the Chinese, either. The synthetic notion of civilization also informs the discourse of Confucian capitalism. The term was popular in English texts in the 1980s to account for the East Asian economic miracle; many of the popular business texts argued that the West needed to learn from Japanese,

Chinese, and Confucian society.[8] Although Confucian capitalism has largely been discredited in Euro-America due to the 1997 economic crisis, such cultural-economic discourses are still popular in East Asia (Jiang and Tang 2000; Higgott 2000). Many promoters of Confucianism are businessmen from Hong Kong, Taiwan, and Singapore; their task is not just to reconvert their compatriots on the mainland but to convert the rest of the world as well (see Tong Yun Kai 1999).

Hence the narrative of conversion spreads Chinese civilization beyond Chinese territory, and works to improve the quality of populations both foreign and domestic through economic and cultural exchange and synthesis. The politics is not just in what is being synthesized, but of who is doing the synthesizing. These can be unequal exchanges. Chinese civilization is still involved in a hierarchical relation to other ways of life: Others (either minority nationalities or Westerners) need to be converted to Chineseness for their own good. Like the use of *Zhonghua minzu*, this is an interesting shift from ethnicity to culture. Still, such a shift can lead to cultural violence and cultural imperialism—not to mention physical violence in both China proper and its periphery.

DIASPORA: GREATER CHINA AS TRANSNATIONAL RELATIONS IN FLEXIBLE CIVILIZATION

The fourth narrative of civilization in China involves a more flexible relationship between populations and territory. Both Tu Weiming and Katzenstein have loosened economic-culture's relation to the state, but they still are transfixed by the stable categories of ethnicity and place. The logic of conversion assumes that there is a stable *thing* called Chineseness, currently located outside the PRC rather than inside it. Thus there is much interest on both sides of the Pacific in diasporic communities, "Chinatowns" in North America, Australia, and Southeast Asia. These discussions often pose an "American" or a "Malaysian" culture against which Chinese civilization must struggle, whether isolated in Chinatowns or assimilated into the greater society (Huang Kunzhang 1998; Wang Gungwu 1991; Ong 1999). The Chinese government certainly understands the "overseas Chinese problem" in terms of a simple self/Other relation, of self-evidently Chinese people living in obviously foreign places (Interviews 1999; interview in Xiamen 2002).[9] Thus President Jiang Zemin went to Yaowarat, Bangkok's "Chinatown," during his September 1999 visit to Thailand, to meet the "overseas Chinese" community.[10]

While this corporatist understanding of society guides policies in places like Malaysia or Indonesia where citizens are sorted by the state according to ethnicity/race, it effaces the practice of Chinese civilization where identity is more social than political. For example, no one really knows the percentage of "Chinese" in Thailand. Ethnicity or race is not a category on the national identity card. This is not a scientific problem of survey methodology, either; rather, it constitutes a cultural and political issue of how to define Chineseness. Likewise, though there is a district in Bangkok known in English as Chinatown, it is not where most people whom one might code as Chinese live or work: in the past thirty years, the new generations have moved out of Yaowarat. More, they have moved out of any stable identity. As products of intermarriage, as well as of other forms of social exchange, the new generations are mixtures of Thai and Chinese that do not make sense in terms of the categories of assimilation or isolation. Being Chinese is already being Thai, and more importantly being Thai is already being Chinese (Suwanna 2000, Interview; Suwanna 1999, Interview). As Kasian explains:

> by now, "Chineseness" has been assimilated into "Thainess" and cannot be easily separated. Therefore now it is difficult to draw a line to divide the *Jek* [Chinese][11] from the Thai and claim that the *Jek* are the national enemies. The boundary of the definition of Thainess has already expanded to include *"Jek"* to unite with the Thai. (Kasian 1999, 41; also see Kasian 1997)

Although he uses the standard "assimilation" vocabulary, Kasian is also calling it into question. As the title of his book, *Civilized People,* tells us, Kasian is redefining practices of civilization in Thailand. This is not civilization conquering the barbarians or selectively combining with Otherness, to synthesize a grand new civilization like the *Zhonghua minzu* (Chinese race) (examined in the last section). Rather, flexible civilization involves a series of mixes for a multiple identity, a blurring of self and Other in the construction and reconstruction of social, economic, and cultural relations. Rather than discovery, entitlement, or synthesis, the diaspora narrative of civilization employs a rhetoric of "flexibility."

This mixing and confusion is not limited to relatively tolerant sites like Thailand. The slippery nature of the diaspora narrative can be seen in overdetermination of names for "overseas Chinese." Just what does one call them: *Huaqiao, Huayi, haiwai Huaren, Zhonghua minzu,* overseas Chinese, or Chinese overseas? (Wang Gungwu 1991; Wang Gungwu 1994; Reid 1997, 33; Kasian 1992, 95–96; Callahan 2003a).[12] *Haiwai Huaren,* the standard term now used in mainland China, is a translation of "overseas Chinese," which in turn is a translation of *Huaqiao* (Wang Gungwu 1991, 236). Within China itself, it is difficult to make clear distinctions between PRC citizens and overseas Chinese: many of the "overseas Chinese investors" are actually local Chinese masquerading as overseas Chinese to obtain the tax rebates and regulatory incentives that foreign direct investment allows (Katzenstein 1997, 13).[13] Inside and outside are in continual exchange, in this circulation of capital and knowledge practices.

Civilization in this sense is not restrictive, but expansive through the exchange and mixing of peoples across borders. While the first three narratives have presented unified Chineseness, this fourth narrative of civilization constitutes a heterotopia itself, entailing a different kind of multiculturalism. One way to loosen the binds of self/Other and civilization/barbarian relations is to look to notions of community beyond nation-state and empire: to, that is, cosmopolitics.

The new cosmopolitans in Euro-America seek to reclaim the concept from transnational capital and imperial power, without resorting to the Kantian abstractions of a rootless identity or a "citizen of the world" (Wilson 1998, 360). Thus, Cosmopolitanism with a capital C is reframed from an ideal into a lowercase practice of everyday life: actually existing cosmopolitanisms (Robbins 1998; Wilson 1998, 360). Cosmopolitan, then, shifts from being singular (one-worldism) to being multiple, from an abstraction to being rooted in the vernacular but not tied exclusively to the nation or the state. Hence, the hyphen in nation-state is questioned but not necessarily erased. This new "domain of contested politics" works in "an area both within and beyond the nation, and yet falling short of 'humanity'" (Robbins 1998, 1, 12). Indeed, as with heterotopia, "nothing is guaranteed, except contamination, messy politics and more translation" (Clifford 1998, 369).

The Chinese diaspora and Greater China are considered strong examples of this sort of rooted cosmopolitanism that helps us question the ontology of One China (Ong 1999; Ong 1998; Schein 1998;

Anderson 1998; Grewal et al. 1999; Walker 1993, 68, 80). In this cosmopolitics, civilization is composed of performative acts of affiliation, rather than fixed by natural categories or fundamentalist ethnicities. There is no contradiction between competing Thai and Chinese identities that needs to be resolved, but an ironic negotiation of practices. Identity is constructed not by who you are or even where you are, but by what you do and who you associate with; the political economy exchanges symbolic capital as well as economic capital. This flexible civilization leads to a robust notion of popular sovereignty, seeing peoples in motion across boundaries not as a problem to be regulated but as a means of accumulating capital and constructing identity.

To understand China and civilization in terms of popular sovereignty, heterotopia, and an open relation to Otherness, we have to go to a different set of texts, both ancient and modern. In this narrative of civilization, we need to switch from the Confucian classics to look at the *Shanhai jing*—the "Classic of Mountains and Seas." The *Shanhai jing* is generally recognized as the first atlas of China; it is useful here because it makes the move from quantity to quality, and from territory to peoples, quite directly. This geography/cosmography maps the world in terms of exotic images of other ways of life, rather than in the flat cartographs characteristic of modernity. This text was described, in the Qing dynasty, as "an ancient geography book containing practical help for worthy projects, and not just fabulous talk" (in Smith 1996, 19; Cao Wanru et al. 1997, 3).

Certainly, the *Shanhai jing* is a text that should not be romanticized; it charts dangers as well as opportunities. It has a curious self/Other relation of eat or be eaten: "An animal like the fox lives here, with nine tails and voice like a baby's. It can eat people, and is eaten to ward off *ku* [spells, poison, worms, insanity]" (*Shan Hai Ching* 1985, 2–3, 9; *Shanhai jing* 1996, 382). In later sections, the text goes far beyond the Middle Kingdom to deal with human-like creatures. They are described as humanoids—the Big People and the Small People—or human-hybrids: three heads and one body, three faces and one body, one face and three bodies, a human face and an animal body, one animal face and a human body, feathered, and so on. Surprisingly, these hybrids are not "barbarians" by definition, for they are often related to Chinese tradition by being classified as descendants of Chinese sage kings. More to the point, one land is called the "Country of Gentlemen"—using the Confucian technical term, *junzi,* for a cultivated person. The actions of this land's people match their name, for they are described as attentive to etiquette: they wear proper clothes, hats, and swords (*Shan Hai Ching* 1985, 216; *Shanhai jing* 1996, 494). Other peoples show their civilization by eating grains (i.e., being settled farmers) and domesticating birds and beasts.

These images of the Other are instructive, for these Others are neither completely human nor completely alien (as Huntington's ontology might lead us to believe). As in Foucault's heterotopia, the inhabitants are a combination, hybrids, part human and part animal. They are not necessarily a simple Hegelian synthesis, centaurs of the East, or an ancient form of the *Ti-Yong* grammar, either. Their multiplicity calls us to question the whole (geo)body that is synthesized, for the creatures can have three heads or nine tails. Rather than alterity being total, there is a grammar of proximity and resemblance in the *Shanhai jing,* giving a new twist to the meaning of geobody (Howland 1996; Thongchai 1994). Identity is thus negotiated around affiliation rather than around natural or stable categories (Haraway 1985). Simply put, difference is not wholly converted into Otherness.

These images of alterity in the *Shanhai jing* are supported by the illustrations of the strange creatures that have been appended to the text for millennia (some argue that the written text was appended to the drawings) (Fracasso, 361–62). In its latest edition, the *Shaihai jing* has entered popular culture. The pictures, like cartoons, come before the text. Indeed, a recent commentary on the text uses the grammar of "civilization and barbarism" to argue for the centrality of the text, in a different kind of ethics than seen in Zhang's *Civilization and Barbarism* (Wang Hongqi 1996, 372).

The *Shanhai jing* shows how Chinese notions of civilization are open to celebrate notions of subjectivity that mix self with Otherness. While nativists tell us that we cannot be half-Catholic and half-Muslim, or be both Thai and Chinese (Huntington 1993; Kasian 1997, 77–78), subjectivity in East Asia is typically multiple. The *Shanhai jing* talks of three-faced people, and in modern times people are a combination of Confucian, Buddhist, Daoist (in China), Christian (in Korea), Shaman (in Korea), and Shinto (in Japan).[14] Identity is related to social positioning and action—when one performs the rituals for each of these civilizations, one is part of that civilization.

In modern times, Aihwa Ong and Donald Nonini's edited volume, *Ungrounded Empires: The Cultural Politics of Modern Chinese Transnationalism,* and Ong's *Flexible Citizenship: The Cultural Logics of Transnationalism* examine the transnational logic of Greater China in helpful ways. Rather than starting in Beijing with a stable notion of a Chineseness that has been lost, as Tu does, Nonini and Ong deploy a different way of talking about identity and political economy that does not rely on the stability of the state (whether nation-state or civilization-state). Rather than seeing Chineseness as grounded in an essential culture, Nonini and Ong figure transnational Chineseness as a mobile practice. This mobility is not just between geographical places, as mainstream analyses of the overseas Chinese tell us, but between identities: there is no essential Chineseness, only multiple ways of being Chinese.

Nonini and Ong look to Chinese identity in diaspora in Southeast Asia, where the Chinese can no longer take for granted that they are civilization incarnate. Rather they are minorities, often figured as barbarians concerned only with money-making rather than with the nation-culture. Suharto's New Order Indonesia was typical in labeling Chinese as "unpatriotic, selfish, materialistic, stingy, cunning, opportunistic, philistine, and, worst of all, 'communist'" (Heryanto 1997, 29). While overseas Chinese promoters trumpet their economic success and power, these diasporic Chinese are actually living in a precarious enclave as an "imagined uncommunity" (Kasian 1997, 78; Interviews 2000; Taiguo puji qiao lianhehui 1999). Their negotiation of multiple identities entails what Nonini and Ong call a Third Culture: not Chinese culture or national culture (i.e., Thai, Malaysian, Indonesian culture) but a third culture that is mobile (Nonini and Ong 1997, 11). The different ways of being Chinese are not based on the possession of a reified Chinese culture but on "the propensity to seek opportunities elsewhere" (Nonini and Ong 1997, 26). This argument deterritorializes identity, for it is no longer tied to coherent categories of space: territory, region, or ethnicity. Indeed, the "elsewhere" is not necessarily territorial, either: seeking opportunities involves "convert[ing] political constraints in one field to economic opportunities in another" (Ong 1999, 134). Thus this deterritorialized understanding of diaspora goes beyond critical notions of rooted cosmopolitics.

But the construction of Chineseness is not always controlled by the "Chinese." Diasporic Chinese are often caught up in the contradictions of their mobile identity when they are defined as a "Chinese" threat by states in Southeast Asia—often as a result of a curious combination of capitalist success and communist danger. Although some people in New Order Indonesia tried to evade the "Chinese" categorization and be simply "Indonesian," the state did not cooperate with its own assimilation policy:

> While the government demands that the ethnic Chinese mix with the locals and give up their Chineseness, most governmental bureaucracies continue to segregate Chinese citizens and process their legal documents separately. These discriminatory procedures can be found in the administration of identity cards, passports, and marriage certificates. . . . No matter how much they "go native," these males will be considered "Chinese" in the government's population registration. (Heryanto 1997, 30–31; Interviews 2000)

This underlines how states use Chineseness to manage populations, whether the term is used as a negative category (as in Southeast Asia) or a positive one (as seen above in Chinese nativism). States have certainly gotten stronger, "but technology and mobility make it harder for them to control and domesticate a population" (Nonini and Ong 1997, 20). In an interesting shift from Seagrave's "invisible empire," here diasporic Chinese often try to evade forms of state power, and compose the "ungrounded empire" celebrated in Ong and Nonini's book title (Seagrave 1995; Ong and Nonini 1997).

The center of this Greater China is not necessarily a political capital city, or even Chinese. Its institutions are not so much state organs as chambers of commerce. Its power works not only through state security services, but through the governmentality of the market, *guanxi* networks, and the family. Its leaders meet not so much at political summits (e.g., ASEAN, ARF, APEC) as in overseas Chinese capitalist conferences organized by the "Chinese World Entrepreneurs." This understanding of Greater China is not just a Chinese variant of capitalism, as in the conversion narrative, but a Chinese practice of globalization as a variety of modernity (Ong and Nonini 1997; Ong 1999; Hamilton 1999; Hamilton 1996; Tu Weiming 1996).

Such a figuration of Greater China is interesting because it contrib-
utes a political-economic factor missing from Tu's "Cultural China,"
and quite different from Katzenstein's regional political economy
of network capitalism. Rather than networking with state power,
here business tries to evade state power—regardless of whether it is
the power of a nation-state, empire-state, or civilization-state. The
slippery nature of identity in this ungrounded empire is the opposite
of that stable Confucian order upon which both Tu and Katzenstein
rely. But it describes the workings of flexible capitalism quite well:
subcontracting, as well as mobile labor and managerial populations
(Dirlik 1998b; Castells 2000; Anagnost 1997: 75–97). The Greater
Chinese capitalist utopia is therefore celebrated in Euro-America
because it corresponds well with the neoliberal ideology of Anglo-
American capitalism.

But I think that the partisans of diaspora often overstate the
case for flexible civilization, disregard the state too easily, and over-
emphasize the wealthy overseas Chinese diaspora as "transnational
yuppies" (Ong 1999, 175) at the expense of understanding how
Chineseness in the PRC figures into the equation. Critical anthropology thus often bypasses the nation-state by jumping directly
from local to global (Weldes et al. 1999). For example, although
Nonini and Ong's argument is transnational, their analysis is limited by the national borders of the PRC. The nation-state needs to
be figured back into the local/global dynamic. However, this can
lead to another problem with analysis of Greater China and overseas Chinese: scholars who reductively frame their examination of
these complex issues in terms of Singapore and its senior minister,
Lee Kuan Yew (Naisbitt 1996; Jones et al. 1995; Ong 1999).[15] Yet
the power of the Chinese economy and civilization grows out of the
network of ties that integrate each of the nodes: not just Singapore,
Hong Kong, Vancouver, and Bangkok, but also Shanghai, Beijing,
Guangzhou, Shenyang, Shenzhen, Xiamen, and so on.

The logic of "flexible civilization" signifies a move away from
territorial sovereignty toward popular sovereignty. Yet in this narrative popular sovereignty does not stand for representative democracy.[16] "Popular" in this case refers to measuring power and authority
according to populations rather than by territory; it is transnational
as opposed to being tied to the nation-state. This narrative also
starts to make the move from populations to be managed by state

power to peoples governed by a more complex set of relations and institutions.

As the following chapters show, thinking of politics in terms of governmentality—where power is not simply restrictive but productive, and comes not just from the state but through social relationships more generally—is helpful to understand Greater China. The state and the market work through regimes of power/knowledge that look to cultural governance in order to regulate not just the individual but other spaces: kinship networks, the capitalist workplace, the nation-state, transnational networks (see Ong 1999). Still, we should be careful with such figurations of flexible diaspora and governmentality. The exuberance of diasporic transnationalism is just as misplaced as the triumphalism of Rising China.

CONCLUSION

This chapter has deconstructed the notion of "Greater China" and regional politics in East Asia. Rather than viewing Chinese civilization as the "answer" to crises, I have reframed it as a "question," reading politics both with and against Chinese civilization. In this way, Greater China is not a territorical place, but a theoretical concept. This concept of "Greater China" is useful in two ways. It demonstrates how civilization is an important part of politics in East Asia—indeed, cultural politics is nothing new in the region, for such issues have been the business of East Asian states for centuries. But it also shows how civilization is not a coherent "thing" but a multicoded set of relationships: nativism, conquest, conversion, and diaspora. All four narratives can be seen as variations of nationalism: affirmative, assertive, aggressive, pragmatic, long-distance (Whiting 1995; Zhao Suisheng 2000; Anderson 1998).

But rather than reaffirming that "the Rise of China" is a typical nationalist narrative, this chapter has shown how "nationalism" as a concept is both too broad and too narrow. The four narratives of civilization are useful because they highlight the different dynamics of civilization/barbarism—different drawings of boundaries, different modes of inclusion and exclusion, different relations of self and Other. Each narrative employs a different rhetoric and logic: discovery, entitlement, synthesis, flexibility. Rather than a coherent "China threat," we have a more complex view of how nativism and conquest narratives guide Chinese foreign policy. Rather than simply thinking in terms of economic opportunities, the conversion and diaspora narratives tell us how economics, culture, and politics are linked in informal as well as formal ways.

While the first three narratives can be read into discourses of unity—a natural, essential, or synthetic identity—the last narrative, diaspora, is more complex. It tells the story of a civilization that is transnational, of self/Other relations that take place not only inside and outside the Asia-Pacific region but also inside and outside personal and group subjectivities. The first three narratives of civilization can be directly related to state-centric Foreign Policy strategies and constituencies in government. The military and propaganda departments characteristically talk in terms of nativism and conquest,[17] while foreign ministry discourse varies between nativism against human rights diplomacy and conversion for multilateral organizations (see Ming Wan 1999, 102–3). The flexible civilization of diaspora, on the other hand, is related to informal foreign relations performances in more economic, social, and cultural spaces.

The move from nativism to diaspora, and territory to populations, might suggest that the historical trajectory of diaspora is the "truth" about Chinese foreign policy. That is not the argument of this chapter. Nor can I say that one can code events according to a single narrative—e.g., that the South China Sea disputes are best understood in terms of the conquest story. In the following chapters, I will argue that these four narratives can help explain the shifts and contradictions in Chinese foreign policy and identity. For example, the most interesting thing about the Chinese reaction to the NATO/U.S. bombing of the PRC's embassy in Belgrade was not the hypernationalism; an appeal to a conquest notion of national humiliation is to be expected in both popular and official space after such an act of war. What is fascinating about the Chinese reaction is how the government shifted the discourse from conquest to conversion. Jiang Zemin very quickly endeavored to shift popular understanding away from demands for military "retaliation" against the American hegemon, to the conversion narrative of economic reform and opening: "We must unswervingly take economic construction as the central task. . . . This is the fundamental guarantee to the invincible position of socialist China" (Jiang Zemin in BBC/SWB 15 May 1999, G2). This time, the state was able to direct discourse:

the way to beat American hegemony was through economic growth, not military battles. Success is the best revenge.

More importantly, as Cheng and Cao point out, cultural cosmopolitanism is intimately related to cultural nativism (Cheng and Cao 1998). This can be seen in how the transnational Chinese public has reacted to various crises. Not surprisingly, overseas Chinese opinion rallied behind mainland Chinese anti-Western opinion in the bombing of the Belgrade embassy (see H-Asia). Much of this rallying was accomplished not in the traditional media but in cyberspace. In the past few years, Internet connection has grown dramatically in mainland China ("Wired China" 2000, 24); it has also expanded among Chinese communities in Taiwan, Hong Kong, Southeast Asia, and North America. Thus "The World Wide Web of Chinese Business" (Kao, John 1993) is not just a metaphor for economic networks, but a common practice.

Many see this expansion of Internet connection and cell phones in China as a threat to state power, and hope the free flow of information will encourage democracy. This is certainly the rationale of the first Chinese cybergroup—*China News Digest* (CND), which uses email to distribute news about China not just into mainland China but around the globe (www.CND.org). Many people frame the politics of cyberspace in terms of control and anti-control: "the government's regulatory and technical measures [seek] to bring the Internet under its control, and the numerous attempts by dissidents [try] to by-pass the official scrutiny and use the Internet as a political tool" (Dai Xiudian 2000b, 190; "Wired China" 2000).

In addition, Chinese groups, both in the PRC and abroad, are maintaining their own sites to promote Chineseness. This not only involves describing the wonders of Chinese civilization and development, but includes nativist links to sites that describe the proper Chinese view of Tibet, the Nanjing Massacre, and other issues (see www.Huaren.org). Examining the cyberspace activity on mainland sites during the 1998 atrocities against ethnic Chinese in Indonesia, Hughes argues that cyberspace was used more for nationalism than for democracy (Hughes 2000: 205-6). Chinese Web sites that now serve as networks for a cosmopolitan community—for example, the World Huaren [Chinese] Federation's www.Huaren.org—were initially organized as a response to the Indonesian anti-Chinese atrocities (Arnold 1998).

But what is curious here is the flow of information and influence. If we agree with the logic of Anderson's critique of "Long-Distance Nationalism," then we see the flow of information and funds from the "outside" back to the "inside." Anderson points out that long-distance politics can lead to extremism as well as democracy, because a lack of residence often means a lack of responsibility. On the one hand, overseas Chinese spread Confucianism or democracy back into mainland China during the 1989 Tian'anmen demonstrations. On the other, the 1992 destruction of the Ayodhya mosque in India was organized and funded in North America and England (Anderson 1998, 73–74). As Anderson concludes, "That same metropole that marginalizes and stigmatizes him simultaneously enables him to play, in a flash, on the other side of the planet, national hero" (Anderson 1998, 74).

But in 1998 it was Chinese at the center in Beijing who were campaigning in support of ethnic Chinese at the periphery. This of course was not done just through the Internet. The PRC Foreign Ministry officially protested to the Indonesian government, and the *People's Daily* commented, "These criminal acts have sparked grave concern and strong indignation among the people in China and the Overseas Chinese societies" (in Vatikiotis et al. 1998). This criticism was a serious departure from Chinese foreign policy since the 1960s; asserting a sovereignty over ethnic Chinese also contravenes the PRC's normalization treaties and nationality law ("The Nationality Law" 1980; Vatikiotis et al. 1998). But in this case the state was following rather than leading nativist sentiment generated, in large part, in cyberspace (Hughes 2000).

Hence cyberspace is an example of a site that effaces the distinctions between cultural cosmopolitanism and cultural nativism, bringing the outsiders back into the center while expanding the insiders abroad: "The tension of the contradiction between cultural nationalism and cultural cosmopolitanism is continuously maintained" (Cheng and Cao 1998, 317). History thus is not a linear process of scientific progress where China struggles on the road from empire to nation-state. Rather it is a field of multiple narrative trajectories that are mobilized, sometimes consciously and sometimes not, for very political purposes.

These ways of understanding civilization are important beyond China. They exemplify current theoretical debates about the global/

local dynamic in their movement from territorial notions of sovereignty, where power is based on an expansion of economic and political relations (which reifies borders), to popular notions of sovereignty, where power is measured by movements of people across borders in a qualitative struggle of cultures and knowledge. This better describes the day-to-day workings of transnational politics, moving from nation-state to civilization-state to transnational economic-culture. Greater China thus provides an example of ethnicity and culture bringing peoples together, rather than separating them as in Canada, Yugoslavia, Burma, and the increasingly (dis)United Kingdom.

Rather than positing an ideal notion of Chinese civilization that would answer the political questions about "war and peace," I have argued for looking to mobility on the margins of Southeast Asia and around the world for a new set of questions. Although some try to use "Chinese civilization" to solve the problem of the "China threat" and world order, I have argued that looking to "civilization" shifts the terrain of the debate to another dynamic of problems and possibilities. Although considering international relations in terms of territorial sovereignty appeals to the solid foundation of geopolitical maps and international law, considering power in terms of populations and knowledge practices asks questions like: who speaks? and what does (political) representation mean? Such questions are increasingly asked on the world stage (and will be considered in the following chapters).

Since we have ended with an examination of the overlapping identities and transnational cacophony of the Chinese diaspora, in the next chapter we will go to a very quiet place, the South China Sea, to both question the exuberance of Chinese transnationalism and examine how the Chinese state employs Greater China discourse to serve its needs as a civilization-state.

3

Sharing Sovereignty: Security and Spatiality in the South China Sea

The collision between an American EP-3 surveillance plane and a Chinese fighter jet over the South China Sea, and this issue's contentious resolution in April 2001, graphically showed how issues of borders, space, and surveillance characterize that vast area. While the United States government insisted that its plane was flying in international air space, the Chinese side insisted that the plane had violated the People's Republic of China's (PRC) sovereign territory both physically and in terms of knowledge practices. Beyond the question of whether or not the U.S. plane was actually in Chinese air space—among diplomats and scholars there were arguments about the status of China's 200-mile Exclusive Economic Zone prescribed by the Law of the Sea—Chinese people felt that the very act of surveillance was an invasion of national sovereignty. There was a very active construction of both sovereignty and space that looked to popular tradition as well as international law. In other words, the United States and the PRC were looking to different mappings of both territory and knowledge to argue their cases (see Ji Guoxing 2001; Valencia 2002).

The disputes over the Spratly Islands (in the South China Sea) between the PRC and Southeast Asian countries likewise propose multiple challenges to the international system both empirically and conceptually. The disputes serve to highlight the theoretical debates over security and sovereignty as well as the tension between peoples and territory, conquest and conversion. China and the other claimant states are very creative at staking a claim on this last terrestrial frontier. State power not only is still present but is developing new strategies, not just as the nation-state of the PRC but also as the civilization-state of Greater China. This chapter thus examines such "dynamic understandings of statehood" (Weber 1995, 11) to see how traditional Chinese concepts of sovereignty are more symbolic than legal-territorial: recognizing China's power here is simply an acknowledgment of China's centrality to the region where neighboring countries pay symbolic tribute to China but otherwise go about their business. Since conflicts of absolute sovereignty are the problem in this region, the chapter argues that traditional Chinese concepts of shared sovereignty and space are useful for explaining/ legitimating a transnational subjectivity that allows for overlapping boundaries in a regional commons.

Mainstream analyses of the South China Sea disputes, on the other hand, frame them as an exemplary post–Cold War conflict; China, Taiwan, Vietnam, the Philippines, Malaysia, and Brunei each have made sovereignty claims on the Spratly archipelago's twenty-five to thirty-five islets. The defining issue of the struggle is economic. The main attractions of the islets are natural resources—fish, oil, and gas—and sea lanes to transport goods between the Indian and Pacific Oceans. The Spratly disputes are part of the general shift from geopolitical competition to geo-economic cooperation. Thus the South China Sea disputes are a case study for the norms of international politics. They challenge international law, specifically the Law of the Sea that took effect in 1994, to sort out sovereignty claims. Both scholars and foreign policy elites use sovereignty's traditional definition of "territory, population, and authority" to frame the issues (see Biersteker and Weber 1996a, 3); in this sense, the disputes are an empirical problem to be solved by drawing stable boundaries in the South China Sea to fairly divide up the goods between the relevant nation-states. Such solutions reify the norm of the nation-state by bringing China into the family of nations (Armstrong 1993).

"Sovereignty" is the obvious tool to use—except in regard to the South China Sea, that is. Close examination shows that it is a space where territorial sovereignty does not make sense. First, there is no "territory" in the South China Sea; most of the islets are under water most of the year. After their fifty-hour trip on a transport ship to the Spratly Islands, a team of Chinese journalists reported that "The island, a terraced reef, did not have a single inch of land above ground. Even at low tide, the terrace is still partially submerged" (An and Xiong 1994, 9; Austin 1998, 132, 159). To build bases on these reefs, army engineers have to work hard: "Concrete caissons towed hundreds of miles by barge from Hainan are sunk onto coral reefs" (Whiting 1998, 299; also see An and Xiong 1994, 9–10; Li and Xiong 1994, 10; Hu Zhanfan 1994, 10–11; Shih Ti-tsu 1975, 10–15; Chinese Ministry of Foreign Affairs 1980, 15–24; *Diaoyutai* 1996). Although such unnatural constructions have no standing in international law (Chen Hurng-yu 1993, 39; Valencia et al. 1999, 45–46), many Chinese texts work hard to turn water into "national maritime territory" that generates the same sovereign rights and privileges as "national land territory" (Ni and Song 1998, 402, 415; Lin and Wu 1988).

Second, there is no population except the literally floating population of fishermen and pirates: "Aside from passing sailors, pirates and fishermen, there is simply nobody in the South or East China Seas" (Godement 1996). Although legally they do not count as settlements, military garrisons try to add substance and stability to sovereignty claims. Chinese texts engage in elaborate historical narratives of travelogues, history, cartography, and archaeology to prove their claims of a Chinese population on the islets (Shih Ti-tsu 1975; Chinese Ministry of Foreign Affairs 1980; Chemillier-Gendreau 1996; Chen Hurng-yu 1993).

Third, there is no authority in the region, either symbolically or materially. Actually it is an area of very obvious lack of authority, for it is the most active region in the world for piracy ("Treacherous Shoals" 1992). As one victim recounted, "the South China Sea [is] infamous for the number and severity of its piracy attacks—from simple armed robbery to hijack, in which the ship itself is stolen and its crew either massacred or set adrift" (Bist 1998, 4). Or, as Chinese fishermen recall: "if you don't run, then there is no other way out. These 'pirates' are vicious, if you let them catch you everything on the boat will be taken, and even the crew will be thrown overboard" (Zheng Degang 1999).

Symbolically, to name is to control (Pan Shiying 1996, 21; Todorov 1984, 28ff). But there are no agreed-upon international names for the features of the region. The names of the islands, reefs, and atolls are not set, for each country has its own set of names—in Chinese, Vietnamese, Tagalog, Indonesian, and Malay, not to mention English. A passage from a Chinese Foreign Ministry report speaks to this confusion by juxtaposing four sets of names: "The Vietnamese authorities allege that Bai Cat Vang and Hoang Sa Chu in the historical records is what they now call the Hoang Sa Archipelago or what is known in the West as the Paracels, that is to say, China's Xisha Islands" (Chinese Ministry of Foreign Affairs 1980, 22). The overdetermination of names thus shows a lack of single sovereign authority: the Chinese, for example, call the Spratlys *Nansha,* or South Sand Islands, and the Paracels the *Xisha,* or West Sand Islands.

The presence of absence in these three categories (territory, population, authority) is neatly summed up by the *CIA World Factbook* entry on the Spratly Islands: most of the commonsense categories for nation-states are said here to not make sense in this area; "NA" (not applicable) and "0 percent" are common entries (CIA 2002). Since there are no obvious referents for sovereignty, each of the claimant states has to work very hard to imagine sovereignty, to imagine communities where there are no communities at all. In this way, the South China Sea disputes challenge the very notion of sovereignty and international law. The *Asian Wall Street Journal* thus doubts the utility of the Law of the Sea itself: "It seems that what the Law of the Sea Treaty has accomplished is to intensify, rather than diminish, off-shore territorial disputes" ("Subic Memories" 1995, 6; Austin 1998, 57; South China Sea Informal Working Group 2001).

In this way, the South China Sea disputes are not an empirical problem but a conceptual issue. Analysts typically note that the South China Sea struggles have broad geopolitical implications indicative of post–Cold War trends (Valencia 1995, 6). Hence, "South China Sea disputes" has become an industry in and of itself, leading to specialized research projects, copious journal articles, and numerous books; Huntington went to the South China Sea for his civilizational war scenario (Huntington 1996, 313ff). Indeed, it is not just the Chinese state, or nation-states in general, that talk about the South China Sea: this slippery space has served as the location for a James Bond film, *Tomorrow Never Dies* (1997), and an action-adventure novel, *Dragonstrike: The Millennium War,*

SHARING SOVEREIGNTY · 61

written by two journalists as a proposal for U.S. security policy (Spottiswoode 1997; Hawksely and Holberton 1997).

Resolving the issues is not just a nuts-and-bolts problem of dividing up goods, but a theoretical problem of understanding how power and authority work in world politics where space is multiple and where "sovereign" claims overlap. More than simply a battle between the Chinese and Vietnamese navies, there is a significant, albeit largely unspoken, struggle between concepts of space. Simply put, the contest is between the master narrative of a horizontal map of geopolitics, on the one hand, and more vertical mappings of ironic world politics, on the other. Thus it is necessary to switch conceptual focus; the horizontal map of unitary state sovereignties is not very helpful in making sense of the South China Sea disputes.

This chapter examines Chinese actions in the South China Sea in terms of a conceptual shift from the Westphalian norms of the nation-state to the Greater Chinese counter-norms of the civilization-state. But before moving from sovereignty to cosmology, it is necessary to examine how such territorial spaces have become a "problem," and how this problematization has set the parameters for resolution. Such a politics concerns much more than who ultimately gets the deeds to the Spratly Islands; indeed, *how* the dispute is resolved is most important.

TECHNICAL PROBLEM: THE CHINESE NATION-STATE IN THE SOUTH CHINA SEA

The hegemonic view of the South China Sea disputes states that the struggle is part of the long process of China shifting from being an empire to, first, a revolutionary state, then finally a member of the "family of nation-states" (Kim, Samuel 1998b; Armstrong 1993; Zhang, Yongjin 1998). The transition from empire to nation-state was not complete when the People's Republic of China (PRC) was founded in 1949. Borders were not well-defined, and this lack of clarity has led the PRC to disputes (and often military struggles) over territorial boundaries with nearly every neighboring state. Sovereignty has been very important in the building of the Chinese national-state, and Chinese foreign policy is characterized, as all agree, by the "centrality of sovereignty issues" (Kim, Samuel 1994a, 5). In China, power and authority rely on a nineteenth-century European notion of absolute sovereignty that entails a firm drawing of national borders, which in turn act as a shield separating domestic from international politics (Kim, Samuel 1994a, 8). Because the Chinese only reacquired sovereignty in 1949, after over a century of division and civil war, it is not surprising that the PRC is loathe to share or divide its sovereignty; indeed, division with Taiwan is still the main issue in Chinese politics (Katzenstein 1997, 21).

Maritime boundaries are the last areas that need to be clarified on (inter)national maps: "the ocean is the last domain on the globe that has been opened up and settled by people" (Ni and Song 1997, 415). The notion of maritime sovereignty is quite recent, dating from 1945 when the United States declared its intention to exercise sovereignty over its continental shelf for the purpose of economic exploitation (Austin 1998, 33, 92). Thus what used to be the shared space of the "high seas" has increasingly become an issue of competitive struggle. The main objective of the United States in the South China Sea is to maintain the sea lanes of communication for its warships as well as commercial traffic; as the crisis in April 2001 showed, this includes airspace. Even though Chinese sources see the United States as the main force behind challenges to its South China Sea claims, actually America has affected the disputes more conceptually than militarily: when it claimed maritime sovereignty in 1945, the United States "opened a Pandora's Box of problems" (Austin 1998, 33).

Islands are increasingly the center of controversy in East and Southeast Asia. China is now concentrating on settling boundaries in the Yellow Sea and the East China Sea as well as the South China Sea (Austin 1998; Whiting 1998, 299). The 1990s were full of such events: the transfer of sovereignty of Hong Kong in 1997 and Macao in 1999, the transnational Chinese confrontation with Japan over Senkaku/Diaoyu Islands in 1996 (*Diaoyutai* 1996), the People's Liberation Army Navy (PLA Navy) firing missiles near Taiwan in 1996 and threats to fire missiles again in 2000, the PLA Navy's battle with the Philippines over Mischief Reef since 1995, the Chinese struggle with the Philippines over Scarborough Shoal in 1997, and so on. Maritime and island disputes are not limited to China; they are part of a more general occupation of all available space on the globe: Korea and Japan, Russia and Japan, are also noteworthy for maritime disputes (Kim, Dalchoong et al. 1996). The South China Sea disputes are, then, both a struggle between nation-states and a struggle to define the (Chinese) nation-state.

The parameters of the debate over the Spratlys are set by the tension between conquest and conversion, between a military solution and a diplomatic solution. As a noted scholar put it, "In sum, China's strategy on this issue appears to combine ambiguity, incrementalism, tactical timing, selective use of force, and 'divide and dominate' tactics" (Valencia 1995, 23; Huxley 1998, 114; Ji Guoxing 1998, 101). Seemingly contradictory pronouncements by Chinese leaders also speak to this tension. In 1984 Deng Xiaoping mused about "the possibility of resolving certain territorial disputes by having the countries concerned jointly develop the disputed areas before discussing the question of sovereignty" (Deng Xiaoping 1994, 59). In 1990 Li Peng applied this formula to the South China Sea disputes: "[U]nder the premise that China has indisputable sovereignty over the Nansha [Spratly] Islands, China is willing to temporarily shelve the question of sovereignty over Nansha so as to jointly develop the resources in Nansha together with ASEAN countries" (Li Peng in FEER 30 August 1990, 11). Chinese actions and utterances of "indisputable sovereignty" and "shelving sovereignty issues" go in opposite directions. This double-coded foreign policy is not an aberration of the South China Sea; Whiting argues that territorial integrity and economic development are the two main themes of post-Deng Chinese foreign policy (Whiting 1998, 289), while Waldron points out that they were the main source of foreign policy debate throughout imperial China (Waldron 1990, 8ff).

The pattern of such aggressive and conciliatory actions often occurs in quick succession in the South China Sea. In 1991 China normalized relations with Vietnam, but then in 1992 China awarded a concession to an American oil company, Crestone Energy Corporation, in an area contested with Vietnam—pledging to defend the concession by military means. In February 1995 China occupied the Philippines-claimed Mischief Reef; then in July 1995 China declared it would use international law and the Law of the Sea to settle disputes at the ASEAN Regional Forum (ARF) meeting; and finally in November 1995 the PRC published its first Arms Control and Disarmament White Paper to reduce tensions. In May 1996 China legislated a "base line" for the Paracel Islands, enabling it to extend its claim in the South China Sea and the right to defend the concession, and then in the same month ratified the Law of the Sea Convention.

Such a military/diplomacy two-step has led to a haunting refrain: "What are China's intentions in the region? Will it be a co-operative benign neighbor as it claims (and as some in the region perhaps too readily accept), or will it seek to dominate and to write its own rules for international conduct?" (Valencia 1995, 6; Austin 1998, 223–52; Cole 2001). Instead of searching for China's singular guiding intent or motive—a project doomed to failure both conceptually and empirically (Foucault 1979; Barthes 1979)—this chapter will examine Beijing's actions to see how they produce meaning as they produce borders. Although China's military officers and diplomats seem to be going in opposite directions, they are all very clearly working within the framework of the nation-state, doing what nation-states do best, establishing and maintaining sovereign territorial boundaries as they produce the "South China Sea," "Greater China," and "the world" in international/intertextual relations (see Der Derian and Shapiro 1989).

Conquest: Military Maneuvers

Military-dominated discourses reaffirm sovereignty through the realist logic of national interest and military force. The Spratlys thus are a technical-military problem that can be solved with the modernization of the navy and the air force. It is easy to read Chinese "aggressive" actions as those of a nation-state laboring to reconquer territories stolen during the imperial era. Many note that the Spratly Islands are the area where China is most likely to use military force to conquer territory. The South China Sea thus is framed as a security issue, the entrance to China's "Southern flank": "In the past 100 years, China has been invaded seven times by foreign troops from the sea. Most of these first entered the South China Sea" (Ji Guoxing 1998, 101, 102). A couplet posted on the wall of a Chinese pillbox in the Spratlys states: "The small reefs should not be taken lightly as their safeguarding concerns three million square kilometers of water; without the reefs, 200 million households will become defenseless" (An and Xiong 1994, 9).

These actions are nationalistic in the sense that they are a reaction to China's humiliation through unequal and disrespectful treatment by European, American, and Japanese imperialists. Such a morally charged narrative certainly guided the discourse of the transfer of Hong Kong, where the hand-over was not presented as an aberration, but was written into a grand narrative of modern Chinese history as the Century of National Humiliation (Wu Chunguang 1998). The Spratly Islands are also framed by this discourse; they first became an issue in 1933 when they were occupied by the French empire (Wu Chunguang 1998, 218; Austin 1998, 133).[1]

China thus starts off with a sense of victimization and entitlement not only from Euro-American imperialist powers but also from the successor states that are now its own Asian neighbors (Wu Chunguang 1998, 219–20). Although books about the South China Sea such as *Pacific Trials* mention the discourse of "national humiliation" (Wu Chunguang 1998), except for minor and confusing references, the South China Sea disputes are not contained in the general narrative of the Century of National Humiliation (*Jindai Zhongguo* 1997, 48; He Yu 1999, 8). Partly this is due to timing. While the "Century" ended in 1949 with the founding of the PRC, the disputes date from the mid-1950s when Vietnam, the Philippines, and Malaysia started to extend influence over the Spratlys (Chen Hurng-yu 1993, 23). Many scholars date the disputes even more recently, as part of a general "rush of claims by coastal states to expansive maritime jurisdictions" to take advantage of the discovery of petrochemicals in the South China Sea in the early 1970s (Austin 1998, 34, 132; Wu Chunguang 1998, 219). As one scholar writes:

> In the South China Sea, the potential conflict over the Spratly (Nansha) Islands has become an emerging security issue for the Chinese defense planners. Vietnam has taken about twenty of the disputed Spratly Islands. The Philippines established the Western Command in 1976 to defend the Kalayaan sector of the islands under its control. In 1988 the sector was converted into a municipal district. Malaysia began to build a military base on Swallow Reef in the mid-1970s, and fortified and expanded its occupation to three other reefs in the 1980s. (Hu Weixing 1995, 122)

China, Hu tells us, did not start this problem but is merely responding to a long list of "incursions" from other countries since World War II: "[I]n 1991 China reiterated its claims over them and the surrounding waters. But, lacking sufficient naval and air force capability, Beijing worries that it may be too late to take effective control of the islets before they are carved up" (Hu Weixing 1995, 122–23). Thus "militarily weaker states are taking advantage of

China's tolerance and restraint by quietly plundering China's oil" (Valencia 1995, 16). According to Chinese sources, the PRC is not being aggressive or expansive, but simply trying to minimize the loss of its "sacred territory" (Wu Chunguang 1998, 221; Stenseth 1999, 38–39; Austin 1998, 302–3; Odgaard 2002, 208; Lee Lai To 1999, 13).

Against this pacific view of Chinese intentions is the fact that China is the only country to use force in the region, first against Vietnam in 1956, 1974, and 1988. Then, in 1995, the PLA Navy clashed with the Philippines over the aptly named Mischief Reef.[2] This event was significant to all claimants because until the 1995 skirmish it was assumed that China would use force only against Vietnam. However, the Mischief Reef confrontation was not an anomaly; it was an outcome of a change in the PLA's grand strategy. The previous plan, formulated in 1965, envisioned a "People's War" against a major (Russian) invasion from the north and west. But in the 1980s, these borders became much less of a security concern (Garver 1998, 122–24). The 1985 plan refocused on the south and east, envisioning the use of rapid deployment forces in small, short, and local wars around China's periphery (Cole 2001, 159–78). The PLA's rising military expenditures have followed this plan; air force and naval capacities are being increased to allow China to control the air and sea in the region, and an eight-thousand-strong contingent of marines is based on Hainan Island for the purpose of defending China's claims (Cole 2001; Valencia 1995, 17). Military bases have been built on the Paracel and Spratly Islands (Whiting 1998, 299).

The discussion of the Spratly Islands and the South China Sea is therefore largely part of the discourse of "naval power." Many of the main sources about the disputes are part of naval history and maritime strategy (Stenseth 1999, 42; Wu Chunguang 1998; Cole 2001). Both territory and identity are thus redefined from China as a continental power to include maritime territory. This redefinition is part of an argument for China to develop a blue-water navy to protect "our second homeland"—40 percent of which is "occupied" (in Stenseth 1999, 47). For example, in *Pacific Trials* Wu tells us that surveys show that 98 percent of Chinese students think that China has 9.6 million square kilometers of sovereign territory. He laments that the students have "forgotten" about the 3 million square kilometers of "maritime territory" because they "do not have the correct maritime attitude to value it." To correct this problem, the Chinese state needs to raise the level of knowledge of maritime territory (Wu Chunguang 1998, 4; Ni and Song 1997, 401–48). In this way, Hainan changes from being "China's smallest land province into its largest ocean province" (Li Yangguo 1998, 14). Again, this redefinition functions not just for the Spratlys but for more general strategic concerns: "to be a maritime great power we cannot be color-blind to blue national territory" (Ni and Song 1997, 405). The security discourse is not just about claiming some territory, but about creating a new frontier mentality.

Such "popular education" in the frontier spirit is one of the tasks of journalists who regularly visit the marines in the South China Sea. Each year or so, journalists sail to the Spratly Islands and write travelogues describing both the exotic charms of the South Sea and the arduous conditions of the heroic soldiers who guard it. The conceptual and identity problems that Wu identifies are graphically shown in these newspaper and television reports. Characteristically, these journalists come from the cold dry North—the Yellow Earth. They are overwhelmed by the vast open waters and exotica of the South China Sea:

> Going out on deck at night, I feel a slight drizzle on my face. In the North at this time of year it would be snow on my face! In our country you can have spring, summer, autumn and winter all at the same time; it is both the vast Yellow Earth and the vast Blue Ocean! . . . Vast emptiness with only row upon row of waves. . . . Here the sky is blue, the water is blue, and coral reef is blue, 1000 km away from the mainland's Yellow Earth. (Ling Xingzheng 1998; also see Zheng Degang 1999)

This vast emptiness is commonly described as the "great treasure house of China," full of unimaginable riches and opportunities (see Li Yangguo 1998, 11–12, 14–15; Sun and Ding 1998, 153).

Like any good frontier, these riches are not just economic but symbolic (see Campbell 1998a). The language of reportage on the Spratly Islands is more lyrical than objective; titles of the resultant articles and books include "Ocean Memories," *Spratly Century Dreams*, "Ripples," "Shouting to the Spratlys," and "Cherish the Reefs with Deep Feelings" (Ling Xingzheng 1998; Gui Hanbiao

2001; "Duanpo" 1998; Liu Shengjun 2000; Li and Xiong 1994, 10). Through the genre of the travelogue, the Spratly Islands provide space for imagining China as a great power, a space that thus renegotiates the borders of Chinese identity. The overwhelming sense of emptiness is seen to be both liberating—due, no doubt, to population pressures on the mainland—and lonely. Both the "special happiness" and "special bitterness" of military service on the Spratlys is neatly summed up in the phrase "the Spratly Spirit"—*Nansha jingshen* (Ling Xingzheng 1998; Zheng Degang 1999).

But the slippery contingency of the Spratly Spirit is quickly co-opted by the Chinese state into merely another slogan. This poem, which prescribes the Spratly Spirit, is prominently posted on an island installation (Ling Xingzheng 1998):

> The Spratly Spirit: patriotism
> Selfless dedication
> Tenacious heroism
> Pioneering work in hardship
> Unity in friendship.

The Spratly Spirit is also summoned beyond the South China Sea. The navy deploys it to rally the sailors and the nation in a diverse set of patriotic tasks that require such "selfless dedication" ("Duanpo" 1999; Chen and Zhang 1998).

Those looking for a China threat thus characterize the South China Sea conflicts in terms of an irridentist China trying to reclaim its ancient empire. This is certainly what is suggested by the "historic claim line" on Chinese maps, a line that hugs the coasts of littoral states and is variously described as a "Chinese tongue licking up the South China Sea" or a "tongue of the dragon" (Stenseth 1999, 13). Alarmist scholars like to quote an internal Chinese document that sees the South China Sea as "survival space," which is then interpreted as the Chinese version of the Nazis' *lebensraum* ("Treacherous Shoals" 1992, 14; Kim, Samuel 1994b, 140). Indeed, the extra three million square kilometers of maritime territory involved "would fulfill our people's hopes" (Wu Chunguang 1998, 4). China, using this logic, threatens to turn the South China Sea into a "Chinese Lake."

Against such an alarmist view of Chinese conquest is the fact that there has been very little actual conflict in the South China

Sea. China has only had violent clashes with the naval forces of other countries twice, in 1974 and in 1988. When compared with that of other countries, China's exercise of its "right to use force to defend territory" is not strange (Austin 1998, 2). Thus, after a detailed analysis of events, Austin finds "no conclusive proof of a pattern of vigorous use of force" by China (Austin 1998, 95). Indeed, although the People's Republic of China has the military capacity to take the islands, the disputes are seen as a political, not a military, question (Austin 1998, 317). Since the late 1990s, the PLA Navy has talked about dividing the spoils equally, in accordance with international law (Gao Weinong 1999; Whiting 1998, 299). Regardless of whether the Chinese actions in the South China Sea are read sympathetically or not, the enduring theme is of the establishment and maintenance of the boundaries of the nation-state. Around the Spratlys, this is not just a scientific act of measuring and marking territory; rather, this security practice requires using more literary tools of "differentiation, classification, and definition" (Campbell 1998a, 199).

Conversion: Diplomacy

In addition to resolving sovereignty disputes, the other element of Deng's official statement points to "joint development" in the South China Sea. The Chinese leadership sees maintaining "good neighborly" relations with Southeast Asian countries as its top priority— although the defense of the "sacred territory'" of the South China Sea comes in a close second (Ji Guoxing 1998, 103). Most Chinese writings about Sino-Southeast Asian relations talk of "regional integration" rather than territorial disputes (Jia Shenda et al. 1998; Che Zhenhua et al. 1999).

Thus, at the same time that China struggles militarily against these nations, it engages them diplomatically. Beijing's relations with its neighbors are certainly the most peaceful since 1949 and perhaps for the past two centuries. Since 1971, when it took over the Chinese seat in the United Nations, the PRC has gradually entered into the international society of nation-states (Chinese Ministry of Foreign Affairs 1999; Armstrong 1993, 176–84; Zhang, Yongjin 1998). As part of the economic reforms initiated in 1978, Deng Xiaoping redirected Chinese foreign policy away from ideology toward pragmatism, declaring that China needed seven decades of peace in order to develop. In moves characteristic of trends in post–Cold War security policy, Deng put economics in command in order to attract foreign investment, trade, technology, and expertise. Indeed, we can even read the discourse of national humiliation in encouraging ways: since the main sources of anger are the "unequal treaties" forced upon China, this would affirm China's interest in "equality" in international relations (see Zheng, Yongnian 1999). Likewise, even militant nativist writers tell us that China is not striving to be "hegemonic" but only wishes for the normal Westphalian practices of equality and respect. China is only aggressive when these sacred ideals have been violated: "China says no, certainly not because it seeks out opposition, but because a more equal setting needs dialogue" (He Beilin 1996, 2).

Thus, alongside its rabid rhetoric and increasing "blue water" naval power, China has been playing the Westphalian diplomatic game of recognizing (and being recognized by) nation-states as an equal sovereign agent (Biersteker and Weber 1996a, 1–2, 285). Since the late 1980s it has established diplomatic relations with all its neighboring countries, including Indonesia, Singapore, India, Vietnam, and South Korea (Lee Lai To 1999, 6, 17, 93).

Many argue that China is being converted to the language of mainstream international relations discourse through its engagement in U.N. activities. A new cadre of Chinese diplomats is joining the practice of international relations through the writing of White Papers on issues such as the environment and human rights (Kim, Samuel 1998a, 23–24, 26–27). In recent years, even the military has been part of this new transparency, with the National Defense White Papers in 1998, 2000, and 2002 and the Arms Control and Disarmament White Paper in 1995 (Interviews 1999). What China needs to do, according to prominent scholars, is to modernize its nineteenth-century notion of absolute sovereignty—to recognize that states cannot control all aspects of political, economic, and social life, because interdependence is the new norm (Segal 1997, 172–73; Kim, Samuel 1994a, 5).

Following this normalization trend, in the mid-1990s China became more active in regional organizations as well. Its status was upgraded to a "dialogue partner" of the Association of Southeast Asian Nations (ASEAN), thus joining Australia, Canada, the European Union, India, Japan, New Zealand, and the United States. In

1997, it joined ASEAN, Japan, and South Korea to form the first truly regional organization: ASEAN plus 3. A regional newspaper commentary declared that "ASEAN-China ties are maturing" (Kavi 1996). It is not just "China" that is "maturing"; the South China Sea disputes are pushing ASEAN in new directions: the 1992 Manila declaration on the disputes was ASEAN's first formal declaration on regional security. The purpose of the ASEAN Regional Forum (ARF), the only viable security organization in the region, was to integrate China into a consultative security community with the hope that it would develop as a "good citizen of international society" (quoted in Yahuda 1995, 145). ASEAN is also working to convert China to the "ASEAN way" of nonviolent and nonconfrontational resolution of problems, perhaps expanding this "way" to an Asia-Pacific Way (Acharya 1997, 340; Narine 1997, 964). As a Thai intellectual states: "ASEAN is using the ASEAN Regional Forum to engage China to ensure that the Middle Kingdom becomes sensitive to the region's needs" (Kavi 1996). In particular, China is increasingly developing expertise in international law in order to profitably use the Law of the Sea to stake its claims for maritime space (Gao Weinong 1999; Pan Shiying 1996; Valencia 1999, Interview; Austin 1998). Indeed, by 2002 the PRC had signed the "Declaration on the Conduct of Parties in the South China Sea" with ASEAN, where all parties pledged to undertake to peacefully resolve disputes through international law and the Law of the Sea ("Declaration on the Conduct of Parties" 2002; Odgaard 2003, 22).

In addition to the track-one diplomacy of ASEAN and ARF meetings, dispute resolution activities are taking place at the South China Sea Informal Working Group workshops organized annually by Indonesia and Canada (South China Sea Informal Working Group 2001). This track-two diplomacy has been hailed as a significant new development not just because it integrates China into multilateral forums (Lee Lai To 1999, 59ff; Austin 1998, 304), but because it also is part of the construction of a new sense of "international society" in Asia and beyond. The disputes that are "located at the junction of outer fringes of China and Southeast Asia" are "a catalyst for initiating fundamental changes in existing patterns of state interaction" (Odgaard 2002, 10, 3; Odgaard 2003, 21).

But while joining the regional structures, attending the conferences, writing white papers, developing a cadre of international law experts, making encouraging statements on general issues, and even signing on to a Code of Conduct, Beijing has resisted multi-lateral solutions to the South China Sea disputes. After eight years of track-two diplomacy, the Indonesian workshops leader was less optimistic about their influence, because China had shown itself "unwilling to agree to concrete moves" (in Stenseth 1999, 13; Lee Lai To 1999, 80). China has encouraged the ambiguity of the South China Sea Informal Working Group; it has realized that, once it specifies its claim, it will have to defend it in the context of inter-national law, and that a claim to most of the South China Sea as historic waters would be very difficult to defend (Valencia 1995, 13). Even the Code of Conduct does not promote multilateral reso-lution (see Odgaard 2003, 22); China still prefers to deal with rival claimants on a bilateral basis. Although Beijing has offered joint development of resources to rival claimants at various times, closer examination shows that joint development is always under Beijing's leadership. One scholar in Beijing compared "joint development" in the South China Sea to a "joint venture" corporation in Beijing: while economic investment and profits are shared, the corporation is still under Chinese sovereign jurisdiction (Interviews 1999).

China further formalized its claim in February 1992, when the National People's Congress passed the "Law of the People's Republic of China on its Territorial Waters and Contiguous Areas." This ac-tion disturbed the region because it unilaterally made a legal claim for ownership not just of the islands in the South China Sea but also for Taiwan, the Diaoyu Islands, Penghu Islands, Dongsha Islands, and "other islands that belong to the PRC" ("Law on Territorial Waters" BBC/SWB 28 November 1992, C1/1–2). But even this ag-gressive unilateral action is still phrased in the familiar language of state sovereignty: the law is "to enable the PRC to exercise its sovereignty over its territorial waters and its rights to exercise con-trol over their adjacent areas, and to safeguard state security as well as its maritime rights and interests" ("Law on Territorial Waters" BBC/SWB 28 November 1992, C1/1–2). The right to defend this sovereignty through military action is included in this law. Once again, both sympathetic and critical readings of China's diplomacy in the South China Sea reaffirm that China is being converted to the Westphalian notion of the sovereignty of nation-states.

To put it another way, Chinese actions in the South China Sea are quite predictable. China is involved in the age-old process of "writing security" (Campbell 1998a). Through its military and diplomatic narratives, China—like the other states in the dispute—is creating a problem in the South China Sea to craft and manage borders that otherwise do not make sense.

Although the South China Sea is commonly seen as one of the main "security problems" in East Asia, in fact there is little actual conflict there. As in the Kasmiri conflict between India and Pakistan, where the greatest casualties are to altitude sickness and frostbite (Krishna 1996, 200–201), in the South China Sea soldiers do not fight each other so much as storms and sunstroke. As the newspaper articles tell us, the main enemy in the South China Sea is the sea itself: "In October 1993, Typhoon No. 20 hit the main pillbox. High waves rolled over the rooftop of the three-story-high building. Erected structures and equipment lying on an area of 600 square meters of the construction site were swept away" (Hu Zhanfan 1994, 11). When the sea does not get you, the sun will: "[W]e heard of instances of asphalt felt melting and thermometers bursting under the scorching sun of the Nansha islands" (Hu Zhanfan 1994, 11; Whiting 1998, 299). The "Nansha Spirit" describes enduring the hardship of the weather conditions, rather than surviving the horrors of battle. Hence equipment upgrading concentrates on stronger air conditioners and better fresh water supplies, rather than on bigger guns (Ling Xingzheng 1998; Zheng Degang 1999; Austin 1998, 312). Indeed, although the South China Sea disputes are a hot topic in English-language security studies journals, the Chinese press, and popular histories, they are not a common item in *Chinese* security studies journals (Stenseth 1999, 36). The *White Paper on China's National Defense 2002* declares, "The situation in the South China Sea area has been basically stable, as the relevant countries have signed the Declaration on the Conduct of Parties in the South China Sea."

In other words, there is no "there" there: in addition to a lack of military conflict, there is no substantial territory to defend, fisheries are depleted, and there is little sign of the promised petrochemical riches. National maritime territory has to be created to manufacture threats to national security that are tied to writing the security of the newly discovered ancient "sacred territory." It is the conceptualization of "security" itself, which creates the subjectivity of the state, that has made "a relatively peaceful area into one of serious security concerns" (Zha, Daojiong 2001, 34). As Walker puts it, "the subject of security is the *subject* of security" (Walker 1997, 78; Campbell 1998a, 199).

The South China Sea disputes thus show how the primary purpose of state security is not to secure a particular nation-state, but to secure the limitation of politics to the spatio-temporal demarcations of state sovereignty that limit identity to citizenship. The very active project of transforming China from a continental power to a maritime power serves as a cogent example of security not *defending* us so much as "tell[ing] us who we must be" (Walker 1997, 71–72; Campbell 1998a, 199). To rethink security—and to rethink the "problem" and "solution" of the Spratly Islands disputes—we have to "rethink the character and location of the political" by asking who or what is to be secured, and under what conditions? (Walker 1997, 69).

While most reconsiderations of critical security studies stop here by questioning the subject of security, I will engage in both criticism and recovery. In the next section we move from the South China Sea disputes as an "empirical problem" of how to fairly divide up the goods, to see the disputes as a conceptual problem of how to write security and sovereignty in different ways. Rather than simply move beyond the state for new post-state concepts of security, we see how modern state subjectivity uses historical trajectories to respond to pressures: we look, rather than to the nation-state of the PRC, to the civilization-state of Greater China.

CONCEPTUAL OPPORTUNITY: MULTIPLE SOVEREIGNTY AND THE CIVILIZATION-STATE

Although the first section of this chapter has argued that China is being converted to Westphalian norms of nation-state activity, it is important to note that such military/diplomatic activity in the South China Sea perpetuates more than resolves the Spratly Islands disputes. A reliance on "sovereignty" and "international law" does more to complicate the issues than clarify them.

Still, many analysts see this as a problem of Chinese nationalism. Valencia, for example, argues that international relations norms are "Western standards and legal precedents" that "have little effect on China" (Valencia 1995, 27). It is often noted that China's main evidence for sovereignty, the historical claim, is not supported by international law, and is increasingly "criticized or even ridiculed" (Valencia 1995, 13; Interviews 2000). Valencia thus concludes that the fundamental question goes far beyond the South China Sea to ask "Is China trying to write its own rules for international order rather than accepting existing norms?" (Valencia 1995, 13). In an analysis more sympathetic to Chinese claims, Austin likewise concludes that if China gives up its "historical" argument for a "legal" one, its claim to the Spratly Islands would be quite strong (Austin 1998, 327). In this way, both the hawks and the doves see the South China Sea disputes as a problem of the particularities of "Chinese nationalism" that can be solved via jettisoning its particularistic stance for the universal rationality of international law.

Rather than question China's particular intentions or culture, I turn this query around to interrogate "international norms." Instead of there being a problem of "Chinese nationalism," the concepts of nation-state, sovereignty, and international law are the main issues. As I argued above, the South China Sea is a space where "territorial sovereignty" does not make sense. According to standard empirical measures, there is no territory, population, or authority there. The South China Sea disputes demonstrate that the "existing norms" of international relations that animate mainstream analysis are far from stable.

This result turns the South China Sea disputes from an empirical matter into a conceptual issue. As Bartelson cogently argues, although sovereignty is the "main question of politics," it is hardly a stable concept (Bartelson 1995, 1–11). Rather than take sovereignty as an empirical scientific question—of looking at the map for natural borders, or treaties for international law—Bartelson shows how sovereignty is bound up in knowledge practices. He argues that sovereignty does not make sense in and of itself, for "sovereignty's main function is to frame objects of inquiry by telling us what they are not" (Bartelson 1995, 51). He writes a genealogical history of sovereignty in Europe, and we could also argue that concepts of sovereignty vary over space as well as time. Just as the Western concept of liberalism has changed from "individual rights" to "states' rights" in its transmigration to China (Hughes 1995, 430), it is important to see how the concept of sovereignty has emerged in China.

Even though Chinese texts are dotted with references to various forms of sovereignty—state sovereignty, territorial sovereignty, maritime sovereignty, economic sovereignty, ideological sovereignty, and cultural sovereignty—it is not clear what the term means in practice. It turns out that sovereignty, as a concept, is no more stable in Chinese than in European languages. *Zhuquan,* the modern Chinese word for sovereignty, has a strange pedigree. It was first introduced through an American missionary's translation of an international law textbook for the Chinese court. Martin, the missionary in question, thought that translating international law was the best way to spread "Christian civilization" to the Chinese elite (Hsu 1960, 126, 130).[3] *Zhuquan* is actually one of the few international law neologisms crafted by Martin that has endured. Therefore modern Chinese dictionary definitions of sovereignty are quite familiar: they appeal to a distinction between internal and external spheres, where a sovereign state must be united domestically, and thus able to defend itself against external forces. Equal sovereignty, the dictionary tells us, is the basis of international law (see *Cihai* 1979). Exemplary sentences characteristically use "state sovereignty" and "territorial sovereignty." It seems that Martin was able to convert the Qing court (and thus Chinese foreign policy) to international law—if not to Christianity in its more spiritual forms.

Indeed, Chinese diplomacy uses the language of liberalism; *quan* is the modern word for rights. *Renquan* is human rights; likewise, international law basically codifies the rights and obligations of states to each other. But the other senses of *zhuquan* come out when *zhu* is added. *Zhu* does not mean state, but ruler. In this way it harkens back to a premodern concept of sovereignty, where sovereign means "king." If we trace the word back two millennia, the classical Legalist text *Guanzi* uses *zhuquan* to describe the power and authority of the sovereign. But *zhu*'s more common meaning is "owner" or "master," in the sense of control over slaves or animals. *Zhuquan* thus are the rights of the master.

Deconstructing *quan* also shows less than liberal roots: the second definition of *quan* is opportunism. Thus *quan* is often more about arbitrary power and authority than about transcendent moral categories of rights. Reading classical and nineteenth-century sources, Roger T. Ames writes: "'*Quan,*' or rights, has generally denoted 'power,' not in the positive sense of legitimated authority but as a provisional advantage that derives from exceptional circumstances"

(Ames 1988, 203). Rather than being a moral category of legitimate power, *zhuquan* sovereignty can be the opposite, immoral "hegemonic" power that operates via coercive force. So, in the end, *zhuquan* can range from familiar senses of "territorial sovereignty," to "the rights of the master," to the more problematic "opportunism of the master." Sovereignty deconstructs itself by its Chinese translation.

Many Chinese considerations of the South China Sea disputes also turn sovereignty from a technical into a theoretical problem. For example, a mass market publication, *Maritime China,* uses the South China Sea disputes as a vehicle to discuss the concept of maritime national territory. The authors do not spend most of their time in recalling the history and statistics of the South China Sea archipelagoes—as expected—but rather in discussing the new set of concepts necessary to make sense of Chinese claims. Ni and Song thus argue that the Chinese need to "establish a maritime national territory perspective" (Ni and Song 1998, 413ff). To establish such a perspective, Ni and Song philologically explore concepts of space by analyzing "the evolution of the concept of 'national territory' *[guotu]*" and how this concept relates to sovereign territory *[lingtu]* (Ni and Song 1998, 417ff). As in *Pacific Trials,* the disputes are figured less as an empirical problem than as a knowledge problem (Wu Chunguang 1998, 414).

In this discussion of Chinese diplomacy, it has been taken for granted that the United Nations or ASEAN would convert China to its model of international relations. But the instability of mainstream concepts, on the one hand, and the increased use by Chinese scholars and officials of traditional concepts, on the other, suggests that conversion can work in different ways: either mutual socialization (Armstrong 1993, 299–311), or Greater China converting the rest of the world to its own model of world politics. An appeal to Asian styles of international politics and diplomacy is not offered only by marginalized scholars but by leaders in both the military and the foreign ministry (Yao and Liu 1998). Indeed, Foreign Minister Qian Qichen declared in 1995 that "the solution to the Spratly question should be sought through bilateral negotiations in an Oriental way" (in Lee Lai To 1999, 38). Public policy studies in the United States also take a political culture approach that respects "Asian diplomacy" where "foreign models do not necessarily apply" (Valencia et al. 1999, 204).

Since many Chinese writers agree with Bartelson's argument that sovereignty is intimately interwoven with knowledge practices, we must recover in more detail how sovereignty and space have operated in China. This attempt leads us back in history to other ideal forms of power and authority, other world orders, and thus away from geopolitics to "cultural epistemology" (Howland 1996, 11). In other words, rather than ridicule Chinese historical claims for their exotic and irrational challenges to the world system (Valencia 1995, 13; Austin 1998, 358), we should explore their particular logic. A long detour into a thick description of traditional Chinese sovereignty and space is necessary to provide a context for rethinking the South China Sea disputes.

Horizontal and Vertical Maps

Cartography is crucial in the discourse of the South China Sea disputes. To locate the Spratly Islands on Chinese maps, it is important to critically examine the logic of Chinese cartography. From the analysis of the *Shanhai jing* in chapter 2, we can see that Chinese maps are concerned more with distinctions between peoples than with boundaries between territories. While it is now taken for granted that cartography is a scientific endeavor devoid of value judgments, there is a strong Chinese tradition of cultural and ethnographic cartography that maps not only places but "power, duty and emotion" (Yee 1994d, 144); Chinese cartography did not map the world as a reflection of how it was but of how it should be (Smith 1998, 96). I will argue that, in unmapping the scientific geography to re-map aesthetic Chinese cosmography, we can see how sovereignty becomes multiple and shared around intersecting peripheries such as the South China Sea (see Shapiro 1997, 171ff).

To demonstrate how this ironic notion of space works in global politics, it is helpful to juxtapose cartographic practices. Comparing two sets maps can help us start to switch from horizontal cartography to vertical cosmology, and from singular sovereignty to ironic space. Indeed, by looking at maps historically, we can begin to recover "the alternative worlds destroyed and suppressed within modern cartography" (Shapiro 1997, 16; Yee 1994f, 228; Smith 1998, 58).

On the one hand, Mark Valencia produces maps noteworthy for

their attention to detail (see Map 3: Valencia 1995, map 6). But the chaotic and overlapping nature (or, as he elsewhere calls it, the "crazy quilt" nature) of the claims—and the garrisons—is also obvious on these maps (Valencia 1995, 57ff). The South China Sea claims are not organized as straightforward spheres of influence extending from established borders. Chinese occupation of islets is not limited to the north but goes deep into the south; likewise, Vietnamese bases are not just in the west, but are in the east as well.

Valencia proposes three scenarios to bring order to this chaos by drawing borders on the map to divide up the territory among the claimant states (Valencia 1995, 57ff). The strategy in each scenario relies on mapping out the South China Sea claims, and fairly splitting the difference between the competing nation-states according to geological and legal measures: continental shelves and baselines. Whiting gives the same advice for solving the Senkaku/Diaoyu Islands dispute with Japan (Whiting 1998, 294).

The solutions are characteristic of a horizontal conception of space. Maps such as Map 3 show how each "scenario" resolves the conflict first by constituting homogeneous horizontal space, and then by dividing it with a simple two-dimensional line boundary. Thus Valencia and others are appealing to a Westphalian mapping of the South China Sea, where claims are based on a "level playing field" of the territorial geography of nation-states. But, as we saw, this does not work very well. Valencia admits that the scenarios would not satisfy the most powerful claimant: when the mappings divide the space according to the boundaries of sovereign states, China does not get even a part of the Spratlys (Valencia 1995, 61; Valencia et al. 1999, 199–223; Austin 1998, 56).

In the end, Valencia argues that the best possible solution is to use the Law of the Sea to set up a "shared regional commons" that would be governed by a regional multilateral resource authority. In this proposal, the disputants would discard sovereignty claims and re-organize the region into a new patchwork of a series of twelve "Joint Development Companies" based on areas of overlapping claims (Valencia 1995, 64; Valencia et al. 1999, 199–223). Costs and benefits would be shared equally between members of each company.

But Valencia and others keep failing to solve the disputes, because the seascape is not singular, but ironic and multilayered: the Chinese, Taiwanese, Vietnamese, Philippine, Bruneian, and Malaysian claims

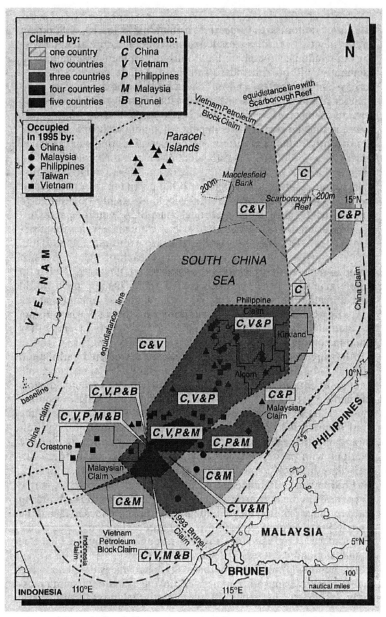

Map 3. Horizontal cartography in the South China Sea. Reprinted from Mark J. Valencia, "China and the South Sea Disputes: Conflicting Claims and Potential Solutions in the South China Sea," Adelphi Paper *no. 298 (1995): 65. Courtesy of Oxford University Press.*

overlap. The problems of the South China Sea are in this way similar to the situation in the former Yugoslavia, which Campbell argues "serves as a powerful example of the limitations and problems associated with international relations' standard modes of representation" (Campbell 1996, 23). The various attempts to solve Bosnian problems through a drawing of stable boundaries between homogeneous ethnic communities kept failing because the ethnoscape of Muslim/Croat/Serb is not singular but ironic and multilayered (Campbell 1998b).

Imperial Cartography and Traditional Concepts of Space

In traditional cartography, it "is difficult to determine where a map of China ends and the world begins" (Smith 1998, 53). The ideology of China as the center of the world, where the main division was between civilization and barbarism rather than between nation-states, is neatly reproduced in imperial Chinese maps. To catch such worlds, it is necessary to unmap the modernization narrative; rather than proceeding chronologically from empire to nation-state, it is necessary to recover a former Chinese understanding of the world and relate it to Greater China in the twenty-first century. The Celestial Empire is now being transformed not so much into a nation-state as into what Tu Weiming calls a "civilization-state" (Tu Weiming 1994a, 14–16).

Still, the Chinese Academy of Social Sciences' (CASS) semiofficial *Simple Historical Atlas of China* maps the imperial dynasties with clear single-line boundaries of a stable geobody—including the South China Sea—in horizontal space (Tan Qixiang 1996). But space and borders were not so simple. Indeed, the differing shapes of "China" in Tan's scientific atlas dramatically show how unstable the geobody has been over time. As we saw in the last chapter, historically it has never been clear what territory the Chinese empire controlled (Waldron 1990, 190). While Chinese claim that Taiwan, Hong Kong, and the Spratly Islands have been theirs "since ancient times," Chinese cartography demonstrates "the perennial problem of keeping China together" (Smith 1998, 61; Yan Ping et al. 1998, 2).

It is curious that the Chinese Academy of Social Sciences' series of *Atlases of Ancient Maps in China* highlights the aesthetic nature of Chinese space better than the CASS atlas (Cao Wanru et al. 1990; Cao Wanru et al. 1994; Cao Wanru et al. 1997; also see Yan Ping et al. 1998; Yee 1996; Yee 1994d; Yee 1994a; Yee 1994b; Yee 1994e; Yee 1994f). While there have been accurate mathematical maps of China and the world since the twelfth century, maps have also been part of a symbolic economy. Indeed, "mathematizing the landscape did not suppress other impulses in China" that were "resistant to the idea that space should be homogenized to aid quantification" (Yee 1994f, 228). Space was seen as "dynamic and fluid" on maps that were not necessarily concerned with telling us how to get from here to there, but (as mentioned above) with "power, duty and emotion" (Yee 1994d, 144; Yee 1994a, 67). Thus, as Yee argues, Chinese maps are not just part of a mathematical tradition, but part of the aesthetic tradition of landscape painting (Yee 1994d; Yee 1996). But it was not a question of being *either* mathematical *or* aesthetic, but of how to be *both* accurate and artistic: "To achieve literacy in traditional Chinese cartography, one needs grounding in the history of science and technology, art, literature, government, economics, religion and philosophy" (Yee 1994f, 228). Chinese space, including the South China Sea, is aesthetic and cosmic rather than mathematical and rational.

A civilization's *mappamundi* can tell us much about its worldview: its view not just of how the world is, but of how it should be (Smith 1998, 52). The hierarchical order of vertical space can be seen in premodern maps of the world such as "Illustrations of the Unity of the Three Powers (Heaven, Earth, and Man)" (Smith 1998, 76; Yee 1994d, 152–figure 6.19; Henderson 1994, 211–figure 8.6). Chinese world maps were laid out in concentric circles not "based on physical or natural features" (Yee 1994b, 76); maps were drawn concentrically with China at the center of the world, Beijing at the center of China, and the Emperor at the center of Beijing (see Cao Wanru et al. 1990, plate 122).[4]

Two of the main cartographic genres speak directly to this Sinocentric ideology that divided populations between civilization and barbarism. While *Tianxia quantu* is often translated as "the Complete Map of All-under-Heaven," more literally it means "the Complete Map of the Chinese empire" (Cao Wanru et al. 1997, plate 83; Cao Wanru et al. 1994, plate 146). While *Huayi tu* is commonly translated as "A Map of China and Neighboring Countries," more literally it means "A Map of Civilization and Barbarism" (Cao Wanru et al. 1997, 7; Yan Ping et al. 1998, plate 35; Cao Wanru et al. 1994, plate 94; Cao Wanru et al. 1990, plates 60–62).

The centrality of the empire comes out in how the maps are drawn. As the unnamed map from 1734 in Map 1 shows, China is presented as an island surrounded by impenetrable barriers. One of the classical idioms for the empire is territory "within the four seas" where civilization floats, surrounded by the empty space of barbarism (Cao Wanru et al. 1997, plate 83; Yan Ping et al. 1998, 152; Cao Wanru et al. 1990, plate 95). Although the world/China maps were often very accurate for the center of the empire, detail thins towards the periphery. *Huayi tu*—Maps of Civilization and Barbarism—such as Map 1, show how the north and the west are framed by the Great Wall (always drawn in, even though it did not exist as a coherent entity) and by the emptiness of the deserts (often drawn as wide impassable "rivers of sand") (also see Cao Wanru et al. 1994, plates 94, 60, 231; Cao Wanru et al. 1990, plate 122). The east and south are framed by seas that form a barrier analogous to the Great Wall—thus the twentieth-century Chinese images of the Spratlys as a Great Wall in the South China Sea.

The sea in the south is not accurate, either: mainland Southeast Asia often disappears entirely. Foreign countries—even Vietnam and India, let alone Portugal, England, and America—appear as small and insignificant islands off the Chinese coast (see Map 3; Yan Ping et al. 1998, plate 87; Smith 1998, 75; Cao Wanru et al. 1990, plates 83–82). Although the "Complete Map of All-under-Heaven" (1644) is one of the first Chinese maps to use a mathematical grid, it combines such scientific accuracy with cultural cartography: "China is located in the center, covering an area bigger than all the other countries put together." As in Map 1, the southern periphery is spotted with island countries from the mythical *Shanhai jing*: the kingdom of inhabitants born with two bodies, three heads, golden teeth; the kingdom of females, of pygmies, of hairy inhabitants, of heart-piercing inhabitants (Cao Wanru et al. 1994, plate 146–p. 3; also see Smith 1998, 75).

Such official cartography continued up to the turn of the twentieth century: the "Complete Map of Imperial Territory" (1899) is quite accurate, but again China is surrounded by blank space (Cao Wanru et al. 1997, plate 129–p. 55). As Smith concludes: "Representationally speaking, there are no obvious borders separating China from Russia or clearly delineating the individual kingdoms and territories of, say, Central Asia, India, or mainland Southeast Asia. Only oceans and seas allow certain countries to appear fully separated from the Central Kingdom" (Smith 1998, 82). Cartographic details are more sparse at the periphery because Chinese administration became weaker as Chinese population thinned.[5]

While borders are the focus of modern mathematical maps, the center was the focus of traditional Chinese cartography. To understand Chinese space, then, we have to go to the center, the capital city. Maps of Beijing show an orderly city with a regular grid oriented on north-south, east-west axes (for examples, see Cao Wanru et al. 1997, plate 160; Cao Wanru et al. 1994, plate 157; Cao Wanru et al. 1990, plates 46–48; Yan Ping et al. 1998, plate 120; Henderson 1994; Meyer 1991). Beijing and other capitals since the Shang dynasty (c.1600–c.1027 BC) have striven for such order, and have served as examples for other parts of the empire (Henderson 1994, 210; Meyer 1991, 12).

Yet the orderliness of Chinese capitals is not an expression of the secular Protestant rationality exemplified by the numbered grids of New York and Philadelphia (Shapiro 1997, 23–24, 26). The *Rites of Zhou*, which is seen as the locus classicus for Chinese capitals, tells us: "This is the place where the heavens and the earth unite, where the four seasons are joined, where the wind and rain come together, where the two principles, male and female, are in harmony" (Meyer 1991, 10; Yee 1994b, 81). The capital, then, is not a political center so much as a cosmic center, a nodal point between the terrestrial and the celestial: "Beijing was the earthly termination of the axis of the universe, the center of the world, the pivot of the four corners" (Meyer 1991, 1; Smith 1996, figure 3.1). The capital is a point on a vertical map for a moral Celestial Empire, "built or reformed to accord with cosmographic strictures" (Henderson 1994, 210). The city was laid out as a cosmic representation to facilitate correlation between the various orders of existence—Heaven, Earth, and Man. Again, one of the popular genres of world maps is called "Illustrations of the Unity of the Three Powers (Heaven, Earth, and Man)."

Emperors "who sat at the pivot of the Four Quarters" would need this cosmological city plan to conduct the proper rituals that mediated between Heaven and Earth (Henderson 1994, 211). Thus, politics followed cosmography: the fate not only of the kingdom but of the world was wrapped up in the royal city (Meyer 1991, 8). This cartography was also more than a Chinese practice—it was a mapping for world politics because the *Rites of Zhou*'s model of a capital city was also used by capital cities in what are now the nation-states of Japan, Korea, and Vietnam (Meyer 1991, 12). This cosmography is not limited by time or ideology, either: many argue that the layout of Tian'anmen Square in Beijing—which was constructed by the communist government in the late 1950s—still looks to such cosmographic models for symbolic legitimacy (Henderson 1994, 227; Wu Hung 1997, 331; Meyer 1991).

Indeed, such vertical cosmographies are not limited to the exotic East; they are also characteristic of medieval Europe. Shapiro notes that "medieval spatial practices had a markedly ethical coding" quite different from modern practices where "space tends to have an air of neutrality, to appear empty of normative imposition" (Shapiro 1997, 20, 15; Bartelson 1995, 91–92). Modern subjectivity is defined by individuality, and is autonomous with sovereign rights vis-à-vis society; hence, moral subjectivity is tied to state boundaries in the horizontal world. But in medieval Europe "a person's worth was derived from his or her place in the universal hierarchy with God at the apex" (Shapiro 1997, 20).

Likewise, the legitimizing vocabulary of the Celestial Empire is focused on the *Tian* (heavens) rather than on the nation-state's horizontal world.[6] The Emperor was *Tianzi*, the Son of Heaven. The doctrine of sovereignty and legitimacy was *Tianming*, the Mandate of Heaven. And as we have seen, the word for the empire was *Tianxia*, All-under-Heaven. This lack of a geographical reference—such as *Roman* Empire or *British* Empire—for the name of the empire, its leader, and its practices was a statement of the region's self-sufficiency, until the nineteenth century. It is uncommon for Chinese world maps to have any reference to the proper names of the Ming or Qing dynastic empires (see Cao Wanru et al. 1990; Cao Wanru et al. 1994; Cao Wanru et al. 1997). There was no concept of "China'" or "Chinese civilization," because in this universal empire, there were only civilization and the barbarians: "The Chinese state was not a state at all, but rather administration of civilized society en toto, the mediator between heaven and earth" (Mancall 1968, 63). In a "highly refined vocabulary of imperial condescension" that stressed both the inferiority and loyalty of foreign rulers, the Emperor was responsible for the management of foreign peoples, all seen as his subjects (Smith 1998, 62).

Thus cartography was part of the legitimization of the Chinese empire. Tributary states presented maps to the emperor as marks of subservience. As the ancient history the *Han shu* put it: "The Son of Heaven receives maps and registers from the four seas" (in Yee 1994b, 77). World maps were not merely strategic or cosmological, so much as part of general claims of feudal overlordship. Virtually all large-scale maps referred to the Chinese tributary system (Smith 1998, 95, 83). These maps were artifacts of both religious and political ritual in a foreign policy performance; the performances were not just among states as in modern diplomacy (see Campbell 1998a; Constantinou 1996, 95–120), but among Heaven, Earth, and Man.

As we saw in chapter 2, all this amounts to a different policing of cultural boundaries. The relations between the civilization-state and the barbarian hordes are neither those of self/Other to be conquered, nor of peaceful coexistence between equal sovereign states. Relations have been characteristically formulated in terms of the governmentality of rituals and family relations. In the civilization-state, the Emperor is the Great Father, the Chinese people the children. The kings of neighboring states are neither equal sovereigns nor "Other" enemies, but are referred to as the Emperor's "younger brothers." The method of dealing with difference was conversion to Chinese civilization more than conquest (Smith 1996, 9; Todorov 1984, 125–82).

In terms of world politics, this means that those barbarians who accepted Chinese culture were reclassified as tributary states. As with medieval Europe, "international" and "interstate" are not proper terms for this system, for those involved did not have the concepts of nation, sovereignty, or the equality of states (Fairbank 1968a, 5; Bartelson 1995, 89). This "tributary system" constructed hierarchical bilateral relations, never multilateral relations, where one partner was always the ruler of China (Mancall 1984, 65). Thus all world politics proceeded through bilateral relations between the center of civilization in Beijing and the barbarians at the periphery. Soon after the unification of the Chinese empire in the third century BC this pattern of world politics became the norm: all foreign missions (including nineteenth-century European embassies) were officially recorded as tribute missions. As Wang Gungwu writes, "The Chinese had begun to believe that the tributary relationship was the only *normal* one that did not conflict with their total view of the known world" (Wang

Gungwu 1968, 41; Mancall 1984, 13–39). Thus the norm was not Westphalian international relations (such as we saw in the first section) but the civilization/barbarian relations of the civilization-state. Since the main focus of political attention was vertical, the horizontal dimensions were secondary, characterized more by aesthetics— cultural anthropology and ritual action—than geopolitics. The main institution dealing with foreign rulers in the Ming and Qing dynasties was called the Board of Rites, and in this tributary system diplomacy was judged on aesthetic grounds (Mancall 1984, 14). Often there were no clear borders, but bands of land in which both sides refrained from occupancy and cultivation, or "a zone in which the people belonged to both countries, or a buffer state" (Yang Liensheng 1968, 22; Waldron 1990, 62ff). Thus as we saw on the imperial Chinese world maps, boundaries between states did not meet in a single straight line. Rather, there were both empty spaces beyond sovereignty, and overlaps where sovereignty was shared (see Tan Qixiang 1996, plates 33–34, 43–44). According to many sources, premodern borders were ambiguous, and sovereignty was multiple, throughout East Asia. So, for example, towns in what is now the nation-state of the Democratic People's Republic of Laos paid tribute to three or four different overlords—in Bangkok, Rangoon, Chiangmai, Hue, and Kunming (Thongchai 1994, 96–101). In Siam (Thailand), boundaries were drawn on the basis of the ethnicity of the population rather than on the topography of mountains and rivers (Thongchai 1994, 63ff).

In Imperial China such ambiguous borders were not problematic; they were characteristic of the system of ironic space (Mancall 1984, 33–39). As the Chinese world maps show, it has been common to frame foreign countries as small islands off the Chinese coast. Historically, in East Asia islands have been part of multiple sovereignty and, like Laos, paid tribute to two or three empires. The Liu Qiu Islands, in what is now the Japanese prefecture of Okinawa, paid tribute to both Beijing and Edo (Tokyo) for nearly three centuries. As an eighteenth-century Japanese scholar noted, Liu Qiu "subjects herself to both countries and pays tribute to them both. She uses the Japanese calendar when she deals with Japan, and the Chinese calendar when she contacts China" (in Sakai 1968, 112).

Although noted scholars see this relationship as "diplomatic evasion" that relied on "confusion" and "deception" (Ch'en Ta-tuan

1968, 159, 162; Sakai 1968, 114), we can also see this as a positive expression of ironic world politics. Indeed, the rulers of the Liu Qiu kingdom tried to play one empire off against the other; when the crisis of modern sovereignty finally came in the 1870s, the people of Liu Qiu still saw China as their "father" and Japan as their "mother" (Sakai 1968, 114). But Liu Qiu's relations with China and Japan were actually quite different. The Chinese treated Liu Qiu as a tributary state, including the rituals of tribute and investiture; Liu Qiu was used by Japan as a conduit for trade with China. The relations between China, Liu Qiu, and Japan are a study in ironic world politics: while the Liu Qiu-ans were culturally Confucian Chinese, they were under the military hegemony of Japan (Ch'en Ta-tuan 1968, 162).

Although China used cultural power in the Liu Qiu Islands, it could also resort to military coercion when necessary (see Johnston 1995). When the Emperor's younger brothers were not willing converts, the Chinese court threatened conquest (Waldron 1990, 85). The Vietnamese king upset the Chinese emperor in 179 BC by calling himself emperor. The Son of Heaven sent a message to remind his younger brother that there could only be one emperor in the world. The Vietnamese king responded sycophantically by assuring the Emperor that he only wanted to serve the dynasty. The Chinese emperor was pleased with this letter, and soon reestablished normal relations. But while the Vietnamese king called himself the "chief of the barbarians" in his letter to the Son of Heaven, back in his own country the Vietnamese emperor still used his ancient title (Mancall 1984, 24–26).

This story shows how submission in the Chinese empire was mostly ritual. If a ruler recognized Chinese culture as Civilization, and paid tribute to the emperor, then the emperor usually left domestic matters alone. Thus recognition switches from a Westphalian ritual of equality and sovereignty, to a recognition of the hierarchy and civilization in the Chinese world order. The Celestial Empire generally exercised a policy of noninterference in the details of local administration. Hence the imperialism of Imperial China was more cultural than administrative or economic, conversion more than conquest. Korea is the best example of a willing tribute to China; while its imperial Confucian culture flourished, it maintained independence in local politics (Kim Key-Hiuk 1980, 8–10; see chapter

4). This imperial weakness was actually a strength: the "rule of son of heaven could be maintained over so broad and diverse a terrain and so vast a population precisely because it was so superficial" (Fairbank 1968a, 8). The empire was unified because local rulers, in both Chinese provinces and tributary states, were left to govern as they saw fit. The emperor exercised few coercive powers but maintained control symbolically.

Although it may seem European cartography has overwhelmed the Chinese world order (Yee 1996, 7–8; Smith 1998, 90), the "one civilization, many systems" model has persevered parallel to Westphalia's "one system, many nation-states" formula. Just because China was brought into international society in the 1860s when the European system of sovereign equality of states was imposed on East Asia, the ancient world order did not end. Rather, the Western system of equal states was superimposed upon the preexisting East Asian system; the new Westphalian system was active only in China-Western relations. Within East Asia the old system prevailed, albeit with some new wrinkles: for example, at the end of the nineteenth century, the Chinese emperor and Japanese emperor competed for the position of universal emperor, the Son of Heaven. What I am calling ironic world politics, Kim Key-Hiuk calls a dualistic system that was partly Eastern and partly Western, partly traditional and partly modern (Kim Key-Hiuk 1980, 328–29). Just as there is a thread joining Roman Law, Christian Law, Natural Law, European Law, and International Law, where ideas have been progressively secularized and deterritorialized (Armstrong 1993, 12–41; Bartelson 1995), there is a thread joining the Chinese Celestial Empire to the more secular, quasi-territorial civilization-state of Greater China.

Still, some have questioned whether the Chinese world order was as historically enduring as its promoters attest. Cumings argues that, rather than "China shaking the world," it has been the world that has shaken China—China has been converted to capitalism (Cumings 1999, 151). Beyond often sterile debates about the continuity or discontinuity with China's imperial past (Mancall 1984, 445–502; Kim, Samuel 1994a, 12; Waldron 1990, 9), works such as Waldron's *The Great Wall of China*, Rossabi's *China among Equals*, and Hevia's *Cherishing Men from Afar* eloquently challenge idealized views of a timeless Chinese world order (Waldron 1990; Rossabi 1983b; Hevia 1995). Rossabi writes, "From the tenth to the thirteenth centuries, China did not dogmatically enforce its system of foreign relations. The Song [dynasty] . . . was flexible in dealing with foreigners" (Rossabi 1983a, 4). But even Rossabi's volume accepts that Chinese dynasties tolerated equal or subordinate relations to "barbarians" and "realistic" foreign policies only in times of weakness: "The Song's military weakness compelled its officials to treat foreign dynasties in China as equals. Thus a true multi-state system operated during Song times" (Rossabi 1983a, 11). Rather than being a multistate system, foreign relations in the Song dynasty were more of a reversal of the imperial hierarchy: Song presented tribute, including maps, to the Jurchen "barbarians" (Yee 1994b, 82; Smith 1998, 61). The concluding essay of Rossabi's volume organizes Chinese foreign policy into yin (weak)/yang (strong) phases, where equality was the pragmatic practice in weak eras but superiority was demanded in strong ones (Ledyard 1983, 313–53).

Since China in the twenty-first century is commonly seen as an emerging economic and military power—entering a yang phase after a long yin phase of national humiliation—according to Chinese historical precedent, Beijing should start demanding superiority, or at least equality with other "great powers." As history shows, after China was humiliated for a century by the Mongolian Yuan dynasty that challenged the Confucian worldview, it reemerged in the Ming dynasty with a revamped Confucian ideology (Wang Gungwu 1968, 34). So the 150 years of Western dominance is not such a long time; current nativist debates among Chinese intellectuals suggest that foreign ideologies of communism and democracy can be discarded as easily as the Mongolian/Buddhist way was overcome in the fourteenth century (Xu, Ben 1998; Zhang Xudong 1998; Zheng, Yongnian 1999). As the last chapter showed, many Chinese scholars and officials are looking to a traditional vocabulary—an imperial vocabulary—to explain both past events and future trends. Traditional Chinese cartography, with its notions of ironic and multiple space, is one of the resources being reconsidered.

IRONIC SPACE IN THE SOUTH CHINA SEA

Although talk of Imperial China sounds very premodern and reactionary (Huntington 1996, 168–74, 218–38), using the civilization-state's practices of multiple sovereignty and ironic space can help explain recent events in the South China Sea. The South China Sea disputes are more complicated than the situation in the Liu Qiu Islands, but the way the PRC is framing the issues is reminiscent of former civilization-states and their relations to the periphery.

For example, in 1993 while the ASEAN Regional Forum was being devised, the Chinese foreign minister warned that "Asian countries should not copy the European models" (in Lee Lai To 1999, 28). At another ASEAN meeting in 1995, at the time of the Mischief Reef crisis, the same minister elaborated, "the solution to the Spratly question should be sought through bilateral negotiations in an Oriental way" (in Lee Lai To 1999, 38). Likewise, the "great ambition" of the authors of *China Can Say No* is to form a different "pattern of world order" (Song Qiang 1996, 30). In both popular and official texts it is common to use the Hong Kong formula of "one country, two systems" as a model for world affairs, "one world, many systems," which has striking parallels with the civilization-state (Li Xiguang 1998, 108ff; also see chapter 5). Hence as Chinese officials and popular authors are looking for a post–Cold War model of regional security, they are consciously looking away from Western models and toward an "Oriental" way (see Acharya 1997). It is telling that Chinese texts employ the tributary vocabulary to include the Spratlys (Ni and Song 1997, 402; Smith 1998, 86).

The civilization-state is willing to be gracious in its imperial sovereignty. This is seen in Deng Xiaoping's oft-repeated statement that China is willing to "shelve" sovereignty for "joint development." And when other countries do not cooperate, China expresses its anger in ways that show imperial condescension. The Chinese government often reminds us how it has shown "tolerance" and "restraint" by not responding to provocative moves by Vietnam and the Philippines.[7] For example, in 1995 the government announced, "We advise the Philippine side not to misinterpret the Chinese side's restraint" (Xinhua in Austin 1998, 89).

But (as the previous section argued) using traditional Chinese concepts of space complicates the issue. We shall now see how these concepts of space can take the Spratlys away from Chinese absolute sovereignty, and, second, how they can give the Spratlys back to China as part of shared sovereignty. Once again, the empirical problems yield conceptual opportunities.

Chinese Maps of the South China Sea

Chinese maps are major sources of evidence in the Spratly disputes (Chen Hurng-yu 1993, 29). The emotional power of maps is striking; the Chinese map hanging on the wall of a pillbox in the South China Sea is encircled with "Motherland in My Heart" (An and Xiong 1994, 9). It is standard for Chinese texts to note how China was the first to map and name the Spratly Islands (Lin and Wu 1988, 140; Lee Lai To 1999, 9; Pan Shiying 1996), but a careful consideration of imperial Chinese maps shows that the Spratly Islands are not clearly part of Chinese territory. Most "Complete Maps of the Empire" only go as far south as Hainan Island. Annotations on many maps tell us that China extends from the Great Wall in the north to Hainan Island in the south (see Cao Wanru et al. 1997, plate 129: 55). As noted above, the periphery was not the focus of such "world maps." "Emptiness" is the theme of "the South" in both traditional Chinese cartography and recent reportage on the "Spratly Spirit."

Due to expanded trade and sea power starting in the Ming dynasty (1368–1644), Chinese cartographers began to produce regional maps of what we now call Southeast Asia (Yee 1994b, 94). For example, the "Map of the Barbarians of the Southeastern Sea" was an important part of the *Complete Terrestrial Atlas* (1553–57) (Cao Wanru et al. 1994, plate 155). Most of the "islands" in the South China Sea are listed as "countries" *(guo)*, which means that they are land-based features, not the reefs that the PRC now claims as the Spratlys. There are no references to the Spratly Islands. More to the point, as noted above, it was common in maps of the time to mix the factual with the fabulous and locate mythical kingdoms from the *Shanhai jing* in the South China Sea (Cao Wanru et al. 1994, plate 146; Smith 1998, 67, 69, 76).

Mapping of the region began again in earnest in the nineteenth century, as China addressed Western incursions. Archipelagoes that could be the Paracels and the Spratlys appear on two such maps first published in 1842: "Map of the Course of Change and Development of Different Countries of the Southeast Ocean" and "Map of Australia and Different Islands" (Cao Wanru et al. 1997: plates 187, 188–p. 65). These maps are framed in the north by Hainan Island, and show in reasonably accurate detail mainland and insular Southeast Asia as well as Australia. The Paracels and Spratlys are marked on both these maps, but their status is not clear on either. Since each is a map of foreign countries, it is more likely that the Spratlys were not seen as part of China, anymore than were other Southeast Asian states.

Another genre of maps is much more detailed and accurate for the South China Sea: *Complete Maps of Coastal Defense*. Ming and Qing dynasty coastal defense maps typically show all the features of the Chinese coast, including bays, estuaries, and offshore islands, from Korea in the north to Vietnam in the south (Cao Wanru et al. 1994, plate 40–p. 24; Cao Wanru et al. 1997, plate 29). These coastal defense maps often appear in atlases that show specific provinces like Guangdong and prefectures like Hainan Island (Cao Wanru et al. 1997, plate 29, 66–68; Yan Ping et al. 1998, plate 115). Initially, coastal defense maps were drawn in the late empire to facilitate security against "Japanese pirates" (who turned out to be Chinese smugglers in disguise) (Cao Wanru et al. 1994, plate 195; Yan Ping et al. 1998, 126–27; Howland 1996). The coastal defense maps, created to defend "China," dramatically confirm how the imperial Chinese concept of space and security was continental rather than maritime. The defense maps went into great detail about islands that were "Chinese," and showed how these islands hugged the coast. Their detail shows how the Qianlong Emperor could confidently tell the British emissary Lord Macartney in 1793 that he knew every island in the Chinese empire, but it also limits the notion of which islands would be included in that empire. Modern atlases of ancient maps pointedly include maps that show Chinese control of disputed territories: Taiwan, Hong Kong, and Xinjiang; hence it is noteworthy that they do not include maps that document the Spratlys as Chinese territory.

Likewise, the popular "patriotic" films that have been produced (ritually) in each decade of the PRC also figure the *Nanhai* (South China Sea) as the waters hugging the Chinese coast. Again, these films are part of security strategy performances (Campbell 1998a, 199). While the coastal defense maps and popular Chinese conceptions of the sea in late imperial times were driven by fears of Japanese pirates, the patriotic films set after 1949 tell stories of maritime militias defending China against the modern Japanese "pirates" in World War II, as well as defending the communist revolution against Nationalist and American bandits.[8]

China has aroused concern among its Southeast Asian neighbors—what some call "cartographic aggression" (in Austin 1998, 331)—by publishing maps that show a "historic claim line" that digs deep into the South China Sea. Indeed, it was this sense of space that justified the PRC government's criticism of the U.S. spy plane for violating China's sovereign territory in April 2001. There is an interesting debate surrounding the origin of China's "historic claim line" that has taken on a life of its own. It was created in the 1930s without the authorization of the central government, but became an aspect on Chinese maps of the Republic of China in the 1940s. These maps also included all of Mongolia and other parts of the Qing empire. Austin points out that, in the 1950s, China (both the ROC and the PRC) repudiated claims to an expansive view of land territories but did not repudiate such claims to maritime territories (Austin 1998, 14–15). It is easy to understand why: there were people to contest Chinese claims to land territory, while sea territory was unpopulated.

The historic claim line is reproduced on each map in the *Simple Historical Atlas of China*. On one, the Spratly Islands are mentioned as part of China since the Liao (916–1125) and Northern Song (960–1127) dynasties (Tan Qixiang: plate 51–52); on this map, the islands are labeled "*Wanli shitang*—10,000-li embankment."[9] The islands appear on subsequent maps of the Jin/Southern Song, Yuan, Ming, and Qing dynasties, and the Republic of China (also see Yan Ping et al. 1998, plate 141). But comparing these maps shows that the islands and their names are unstable: mostly, the Spratlys are called the "1,000-li embankment" *[Tianli shitang]*, and the Paracels are the "10,000-li reef" *[Wanli changsha]*, but often the Spratlys are called the "10,000-li reef," and the Paracels are the "1000-li embankment." At other times, the same set of names is used for different features. None of these names—10,000-li reef, 1000-li reef, 10,000-li embankment, 1,000-li embankment—has any stable reference of a proper name either. Nansha and Xisha are relatively recent designations, only coined by the government of the Republic of China in 1947 (Zheng Ziyue 1947; Chen Hurng-yu 1993, 24). The Chinese Ministry of Foreign Affairs report states that the "Xisha and Nansha Islands were variously named," and then lists seven traditional names (Chinese Ministry of Foreign Affairs 1980, 16). Hence the common argument that China was the first to name the islands may very well be correct; the problem is that it kept naming them again and again.

The overdetermination of names in Chinese speaks to the uneasy fit between imperial maps and modern maps. As we have seen, premodern Chinese maps appeal more to landscape art than to mathematical science. The celebrated journeys of Admiral Zheng He in the Ming dynasty utilized sophisticated astronomical and compass readings, but his maps—which are presented as evidence for South China Sea claims—were "drawn with the method of landscape painting" (Cao Wanru et al. 1994, plates 168ff–p. 38). As we saw with the repeated references to the mythical geography of the *Shanhai jing*, traditional Chinese maps characteristically are based on literary sources rather than surveys (Waldron 1990, 24; Smith 1998, 94).[10] Indeed, one of the main traditional modes of geography was the travelogue that both privileged personal experience and served as official document, often published and widely quoted (Howland 1996, 4, 105). Hence the modern reportage of the Spratlys continues a traditional mode of representation bringing the exotic into the familiar. One analyst criticizes this practice by noting that in the Chinese maps and travelogues "the toponymy of the islands varies with the grand fantasy" (Chemillier-Gendreau 1996, 60). They therefore are not a very reliable guide for making territorial claims according to international law. Curiously, the Chinese government and scholars make the same criticism of unreliability of Vietnamese maps (Chinese Ministry of Foreign Affairs 1980, 22; Lin and Wu 1988, 132).

Cartographic Conceptual Opportunities

In an effort to stake a claim to the archipelagoes in the South China Sea, Chinese texts mix the metaphors of international law and local history, science and poetry, cartography and landscape painting. Although this is taken by many to be a problem, it actually emphasizes how international law has its own (European) aesthetic and history (Gong 1984, 24ff; Keene 2001).

Chinese texts often criticize international law as the tool that Western imperial power used to "carve up" the rest of the world.[11] But, for the Spratlys, they employ the logic of conquest and imperialism. Pan Shiying, a well-respected expert on the disputes, writes, "The practice of the discovery of the New Land showed that when European navigators discovered a new area, their home countries claimed the sovereignty over that area" (Pan Shiying 1996, 31–32; Austin 1998, 339–41). Although this argument for sovereignty has not been recognized for hundreds of years—since the passing of the Age of Discovery—the Chinese claim still appeals to it. Indeed, though Chinese foreign policy is wholeheartedly anti-imperialist, Pan uses the examples of how the British, French, American, and Dutch empires acquired "overseas territories" as evidence for Chinese sovereignty over the Spratlys (Pan Shiying 1996, 28–41).

More to the point, many Chinese scholars also refer to Chinese imperial practices as a legitimate part of international law. Responding to the foreign minister's call for the use of the "Oriental way," such legal scholars employ "intertemporal law," which states that "a judicial fact must be appreciated in light of the laws contemporary with it, rather than the laws in force at the time when a dispute arises" (Chen Hurng-yu 1993, 32; Pan Shiying 1996, 27). Chinese claims that do not accord with Western notions of international law thus are judged as "not strange for any Asian nation in ancient times" (Lin and Wu 1988, 22). In this way, the tributary system of the Chinese empire is resurrected via intertemporal law.

Once we make the shift from (European style) international law to (Chinese style) intertemporal law, history becomes central. As we see in the following chapters, history has long been a central mechanism for legitimacy in East Asia. History is the basis of South China Sea claims for both China and Taiwan. While other states use legal and scientific categories—the geology of continental shelf and the Law of the Sea's category of Exclusive Economic Zones[12]—China uses cultural categories.[13] Evidence is compiled from historical documents, travelogues, maps, and archaeological digs to prove that the region has been Chinese "since ancient times" (Lin and Wu 1988; Pan Shiying 1996; Shih Ti-tsu 1975; Chinese Ministry of Foreign Affairs 1980; Valencia 1995, 6; Chen Hurng-yu 1993, 29ff). Even the texts that concentrate on law and science have to start with a detailed historical argument (Pan Shiying 1996; Si Tuxiang 1996).

For example, Chinese archaeologists have dug up the following relics from the Paracels: chinaware, copper cash, and bits of broken iron pans from the Tang and Song dynasties. A Chinese temple was excavated on another Paracel island, but no one can determine whether it is from the Ming or Qing dynasty (Chinese Ministry of Foreign Affairs 1980, 16; Chen Hurng-yu 1993, 33). Because none of the reefs in the Spratlys that China occupies is above sea level, there are no comparable digs there. In the 1990s, Vietnam, too, started to use archaeology to justify its claims; this shows how the Imperial Chinese world order, of which Vietnam was a part, is reasserting itself ("Vietnam . . ." 1996; Chemillier-Gendreau 1996).

China's treatment of Vietnam in the disputes also has echoes of imperial times. While hailing its own restraint, China reserves the right to intervene to protect its sacred territory. Certainly nonintervention is one of the defining features of the Westphalian system of equal sovereign states. "Nonintervention" was also prominent in the hierarchical Chinese world order. In both cases, intervention is occasionally necessary not just to guard the geographical borders but to uphold China's cultural boundaries and identity. In Imperial China, it was the civilization-state that decided where the inside/outside borders lay, and when intervention was necessary and proper. The punitive expedition to Vietnam in 179 BC mentioned above has important parallels with the Chinese invasion of Vietnam in 1979. In both cases China felt that Vietnam was becoming a disrespectful regional hegemon, and used the same family-based discipline to correct this challenge, with the same mixed results.

While China was engaged in a bitter border war with Vietnam in the late 1970s, it was also involved in a vociferous discursive battle over the Spratlys and the Paracels. The Chinese Ministry of Foreign Affairs' report "China's Indisputable Sovereignty over the Xisha and Nansha Islands" was published in response to the Vietnamese Foreign Ministry's White Book "Viet Nam's Sovereignty over the Hoang Sa and Truong Sa Archipelagos" (Chinese Ministry of Foreign Affairs 1980, 15). The Chinese report states:

> The Vietnamese authorities cherish regional hegemonic and expansionist designs. While stepping up aggression and expansion in Indochina and Southeast Asia, they illegally occupied some islands of China's Nansha island group in 1975. . . . (15)

Thus it was within China's remit "to stop Vietnam's expansionist atrocity and even to punish it severely" (in Austin 1998, 82).

Likewise, the PRC's insistence on solving the disputes through bilateral negotiations with each country, rather than through multilateral regimes, parallels the civilization-state's tributary system. When the tributary system worked, it was to mutual benefit; when it did not work, the Chinese used their own practice of divide and rule, "using the barbarians to fight the barbarians." This helps explain China's insistence on bilateral relations for solving the South China Sea disputes, and underlines how such resolution is the "Oriental way."

It is noteworthy that China and Taiwan present a united front in demanding full sovereignty along the "historic claim line" that hugs the borders of the littoral states. This is one of the few issues where Taipei and Beijing cooperate on the international stage. As Chen's article, which compares the two policies, concludes, "One thing we are sure of is that the two sides should work together to cope with challenges from the littoral states of the South China Sea" (Chen Hurng-yu 1993, 53; Lee Lai To 1999; Austin 1998).

This Oriental way, promoted by the Chinese civilization-state, can also help us rethink the subjectivity of security in terms of shared sovereignty. A map of the South China Sea claims clearly shows how borders overlap. As we have seen, from a horizontal point of view, this is problematic. Valencia argues that the best possible solution is to use the Law of the Sea to set up a "shared regional commons" that would be governed by a regional multilateral resource authority. In this proposal, the disputants disregard sovereignty claims, and reorganize the region into a new patchwork of a series of twelve joint development companies, based on areas of overlapping claims (Valencia 1995, 64; Valencia et al. 1999, 199–223). As we saw above, costs and benefits would be shared equally among members of each company. Here, Valencia is loosening his definition of the concept of sovereignty; in a later work, he prevaricates: "Although *operational* sovereignty would be curtailed, *formal* sovereignty would be unaffected. The *formal* sovereignty issue would have to be decided by future generations" (Valencia et al. 1999, 215). Thus, via the horizontal maps, sovereignty soon springs back to its formal definition. Valencia tries to solve this problem with the multiple ownership of the joint development companies (see Map 3)—which seem to be working according to the same logic as multiple sovereignty in Laos and the Liu Qiu—but he is unable to justify these joint development companies in terms of standard sovereignty arguments.

Hence the vertical maps of the civilization-state that allow for such multiple sovereignty are useful. Vertical maps can make sense of the contradictions in Deng Xiaoping's statement about the disputes. Rather than "indisputable sovereignty" and "shelving sovereignty issues" being incommensurable opposites (Ji Guoxing 1998, 101), these statements accord well with the civilization-state's tributary relationships. But what Beijing means by "joint development," with itself in control after all parties recognize Chinese sovereignty, might not be as threatening as it sounds. Some Chinese scholars feel that China should make foreign firms engaged in oil prospecting in the Spratly Islands under Vietnamese contracts admit that the islands are Chinese territory; if these firms are willing to recognize Chinese sovereignty over the islands, Beijing can allow them to continue prospecting. Pan Shiying gives the example of how the American oil prospecting company, Crestone Energy Corporation, switched from a Vietnamese to a Chinese contract in 1992 (Pan Shiying 1996, 1–8). Others suggest that once the contracts signed with Vietnam expire, new contracts can be signed with Beijing (Chen Hurng-yu 1993, 48).

The control, then, could be simply an acknowledgment of China's centrality to the region—a payment of symbolic tribute to China. As most historians state, the tributary relations benefited the Chinese culturally but the tribute states economically (Mancall 1984; Cumings 1999, 169). These are not equal relationships, for the other states would have to recognize their "inferiority and loyalty" to the Chinese civilization-state (Smith 1998, 62).[14] Moreover, the series of joint development companies—each of which would include China—certainly sounds reminiscent of the tributary system's administered economy of feudal overlordship (Mancall 1984, 40–64). Still, the South China Sea claims could be sorted out to mutual benefit, according to the idealized view of the civilization-state. The "shared regional commons" that Valencia suggests, or the "pooling sovereignty" of the Indonesian Workshops (South China Sea Informal Working Group 2001), could actually work out better using the civilization-state's aesthetic practice of multiple sovereignty, rather than by using international law's un-ironic abstractions of absolute sovereignty.

CONCLUSION

This chapter has shown how Greater China can work in quite different ways in the South China Sea. While many discussions of Greater China highlight the economic culture of diasporic Chinese, here we have seen how imperial notions of ironic space are employed by a civilization-state. The South China Sea disputes served as an example to explore the empirical and conceptual issues raised by the interrelationship of the historical trajectories of conquest and conversion. In the first section, the mainstream analyses based on military and diplomatic performances were considered. Rather than being a threat to regional security and international norms, I concluded, the PRC's performance in the South China Sea has actually been a case study in the creation and defense of state security.

While most critical reconsiderations of security conclude by questioning the subject of security, I have in the second section moved from the South China Sea disputes as an empirical problem (of how to fairly divide up the goods) to a conceptual problem of how to write the subject of security and sovereignty in different ways. Certainly, many take for granted that "conversion" involves the PRC slowly adapting to the discourse of mainstream international relations, but in the second section I explored another kind of conversion. Traditional Chinese cartography and imperial Chinese ritual were recovered to see how their ironic space allowed for shared sovereignty in the civilization-state. Hence, I argued that the conflict is not so much between the navies of Vietnam, the Philippines, and China as between premodern and modern concepts of space, sovereignty, and power. This is not to argue that the Chinese claims are weaker than those of the Philippines or Vietnam; the same arguments could be made to question Vietnamese claims, for example. Rather, by deconstructing the main debates that are employed by strategic studies and diplomacy, I have been able to examine how culture works in East Asian power relations. Although China pursues a policy of anti-imperialism, it still looks to its own empire to recover vocabulary and concepts for international politics.

Undoubtedly, there has been a shift from a premodern to a modern style of border measurement and mapping in East Asia. But since most analysis of the South China Sea disputes takes the modern modes of nation-state sovereignty and security for granted, I excavated the civilization-state of Greater China as an alternative mode of power and authority. An appeal to the historical trajectory of conversion is more than just residue from Imperial China that will wither away with modernization. Although the Chinese military certainly does make aggressive statements from time to time, Cumings reminds us that "[Chinese] heritage also teaches them the ultimate weakness of a power that only expresses itself militarily" (Cumings 1999, 168). Indeed, some Chinese elites are exploring traditional modes of conflict resolution that rely on multiple sovereignty and ironic space. Using irony in world politics is, of course, a risky venture. Irony works for those who appreciate the multiplicity of the system; to others, such multiplicity is a contradiction that is coded as a "problem" that has to be resolved (e.g., Ch'en Ta-tuan 1968, 159, 162; Sakai 1968, 114). But the benefits of ironic practice are also manifest: such a cosmopolitan approach is certainly more flexible and pragmatic (see Waldron 1990, 180–81). As a working version of a non-Enlightenment system, the civilization-state constitutes one of the few challenges to "globalization" and American hegemony; the nativists in China certainly see themselves in this light. Thus a resistance to the global system comes not just from the margins, as is commonly argued (Shapiro and Alker 1996; Hardt and Negri 2000). As chapter 2 demonstrated, resistance can also come from alternative systems that occupy the center of a different space, a parallel modernity in the present. In switching from geography to cosmography, we can see how sovereignty becomes multiple, and shared around intersecting peripheries such as the South China Sea. Such a vertical imagining of communities effaces the boundaries between domestic and international relations, and thus alters political subjectivity and space as well.

Since this chapter has dealt with an idealized notion of the civilization-state, it is necessary for the following chapters to take a more critical stance. The empirical and conceptual challenges that South Korea, Hong Kong, and Taiwan pose to Greater China will be examined to see how the practices of the civilization-state continue to frame contemporary politics in East Asia. The current chapter has examined Chinese identity as it is constructed in an empty space—where no one can talk back—but chapter 4 will examine the influence of the transnational discourse of Confucianism on identity production in South Korea, where people are very vocal. South Korea is not a unique case; the arguments apply for other East and Southeast Asian societies employing Confucian rhetoric (see Elman et al. 2002).

4

Modernizing Confucianism: Trans/national Identity in Korea

Mainstream studies of Sino-Korean relations neatly fall into two categories. One is organized around geopolitical security, and looks to the Korean War to figure the continuing struggle on the Peninsula as the last outpost of the Cold War. The other is inspired by political economy, and looks to the burgeoning trade and investment ties between South Korea and the People's Republic of China (PRC) (Lee Chae-Jin 1996; Liu Jinzhi et al. 1998). Indeed, the main stories in Korean newspapers about the reversion of Hong Kong in 1997 concerned not human rights or democracy but the transfer of defectors from North Korea[1] and the future of economic ties.

Studies of Korean national identity have also followed the well-worn paths of Cold War security and development studies. The narratives of nationhood on the Korean Peninsula are intensely political acts. Both the Democratic People's Republic of Korea (DPRK, or North Korea) and the Republic of Korea (ROK, or South Korea) invest scarce resources in the symbolic construction of cultural identity and political legitimacy. The South built its official identity against the alterity of Soviet social imperialism, the North against the Other of American/Japanese neocolonialism. In South Korea, the United States has had a hegemonic influence on the academic discourse. As Robinson explains:

> U.S. security interests and military preoccupation in the Korean War
> spawned an enormous literature on the conduct of the Korean War,

general security problems and North-East Asian regional politics. The dramatic economic growth since the 1960s gave birth to a similarly large development literature. However, the hundreds of books on these topics tell us very little about the Korean people, their culture, ideas and historical memory. (Robinson 1996, 33; Cumings 1999, 173–204)

Robinson suggests that we resist the master narrative of Korean nationality through excavating the silences it has produced in social movements of folk culture, farmers, women, and so on (Robinson 1996, 33–35; Bhabha 1990, 3; Callahan 2002a).

But such counterhegemonies of resistance focus too tightly on the neocolonialism from the "West" of the United States and Japan (Robinson 1996, 34; Paik Nak-chung 1996; Cumings 1999). They ignore the important role that China has had in the definition of Korea, and how arguments that look to "difference" are deployed in South Korea not just by marginalized subalterns, but by counter-elites. In this chapter, I take a different approach to politics on the Peninsula, framing my analysis in terms of the complex intercultural relations of Confucianism in China and Korea. To gain critical distance from Confucianism, most texts compare it with liberal democracy, but this chapter goes to South Korea to gain critical purchase on Confucianism and East Asian economic culture in an argument that also applies for analogous sites such as Japan and Vietnam. Sino-Korean intercultural relations highlight two important issues in political theory and international relations: the transnational nature of world politics, and the limits of framing analysis in terms of East-West and tradition-modernity distinctions. Once again, "The primary issue is not politics and diplomacy; it is the cultural epistemology that informs certain forms of interaction" (Howland 1996, 2).

This chapter examines how Confucianism acts as a transnational discourse in the construction of identity in Korea. Confucianism in Korea problematizes the standard notions of Greater China, which, as we saw in chapter 1, are based on shared Chinese ethnicity. Korea fits into Greater China on the basis, rather, of shared culture. Here we examine how South Koreans use Confucian discourse in their own narratives of nativism, conquest, conversion and diaspora; this complicates discursive power relations, for Koreans can use Confucianism to form a "Greater Korea" which uses the same logic as Greater China even as it contests it. As we shall see, this is a very messy business that stretches the existing vocabulary of tradition and modernity, while creating a new vocabulary of heterotopic phrases in both Korean and English: "the Confucianization of Korea," "the Koreanization of Confucianism," "modernizing Confucianism," and "Confucianizing modernization."

The Kyongbok Palace at the center of Seoul provides a helpful metaphor to guide our attention away from the clear Cold War divisions to grasp the ironies and ambiguities of politics and civilization in Korea. The palace and its surrounding city plan are an integral part of the narrative of Korean national liberation, as well as of the cosmological narrative of Confucian civilization (Bhabha 1990; Meyer 1991). In the twentieth century, the Kyongbok Palace in Seoul has been a guiding symbol of Korean independence and identity—the National Museum has been housed on palace grounds since 1908. But like most national identities, Korean identity is a construction—and not a stable construction, either. The palace itself has not been constant but has been constructed, deconstructed, and reconstructed again and again over the past six hundred years. Thus one could argue that the palace's history is indicative of the history of Korean nationalism, along the lines of the dynamic historiography of Sin Ch'ae-ho, a nationalist historian of the early twentieth century: "Those who do not know how to build do not know how to destroy, and those who do not know how to destroy do not know how to build. Construction and destruction are different only in appearance. In the mind, destruction is immediately construction" (in Em, Henry 1999, 361).

Kyongbok Palace was first constructed in the fourteenth century as the seat of the newly established Choson dynasty. It was destroyed by the Japanese invasion of Korea in 1592–98. The palace was then reconstructed by an unpopular regent in the 1880s as part of a reassertion of Korean orthodoxy against both foreign threats and internal dissent. It was destroyed a second time by the Japanese during their colonial rule of Korea from 1910 to 1945. This time, the Japanese did not just destroy the palace; they displaced it by building their colonial headquarters on the palace grounds, turning it from a royal city into an imperial node. In *Architecture and Authority in Japan,* Coaldrake argues convincingly of the link between public buildings and power in Japan; and architecture certainly was part of the colonial regime in Korea (Coaldrake 1996, 1–15). The destruction of the palace and construction of colonial headquarters was generally seen, by both the Japanese and the Koreans, as an effort to spiritually and symbolically colonize the Korean people.

The palace started to be rebuilt in the 1960s by the Park Chung-hee regime as part of its authoritarian-bureaucratic capitalism. The reconstruction proceeded in earnest, as a cultural measure of South Korea's economic success, up through the 1997 financial crisis. In the mid-1990s, the Koreans reconstructed their national identity through a deconstruction of their colonial relationship with Japan: in 1996 the Japanese colonial headquarters was pulled down with great fanfare. This very public act was applauded by many newspapers and scholars (although not by all) as a reassertion of Korean symbolic sovereignty. An editorial in South Korean's leading newspaper wrote: "Given that the Japanese intended to obliterate Korean aspirations for independence by destroying the royal palace and the Seoul fortress, it was only natural to demolish the former colonial headquarters as a symbolic gesture of closing a painful chapter of Korea's history" ("Demolition of Old Colonial Headquarters" [editorial] 1996).[2]

The Kyongbok Palace therefore is an important part of the narrative of Korean national identity. The Other is clearly Japanese imperialism (throughout history), and the Koreans have constructed a national self by transforming royal symbols into national symbols (see Anderson 1991; Thongchai 1994). Indeed, there are powerful arguments that state that contemporary forms of Korean national discourse are in large part products of the Japanese colonial project (see Em, Henry 1999, 353–54; Tanaka 1993, 82–85, 247–50).

But both the style of the palace, and its placement in the royal city of Seoul, raise a different set of questions of Otherness and identity, questions that focus on China rather than Japan. Rather than being national, the implied narrative is cosmological. As we saw in chapter 3, the capital is not the political center of the nation so much as the palace is the cosmic center, a nodal point between the terrestrial and the celestial. Thus, politics follows cosmography; the fate of the kingdom is wrapped up in the royal city centered on the palace (Meyer 1991, 8). The *Rites of Zhou* is not limited to inspiring Chinese capitals, but shaped capital cities and palaces in Korea; in particular, the Kyongbok Royal Palace follows this cosmic geography. Confucianism is tied up even more intimately with the palace. The *Rites of Zhou* was praised by Confucius and, as we shall see, the Choson dynasty that built the palace is known in Korea as the quintessential Confucian dynasty. When the regent reconstructed the palace in the 1880s, he was also reasserting Confucian ortho-doxy against enemies both foreign and domestic.

The most recent reconstructions of Kyongbuk Palace likewise have accompanied a renewed interest in Confucianism in Korea. For example, the inaugural editorial of the Korean intellectual journal *Tradition and Modernity* directly links the demolition of the Japanese headquarters with the reassertion of Confucian values. The editors use the palace to represent Korean Confucian culture, and argue that it must be reconstructed, just as Confucian tradition needs to be reconstructed in Korea ("To Put Rightly What This Era Requires" 1997, 13–23). Indeed, the end of the military period of South Korean politics in 1987/1992 presented two options; the opposite of military dictatorship is not only liberal democracy but also elite Confucianism. Although the 1990s was characterized by President Kim Young-sam's push for globalization in Korea (Kim, Samuel 2000a; Kim Young Sam [n.d.]), Kim Young-sam, President Kim Dae-jung, and editorial writers increasingly used a Confucian vocabulary in discussing political problems and solutions.[3] The financial crisis of 1997 quickly became an identity crisis about how to deal with capitalist modernity in a proper Confucian style (Higgott 2000; Kim Young Hie 1998; Junn Sung-chull 1998). This renewed interest in Confucianism, in-dicative of the tensions between tradition and modernity, has not just come out in new journals with names like *Tradition and Modernity*; it was also wonderfully reproduced on the (re-)construction site at the Kyongbok Palace, where the ancient buildings were framed by cranes of the capitalist conglomerate Hyundai, which were labeled "HYUNDAI," which means "modern."

Therefore, though Japan is the most obvious focus of Othering in the discourse of Korean identity, this assertion is largely limited to the twentieth century. Discussions of Korean national identity that look to both the past and the future address the curiously complex relationship Korea has had with China not only politically but cul-turally (see Kim Key-Hiuk 1980). Indeed, though the United States is the most obvious target for charges of cultural imperialism, the Chinese empire was, as I argued in chapters 2 and 3, organized around cultural imperialism, and traces persist not merely as residue from the past but as clues to the future.

There are, of course, many facets to the Korean-Chinese interaction. I focus on the place of Confucianism in Korean identity because, on the one hand, it is "obvious" to Koreans that theirs is the most Confucian country in the world, and, on the other, because Confucianism presents the most problems for national identity construction. Although much work has been done to naturalize a unique identity in Korea, the anxieties about Chinese influence are manifest. At various times, Korean intellectuals have referred to their country as Little China, the eldest younger brother and first tributary in the Chinese empire:

> The Korean elite in particular would have found the idea of nationalism not only strange but also uncivilized. Since at least the seventh century the ruling classes in Korea had thought of themselves in cultural terms less as Koreans than as members of a larger cosmopolitan civilization centered on China. . . . To live outside the realm of Chinese culture was, for the Korean elite, to live as a barbarian. (Eckert 1991, 226–27)

This anxiety is not unidirectional, and can help us understand the practices of identity formation in China, as well. Chinese intellectuals assume that Confucianism is an integral part of Chinese civilization that Others (e.g., Koreans) can only (imperfectly) copy. Intellectuals in the PRC see Korean Confucianism as, like overseas Chinese cultural activities, derivative (Qi Mei 1998). Thus, Chinese elites are concerned when other Asian countries try to assume the mantle of Asian or Confucian civilization (Kim Hong-kyung 1997, Interview; Kwon Tai-Joon 1997, Interview; Howland 1996).

The introduction to a recent Chinese novel, *Confucius*, by Yang Shu'an gives some sense of this anxiety of loss and recovery. In a discussion of a contemporary Japanese novel, also named *Confucius*, the Chinese editor writes:

> Inoue Jiyoshi's novel *[Confucius]* is a masterful work, filled with deep philosophical truths expressed with skill and grace. After I read this work, I felt my soul had been deeply touched. But upon further reflection, I immediately realized that this was still a book written by a foreigner. Confucius came out of China, so why hadn't a Chinese writer sought to depict this Chinese philosopher? Just at this time, I received a manuscript of Yang Shu'an's novel *Confucius*. (Miao Junjie 1993, 5)

Rather than seeking to find and define what Confucianism *really* means in contemporary Korea, Japan, Vietnam, or China (Elman et al. 2002), this chapter traces the discursive economies of Confucianism's use by various groups. This analysis is divided into three parts that address the function of Confucianism in three overlapping social spaces. In each section I address questions of difference and Other, authenticity and history. The first section examines the official discourse of Confucianism through government publications; I show how official discourse utilizes a curiously hybrid historiography to take Confucianism from China and turn it into the basis of a unique Korean national identity. The second examines Confucianism in mass culture to see how the media and the chaebol-conglomerates present and represent Confucianism, and argues that these entities use the logic of national discourse to construct an East Asian regional identity, then commodify Confucianism through Confucian capitalism. The third section looks at how scholars write about Confucianism and relate it to Korean national identity; some are trying to recapture the past to decolonize Korea from the influence of "Americanization," and others are more self-consciously utilizing critical discourse to gain a posttraditional sense of Confucianism.

The chapter concludes that, though it is common to read articles that propose Confucianism as an "alternative" to the ideologies of liberal democracy or communism, Confucianism makes the most sense when we cease looking at it as if it were a metanarrative that could meet all ideological needs. Rather than trying to understand "Confucianism in Korea" as a whole, or to define something grand like "Korean Confucianism," we can use Confucianism as an analytical tool to understand something else: to use Confucianism to work self-consciously for the specific project of building democracy in Korea, and to examine the slippery relation among culture, ethnicity, and nationalism in the following chapters.

FROM THE CONFUCIANIZATION OF KOREA TO THE KOREANIZATION OF CONFUCIANISM

Confucianism, as we have seen, is part of a cosmology that places China at the center of the universe not as a nation-state in geopolitics, but as a "civilization-state" in geomoral politics (Tu Weiming 1994a; Howland 1996, 11). Imperial China's relations with its neighbors were characterized by hierarchy and unification, rather than by the

Westphalian model of equality and differentiation. Diplomacy was ordered along a conversion narrative where world affairs proceeded through bilateral relations between the center of civilization in Beijing and the tributes/barbarians at the periphery. In this conversion narrative, the classical Chinese notion of power was intensely discursive— *wen* means both civilization and writing—and struggles over culture and ideology have characterized Chinese politics in the twentieth century as well.

Korea was a willing tribute, seen as the eldest younger brother in the imperial family. This perspective started to break down at the end of the nineteenth century as Euro-American and Japanese imperialism challenged the East Asian world order (Kim Key-Hiuk 1980). Many vassal states used the Western concepts of international law to reorganize their relations with the Qing Empire in Beijing. But, as the Japanese example shows, there was not a simple process of Westernization. Confucianism itself was revalued as part of the disintegration of the Chinese empire. Nationalist scholars and government officials in Meiji Japan labored to reframe Confucianism. From a universal doctrine that placed China at the center of the cosmos, Confucianism was refigured into an ideology that was the product of a series of historical events. Confucianism was thus separated from essential Chinese identity through historicization; this particular history was a narrative of China's decline and Japan's rise. The history served to preserve certain aspects of Confucianism in Japan, while separating Japan from China. In other words, these Japanese scholars used nativistic strategies to figure Japan as both "modern" and "Confucian" in order to resist the power of both Chinese and Western imperialism (Tanaka 1993, 115–52).

Confucianism in Korea has also deployed itself consistently as a historical narrative to move from conversion in Chinese civilization to Korean nativism. While Chinese texts use "history" to consolidate territory—the South China Sea claims, for example— "history" is used in official Korean texts to differentiate territorial cultures. Much as in Japan, such narratives are nativistic inasmuch as they function to locate Korean Confucianism as an independently evolving phenomenon rather than a derivative of universal (Chinese) civilization. Confucian narratives in Korea can be seen as "events" in that they have been provoked by particular struggles: for example, the desire of the Koreans to credit themselves with maintaining Confucianism against the barbarian Manchurians of the Qing dynasty, as well as with preserving Confucianism during the Communist regime in China, especially during the Cultural Revolution ("Preface" 1996, 3–4). Indeed, official ROK Cold War discourse used slogans that reversed the civilization/barbarian, center/periphery metaphors of Imperial China: "Smash the Chinese barbarians" (in Cha, Victor 1997, 2). Since Confucian rites are "no longer performed in China where they originated" (Art Space 1996, 150), Koreans see themselves as "inheritors of the Confucian heritage" (Deuchler 1992, 24; Nah Seoung 1996, 59). Rather than being absorbed by Confucianism—as the standard conversion narrative of Imperial China states—Koreans nativists have, as they thus argue, absorbed Confucianism into their national identity—albeit through a curious historical process.

Reading the Official Texts

To examine the interplay between Confucianism and Korean identity, it is useful to conduct a textual analysis of two books published in 1996 by South Korean government organizations and one published by a national/transnational organization: (1) *Religious Culture in Korea,* produced by the Ministry of Culture and Sports; (2) *Thought and Religion,* the second volume of the Korea Foundation's encyclopedic *Korean Cultural Heritage*; and (3) the Korean National Commission for UNESCO's 1983 publication, *Main Currents of Korean Thought.*[4] These texts are interesting because they hover between the lines of government propaganda (Korean Overseas Information Service 1997), and critical scholarly study (de Bary and Haboush 1985; Choung and Han 1996).

At first glance, the two official texts appear to use quantitative analysis and comparative methods to understand Korean religions. The opening chapter, "Outline of Religious Culture," of the South Korean Ministry of Culture's book quickly moves from the natural science of a satellite photograph of Korea (the first image in the book) to social science. The "objectivity" of the photograph[5] leads smoothly into an analysis that appeals to statistical methods and categories to measure religious belief in terms of statistics taken from surveys and censuses, complete with tables that list "The Present Status of Religious Orders and Organizations," "Number of Believers of Each

Religion," and "Present Status of the Korean Religions per Year" (Yun Seoung-yong 1996, 8, 9, 10).

Then, after a general introduction, the chapters in both official books are organized topically (in the comparative style of Religious Studies texts) according to religion. The tables of contents list chapters on specific religions: Buddhism, Confucianism, Catholicism, Protestantism, Shamanism, and so on. This is not an obvious ordering; it demonstrates that discussions of religion already involve discussions of history. Even though each of these religions has adherents today, the narrative of Buddhism refers not just to spiritual ideas and practices across time but to the United Silla dynasty (668–935 AD). Likewise, when authors write about Confucianism they already are discussing the Choson dynasty (1392–1910 AD); when they write about Catholicism and Protestantism they already are discussing the coming of the West in the nineteenth century.

Confucianism involves certain forms of temporality, reflected in the organization of these official texts. Alterity is expressed not just in terms of geographic space, but of time as well: Koreans replaced the Chinese dynastic calendar with a Korean national calendar as part of separation from the empire (Kim Key-Hiuk 1980). Rather than use the homogeneous empty time characteristic of modernity, the narrative of the Confucianization of Korea involves sacred time "in which cosmology and history were indistinguishable" (Anderson 1991, 36). East Asian forms of dynastic historiography relied on cyclical notions of time; dating was internal and self-referential, according to the reigns of Chinese emperors and Korean kings. The Chinese word for time (shi) also means "season" and "era." The fourteenth-century Chinese novel Romance of the Three Kingdoms begins with a cyclical concept of history: "In general, the world must unite when it has long been divided and it must be divided when it has long been united."

Dynastic historiography, then, involves a cyclical narrative where the new dynasty is formed out of the ashes of an exhausted, corrupt regime. Dynasties start out strong because they have had to forcibly unite the empire, but after enjoying the fruits of state power they become soft and weak and eventually are overthrown by a new vibrant power, which will, in turn, establish the next dynasty. The narrative of the official dynastic history is characteristically compiled/written by the victors, the new dynasty, to assess the faults of the previous regime and justify its overthrow (Twitchett 1992; Beck 1986). Thus

Confucian patterns of historical scholarship were engaged in the task of "identifying the legitimate dynasty . . . then recounting how the rulers attained, maintained, and lost the Mandate of Heaven through a moral appraisal of their actions" (Schmid 1997, 29).

In these official Korean texts, the historical narrative deviates from the Chinese norm. It is not just the kings who are strong or weak, but their philosophical-ideological systems that are virtuous or corrupt: the official narrative tells us that both Buddhism and Confucianism started out vibrant and strong in their respective reigns as state religion, at the beginning of their dynasty; they were a means for uniting the Silla kingdom (for Buddhism) and the Choson kingdom (for Confucianism). But in the course of hundreds of years in power, both became corrupt, factionalized, empty, and weak, leading to disunity. Just like the dynasty itself, a dynasty's thought system needed to be replaced (Park Sun-yong 1996, 138; Yun Sa-soon 1996, 113). In China, while dynasties came and went, imperial Confucianism lived on (we are told) as a guiding theme in "5,000 years of Chinese civilization," waxing and waning but never disappearing. However in Korea, Confucianism is tied to one dynasty, the Choson dynasty. The founding of the Choson dynasty (1392–1910) is figured as a Confucian event, the Confucianization of Korea (Deuchler 1992, 27). When the Choson dynasty fell in 1910, so did Confucianism.

Religion in Korea, then, is intimately tied to political power. Religion is not pure or otherworldly, according to the official narratives, but part of historical struggles for political supremacy: "Korea was transformed into a Confucian country for political and social reasons" (Hwang Sun-myung 1996, 24). This is because both Buddhism and Confucianism have at various times in Korean history been official state religions. Even the introduction and success of Christianity in the nineteenth century is tied to changes in the relationship between state power and religious belief: the books tell us that it was the French imposition of "freedom of religion" in 1884—meaning the absence of a state religion—that led to the rise of Christianity in Korea (Yun Seoung-yong 1996, 18–19). This is not simply an argument against "cultural imperialism" characteristic of postcolonial criticism (Tomlinson 1991). Rather it is about domination in more direct form: "Christianity served as an avenue of economic and political imperialism" (Park Sung-bong 1996, 18).

As it approaches the twentieth century, the dynastic historiography of orthodoxy begins to break down in the official texts. It is no longer cyclical, for a new orthodoxy is not put into place with the new regime of "freedom of religion." On closer examination, the historical narrative written in these two texts is not an East Asian–style dynastic history so much as a nineteenth-century style European progressive national/universal history (see Duara 1995, 17–50). In this respect, it signifies a shift from an imperial (Chinese) concept of space and time to a national (Korean) concept of space and time. In other words, the historical narrative uses time to establish place—the modern Korean nation (Schmid 2002; Em, Henry 1999; Lee, Peter H. 1996, 386–400).

Rather than being a cyclical historiography, the narrative is teleological in a nativist way: always pointing to the uniqueness of Korea. This discourse of national essence comes out well in the volume compiled by the Korean National Commission of UNESCO in 1983—the time when UNESCO's campaign against cultural imperialism was at its high point. The secretary-general's foreword tells us that the volume is "dedicated to seeking the real character of Korean culture . . . baring the roots of Korean tradition . . . to reveal the framework of traditional thought which is fundamental to any understanding of Korea's past and present" (Bong Shik Park 1983, v).

What makes these official texts interesting is that such an authentic national mind, essence, or history is not at all obvious in Korea. Nearly all the authentic national materials have been imported. They were not imported from some distant "abroad" (like Euro-America) that would make it easier for Korean elites to pick and choose according to the explanations of "selective cultural assimilation" popular for explaining the economic success of Japan and Korea (see Kim Kyong-Dong 1994). While Euro-American civilization can be "deterritorialized" because it traces its origins to fallen empires—Greece, Rome, and Christendom—Confucianism cannot, since China is still a political, economic, and cultural power in East Asia. The relation between Chinese civilization and an East Asian civilization is uneasy (see Yamazaki 1996). The genealogy of Korean authenticity is always tied to power, and more specifically to Chinese power; Buddhism, Daoism, Confucianism, and even Catholicism came to Korea through Chinese mediation. Indeed, the first third of the Ministry of Culture book's article on "Confucianism" is about China (Nah Seoung 1996, 57–60).

Thus the anxiety of influence: what do you do when your unique national materials are so obviously foreign? One strategy that the texts use is to celebrate the diversity of Korean spiritual life, and the remarkable tolerance that it entails. The Ministry of Culture's book proudly states that "Korean religion is a kind of reservoir of classical religions" from both East and West (Yun Seoung-yong 1996, 12), and the Korea Foundation's book notes that "Few countries can boast as rich a religious spectrum as modern Korea" (Chung Chin-hong 1996, 221). And indeed, the multicultural, pluralistic environment in South Korea where no one religion dominates is quite a fascinating accomplishment, worthy of praise and study.

But as the page numbers from the quotes above attest, this strategy of celebrating diversity largely comes in the introductions and conclusions of the texts. The main argument is quite different, and much more exclusive, pointing to the homogeneity of the Korean culture and "race" (see Grinker 2000). This argument is part of the state's management of the Korean knowledge project that labors to define singular "correct" views of Korean national history, culture, identity. The underlying historical narrative of such texts uses *time* to historicize Confucianism and thus separate it from China. This narrative tells us that even though Confucianism started out in China, Koreans have taken the philosophy to its most highly developed state:

> Though the concepts themselves were not original, [Korean philosopher T'oegye] developed and consummated them, picking up and making up for the philosophical issues Chinese Confucians left behind. . . . It can be said that the debate itself raised the level of the study of Confucianism in general and, in a sense, symbolized the Koreanization of Confucianism. (Nah Seoung 1996, 64)

Other stories rewrite the genealogy of Confucianism, changing Chinese origins to Korean ones to insist that Korean Confucianism predated Confucius, making Korean Confucianism "more advanced" than Chinese Confucianism (Yun Sa-soon 1996, 113). In this way, Confucianism tends to fade into the background, while history itself becomes the subject, nationalism becomes the religion, and sovereignty becomes the objective.

In such official "religion and thought" texts, Buddhism, Confucianism, and Christianity are useful and interesting only in so far as they are patriotic and thus fit into the master narrative of Korean nationalism. The Confucian virtues of loyalty and filial piety are reframed from pillars of civilization and family life into pillars of national sovereignty: "they help us recognize our home and nation, repel invasion, resist oppression by outsiders, and guard our national sovereignty" (Suh Kyoung-yo 1996, 33; Yun Sa-soon 1996, 108–9). Such an incongruous use of international relations vocabulary—sovereignty, foreign invasion, etc.—in a religious-studies context characterizes the discourse. "Confucian Thought and Korean Culture" appeals to the language of nationalism and sovereignty in an effort to shift from the Confucianization of Korea to the Koreanization of Confucianism:

> Confucianism served as a national belief system and can therefore be seen as a body of *Korean* thought. Korean Confucianism is closely related to the formation of a sense of national selfhood and to the establishment of a sense of sovereignty. In other words, although Confucianism was originally an imported thought system, it has become a Korean body of thought inasmuch as it has had a strong impact on Koreans' view of their national livelihood and their historical view of themselves as a people. (Yun Sa-soon 1996, 112, emphasis in original)

The Confucian narrative ends with another national event, the Japanese colonization of Korea in 1910. The common reason cited for the disenchantment with Confucianism is that it could not resist Japanese aggression: "Needless to say, the loss of national sovereignty was far graver than the collapse of the Five Moral Disciplines [of Confucianism]" (Yun Sa-soon 1996, 112). Once the five-century-old Choson dynasty was extinguished by the Japanese empire in 1910, the narrative tells us, Confucianism waned as well. According to the Overseas Information Service's *A Handbook of Korea*, Confucianism disappeared completely there in 1910 (in Robinson 1991, 210). The connection between these two events is clearly drawn by Yun Sa-soon: since "Neo-Confucianism was the governing principle of the Choson dynasty . . . [it] must be responsible for this historical fact" (Yun Sa-soon 1996, 112).

But to paraphrase Mark Twain, reports of the death of Confucianism were a bit premature. Confucianism would rise again as a central theme in various narratives of identity in Korea. Confucianism thus has been transformed, through a peculiar historical reading, from Chinese civilization into Korean tradition and thus a primary source of Korean national identity. The narrative in this way shifts from conversion to nativism. Other Korean discourses move from nativism to conversion, but with a twist; here conversion is not to Chinese civilization, but to Korean-style Confucian capitalism.

TRANSNATIONAL CONFUCIAN CAPITALISM: FROM GREATER CHINA TO GREATER KOREA

Philosophers characteristically point to the sixteenth century as the high point of Korean Confucianism (de Bary and Haboush 1985; Choung and Han 1996; Choi Kun Duk 1998). They recall how T'oegye expanded the notion of Confucianism far beyond his Chinese precursors in Song Neo-Confucianism (Kalton 1994; Nah Seoung 1996, 64). But the official texts dwell on the ideological aspects of Confucianism: *ch'ung hyo* (Chinese: *zhong xiao*), loyalty to the state, and filial piety. Even though loyalty and filial piety are very clearly orthodox Confucian virtues, the Korea Foundation volume places "Loyalty and Filial Piety and the Sonbi Spirit" not in the section on "Confucianism" but in the first section on "Fundamental Principles" (Suh Kyoung-yo 1996, 30–35). In the same spirit, the semiofficial Academy of Korean Studies (AKS) elevated filial piety to new heights with its international conference on Filial Piety and Future Society (1995), cosponsored by the Korean Broadcasting System (KBS) and the Samsung Welfare Foundation (SWF).

Therefore, filial piety is not just a preoccupation of the official government publications; it forms an important theme of those modernizers of Confucianism who talk about Confucian capitalism and Confucian democracy. Here, rather than referring to informal overseas Chinese networks (such as we saw in chapter 2 of this book), Confucian capitalism describes the Korean-style developmental state model (see Kim, Samuel 2000a; Kim Kyong-Dong 1994). Confucian capitalism, as a mode of governmentality, thus shows how the state, business, and media work together in the service of a particular cultural epistemology:

> KBS has set the expansion of filial piety as one of 10 planning themes for 1995, and has already broadcast several special programs on filial piety. SWF has also tried to plant filial piety into ordinary

life through instituting and implementing the Filial Piety Awards for the last two decades. And AKS, since its opening in 1978, has studied the essence of traditional culture such as filial piety, and the means for implementing it. (Yung Dug Hee 1995, iii; also see Hong Doo Pyo 1995, vii)

The Confucian narrative in the past decade has been characterized by a series of "events." In this section I analyze conferences organized by the *Dong-A Ilbo (East Asian Daily News)* (August 1996) and the Asan Foundation (July 1997), and relate them to broad political-economic trends in Northeast Asia. I consider these two conferences not just for their academic content, but as social events in mass culture since they were organized by nonacademic organizations in the mass media and business. Here, then, I am appealing to the Frankfurt School's notion of mass culture as an industry organized for the people, but not by or of the people. In that way it overlaps with the elitist aspects of Confucianism that aim to manage not just political economy but knowledge practices. This section concludes with a comparison of the Confucian capitalist ideals, on the one hand, and case studies of chaebol management style, on the other.

First, I must note that audience for these texts is different from that of the official texts: while the official books are directed abroad, primarily at Euro-America, the mass culture of these conferences is directed at Koreans and East Asians: the general public, in particular teachers. But these conferences look to the West, as well; the resources of the *Dong-A Ilbo* and the Asan Foundation allowed them to invite scholars from abroad, to translate and distribute the texts as well as to provide simultaneous interpretations of the conference activities. More important, the discursive organization of the papers was characteristically fixated on the West, in the language of the Pacific Century discourse that appeals to tropes of "response" and "challenge" (see Dirlik 1998a, 3–72). For example, the Asan Foundation's symposium was called "The Challenge of the Twenty-first Century, the Response of Eastern Ethics"; it is quite clear that the response is also to the Western challenge (Asan Foundation 1997a).

Although the papers in both conferences were diverse, as a discourse they are involved in two clear projects. The first involves switching from the nationalist discourse of the Koreanization of Confucianism to a regional discourse of East Asian World Order—

but this time under Korean rather than Chinese discursive control. The second involves engaging in the discourse of Confucian capitalism. Both these projects entail discursive moves from figuring transnational relations as "Greater China" to "Greater Korea."

The switch from a nationalist to a regional discourse can be seen most clearly by looking at the lists of scholars invited to the conferences. Both the *Dong-A Ilbo* and the Asan Foundation made sure to invite noted scholars from South Korea, China, and Japan. The contents of many of the papers also appeal to East Asian solidarity. This solidarity is possible, according to papers and interviews, because of the waning of Western ideological hegemony—in direct contrast to Fukuyama's "End of History" thesis. This solidarity takes particular forms, for the discourse appeals primarily to Confucianism. Although Daoism and Buddhism were included in both conferences, Lee Chong-Suk, the organizer of the *Dong-A Ilbo* event, made it clear that Confucianism was the focus since "Confucianism is the most practical and realistic" (Lee Chong-Suk 1997, Interview).

Indeed, the event itself and the choice of Confucianism were quite political. Lee Chong-Suk explained that the conference was the result of a joint project between the *Dong-A Ilbo* and the *People's Daily,* the flagship newspaper of the Chinese Communist Party, to try to deepen the relationship of the two countries after diplomatic ties were normalized in 1992. This "normalization" was also a mass cultural event; it was "couched in language celebrating the restoration of historical ties and common Confucian traditions, with only passing reference to an 'unnatural and abnormal' past" (Cha, Victor 1997, 7; PRC-ROK Joint Communique in BBC/SWB 25 August 1992, A2). In his speech announcing the event, the South Korean president stressed that "Korea and China have neighborly and friendly relations with deep ties as closest neighbors historically, geographically and culturally for thousands of years" (No Tae-u in BBC/SWB 25 August 1992, A2). Ties between the PRC and the ROK thus were established via the characteristic Renan-ian calculation of memory and forgetting: remembering a traditional "historical affinity" while actively forgetting the more recent struggle of the Korean War (Renan 1990, 11; Lee Chae-Jin 1996, 126).

This regional discourse, which uses the "historical, geographical and cultural affinity" between China and Korea as a means of overcoming the conflicts of twentieth-century European ideology (i.e., communist vs. capitalist) to "facilitate cooperation in the twenty-first century," continues to circulate alongside the expected references to sovereignty and "the Charter of the United Nations" ("Upgrading of Ties" [editorial] 1998; Korea-China Joint Statement 1998, 152). The fact that left-wing President Kim Dae Jung read from the same script as a previous right-wing president on his 1998 state visit to Beijing reinforces the notion of this historical and cultural articulation of diplomatic discourse. Kim told students at Beijing University: "China and Korea have maintained the closest relations—geographically, historically and culturally—of any two countries in the world over the past 2,000 years" (in Chon Shi-yong 1998). Thus it is not surprising that *Dong-A Ilbo* and the *People's Daily* decided that Confucianism and social development were shared issues between the two countries, and the title of the 1996 conference was "Oriental Thought and Social Development" (Lee Chong-Suk 1997, Interview).

The *Dong-A Ilbo* project, which organizes a biannual conference, has been expanded to include the *Asahi Shimbun*, Japan's most influential paper, and looked for a suitable Vietnamese partner. The East Asian regionalism, in Lee's description, is a simple expansion of the logic of Korean nationalism. Although Koreans like to point with pride to their unique Hangul script, Lee states that East Asian countries are united in their use of Chinese characters; they have a common language, so they have a "common pride." This idea mirrors the traditional notion of imperial Confucian civilization based on *tongwen*, which means not just "shared language" but "shared Civilization" (Howland 1996, 54–57). But there is an important deviation for the Korean organizers: in expanding Confucianism from "Korean" to "East Asian," the *Dong-A Ilbo* conference organizers are conspicuously not reverting to a view that Confucianism is Chinese. The shared civilization is not just for East Asia either; Confucianism in such conferences is being universalized, a transnational resource for all civilizations as the world faces the problems of modernity: thus we have "the globalization of filial piety" (Hong Doo Pyo 1995, viii).

Shared civilization is most evident in the second theme of these two social events: the economic dynamism of East Asia due to "Confucian capitalism." With the crisis of capitalism in East Asia, there was a critique of Confucian capitalism as crony capitalism—but Korean responses were also vociferous (Kim Young Hie 1998;

Junn Sung-chull 1998; Fukuyama 1998; Higgott 2000; Kang 2002). The Confucian capitalist theme does not come out so much in the conference papers as in the events themselves. Each conference only includes one paper that directly addresses the question of the relation of Confucianism and economic development, a question that has fascinated scholars for the past two decades, and these two papers are the weakest of the collections. Most of the other papers simply take Confucian capitalism for granted, and this perspective was echoed in Lee's conceptual organization of the *Dong-A Ilbo* conference: "I'm sure that Confucianism and economic development are closely related." This Confucian capitalism goes back to the primary Korean Confucian virtues of *ch'ung* and *hyo* (loyalty and filial piety) and the metaphor of "harmonious family life" for social and economic organization. Lee feels that Confucianism is the opposite of individualism; he states that the aim of the *Dong-A Ilbo* conference is to establish a balance between political conflicts and the interests of the group that is based on the sacrifice of the individual (Lee Chong-Suk 1997, Interview).

This view of Confucian capitalism, which combines the collectivist corporate cultures of East Asia with the individualistic ones of America, is backed up by management studies—some also published by *Dong-A Ilbo* (Shin and Kim 1994; Shin 1992). The massive capitalist conglomerates in Korea—chaebol—are well-known for appealing to family metaphors to regulate their managerial and working-class staff (Janelli 1993). Thus it is not surprising that the Asan Foundation, which organizes and funds the charitable activities of the massive Hyundai Corporation, is involved in organizing conferences on "Eastern Ethics." The conference here discussed was to celebrate the twentieth anniversary of the Asan Foundation, and was blessed by Hyundai's founding chairman, Chung Ju-Yung.

Such conferences run parallel to the chaebol's business activities, often acting as intellectual support for the regionalization of the South Korean economy into China. Again, the growing ties are not just economic but ideological. It is common for South Koreans to employ the conversion narrative in economic encounters with China—conversion to capitalism, Korean-style. Although there was much talk in the 1990s of a "globalization" of South Korea that refocused foreign policy to issues beyond the Korean Peninsula, much of South Korea's economic activity remains concentrated in the East Asian region (Kim, Samuel 2000a). This expansion of the Korean economy takes advantage of "economic complementarities" along similar lines to the regionalization of the Taiwanese economy into Southeast China (discussed in chapter 1). The "natural" ties between Taiwan and mainland China were disrupted for nearly forty years by the civil war between the Nationalists and the Communists, but once Taibei loosened travel, trade, and investment restrictions in the mid-1980s, informal ties warmed, leading to an explosion of commercial and social contacts (Shambaugh 1995a).

Likewise, since relations between South Korea and the PRC warmed in the 1980s there has been an phenomenal growth in travel, trade, and investment. This was not just an economic policy for South Korea, but a geopolitical one. Contacts between the PRC and South Korea served to slowly wean Beijing away from Seoul's rival regime in North Korea; by 2002, China–South Korea trade was worth more than fifty times China–North Korea trade (Snyder 2003). In the first four years after the normalization of relations, South Korean travel to China increased by more than ten times: 43,000 in 1992 to 534,000 in 1996; Chinese travel to South Korea doubled to 91,000 in the same period (Köllner 1998, 2). By 2001, tourist arrivals from South Korea to China reached 1 million, while the number of Chinese visitors to South Korea was more than 400,000 (Snyder 2001).

Since 1992, trade has also skyrocketed; South Korea's trade with China (including Hong Kong) is on par with South Korea's number-one trading partner, the United States (Köllner 1998, 3). In the first eight years after normalization, bilateral trade experienced a tenfold expansion. After a sharp decline in 1998 due to the financial crisis, trade surpassed its 1997 level in 1999, and in 2000 alone it expanded by 30 percent to reach $30 billion; in 2002 it grew to $38 billion (Snyder 2001; Snyder 2003; also see statistics at www.strategicasia.nbr.org). Just as Taiwanese investment is concentrated in the southeast, especially Fujian province, South Korean investment is concentrated in the northeast, including Jilin and Shandong provinces—accounting for nearly three-fourths of all investments by the end of 1996 (Köllner 1998, 5; Lee Chae-Jin 1996, 160). Although the shift of chaebol capitalism from domestic to international business was seen as part of the frenzy for globalization in the 1990s, most of the chaebol's foreign direct investment went to China (Kim, Eun Mee 2000; Lee Chae-Jin 1996, 163).

Just as "Greater China" relies on transnational ethnic, cultural, and geographical affinities, so does the emerging "Greater Korea." Korean Confucian capitalists, especially in the small and medium enterprises (SMEs), rely on China's two million ethnic Koreans—a major "national minority" in China's Northeast—as middlemen, employees, and business partners (Köllner 1998, 6). As of 1993, the majority of the "Chinese" employed by South Korean business (thirteen thousand in 1992 and twenty thousand in 1993) were bicultural, bilingual ethnic Koreans (Lee Chae-Jin 1996, 149, 158). Korean public opinion takes particular interest in the major enclave of ethnic Koreans in Yanbian county of Jilin province. Just as Thais and Malays study Mandarin to take advantage of "Greater China," both ethnic Han and ethnic Korean Chinese youths in the northeast are learning Korean. Just as Taiwanese businessmen set up parallel families on the mainland, "local girls" in northeast China are marrying South Korean businessmen to participate in Greater Korea (Lee Chae-Jin 1996, 160).

Within South Korea itself, ethnic Korean migrant workers from China and the former Soviet Union are favored by SMEs over other Asians—in part because employers feel that they do not "disturb Korean homogeneity" (Moon, Katherine 2000, 157). In 1998, the South Korean government tried to turn these informal preferences into legal rights as part of a new regime of "transnational citizenship" that would "extend many of the benefits of Korean citizenship to ethnic Koreans abroad" (Moon Myung-ho 1998, 120). This movement of Koreans across borders was due initially to pressures from the Japanese empire, and then from the Korean War (Kim Ji-soo 1999). Since 60 percent of overseas Koreans are citizens of other countries—primarily China, Uzbekistan, and Kazakstan—this new citizenship policy caused a diplomatic crisis (Kim, Samuel 2000a, 262–63). These policies mostly concern China, which has the largest concentration of overseas Koreans in the world, 2 million out of 5.7 million.

Due to vociferous protests from the Chinese government, the bill was revised to give "overseas Korean" status only to those once citizens of the Republic of Korea, which was founded in 1948. In this way, neither the Korean Chinese nor the North Koreans qualified; thus the main beneficiaries of the new status are overseas Koreans who fled the Korean War to North America and are relatively more prosperous. With the 1999 law, all Korean Chinese have more rights and privileges than ordinary immigrants, but the diasporic politics favors the wealthy in the West over the impoverished in North Korea, China, and the former Soviet Union.

Such transnational ties can go beyond cultural-economic spheres to Korean territorial irredentism. Although many Korean Chinese trace their movement into Manchuria to the early-twentieth-century pressures of Japanese imperialism, many Korean nationalists talk of reclaiming Chinese territory that both North and South view as the birthplace of the Korean nation (Schmid 2002, 224–36; Cha, Victor 1997, 19; Banning and Glaser 1995; Em, Henry 1999). Even though a Korean regime has not controlled Manchuria since 926 AD, the roots are seen as ancient: Korea's mythical progenitor, Tan'gun, the focus of much nationalist ideology, is said to have been born in what is now Manchuria (Lee Kyong-hee 2000; Jeong Young-hun 2001; Schmid 2002, 229–33).[6] This is not just an academic argument. According to one report, North Korea successfully renegotiated its disputed border with China "by asserting that Korea's progenitor was born at Mt. Paektu" (Kim Ji-ho 1999). There is a social movement, called Tamul, in South Korea that seeks to "reclaim" parts of Manchuria. Both North and South are reimagining Korean space by appealing to a continental historical perspective that looks to ethnic Korean populations in place of the mainstream peninsular view that looks to the state (Schmid 2002, 233–36).

In this way, Korean nationalists use many of the same historical and nativist types of arguments to claim parts of Manchuria, that we saw the PRC use to claim the South China Sea. Just as Southeast Asian governments are wary of overseas Chinese populations, the PRC is getting nervous about South Koreans "stir[ring] up nationalist sentiments among ethnic Koreans in China" (Moon Myung-ho 1998, 121). While the transnational practice of Greater China expands Chinese influence, the Greater Korea project threatens to unmap the PRC.

The Political Economy of Filial Piety

Back in South Korea, the chaebol have been involved in social engineering projects in the domestic sphere. Beyond the conference on Eastern Ethics in the Twenty-first Century, the Asan Foundation has been involved in many other projects for social welfare. The Filial

Piety *(hyo)* Award is one of the results of earlier Asan symposia that addressed the problems of the elderly, retirement, the family, and women. The Filial Piety Award is the best example of how a definitively modern chaebol appeals to traditional culture. It should be noted that Hyundai is not alone in such activity: the Samsung Welfare Foundation has been giving out Filial Piety Awards for more than twenty years, and Daewoo Foundation funds *Tradition and Modernity*. It is important to note that these foundations are not independent of the chaebol, but are "tightly managed by their parent companies" (Park Tae-Kyu 1995, 585; Kim Kyong-Dong 1997).

The Asan Foundation's Hyo Award, which was created in 1991, aims to promote "the expansion of hyo culture" that Asan sees as the "prime virtue of our tradition" (Asan Foundation 1997b). Still, due to the rapid industrialization and urbanization that have involved "indiscriminately importing the negative elements of modernization and western culture," the number of people who practice hyo virtue has been declining (Yung Dug Hee 1995, iii). This is not just a moral problem, but a practical one: since nuclear families exclude grandparents, people are no longer taking care of the elderly. Thus Chung Ju-Yung established the Hyo Award system, which in its first five years distributed 148 awards of between 10 million and 20 million won each for a total of 1,277,030,000 won (US$1,596,278 at the August 1997 exchange rate) (Asan Foundation 1997b).

Surprisingly, the prizes did not go just to filial sons, as one would expect since the classics tell us that the filial relationship is between fathers and sons. (Indeed, the Chinese character for filial piety contains "son" as an element.) Rather, many of the prizes went to filial daughters-in-law who live in extended families, respect parents and elderly people, and teach hyo culture to the next generation. Hence, this project is a direct reaction to the breakdown of a patriarchy that depends on the unpaid labor of women; rather than using the stick of cultural and legal sanctions (which served well in controlling female factory workers), the chaebol appeal to the carrot of material rewards. Thus as in the Chinese diaspora, "Filial piety has been bent and channeled to serve the governmentality not only of the family, but of global capitalism as well" (Ong 1999, 127).

Events such as the Hyo Award and international conferences are indicative of the logic of Confucian capitalism that aims to Confucianize modernization. To put it another way, the problems that the *Dong-A Ilbo* and the Asan Foundation highlight are not limited to liberalism or individualism (and thus easily criticized as Westernization) but are more characteristic of modernity, which is not so closely linked to territoriality. As Chung Ju-Yung said, the problems come from industrialization and urbanization. He and others certainly do not question the grand project of modernization, and the rapid economic growth that it has brought to Korea. We can see the tension by looking at the cover of *Tradition and Modernity*, which appeals to tradition as handmade paper: it utilizes ancient images, yet all the advertisements are for modern capitalist commodities: high-rise condos, mobile phones, cars, satellite communications, computers, and credit cards. Rather than engaging in a sustained critique of modernity (Han Sang-Jin 1998), industrialists are seeking to Confucianize modernization, to use Confucianism as an ideological crutch to deal with the problems that industralization has created.

This is a major shift from the *ti-yong* (Eastern essence–Western technology) formula of conversion that has been guiding image of cultural synthesis in East Asia for more than a century (Levenson 1966, 59–78). Whereas Western science and technology used to be utilized to preserve and enhance East Asian spirit and culture, now Confucian ethics are appealed to in order to preserve and enhance capitalism. In other words, Confucianism is being commodified as a consumer product. This can be seen in how the meaning of "value" is changed from moral and aesthetic to instrumental and exchange: the moral value of filial piety is rewarded with cash: 20 million won. Chaebol Confucianism concerns how to make money by using Confucianism as an ideology to better control managers and workers, both politically and economically, as well as to encourage people to consume in particular ways (Lee Seung-Hwan 1997).

Such a commodification of Confucianism and Korean traditional culture is not strange. The Korean Confucian sage T'oegye graces the 1000-won bill, and, in a roundtable discussion commemorating Korea's Year of Cultural Heritage (1997), the aesthetic value of Korean porcelain was proven by the cash value it fetched at an auction in New York (Chung Yang-mo 1997, 8). Hence the commodification of Confucianism is not just for the local market, but follows the Korean model of export-led economics, expanded to cultural activities. As we saw earlier in this section, one of the main arguments of the media and the chaebol Confucians is that Confucianism is universal and thus exportable—with Korean branding. In official circles in Seoul, "globalization" often referred to promoting Korean culture on the world stage beyond the Peninsula, wonderfully reproducing the Confucian import/export economy of the conferences in still another variation of Greater Korea. Again we see "the globalization of filial piety."

Actually, the discourse of Confucian capitalism and the developmental state was waning even before the 1997 economic crisis (Gills and Gills 2000). Although it appeals to the authentic categories of indigenous, national, or regional culture, the argument for Confucian capitalism was, as we saw in chapter 1, first made and popularized in the United States—Confucianism is perhaps a more important American ideological export than democracy (see Dirlik 1995; Callahan 1996a). The argument was formed twenty years ago by American political economists searching for an explanation for East Asia's rapid development; their solution became the capitalist utopia of the "Pacific Century." But it is quite odd that it still was being presented in Korea in 1997 as either a new fad or "obvious."

The cultural argument for capitalist success could only explain so much, and the contradiction between the militaristic developmental states and the notion of civilian bureaucracy so dear to Confucians became too great. Indeed, more critical analyses of the rapid growth of chaebol—especially Hyundai—point to the military methods augmented by Confucian rhetoric of industrial peace and harmony. A case study of the inner workings of a chaebol argues that lower-level managers do not understand their work experience in terms of the Confucian family metaphor. Rather, these young men speak of work in terms of the military metaphors acquired during compulsory military service (Janelli 1993).

Even those who maintain that Korean corporate culture draws on collective Confucian values now say that changes are being made (Kim, Samuel 2000a). There is evidence for this in scholarly studies, as well as in pronouncements from the chaebols themselves. In the year leading up to the 1997 crisis, both internal newsletters that tell chaebol lower- and middle-managers how to think and act, as well as external pronouncements to the world, suggested that Confucian capitalist ideology was passing. Hyundai Housing and Industrial Development's public relations magazine's "humorous account" of the changing demands on workers was summed up:

In a world where creativity and individuality are the keys to success, the stoically uncomplaining grunt who blindly follows his superior's orders would not be able to survive today's cut-throat business environment. The ideal worker of the past is already an obsolete figure in this fast-paced, modern society. (Yoon Yeong-il 1997, 8)

This complete turnaround in corporate culture is shared by Samsung Electronics chairman Lee Kun-hee's serialized commentaries such as "Great Changes Engulf World as New Epoch about to Dawn," "Globalization Strategies," and "The Spirit of Rugby" (Lee Kun-hee 1997a; Lee Kun-hee 1997b; Lee Kun-hee 1997c). The last article is noteworthy, for Lee switches the definition of teamwork from the Confucian spirit to the Rugby spirit.

These shifts away from Confucian capitalism are confirmed by scholarly studies that show that collective models of organization and corporate culture are being modified (Shin Yoo-Keun 1997, Interview). What is interesting is that this shift is not seen as a threat. It is not framed in terms of a crisis of Westernization or the loss of traditional culture, but rather as a phenomenon that requires a change in the leadership style of managers. The solution is not to dig in one's heels to fight foreign development/business models, but to organize "corporate leadership training programs [that] should focus on a change in leadership from the authoritarian toward democratic consultative styles" (Shin and Kim 1994, 205–6).

I have been arguing here against popular notions of East-West conflict, and their attendant categories of cultural imperialism and cultural nativism. I have recounted mass cultural events, to show how Confucianism has been resurrected and revalued in the late twentieth and early twenty-first centuries. Although used in the late nineteenth century to separate Korea from the Chinese empire, Confucianism lately is being used by the media and chaebol to relink Korea with China in a transnational discourse that, emanating from various centers, at times posits a Greater Korea to contest Greater China. Here we not only have the flexible capitalism of "globalization" but a flexible civilization of Confucianism. This discourse is articulated in a series of "events" where the newspapers and chaebol use Confucianism when profitable, and disregard it when not—appealing to non-Confucian discourse (calling it modern, scientific, capitalist) when this suits them.

MODERNIZING CONFUCIANISM: CONFUCIAN SOCIAL SCIENCE

The other main theme of Confucianism in Korea is also a response to the pressures of globalization. Modernizing Confucianism takes it beyond the economic model of Korea and East Asia to make it be a universal ideology, a world-class civilization—and one specially suited for Korean social and political development (Hahm 1997a). This section examines two prominent examples of academic discourse of Confucianism that have become popular movements: the Sung Kyun Kwan Confucian Foundation and the founding of *Tradition and Modernity*. These organizations, because both blend academia and projects for social reform, are examples of activities characteristic of Confucian scholar-officials.

The Sung Kyun Kwan Foundation is commonly taken as the representative of Confucianism in Korea because of its traditional historical position. Sung Kyun Kwan is the name of the official Confucian academy founded in 1398 by the first ruler of the Choson dynasty. This traditional Confucian academy has grown into Sung Kyun Kwan University (founded in 1895), which includes programs in natural science and engineering in addition to humanities and social sciences. The university has the highest concentration of Confucian scholars in Korea, and includes an Institute of Confucian Philosophy. This Institute is located next to the ancient ceremonial buildings that contain the sacred tablets of Confucius and his disciples; each year, Confucian priests still conduct the proper rituals (see Qi Mei 1998; Choi Kun Duk 1998).

In 1995 Confucianism was officially declared a religion. This was not done by the government, but by the Sung Kyun Kwan Foundation.[7] Rather than responding to questions of national/regional identity or political-economic models, this aspect of the Confucian revival in Korea came in response to social issues: the rises in youth crime, sex crime, and the divorce rate that were publicized in the media (Cho Soon-Kyoung 1997, Interview; Yung Dug Hee 1995, iii; Nah Seoung 1996, 67). The worst examples of the stresses of modernization and urbanization were celebrated cases of patricide—sons killing fathers for an inheritance. According to Confucian ethics and filial piety, this is the most serious crime imaginable, and a cause for much reflection among Confucian elders as well as the general public (Hwang 1997, Interview).

In response to such problems, the Confucian Foundation gathered in 1991 to discuss how to modernize the organization and popularize Confucian teachings among the youth (Kim Kwang-Ok 1996, 202, 204). The resultant revival has used summer camps, public lectures, and teacher training courses to instruct young people in Confucian ethics (Kim Cheol-Hyeon 1997, Interview; Kim Kwang-Ok 1996, 213). For example, Confucian associations are altering their exclusive ritual culture to expand participation: "In principle the ritual is observed only by Confucians, but it was opened to high school students in order to give them an opportunity to be exposed to their tradition and history" (Kim Kwang-Ok 1996, 210).

Kim Kwang-Ok argues that such a regeneration of Confucian culture is changing the nature of a tradition previously "the exclusive asset of [a] particular privileged class" (Kim Kwang-Ok 1996, 202). The meaning and scope of Confucianism in Korea is expanding to include new groups. The Confucian Foundation, as a voluntary association, is working as an element of civil society through this revival project. Sometimes it is a very powerful element: for example, the Confucian Foundation protested when the Korean Supreme Court struck down the provision in the marriage law banning marriage between persons with the same family name and lineage. The Confucian Foundation stated that "The ruling is an outright challenge to the only remaining instance of public morality handed down for centuries. We, the ten million Confucian followers, will fight against it, resorting to all possible means" (in Hong Sun-hee 1997, 3). Although these "Confucian elders" seem to be appealing to orthodoxy, they are actually working as an example of a Confucian civil society; the Sung Kyun Kwan Foundation is a pressure group that protests in front of the National Assembly, and is backed up with the power of its influence over votes in the rural areas (Lee Seung-hwan 1997, Interview).

The Sung Kyun Kwan University has been active in (inter)national politics as well. The president of the university used the six hundredth anniversary of the founding of the Confucian academy to initiate the first links between North and South Korean universities, in 1998. Confucian tradition served as a bridge to bring the "Korean nation" together: "Sungkyunkwan University in Seoul has established a sister relationship with Koryo Sungkyunkwan (University) in Kaesong, North Korea" (*Korea Herald* 5 September 1998; Shin Hye-son 1998).

Such a use of Confucianism to facilitate reunification is supported by both conservative and progressive scholars in Seoul (Hahm 1997, Interview; Park Myoung-kyu 1997, Interview). These links are possible since, unlike the PRC, North Korea was never "overtly critical of traditional Confucian values" (Kim Kyung Hyun 1996, 105). Indeed, some note that North Korea is more Confucian than South Korea—and has been becoming more Confucian since the death of Kim Il Sung in 1994 (Armstrong 1998, 44–45).[8] Although Confucianism as a common culture between North and South can be used as a bridge for reconciliation, Grinker points out that such arguments rely on a romanticized notion that traditional Korean identity has been "frozen" in North Korea by communism (Grinker 2000, 12).

The second example of the Confucian revival in academia is the journal *Chontonggwa Hyondae (Tradition and Modernity)*, the first issue of which was published in June 1997. This journal is an important departure from earlier revivals of Confucianism, led by old conservative men who took it as their duty to instruct the youth. *Tradition and Modernity* brings together young scholars who have used their elite education—most have Ph.D.s from the United States—to reconsider the worth of Korean tradition. The journal itself is quite successful; the first issue sold about three thousand copies, and five thousand copies of the second issue were printed. Its first issue was widely publicized, at great expense, with part of a generous grant from the Daewoo Foundation, which funds the journal. (It is no coincidence that Daewoo was also the most active Korean investor in China at this time.) Although the journal is managed and written by scholars, its target audience is much wider: the Korean intelligentsia, especially teachers. Thus, whereas the Asan and *Dong-A Ilbo* Conferences were events that generated texts, *Tradition and Modernity* is a text that has generated a social event through its mixing of academic and popular culture in a mass market magazine for the intelligentsia.

Its purpose, according to editor-in-chief Hahm Chaibong, is to "reintroduce Confucianism into public discourse" because Confucianism has been ignored by social scientists and politicians since the fall of the Choson dynasty in 1910 (Hahm 1997, Interview; Hahm 1997a). Finding the Left/Right framing of political and social events unsatisfactory, Hahm felt that Korean politics should be considered in terms of the relation of tradition and modernity. *Tradition and Modernity* is then a product of post–Cold War discourse (even though the Cold War is not over on the Korean Peninsula). Like publications of the Chinese nativists (examined in chapter 2), the publication comes out of an academic atmosphere characterized by postmodern/postcolonial criticism of the Enlightenment and a deconstruction of universals—including human rights and democracy (Lee Seung-hwan 1997, Interview; Jang Dong-Jin 1997, Interview; Hahm 1997, Interview; Cho Soon-Kyoung 1997, Interview; Hahm 1997b, 1–3).

This new journal is interesting because it frames issues in terms of time rather than space; it can deal with the problems of modernity, rather than being limited to nationalist appeals against Westernization. Like *Guoxue* nativism in China, it is part of a broader project to find a new vocabulary of social science concepts that can better address problems and possibilities in East Asia (Lee Su Hoon 1998). Even so, Cumings notes, the postmodern turn has ironically revived the vocabulary of 1950s modernization theory just as Korea has slipped from an economic success to a failure (Cumings 30 July 1998: personal correspondence).

It is clear that the "tradition" in *Tradition and Modernity* is Confucianism: the first issue contains eight specially commissioned articles on Confucianism in the modern world. Titles include: "Confucianism and Globalization: Problems of Particularity and Universality," "Anti-Confucian Politics: Contradictions of Political Argument in Korea," "Liberalism and Confucianism: Meeting, Conflict, and Compromise," "The Possibilities and Limits of Confucian Capitalism," "Can Confucius Be Revived?" "Modern Moral View and Confucian Moral View," "Education of Leaders in the Choson Dynasty and Universal Education in Modern Times," and "Who Dares Bring Disgrace on Tradition?"

There are problems with *Tradition and Modernity* that are instructive for analyzing other studies of Confucianism. As we have seen, traditionally the Confucian academy of Sung Kyun Kwan represented Confucianism in Korea, and one would expect that the academy's faculty would be part of the discourse. But generally, they are not. None of the contributors to the first issues of *Tradition and Modernity* are from the Confucian Foundation. Neither the Confucian Foundation nor Sung Kyun Kwan University was involved at all in the organization of the joint conferences of the *Dong-A Ilbo* and the *People's Daily* (Lee Chong-Suk 10 November 1997, personal correspondence). The Sung Kyun Kwan Foundation did not participate in the Asan Foundation conference either, and only marginally participated in the Academy of Korean Studies "Filial Piety Conference" in 1994.[9] Thus, the professional Confucians are largely absent from current discussions. Rather, the modernizers of Confucianism are social scientists trained in the West. Although they take the Confucian tradition as their own, and assume familiarity with it, they still come at tradition and Confucianism as "exotica" and "foreign studies" (Kwon Tai-Joon 1997, Interview).

Such a romanticization of the past causes numerous problems: the discussion begins from the position that social science is hostile to Confucianism. Since the modernizers' purpose is to reintroduce Confucianism into public discourse and social science, they have to show how "good" Confucianism is. But such an utopian approach can lead to an unbalanced analysis characteristic of postcolonial criticism in general and "Confucian democracy" discourse in particular: the modernizers examine the limits of modernity and the limits of democracy, but they do not consider the limits of Confucianism, which is being univeralized (Callahan 1996a; Dirlik 1997). If theirs was a new line of analysis, we could forgive such problems; it is certainly hard to get it right the first time. But these scholars are starting from a false premise (as we saw in chapter 1). Social science is hardly hostile to Confucianism; rather, influential segments of the academy have actively promoted Confucianism for decades. Thus the journal is largely a rehash of old arguments imported from the West—even as the contributors are searching for a new/old vocabulary (Dirlik 1997).

Another problem with the journal's analysis concerns selectivity; it primarily considers Confucianism, whereas many female scholars are looking to Buddhism and liberalism. Like the official histories, the analysis tends to deny the multiplicity of tradition in Korea, a multiplicity that is Korea's major strength and resource. More important, nativism in the form of cultural nationalism and the resurrection of "tradition" for political purposes is nothing new in Korea. The 1970s and 1980s witnessed a very vibrant *minjung*— popular masses—movement that looked to the folk culture shared by all Koreans. Rather than look to Confucianism, for example, this nativism looked to shamanism. The *minjung* as a counterculture grew out of the collapse of values that were taken for granted in the family and school. The task was to break up the orthodoxy, and thus question elitist conceptions of self. This was done through subaltern discourse that examined identity from the viewpoint of the non-elite and stressed radical openness, solidarity, and justice (Han Sang-Jin 1997a, 86; Abelman 1993; Koo 1993; Kim Kwang-Ok 1997). Such discourse questioned the Confucian elite's role of being "the voice of the people," to encourage the people speak for themselves. But with the passing of the Cold War certainties of Right and Left, culture has shifted from a radical tool to a conservative weapon, from a source for grassroots *minjung* national identity to a source for elite Confucian regional identity (Callahan 2002a; Rozman 1991b). While the discourse of Confucianism certainly serves to decentralize power from the West and globalization, it recentralizes power in East Asia not for the masses but for the elite.

The discourse of the modernization of Confucianism is likewise selective about "modernization": women and children come last. The editorial board of *Tradition and Modernity* is still all men, a feature noted by feminist scholars in Korea (Cho Soon-Kyoung 1997, Interview). Social movements and labor unions are disqualified in the journal's appeal to Confucian capitalism and Confucian democracy. Because many of the articles appeal to loyalty and filial piety as definitive of Confucianism (Callahan 2002a, 295–305), legitimate criticism can only come from the neo-mandarin watchdogs in the media and the academy (Lew Seok-Choon 1997, 93).

Here the project of Confucian social science is similar to that of Confucian capitalism: to reestablish the patriarchy. This certainly was an important part of the response to *Tradition and Modernity*. The journal was most popular with right-wing, traditional, and hypernationalist groups; Hahm received many invitations to speak at their meetings, as well as at government agencies (Hahm 1997, Interview). In this way both academic projects neatly follow the state management of the knowledge project with its aim, according to one Korean official, to "correct distorted views of Korea" (in Holloway 1997, 30; Cumings 30 July 1998, personal correspondence). This governance of the Korean knowledge project through organizations like the Korea Foundation—which funded the research for this chapter—has been criticized in recent years (Cumings 1996; Rubin 1997; Holloway 1997).

There are two distinct streams of culture in Korea. As we have seen, the atmosphere of official, corporate, and intellectual discourse is very open to Confucianism. But the mainstream culture is another matter. Confucianism is not represented in popular culture as a positive force; it exists primarily in terms of rebelling against the father or the local magistrate (Kim, Samuel 2000a; Lee Seung-hwan 1997, Interview; Kim Hong-kyung 1997, Interview). Although there are artifacts of Confucian popular culture—including comic books, novels, films, and television series (Cai Zhizhong 1987; Inoue 1992; Yang Shu'an 1993; Yang, Edward 1994)—all over the world, translated into dozens of languages, such cultural products are not popular in Korea.

Popular culture in Korea, as elsewhere, is increasingly guided toward the "youth." To them, the only thing Confucianism has to offer is *hyo*, which is not very attractive. As in the rest of East Asia, there are particular problems convincing young women about the virtues of Confucianism. Many feminist scholars in Korea are involved in projects that criticize Confucian patriarchy, and look for answers either in liberalism or in Buddhism (Cho Soon-Kyoung 1997, Interview; Northeast Asian Women's Studies Association 1994). We have seen how Confucian modernizers have tried to perpetuate and/or re-create Confucianism through activities such as the Hyo Award and the targeting of teachers, but this does not seem to be working.

Part of the problem is in the approach that many writings on Confucianism take. As happens with "history" in China, articles look to "tradition" as something not just whole but continuous. The writers justify their arguments on what Koreans *really* are and what they *really* do, and lament any break with tradition. But we can only talk about modernizing Confucianism because there has been a break with tradition: and I would argue that this break is not a problem—rather, it is enabling and empowering. Once we start talking about "tradition," we have already made a break with the past where tradition was taken for granted and thus did not need to be named. Choice is a peculiarity of modernity (Giddens 1990). Once the orthodoxy of state religion has been broken, people can pick and choose from the elements of Confucianism. In other words, you can only modernize Confucianism, and have it speak to modern issues, once a critical break has been made, and the discontinuity recognized.

Although Korean scholars increasingly take Confucianism for granted, and say that they are standing on their Confucian foundations to pick and choose from Euro-American modernization/

enlightenment, they are actually picking and choosing from Confucianism from the standpoint of their modern/postmodern condition. Once we recognize this peculiar relationship between tradition and modernity, we can reexamine tradition without necessarily having to recreate it. But *Tradition and Modernity* is caught in the cycle of orthodoxy: it sees social science as hostile to Confucianism, so it responds by promoting Confucianism. This is exemplary of a simple reversal; rather than looking at Confucianism anew, the writers either worship Confucianism or smash it. This is indicative of the relation between colonization and decolonization: colonization imposes boundaries of self/other, civilized/barbaric, traditional/modern, empire/nation. Decolonization typically accepts these boundaries and organizes resistance around their reversal, in "emancipation through mirroring" that entails a "mix of defiance and mimesis" (Pieterse and Parekh 1995, 11). Decolonization, then, continues to reproduce the power of domination.

The postcolonial, in this sense, has a more fluid relation to boundaries than the "confrontation and reconquest" characteristic of colonization and decolonization. For Confucianism in Korea, this sort of postcolonialism would entail a new angle of analysis that neither worships nor discards Confucianism, but comes at Confucianism (and Buddhism or shamanism) anew, not to reclaim the old as a pure, natural, or national tradition but as an ironic, mixed, and dirty practice. Korean social scientists are part of this heterotopic irony with their Western training and Korean socialization.

This effort to deal with Confucianism in its complexity, as noted in this volume's introduction, is analogous to Benedict Anderson's plea for social scientists to decapitalize "Nationalism-with-a-big N," and thus remove it from the list of ideologies: "It would, I think, make things easier if one treated [nationalism] as if it belonged with 'kinship' and 'religion,' rather than with 'liberalism' or 'fascism'" (Anderson 1991, 5). Likewise, it is more profitable for us to view Confucianism is the same light: as one category among many, rather than as a hegemonic metanarrative.

Many Korean scholars are responding to this challenge in interesting ways (sometimes within *Tradition and Modernity* as well). Rather than taking Confucianism for granted as the bedrock of their (national or regional) identity, they are using it as a tool for very specific projects of cultural construction and analysis (see Chaiwat

1992). In *Tradition and Modernity,* Lee Seung-Hwan's article, "Who Dares Bring Disgrace on Tradition?" takes such a critical view of Confucianism. He warns against a simplistic division of philosophy and practice into tradition and modernity, East and West, and suggests that hybrid forms of Confucianism, liberalism, and other discourses are necessary to meet the needs of contemporary Koreans (Lee Seung-Hwan 1997). In "Anti-Confucian Confucian Politics" Kim Byung-Kook uses Confucianism as a category to understand the ironic success/failure of political parties in Korea, which is due to the morality/regionalism of Confucian society (Kim Byung-Kook 1997). In a similar way, Cho Hein utilizes Confucian modes of criticism and interaction for the project of unearthing "The Historical Origin of Civil Society in Korea," while still noting that "we in no way presume Confucianism to be the only possible source of civil society in the East" (Cho Hein 1997, 24).

Most interestingly, Han Sang-Jin uses de-essentialized critical social theory to analyze Confucianism as a resource for identity within the dynamic of globalization and tradition. Han seeks to use Gidden's posttraditional approach to refigure Confucianism in global discourse. He hopes to get beyond the conservative project of a "Confucian alternative" to Western democracy, which he feels risks re-Orientalizing Asians (Han Sang-Jin 1997b, 2; Kim Yung Myung 1997, 1132–34). By writing a subversive genealogy of Confucianism in East Asia, Han argues that "Confucianism has not just legitimized authoritarian regimes, but criticized them" (Han Sang-Jin 1997b, 10). Thus the notion of a normative Confucianism can be resurrected as a critical tool for assessing politics, and pushing for a more open, pluralist politics (see Kim Dae Jung 1994). As mentioned above, progressive scholars are also considering how Confucianism can be used for reunification with North Korea, as well as for maintaining peaceful relations with China and Japan (Park Myoung-kyu 1997, Interview).

Of course, as we saw above, the capitalist conglomerates are already using Confucianism in this hybrid fashion. Although the chaebol insist that they are being true to Confucian orthodoxy, chaebol Confucianism (as opposed to Confucian capitalism) picks and chooses from among the Confucian virtues for discourses to advance its project of profit and control. Likewise, the state selectively uses filial piety and loyalty for its own purposes; this is shown in the second issue of *Tradition and Modernity, Political Power in Korea*, which, for example, looks to elite notions of addressing corruption, rather than to popular civil society (Son Moon-ho 1997; Kim Myong-ha 1997; Hahm 1997c).

Hence, I would argue that, though Confucianism is often seen, for good reason, as "conservative," the politics is not in Confucianism itself. Confucianism is neither naturally authoritarian nor democratic. Like most enduring social practices, it is complex and contains contradictory elements. The politics comes in with what we choose to use Confucianism to promote: nationalism or transnationalism, patriarchy or democracy, capitalism or civil society. None of these projects is natural, and they all need the legitimacy that discourses like Confucianism can provide.

CONCLUSION

Diasporic Chinese are the lead characters in the narrative of Greater China in both its alarmist and triumphalist forms, and Confucianism is characteristically figured as the foundation of their strength (Bolt 2000; Huntington 1996; Tu Weiming 1994a). But this chapter has shown how Confucianism is far from stable enough to serve as a solid foundation. It has problematized the standard notions of "Greater China" based on shared Chinese ethnicity, because Korea acts in Greater China on the basis of shared civilization. This chapter thus has used the Korean example to show how Confucianism works within temporal and spatial contexts as part of class, national, regional, international, and transnational identity in East Asia more generally, at times weaning Confucianism away from China to form a Greater Korea that works along much the same logic as Greater China. But this is not the sole ambition of Confucianism in Korea.

To recount the tactics of governmentality in Korea: the state uses Confucianism in a nativistic way to overcome postimperial anxieties, to separate Korea from American, Chinese, and Japanese empires and thus produce the nation-state. Confucianism is also mobilized by diplomats and transnational capitalists to change the subject of PRC-ROK relations from Cold War rivalry to more harmonious relations in the past. This is both a national and an international project of conversion. On the one hand, Confucianism as "Korean tradition"—specifically via the institution of the Sung Kyun Kwan

Confucian academy—is used as a "nonpolitical" means to establish ties between North and South Korea. Such contacts take place in the context of a shared suspicion of a renewed Chinese hegemony in Northeast Asia that favors a divided Peninsula. On the other hand, Confucianism was used according to the logic of "shared civilization" to facilitate official ties between the Communist PRC and the anti-Communist ROK—often against the rival Korean regime, the Communist DPRK.

Still other groups use Confucianism in a transnational fashion to promote various political and economic projects—which are neither "for" nor "against" the cultural or territorial entities called "Korea" or "China." The chaebol conglomerates in Korea use Confucianism as "Oriental tradition," to facilitate links with comparable Chinese elites. Rather than being part of the economic culture of Greater China in Southeast China, I have argued, they are better described as being part of a Greater Korea project encouraged by the substantial ethnic Korean presence in Northeast China. Although there is talk of Korean irredentism in Manchuria, this misses an important point—territorial sovereignty is not the issue, so much as are the workings of flexible transnational capitalism produced by flexible transnational civilization.

Likewise Confucianism is used by elites in Seoul not to argue for "Korea" against "China" (or the United States), but for specific political projects: patriarchy, reunification, peace, and even democracy. These take place not in national space so much as in trans/national space. Once again, this usage shows the malleability of Confucianism as a discourse. It can be coherently used for national, international, or transnational projects. It is so meaningful, and thus powerful, just because it is so empty and flexible. In this way, the vibrant discourse of Confucianism in Korea demonstrates the contradictions and evasions, the negotiations and assertions, within East Asia that mainstream (East/West) analysis obscures.

This more robust understanding of the knowledge practices of the Chinese empire and the South Korean nation-state have enabled me to unpack important aspects of Sino-Korean relations. A critical use of this Greater China discourse can also help us to reframe the analysis of Hong Kong from issues of territorial sovereignty to that of civilizational security in the next chapter. Chapter 5 displaces common views of Hong Kong that place it at the center of an East-West conflict between the United Kingdom and the PRC, to see the intra-cultural relations of Beijing and Hong Kong.

In the previous chapters, I have decentered, denaturalized, and decapitalized guiding concepts such as civilization, Confucianism, and Greater China. This will help me in chapters 5 and 6 to problematize the tight links between nation and state, culture and ethnicity, that the PRC tries to enforce in its relations with Hong Kong and Taiwan.

5

Harmonizing Boundaries:
Civilization and Security in Hong Kong

Hong Kong is both fascinating and frustrating. It does not fit into standard political science vocabulary, either for domestic politics or for international relations (Yahuda 1996, 40ff; Abbas 1997a, 3ff). Although many scholars work hard to locate it, Hong Kong defies the standard conceptual maps defined by empires and nation-states. Certainly, it was legally part of (the British) empire before 1997, and is part of (the Chinese) nation-state after 1997, but in practice it is both and neither. It is an anomaly: for the first time, the colony returning to the imperial center was more advanced than that center (Abbas 1997a, 3).

In practical terms, the search for Hong Kong studies leads to strange and unexpected sites. The conceptual formula employed to regulate the Beijing–Hong Kong relationship, "one country, two systems," is perplexing—not just for Hong Kong, or even for Taiwan and Greater China, but for identity politics and international law in general. Certainly, "one country, two systems" is now part of propaganda, a slogan reproduced in all areas of public discourse, even receiving the honor of its own commemorative postage stamp in China. But it contains interesting possibilities for alternative understandings of self/Other relations. The formula is the opposite of the Westphalian system: one system, many countries. Since "one country, two systems" contains fruitful ambiguities, it provides opportunities for both an engagement with the Other and a reassessment of the self.

In chapter 4 we saw how the "Confucian Civilization" promoted by Greater China enthusiasts was denaturalized as it was employed by Korean groups; this chapter extends such a critical approach to examine how cultural categories likewise produce and differentiate "Chinese" peoples in Hong Kong. Thus this chapter further twists the four narratives of nativism, conquest, conversion, and diaspora, to see how they produce Hong Kong and mainland China. To summarize, the first section considers how "Hong Kong" is deployed in the British imaginary. Although the territory is the product of a conquest narrative of expanding empire, we will see how British discourse employs the logic of conversion in its "civilizing" mission. On the other hand, "Hong Kong" is employed in the Chinese imaginary as part of the nation-building project. Thus, in the second section we see how the People's Republic of China invokes a nativist narrative to welcome Hong Kong back as a part of the homogeneous Chinese nation: One China. But with "one country, two systems," China also shifts to conversion in its rhetoric of (imperial) harmony. The "Return of Hong Kong" narrative updates the traditional Chinese tributary system, examined in chapter 3, to the late twentieth century.

Local Hong Kong narratives, on the other hand, are fascinating because they are contested. Section three shows how they appeal to combinations of the narratives of nativism, conquest, conversion, and diaspora. Lines of civilization and barbarism are still drawn, but in unexpected places. In this way, Hong Kong provides excellent terrain on which to further explore the issues of nation and state, culture and ethnicity, territory and population, temporality and spatiality.

In this chapter, then, I interrogate modes of understanding, the discursive economies that produce identity politics in these three imaginaries. Although there was much talk about an East/West conflict with the handover of Hong Kong in 1997, Yahuda presciently notes that the main issues of the handover do not concern Sino-British relations but the challenge of how the two systems understand each other: how Hong Kong understands China, and how China understands Hong Kong (Yahuda 1996, 43). Since most analyses of Hong Kong focus on Sino-British relations, this chapter focuses more on Beijing–Hong Kong relations. A short summary of the dominant themes in the British imaginary will be followed first by a longer treatment of the Chinese imaginary, and then by an in-depth discussion of the Hong Kong imaginary.[1] Indeed, Hong Kong and China are not simply understanding each other, but *producing* each other, through the various discourses: "one country, two systems," the Basic Law, "Hong Kong people running Hong Kong," a "high degree of autonomy," the "Return of Hong Kong," the "Hong Kong way of life," and so on.

To interrogate these understandings and productions, we need to switch from Beijing's overriding concern with "national unity and territorial integrity" (*Basic Law* 1991, 4) to see how "one country, two systems" works. We need to switch from understanding Hong Kong in terms of universal rationalities of law and history, to imagining the territory via the ambiguity of stories—the numerous stories that point to contextuality and contingency. Although this may sound far-fetched, the documents themselves lead us from the legal-constitutional to the metaphorical, from diplomatic history to cultural studies; the "Hong Kong way of life" became a legal and technical term in both the 1984 *Sino-British Joint Declaration* and the *Basic Law*. This conceptual move requires a shift from a Western social science vocabulary to a classical Chinese vocabulary of harmony and hegemony, a shift from the hegemony of single-ordered master narratives to the harmony of multiple metaphors described in the Confucian concept "harmony with difference." Confucian harmony is not just a conceptual issue: it is a practical issue, because "harmony with difference" has important parallels with "one country, two systems." Here, harmony is not the "answer" to a Hong Kong "problem"; rather, like civilization, it provides us with a different set of questions.

To make a transition from the standard concepts of international relations and political science to such a critical approach, I first need to line up and deconstruct mainstream discourses: the usual suspects of "evil empires" and a "victimized" Hong Kong. Indeed, it turns out that most texts do not talk about Hong Kong as *Hong Kong*, but Hong Kong as a metaphor for something else: Hong Kong is variously figured as a barren rock, a floating island, an example of a benevolent empire, the key to Chinese foreign policy, a model for reunification with Taiwan, the end of Western empire, and the beginning of the Pacific Century (Mathews 1997, 5; Barmé 1997; Xi Xi 1997; Ma Jian 1997; Yahuda 1996, 19, 21–22; Yahuda 1997; Brown and Foot 1997; Naisbitt 1996).

Such metaphors rely on the binaries of Enlightenment discourse: the rationality of (British) law and the singularity of (Chinese) history, typically bolstered by stereotypes of West and East (see Patten 1998). It is common to see Hong Kong written into romances: "Of all the romances of modern history, the chronicle of Hong Kong since 1841 is surely one of the most alluring to the imagination" (Blanden 1959, 1). In a more technical sense, "romance" refers to a quest involving two main characters, a hero and an enemy in an un-ironic struggle. In such an adventure tale, the hero represents youth, angelic spirit, spring, dawn, order, fertility, and vigor, while the enemy is the opposite: old age, the demonic, winter, darkness, confusion, sterility, and moribund life (Frye 1957, 187–88, 195; also see Wasserstrom 1994; Callahan 2002b). As we shall see, both the British and Chinese imaginaries are transfixed with the romance of Hong Kong in their respective frontier economies of civilizational security. In the mainstream discourse from both China and Euro-America, self/Other relations are clear: a civilized self and a barbaric Other.

Both the British and the Chinese discourses rely on the notion of Hong Kong as real estate rather than population; it is a thing to be "owned," taking part in an economy of exchange; it is a commodity to be "handed over" in 1997 as part of perhaps the most lucrative real estate deal in history.[2] In the concluding section, I switch from this hegemonic territorial view of Hong Kong to consider how the people of Hong Kong fit into these politics via a discursive economy of harmony. In this way we can move from the often virtual politics of the elites defining a "Hong Kong way of life" to the visceral politics of who has the "Right of Abode" in Hong Kong. We can see how territorial and popular sovereignty are related in slippery ways. As Umberto Eco writes, the main political concern is not about who speaks but about who dies (in de Lauretis 1987, 65)—or in this case who lives, who *can* live in Hong Kong.

BRITISH IMAGINARY: LAW

Although Hong Kong is commonly known as the Pearl of the Orient, in the British imaginary it is often described as the Pearl of the Empire, a "justification for the idea of imperialism itself" (Morris 1990, 305; Tambling 1997, 364; Courtauld et al. 1997; Blyth and Wotherspoon 1996).[3] In this story, Hong Kong is figured as wholly a British creation.[4] John Luff ends his 1959 book *The Hong Kong Story* with the following passage: "This then was Hong Kong, this that you see is Hongkong. Gaze well around, for all you see began in the minds of English men, just over a century ago" (Luff 1959, 102).

Thus Chinese people are either totally invisible—missing, even though they are over 95 percent of the population, or present only as servants. The following passage from the 1997 special issue "Hong Kong: A New Beginning" of the *Far Eastern Economic Review* gives a good sense of the racial hierarchies that are an integral part of British imperialism:

> Far from hating and despising the ordinary Chinese, the British merchants who came to Macao and Canton in the early 19th century actually liked, and in some ways greatly admired, them. They became very fond of their Chinese interpreters, assistants and servants, and were outraged by the cruelty often visited on them by Chinese officials. (Johnson 1997, 9, 12)[5]

This passage also demonstrates that Empire was a moral project that involved "civilizing the barbarians" and thus saving the Chinese from themselves (also see Patten 1998, 249).[6] Johnson argues that "The truth is that colonialism at its best, and Hong Kong was an outstanding example, is an attempt to export a system of superior political, economic, and often cultural ethics to societies which have been denied them" (Johnson 1997, 8).

Thus much of the discourse surrounding the handover in 1997 was not just anti-PRC or anticommunist, but anti-Chinese (see Bernstein and Munro 1998, xiv). Percy Cradock, a well-known "China expert" for the British government, famously said that China's rulers "have always been thugs, are thugs, and always will be thugs" (in Mirsky 1997, 140; also see Cradock 1999; Cradock 1997; Patten 1998). Editorials in Euro-America complained about the British government's "appeasement" of an evil China, comparable to giving Hitler the Sudetenland in 1938. Rather than a "handover," the transfer was framed as an invasion, a conquest, a "takeover"—and even a "Chinese takeway" (see Knight and Nakano 1999, 64–67; Cradock 1999, 214, 223; Chow, Rey 1998; Theroux 1997). The chorus of anti-Chinese curses grew so loud in 1997 that "China hands" had to write special articles to counter the "gloom and doom" scenarios for Hong Kong (Ching, Frank 1997; Knight and Nakano 1999; Cradock 1997).

In the racial and moral hierarchy of British imperialism, the Orient is a corrupt foil to the civilization of the West. If barbarism is defined by corruption, then civilization is defined by the rule of law (Gong 1984, 14–15; Keene 2001, 90–6; Munn 1999, 46). The British occupation of Hong Kong relied on the international law of three treaties signed in 1840 (for Hong Kong island), 1860 (for Kowloon), and 1898 (for the New Territories). Even when Britain agreed to return Hong Kong, it was done through a treaty: the 1984 Sino-British Joint Declaration. Indeed, some take Beijing's increasing participation in such negotiations as a sign that it has been converted to the rules of international society (Kim, Samuel 1998b).

As many have remarked, in Hong Kong the "principle ideology is the Rule of Law," which is the "cornerstone of society" (Ghai 1998, 11; Liberal Party in Chan, Fu, and Ghai 2000, 228). The rule of law thus is seen as the key to everything: while Hong Kong is often figured as a site of laissez-faire capitalism, freedom, or democracy in Asia, these all are secured by the civilization of the rule of law.[7] The British government declared that, though its legal responsibility ended in 1997, it still had "an enduring political and ethical commitment to Hong Kong" (Foreign and Commonwealth Office 1997–; see Cradock 1999, 211). Thus there is a peculiar circular logic: civilization employs law to gain imperial sovereignty; then, once legal sovereignty is gone, we go back to the morality of "civilization." Such circularity makes it clear that the imaginary is dictated by neither civilization nor law but by modes of British control. The British imaginary thus moves from conquest to conversion in the service of imperial power.

BEIJING IMAGINARY: HISTORY

Although China was often presented in Euro-America as conquering Hong Kong in 1997, its own understanding of the transfer was very clearly in the nativist mode. Even so, Hong Kong studies are hard to find in the academic centers of Beijing. Hong Kong studies are not located in law departments, because both the official and popular Chinese views of Hong Kong start from the premise that the three treaties were unequal and thus illegitimate. Actually, the phrase "gunboat diplomacy" comes from this experience. Although (as we saw in chapters 3 and 4) the Chinese empire was built on grossly unequal relations with neighbors in Korea and Vietnam (Kim Key-Hiuk 1980), neither the Nationalist nor the Communist regimes recognized the Hong Kong treaties as valid. Indeed, one of the first things that Beijing did after entering the United Nations General Assembly in 1971 was to have Hong Kong and Macao taken off the "colonial territories" list of the United Nations Committee on Decolonization. Hong Kong is not found in political science or international politics departments, either; as a characteristic problem of inside/outside, Hong Kong is neither domestic nor international politics.

I finally found Hong Kong in the history departments. Throughout the literature in China, Hong Kong is framed as a historical problem, a "historical legacy" of imperialism. The British occupation of Hong Kong is seen as a "historical anomaly." Even Beijing's legal arrangement for Hong Kong, the Basic Law, which serves as Hong Kong's mini-constitution, is framed by history. Its preamble begins, "Hong Kong has been part of the territory of China since ancient times; it was occupied by Britain after the Opium War in 1840" (Basic Law 1991, 3). Thus the Crown Colony of Hong Kong compromised both the territorial and the cultural security of China.

This historical problem demanded a historical solution. So in 1983 the Second Section of the Foreign Relations Division of the Institute of Modern History at the Chinese Academy of Social Sciences (CASS) in Beijing began its "Hong Kong History Project." The timing is telling: between Britain's statement in 1982 that it would negotiate Hong Kong's future, and the signing of the Joint Declaration in 1984. This project was part of the new relations between Beijing and Hong Kong. The Institute of Modern History worked with a noted historian from the University of Hong Kong to produce two books, *Hong Kong in the Nineteenth Century* and *Hong Kong in the Twentieth Century* (Yu Shengwu and Liu Cunkuan 1993; Yu Shengwu and Liu Shuyong 1995). The team did not share only resources and documents, but ideas and interpretations. Both sides were proud that the two books were published not just in Beijing for a mainland audience but in Hong Kong for a broader audience (Fok Kai Cheong 1999, Interview; Interviews 1999). A younger member of the research group went on to publish books and articles in English and Chinese (Liu Shuyong 1998; Liu Shuyong 1997a; Liu Shuyong 1997b; Liu Shuyong 1996). The project showed that the CASS has a long-term commitment to Hong Kong studies; the third generation of

Hong Kong scholars is being trained in Beijing, in cooperation with Hong Kong (Interviews 1999).

An examination of the two texts shows that they are not "the history of Hong Kong" so much as they are writing Hong Kong into Chinese history, both ancient and modern (also see Fok, K. C. 1990; Tsai, Jing-fang 1993). Ancient history is written to counter the view that Hong Kong was a barren rock before the British regime; as occurred regarding the South China Sea, discussions typically begin with statements that the territory "has been part of the territory of China since ancient times." Thus, the dynastic histories are combed for references of Chinese administration of the region we now call Hong Kong, traditional maps that include Hong Kong are republished, and archaeological projects document "Chinese" settlements dating back six thousand years.

For modern history, Hong Kong is written into the Chinese revolution. But the historiography is more complex than that, and to understand the relation of revolutionary history and civilizational security, it is necessary to take a detour into Chinese historiography. However, this is a different sort of historiographical struggle than we witnessed in the last chapter. While Japan and Korea had to differentiate themselves from "China" to be modern, the switch from cyclical to linear historiography in China itself was a matter of more complex self/Other relations. In other words, there has been a more thorough examination of the Chinese self, and a more peculiar Othering.

It would not be an exaggeration to argue that the master narrative of modern Chinese history is the discourse of the "Century of National Humiliation." This phrase is often mentioned not just in discussions of Chinese nationalism but also of Chinese foreign policy (see Zhao Suisheng 2000, 2; Bernstein and Munro 1997, 19; Huntington 1996, 229; Nathan and Ross 1997; Callahan 2004a). Indeed, the English title for a book called *A History of National Humiliation* is *A History of China's Modern Foreign Relations* (Jiang Gongsheng 1927). Yet the discourse of National Humiliation has itself received scant critical analysis (see Cohen 2002; Callahan 2004(a); Luo Zhitian 1993; Pye 1992, 67–84). Modernity, humiliation, and nationalism are linked to guide not just historiography but the Chinese imaginary that has important institutional links leading us directly back to Hong Kong (Callahan 2004a). In short, there is a network of ties among the discourse of National Humiliation and its institutional base in national history museums whose leaders are graduates of Renmin University's Party History Department, whose professors constitute an influential cadre of Hong Kong experts.

Recalling the discussion in chapter 2, the narrative of the Century of National Humiliation starts with the Opium War in 1840, which is commonly seen as the beginning of the end of Chinese supremacy. As well as being the beginning of colonial rule of China, 1840 is taken as the beginning of the era of "modern history" in China.

Actually, the discourse of National Humiliation does not start with the Opium War but by giving an ahistorical report of the glories of Chinese civilization and its five-thousand-year history; the written texts are often accompanied by maps that show the Chinese empire extending far into Siberia, Central Asia, and Southeast Asia (*Jindai Zhongguo* 1997; Cao and Huang 1932, iii). The discourse then recounts how, at the hands of foreign invaders and corrupt Chinese regimes, sovereignty was lost, territory dismembered, and the Chinese people humiliated in a direct link of the soil with the spirit. This tale is characteristically written according to diplomatic historiography: a linear narrative recording the wars, invasions, occupations, lootings, and unequal treaties that China suffered at the hands of predatory imperial capitalism (see He Yu 1997). The century ends with the establishment of the PRC in 1949. At this founding moment, National Humiliation was linked to "national salvation" when Mao Zedong famously declared from the Gate of Heavenly Peace, "Ours will no longer be a nation subject to insult and humiliation. We have stood up."

The long-term aim of the National Humiliation narrative is both political and cultural: to "cleanse National Humiliation" the Chinese government needs first to unite the lost territories under Beijing's leadership, and second to achieve social and economic development. "National salvation" thus is the discursive twin of National Humiliation. "National salvation" discourse has inspired the economic reforms of the Deng and post-Deng era, but it can also encourage a military reconquest of lost territories. During World War II, a patriotic banner pictured a heroic Chinese soldier holding up a decapitated Japanese head as a trophy. The banner reads "To wipe out our humiliation with our enemy's blood" ("Rise of Modern China" 1999). As we saw in chapters 2 and 3, National

Humiliation discourse still shapes China's territorial conflicts and border wars (Ji Guoxing 1998, 102; Wu Chunguang 1998). On the other hand, in 1997 Jiang Zemin told the Fifteenth Party Congress that living a "relatively comfortable life" also serves to cleanse National Humiliation (in BBC/SWB 15 September 1997).

This narrative is painstakingly reproduced in museums, textbooks, popular history books, and feature films, as well as specialized National Humiliation dictionaries, journals, atlases, and pictorials (Hu Huiqiang et al. 1998; Mitter 2000; Guo Qifu 1996; Zhongguo geming bowuguan 1997; Jiang Gongsheng 1927; Cao and Huang 1932; He Yu 1997; He Yu 1999; Xie Jin 1997; Chen Chengxiang et al. 1993; *Guochi* 1915; *Jindai Zhongguo* 1997; Zhou and Zhang 1997). Thus National Humiliation is not just "the standard view of Chinese Communist historiography" or "stale Maoist ideology," as many Euro-American scholars assume (Yahuda 1997, 209; Schell 1999; Weigelin-Schewiedrzik 1993, 164–71). Until 1940, Republican China commemorated a National Humiliation Day each May, and National Humiliation is the leading topic in a book by Mao's rival, Chiang Kai-shek (Chiang Kai-shek 1947, 44–75; Liu Zhen 1993, 210). National Humiliation is, then, a guiding discourse in the Chinese imaginary.

The best place to see this narrative is the Museum of Revolutionary History, which sits on the east side of Tian'anmen Square (see Hu Huiqiang et al. 1998; *Zhongguo gemingshi* 1990). In English it is called the Museum of Modern History, with the dates 1840 to 1949. The museum was founded in 1950, and transferred to its present site in 1959 as part of the celebration of the tenth anniversary of the founding of the PRC (Hu Huiqiang et al. 1998, 1–8). The museum is well organized, gathering together fascinating artifacts to guide visitors through modern Chinese history along the linear narrative of revolution: year by year, event by event, atrocity by atrocity. The impact of this narrative is quite strong: the phrase "never forget National Humiliation" is repeatedly inscribed in the comment book at the end of the exhibit. While the Traditional History Museum has been revised since the Cultural Revolution, the Revolutionary History Museum's exhibits have not been changed (Wu Hung 1997, 333; Mitter 2000, 281; Hu Huiqiang et al. 1998, 3).[8] The discourse of the Century of National Humiliation is treated as natural: there is very little irony or critical commentary on it (see Callahan 2004a; Wang Shuo 2000).

But this discourse has a history too: though the dates of the century are 1840 to 1949, the term was first popularized in 1915 to oppose Japanese aggression. At the time, there was a debate about timing: on which day should the humiliation be commemorated, May 7, when Japan made its demands that seriously compromised Chinese sovereignty, or May 9, when the Chinese president accepted them? Self or Other? National Humiliation Day was celebrated on May 9, as part of self-criticism. Although the discourse is now quite official, it began in 1915 as a counterhegemonic popular movement that involved textbooks and popular education campaigns (Luo Zhitian 1993, 310–12).

National Humiliation and "national salvation" are part of the process of nation building. In classical Chinese texts, "humiliation" is commonly deployed in the building and guarding of social boundaries: male/female, proper/improper; inside/outside (Geaney 2000). It is therefore not surprising that the modern discourse of National Humiliation is involved in building and guarding national borders. The transition from empire to nation-state had only just begun in 1911 in China, just four years before the 1915 challenge from the Japanese empire. This was a credible threat to territorial integrity and civilizational security—by 1910 the Japanese empire had swallowed Korea whole; Japan's demands would transform China into a Japanese protectorate.

National Humiliation thus can tell us much about the relation of historiography and identity. On the one hand, though official readings of "Japan" and "Korea" have their own variants of National Humiliation discourse (Grinker 2000, 73–98; Thorsten 2004), they still look to discontinuities and disjunctures to create a linear modern history of their distinct nation-states that are differentiated from transnational (Chinese) civilization. On the other hand, even though official historiography in China uses the disjunctures to likewise script a "nation-state" (see Duara 1995; Unger 1993), it also uses this peculiar linear reading of modern history as a way of recapturing past glories, rereading them into its own celebratory "rise of China." While, in chapter 4, history was separated from cosmology in the service of the (Korean or Japanese) nation-state, here history is rejoined to cosmology in the service of Greater China. While Japan and Korea make an "Other" of China to establish themselves, China needs to not only "Other" Japan and the West but "Other" itself through a thorough self-criticism: "national humiliation" is necessary for "national salvation."

And Hong Kong is necessary for both. It is the alpha and omega of the discourse of National Humiliation. The title of one book tells us as much: *Conclusion of the Century of Humiliating History: The Hong Kong Problem from Beginning to End* (Li Hou 1997). Hong Kong enters the discourse most recently, as the narrative of the "return of Hong Kong." Like the more general discourse of National Humiliation, the "return of Hong Kong" discourse works in many public spaces: catechisms, books by government officials, academic works, popular journalism, military culture, television programs, novels, feature films, and so on (*Xianggang zhishi* 1996; Hong Kong Society and Culture Section 1997; Li Hou 1997; Zhou Yizhi 1996; Qi Pengfei 1997; Wang Pujun 1997; *1997: 5000 years ago* 1997; Li and Hu 1997; Central Television Overseas Center 1998; Liang Fengyi 1997; Xie Jin 1997). More than one Chinese book declares that 29 August 1842, the day of the signing of the Treaty of Nanjing, which ceded Hong Kong to the British, was the "First Day of the Century of National Humiliation" (He Yu 1997, 43). So Hong Kong is on page one of the discourse of National Humiliation. Hong Kong, thus, is not a place or a people but a problem, an obstacle to the natural national narrative of Chinese history. Deng said that this obstacle needed to be removed by any means necessary, even at the risk of destroying Hong Kong itself (Deng Xiaoping 1993; also see Cradock 1999, 172). In echoes of Mao's 1949 founding speech, Jiang Zemin's 1997 handover speech has all the code words in one sentence: "the occupation of Hong Kong was the epitome of the humiliation China suffered in modern history" (Jiang Zemin 1997, 2).

Like the British imaginary, this nationalist discourse sets a strong "romance" tone; it uses the charged moral language of the Opium War, invasion, loss, rape, and atrocity. Rather than tell of British saving Chinese from themselves in Hong Kong by civilizing the Chinese barbarians, National Humiliation lists the barbaric acts of the Western and Japanese imperialism. Thus Hong Kong is figured as a decadent and immoral place, a site of gambling and prostitution. As Deng Xiaoping famously said, after the handover "The horses would keep on racing, the dancers would keep on dancing." Grassroots Chinese views are similar: a brothel on the main street of a provincial capital in central China advertises itself as a "Hong Kong–style" establishment. Indeed, because of their long contact with the barbaric foreigners, Chinese in Hong Kong are not to be trusted either, and thus are divided up in the "return of Hong Kong" discourse into the "pro-British" and the "patriotic" factions (see Zongzheng 1997).

Such public histories (White 1997) of Hong Kong come out of different institutions—not the Institute of Modern History at CASS, but the Chinese Communist Party History Department at Renmin University of China in Beijing. Most leaders of national museums and propaganda departments are graduates of this department, including the head curator at the Revolutionary History Museum in Beijing. The Party History Department (the only one in China, and perhaps the world) set up the discourse of modern Chinese history in the 1950s: the "century" was defined as 1840–1949 to justify "liberation" (see Weigelin-Schewiedrzik 1993, 153–54, 157). In Taiwan, on the other hand, the "century" was generally seen as 1840–1942 to highlight how the Nationalist regime had renegotiated the old "unequal treaties" during World War II. Both sides have the same beginning date though they have different end-dates; this fact shows how Century of National Humiliation discourse defines a Chinese imaginary.

Although that century is supposed to have ended in the 1940s, the discourse is continually redeployed: in the PRC, 1997 is seen as another "final" end point in cleansing National Humiliation, while Taiwan saw itself as humiliated again in 1971, when it was ejected from the United Nations in favor of the Beijing regime. As a Taiwanese *History of National Humiliation* tells us: "Since October 1971 when it entered the UN, the fake Communist bandit government has troubled the world and humiliated our nation" (Liu Zhen 1974, 313).

The Party History Department in Beijing is tied into the political economy of the university, teaching one of the four required courses, Party History (see Weigelin-Schewiedrzik 1993, 157–58, 172). Even so, the prospects of the Party History Department were not good in the early 1990s. Not many people wanted to major in Party History, fearing that they could not obtain good jobs with such a degree; since student numbers were falling, the university told the department to create new courses that would attract students. This crisis occurred in early 1990s, just as interest in Hong Kong was growing. Hence, the department added a Hong Kong, Macao, and Taiwan Studies minor to the Party History Degree. In addition to studying Mao Zedong Thought and Deng Xiaoping Theory, students now take courses in the politics, economics, society, and culture of Hong Kong, Macao, and Taiwan; hence, the Party History Department has a particular way of studying Hong Kong. This is because the main Other is not Britain but the Nationalist Party in Taiwan. Thus the Party History Department studies the unification policy of the Chinese Communist Party and that of the Nationalist Party, rather than the unification policies of the PRC and Taiwan (Interviews 1999; Interviews 2001).

Once Hong Kong was returned to Chinese sovereignty in 1997, the historical problem was solved. Professors in the Party History Department were no longer interested in Hong Kong for research and consulting (though they still teach the courses). Indeed, one official in the PRC's Hong Kong and Macao Affairs Office stated that Hong Kong was only a small part of a huge country: China had other historical problems to address. The problem shifted first to Macao (which reverted to the PRC on 20 December 1999) and finally to Taiwan. Reunification with this "renegade province" has been declared one of the three sacred missions of the twenty-first century, but has no set deadline (see Taiwan Affairs Office 2000).

To summarize, the Century of National Humiliation is a single-ordered linear master narrative characteristic of national history, as opposed to the circular time of dynastic history. This is also a specific kind of national history: a romance of struggle between good and evil, where one side wins totally. In this way, it is like the British narrative of "good" (civilization and law) vs. "evil" (barbarism and corruption), except here it is the colonial foreigners who are barbaric. It proposes a Hong Kong variant of the nativist One China Principle for unification with Taiwan: Chinese people are seen as homogeneous. This narrative has an institutional base that facilitates its reproduction and circulation: in policy papers written for the government, pamphlets restricted to the People's Liberation Army, popular history books, television programs, and national museums. Hence, Hong Kong does not have the starring role in the "return of Hong Kong" narrative; rather, it is part of the supporting cast of a key master narrative of the Chinese revolution. Once Hong Kong was recovered and the problem of temporal disruption was resolved, the linear narrative of Chinese history could take its natural course.

Revolutionary History's Road Trip

Although the master narrative of modern Chinese history is not critically examined on the mainland, it provokes interesting responses when it travels "abroad." In 1999 an abridged version of Beijing's Revolutionary History Museum was exhibited in Hong Kong as "The Rise of Modern China: A Century of Self-Determination." It can help us probe how historiography and museology are part of governance, how they produce and maintain the new boundaries between the mainland and Hong Kong.

The Hong Kong Museum of History closed down in 1997. Its permanent exhibitions, including a rewritten "Story of Hong Kong," reopened at the new site in 2001. In the interim, the space was filled with special exhibitions. Since 1999 was a special year for China—marking the return of Macao, fifty years of the PRC, and the millennium—a curator decided to organize an exhibition about modern Chinese history in cooperation with the Revolutionary History Museum in Beijing. (This is the first exhibition on modern Chinese history in Hong Kong, which shows how the British colonial regime also employed a restrictive cultural policy.) For special exhibitions, the Hong Kong Museum of History usually lets the partner museum organize the show. But since the topic and timing were sensitive, the curator felt he had to rework the Beijing exhibition for audiences in Hong Kong. After much hard negotiation with the Revolutionary History Museum, the curator was pleased that he had maintained the integrity of his exhibition (Ng 1999, Interview).

Although it was compressed into a smaller space, the exhibition in Hong Kong was quite similar to that in Beijing. It was introduced as a way for Hong Kong people to get to know the motherland, and was specifically aimed at school children. But the similarities with Beijing are less interesting than the differences. On the one hand, there are glaring absences that cannot be explained by compression. On the other, while the "Rise of Modern China" was compressed spatially, it was expanded temporally. It has the same beginning as Beijing's exhibition, but a different ending.

In both places, the exhibition of modern Chinese history starts with the Opium War, but in Hong Kong something is missing. As we saw above, Hong Kong itself occupies a pivotal place in modern Chinese history. But it is not mentioned in the first section of the exhibit, "A Nation on the Verge of Subjugation": the Opium War and the Treaty of Nanjing are there, but not Hong Kong. It only surfaces as part of the nationalist historiography where Hong Kong makes positive contributions to the revolution.

The second difference concerns endings. In Beijing the exhibition ends in triumphal mode with Mao declaring the foundation of the PRC: there is a grand painting of Mao reading the famous speech. Thus there is no modern history after the revolution. As noted above, the exhibition has not been changed since 1959, and modern history typically does not go past 1949 in other museums either (see Zhongguo geming bowuguan 1997).

On the other hand, the Hong Kong exhibition continues beyond 1949, first displaying the golden years of the revolution, land reform in the 1950s. Then it records a "tortuous road gone astray," with displays on controversial events like the anti-rightist campaign of 1957, the Great Leap Forward, the Cultural Revolution, before moving on to the reform era. There were some arguments with Beijing over bringing history up to the present; the curators in Beijing would rather that such "mistakes" not be discussed in public. But the most interesting thing about the exhibition is how it ended—not in 1999, either for the end of the twentieth century or for the fiftieth anniversary of the PRC, but in 1997, with the handover of Hong Kong. As Mao's 1949 speech ends the Beijing exhibition, Jiang's 1997 speech ends the Hong Kong exhibition.

Rather than being a different kind of history, this exhibition returns to the logic of the Revolutionary Museum in Beijing. Like "1949" for the PRC, "1997" is the end of history for Hong Kong. Once again, the historical problem is solved, the historical anomaly resolved, and history can rejoin its natural nationalist trajectory. On the way out of the exhibition, viewers walk through a tunnel with photos of happy Chinese and the PRC's achievements over fifty years—but is this a Marxist or a capitalist utopia?

The Hong Kong Clock and the Poetics of Time

This tension between progressive national history and utopian anti-history corresponds to the Hong Kong Clock that graced the symbolic center of China from 1994 to 1997. It was placed in Tian'anmen

Square in front of the Revolutionary History Museum and Traditional History Museum. But it was a peculiar clock. Rather than moving forward to measure progressive elapsed time, it counted back to zero. When zero was reached on 1 July 1997, Hong Kong officially rejoined the motherland, signifying completeness: One China. Once that historical problem was solved, Chinese history could resume its continuous linear progress.

Hence the clock was not involved in time-keeping so much as in reversion to an imperial mode of time-telling. Time-telling involves setting up a timetable as part of a strategy of governance. In addition to telling the Chinese public of the impending return of Hong Kong, the clock also told Hong Kongers of the changes to come. The clock appeared not in 1984, with the signing of the Sino-British Joint Declaration, but in 1994, as a response to Hong Kong Governor Chris Patten's democratization proposals. Thus the clock functioned as a document declaring "The Chinese Government Resumes Exercise of Sovereignty over Hong Kong" (Wu Hung 1997, 349, 337; also see Liu Shuyong 1997a). The clock was so popular in China that it was reset to count down to the reversion of Macao on 20 December 1999. Linear time was being used (as we saw in chapter 4 for Korea) to establish space—the territoriality of "One China."

This political use of time going backward, forward, and in circles added to the millennial fever in Beijing (Xi Mi 1999). There were countdowns to the fiftieth anniversary of the founding of the PRC in newspapers and on television news in 1999. Time was loosened from scientific and rational calculations to become more figurative and rhetorical. Just when does the Century of National Humiliation begin and end? The dominant discourse has it begin in 1840 and end in 1949 (after 109 years). It was common during the lead-up to the Hong Kong handover to see the century as lasting from 1898 to 1997, with the end being the 99-year lease on the New Territories. Or was the end the closing of the twentieth century, as in the Hong Kong Museum of History exhibition and some popular histories of National Humiliation? (He Yu 1999).

From National History to Family Harmony

This poetics of time provides a critical gap in the linear modernist history narrative. As mentioned, the Hong Kong handover marked the first time that a colony returning to the imperial center was more advanced than that center (Abbas 1997a, 3). Hong Kong was figured as an obstacle to history before 1997, but since the handover Hong Kong has been reframed from history to harmony, and from nation-state to civilization-state to family-nation. Hong Kong is often represented in both the mainland and Hong Kong as a lost child. The official PRC slogan was "Welcome Hong Kong back into the bosom of the motherland." Thus, though Hong Kong was not necessarily returning to the Chinese empire, it certainly was returning to the Chinese patriarchy. Patriarchy is a system that values (older) generations as well as (the male) gender (Callahan 2002b). The central government and Chinese civilization are the parents, while Hong Kong is the child (see Yahuda 1996, 139). Thus the language of a generation gap is used rather than that of a cultural or economic gap.

Family rhetoric is part of the traditional Chinese social grammar of harmony. As noted in chapters 2 and 3, the Chinese empire employed harmonious family metaphors to justify its hierarchical tributary relations; chapters 1 and 4 showed how the family is a model of governmentality in Confucian capitalism as well. Recent South Korean governments have also "use[d] familial or Confucian terms" to criticize "students as irresponsible children" (Grinker 2000, 3). For Hong Kong, China did not allow the territory to represent itself in the negotiations between Britain and PRC, for Hong Kong was seen as resembling a child who needed to be represented for its own good. Since the handover, the chief executive of Hong Kong, Tung Chee Hwa, often talks about Hong Kongnese as children; his critics are like unruly teenagers. During the Right of Abode controversy in 1999, a pro-China elite in Hong Kong compared Hong Kong's chief justice to "a little boy who had not asked his mother, China, for permission before making an improper decision" (Ching, Frank 1999f, 262). In 2000, Jiang Zemin criticized Hong Kong journalists for being childish, saying they were not well-prepared and they lacked professionalism (BBC/SWB 28 October 2000).

The grammar of a harmonious family thus is used for political order. Some scholars have noted the parallels between the Dengist formula "one country, two systems" and the Confucian formula "harmony with difference." Confucius tells us, "The exemplary person harmonizes with others, but does not necessarily agree with them; the small person agrees with others, but is not harmonious with them" (Confucius 1979, 13/23). Agreeing with people means that you are the same with them, here uncritically the same. The opposite of harmony is not chaos, but uniformity and homogeneity. In the Chinese vocabulary this is often described as "hegemonic"— *bawang*.

Hegemony is not a neutral or progressive term in either classical or modern Chinese. Rather than looking to positive Gramscian notions of hegemony, we can better translate *bawang* as tyranny, describing illegitimate and immoral rule. As the ancient philosopher Mencius says:

> One who uses force while speaking of benevolence will become a hegemon, but to do so he must first be the ruler of a state of considerable size. One who puts benevolence into effect through the transforming influence of morality will become a sovereign king, and his success will not depend on the size of his kingdom. (*Mencius* 1970, 2A/3)

"Hegemony" has been used in the past few decades by the PRC to criticize "world domination" first by the Soviet Union and now by the United States (Liang Shoude 1996, 300; Zheng, Yongnian 1999). China often declares that, even when it becomes an economically developed world power, it will never be a *hegemon*.

Harmony, on the other hand, allows us to preserve difference in our ethical relations with Otherness. It appeals to aesthetic order rather than logical order (Hall and Ames 1987, 165ff). Harmony is not a concept for the reduction and definition of a single-ordered discourse; rather, it involves a process of negotiating elements so that they work in a happy multiplicity: "Harmony is certainly fruitful, whereas sameness is barren. . . . A single note is not pleasing to the ear; a single object is not rich in design; a single flavor is not satisfying to the palate; a single opinion about things does not make a conversation" (*Guoyu* 1978, SPTK 16/Zhengyu). The *Zhuangzi* describes such a politics of multiplicity that values difference:

> Collective communities bring together one hundred people in ten families to constitute a tradition. Their tradition constitutes their similarities by combining their differences; it constitutes their differences by scattering their similarities. . . . Each person pursues different goals: having what is deviant, they have what is correct. (*Zhuangzi* 1985, 72/25/59)

Although theirs is not the official view, a number of well-placed scholars and public intellectuals in mainland China and Hong Kong appeal to the notion of "harmony with difference" to explain "one country, two systems" (Li Changdao 1999; Wan Lifeng 2000; Luo Chenglie 1997; Tang Weilun 1997; Li Tianchen 1997; Tong Yun Kai 1999). In this way, Hong Kong can continue to follow its own way while being a part of China, being both patriotic and Confucian in a socialist state. Indeed, Tang argues that "one country, two systems" operates according to the grammar of yin and yang, which are opposites but not completely separate. They are complementary: in the midst of yin there is yang, and vice versa.

Likewise, the socialist and capitalist systems of mainland China and Hong Kong were already related long before the handover; without reform and opening in the mainland, Hong Kong would not have prospered. Without Hong Kong's investment, the mainland economy also would not have developed so quickly. Tang predicted that, after the return in 1997, the mainland and Hong Kong would work together even more (Tang Weilun 1997, 529). The formula is not solely for Beijing–Hong Kong relations, but for world politics in general: "On the increasingly pluralist international stage, we need Confucius's 'harmony without uniformity' to address the cultural contradictions presented by different countries" (Tang Weilun 1997, 529; Liang Shoude 1996, 305; Tong Yun Kai 1999, 6). Liu most directly uses the "harmony without uniformity" formula to argue that it constitutes an alternative to the Westphalian world order (Liu Zhiguang 1992, 224–29). Key Chinese intellectuals such as Fei Xiaotong agree that "harmony with difference" is necessary to quell international violence in the era of globalization (Fei Xiaotong 2001, 16).

Here, Chinese intellectuals see reunification in terms of a continuing encounter with difference. But "harmony" has its own politics. Traditionally, harmony was the logic of empire building: "Harmony is the workable way of the empire" (*Zhongyong*, ch. 1, in de Bary 1960, 119). Other key passages relate it to the expansionism that Mencius criticized as hegemonic: "Your state is too small and is inadequate to have the full complement of the necessary ingredients [for harmony]. It is only once you are the Emperor that you would have the full complement" (*Lüshi chunqiu* 1996, 210). The *Guoyu* passage cited above puts this into the context of empire: "A situation like this has the greatest degree of harmony. Why is this?

The former [sage] kings took their wives from different clans, and sought tribute from outlying regions."

Hence harmony is not metaphysical but very material; the border between harmony and hegemony is not clear at all because harmony is contextual, and is judged from a point of view. Beijing often sounds as if it is including Hong Kong as one element in its national harmony. With this Beijing-centric ordering, the narrative switches from nativism to conversion, re-employing a vocabulary from Chinese civilization and empire. People in Hong Kong reverse this Beijing-centric logic to see their "periphery" as the center in judging harmony (Tu Weiming 1994a). Rather than the socialist PRC infiltrating Hong Kong, the situation is that some people in Hong Kong are trying to convert the mainland with Confucianism and capitalism (Tong Yun Kai 1999; Tang Weilun 1997, 525; Mathews 1997). In this figuration, Hong Kong becomes the capital of Greater China (Yahuda 1995).

HONG KONG STORIES

The production of the "Rise of Modern China" exhibition at the Hong Kong Museum of History demonstrates how Hong Kong and Beijing negotiate issues of identity in semi-official space. But there are many other spaces of encounter, some not so obvious. Chan Goh's widely acclaimed film *Made in Hong Kong* (1997) addresses the relation between Hong Kong and the mainland in more figurative ways. Chan's film does not talk about Beijing–Hong Kong relations directly but metaphorically—neither the British nor the Chinese regime is mentioned.

The title is telling: "Made in Hong Kong" is not just local but global. It is the caption stamped on billions of commodities distributed all over the world. It refers to the success story of Hong Kong as a commercial power. But in the 1990s, industry went north into mainland China as part of the regionalization of the Hong Kong economy in Greater China (Rowley and Lewis 1996; Ash and Kueh 1995; Ngo 1999). Now Hong Kong is defined by a service economy, moving from industrial capitalism to transnational and finance capitalism. Indeed, the film is also a story about finance capitalism. But rather than in high finance, the action takes place in low finance. The main character, Autumn Moon, is a small-time hood who spends his days as a freelance enforcer collecting debts for Big Brother Wing, a loan shark in the Triads.

In following the comical adventures of Moon's everyday life, *Made in Hong Kong* gives a stunning critique of the regimes of law and family, the two main supports for the Hong Kong success story. The film begins with Moon telling how he has dropped out of school but does not want to join the Triads. Like Hong Kong in the 1990s, he was between two hegemonic regimes. Along the way, Moon befriends a retarded boy, Sylvester, who is repeatedly beaten up by the poster boys of Confucian capitalism, uniformed high school students. Through their loan sharking, the two meet the third main character, Ping, a pretty girl who has kidney disease. These three outsiders come together to track down the story of why a good middle-class girl, Susan, has committed suicide.

In the course of the film, each of these characters' families breaks down. At the beginning, we are shown how even a model family is fragile: Susan abandons her caring parents by jumping off a building. Moon is abandoned first by his father, then by his mother. Ping's father has likewise gone, leaving her and her mother with a heavy debt to the loan shark. Sylvester's parents deny even knowing him. The reaction of such abandoned children is often the Confucian hyper-crime of patricide: as Moon is en route to kill his father, he witnesses a school boy chop up his own incestuous father in a public toilet. Even the imagined family of the mafia with its law-like codes breaks down: Moon kills his boss Wing at the end of the film. Hence, like family, law is a dysfunctional idea. With all the gangland violence, the famous Hong Kong police rarely appear in the story. The film ends with a voiceover of People's Radio (Hong Kong) broadcasting Chairman Mao's speech about the "energy of youth" saving the nation.

As a curious combination of genres that tests the limits of gangster comedy and teen adventure film, *Made in Hong Kong* problematizes both the British discourse of law-abiding capitalist Hong Kong and the Chinese discourse of nation-family. Both British and Chinese parents are shown to be irresponsible toward the children of Hong Kong. The three main characters have to negotiate their own harmony based on friendship, bringing together their Otherness to form a local self, as we saw in the *Zhuangzi* passage cited above.

Made in Hong Kong serves as an example of the discursive politics of a Hong Kong imaginary that is not guided so much by the official, stable, and authoritative master narratives of law or history as by the many stories, the various contradictory narratives, of the people who look to variations of nativism, conquest, conversion, and diaspora. Many note that, while "outsiders use grand narratives to describe Hong Kong," natively produced "Hong Kong epics" do not exist (Ip Iam-Chong 1998, 46, 48; Abbas 1997b, 303; Cheung, Martha 1998, ix). Although some see this lack of "national identity," "national history," and epic film as a problematic mark of marginality, others use the fact to refigure Hong Kong's position in transnational identity politics (Ip Iam-Chong 1998, 48; Man and Lo 1998, 4–5).

In describing popular resistance to a Hong Kong government policy (see below), one scholar notes a shift from the master narratives to the decentered resistance of stories: "More and more, we like to tell stories, including other people's stories, our own stories, big stories, and small stories. I don't know if this is what you call a 'cultural movement,' but it seems to be a 'cultural resistance'" (Pun Ngai 1999, 116). Thus, rather than as a response to the hegemony of law, history, and family with a counterhegemony, the Hong Kong imaginary is better understood as a weaving together of these stories in a contingent harmony. This harmonizing does not discard law, history, or family; they are important ingredients in the Hong Kong harmony, but none is hegemonic.

Some write a counter-history for a distinct Hong Kong identity, to carve out a distinct "Hong Kong way of life" separate from the master narratives of Chinese civilization represented by the PRC or Taiwan (Feng Renzhao 1998; Luk Hung-Kay 1998).[9] They state that Hong Kong is not a badge of humiliation: "We truly do not have to bear the cross of National Humiliation created by an earlier generation. In fact, historically, neither the KMT [Nationalist] nor the Communist regime had ever discharged its obligation to the Hong Kong people" (Feng Renzhao 1998, 39). This response to Chinese nationalism employs Hong Kong nativism. It is common for Hong Kong historians to use archaeological digs to prove the region's six thousand years of history both to problematize the British discourse of a "barren island" and to upstage the mainland's five thousand years of civilization. They thus aim to transform Hong Kong from an *object* of history into a subject, to give Hong Kong itself the starring role in Hong Kong Studies. Even though the best way to respond to the British regime was through engaging the master narrative of law, this group of scholars has engaged China's narrative of history with history. But Hong Kong's nativism is not so strong as it is on the mainland or in Taiwan or South Korea.

Rather than directly engaging the macro-narrative of history, others have been looking to the numerous micro-narratives. They switch from the professional historians' kingly epics to figure history as an accumulation of local and oral histories/herstories (Luk Hung-Kay 1998, 14; Leung, P. K. 1998, 3). Such stories often play off from official texts. Indeed, the "Hong Kong Story" itself is an industry, producing dozens of books, television series, and so on.

The Hong Kong story started out as the tale of the success of British imperialism, and was reasserted in 1997 (Luff 1959; Courtauld et al. 1997). It also was used by the Chinese media to give popular appeal to the "return of Hong Kong" narrative (Central Television Overseas Center 1998; Li and Hu 1997; Ma, Eric 1999). In Hong Kong itself, "Hong Kong Story" was the name of the permanent exhibition in the old Hong Kong Museum of History—an exhibition that was rewritten, but not renamed, for the museum's reopening in 2001. A popular author, Xiao Si, plays with the original "Hong Kong Story" exhibition in her book *Hong Kong Stories*. Commenting on a visit to the exhibition, she is dissatisfied with the orderly "Hong Kong Story." Although not false, Xiao Si declares, "It's not true enough." To get a fuller sense of Hong Kong, Xiao Si moves from the official history to her own memories, from the sterile state institution to a neighborhood Chinese pharmacy with its catalog of colors, sounds, and scents. By moving from history to stories, Xiao Si moves from a scientific search for clarity to celebrate the ambiguity, the haziness of Hong Kong identity (Xiao Si 1998, 59).[10]

> I often say to friends, Hong Kong is a hazy city; those of us who were born-and-raised here also have this kind of hazy nature. It is not easy to understand Hong Kongers, because we ourselves have no way to explain ourselves clearly. Born in this place, raised in this place, blood and guts mixed together, we are stapled together with Hong Kong in a tangle of love and hate. To her [Hong Kong], we are sometimes very arrogant, sometimes very humble. This contradiction is tangled into an unresolvable knot. (Xiao Si 1998, 3–4)

While the PRC uses history to "resolve" the Hong Kong problem, Xiao Si sees the situation as unresolvable. To give a sense of Hong Kong and Hong Kongers, Xiao Si tells stories—layer upon layer of stories, stacked up like the skyscrapers and hills in the cityscape (Xiao Si 1998, 3, 59). These stories of everyday life do not ultimately settle on a master narrative to define identity as citizenship; rather, they work together in a fluid harmony (also see Leung, P. K. 1998).

Often the Hong Kong story is involved in farcical history, which has the effect of undermining national history. For example, in 1997 a group of artists fabricated their own ancient history of Hong Kong in an exhibition called "The Prehistoric Hong Kong Museum" (Gao Minglu 1998, 210; Clarke 1998, 177). Likewise, in *The Atlas: Archeology of an Imaginary City,* Cheung uses imagined maps to retell a Hong Kong story. He thus twists the language of cartography, which characterizes both the discourses of the British Empire and National Humiliation, to spin absurd yarns. "Possession Street" commemorates the British landing in 1840 to occupy Hong Kong, and Cheung tells us:

> The British probably did well to steer clear of this place for the word "possession," besides meaning ownership and control, also refers to the condition of being under the control of an evil spirit, or to madness. . . . Professor S. Clark, who taught at the History Department of the University of Hong Kong before the Second World War . . . suggested changing the name to "Exorcism Street" to restore rightful order of things. In Chinese, "exorcism" translates as *gon gwei,* which means "to chase away ghosts, evil spirits, and foreign devils." (Cheung, Dung Kai 1998a, 42)

Other stories take the Chinese classics and rewrite them both with and without reference to Hong Kong (Cheung, Dung Kai 1998b; Hung, Eva 1999; Clarke 1998, 178). For example, one tale appeals to both Chinese civilization and the rule of law; the honorable Judge Bao, a character in Chinese mythology who is popular throughout Greater China via a Hong Kong television series, is transformed into a buffoon. Judge Bao is called into a custody battle to judge who is the proper mother. But he is fooled because he would not listen to the child: "Oh dear, Judge Bao, Judge Bao, I thought you were supposed to be such a clever and able scholar, but actually you are a fake and a phony, you're really up the creek. . . . It no longer matters who is my true mother. What really matters is the right to choose" (Xi Xi 1997, 103, 106). As with the Hong Kong populace, the issues concerned not choosing the natural master so much as "choice" itself. This use of voiceless and abandoned children to represent Hong Kong is a common theme in the film and literature of the period leading up to the handover (see Xi Xi 1998).

Before 1997, Hong Kong stories addressed anxiety, uncertainty, and powerlessness, the black hole at the end of empire. But, in fact, 1 July 1997 came and went; there was much hoopla, but very little change in day-to-day life. Indeed, the Basic Law was written for the curious situation of a transition without change, a transition that stressed continuity (Ghai 1998, 9). The code words for Hong Kong continue to be "stability and prosperity." The People's Liberation Army (PLA) entered Hong Kong with a flourish for the mainland audience, but quickly disappeared to its barracks on Stone Cutter's Island.

Hong Kong's high degree of autonomy according to "one country, two systems" seems to be working; Beijing has not interfered with Hong Kong after all (Chow and Fan 1999a, xxvii, xxxvi). Many people in Hong Kong are actually pleased with the mainland discourse of the "return of Hong Kong," because it meant that, after the "history problem" was solved, Beijing would no longer care about Hong Kong; the Hong Kongers would be left alone.

This stability is certainly good for the Hong Kong people, but many have pointed out that it was bad for Hong Kong culture. Interesting films, for example, were produced between the 1984 Joint Declaration and the handover in 1997. Part of this cultural production stemmed from a need to create and justify the Hong Kong "way of life" referred to in the Joint Declaration and the Basic Law: "'cultural identity' is the first line of defense against total political absorption" (Abbas 1997a, 142; Man and Lo 1998, 3–4). The tension and uncertainty in *Made in Hong Kong* produced vibrant culture. But with the smooth transition, this energy is gone—with disastrous consequences to the film industry (Abbas 1999, Interview; Pun Ngai 1999, Interview). "Hong Kong" was seen as a historical problem by Beijing that was resolved in 1997. But in Hong Kong, "1997" was seen as a problem, one that dissolved the Hong Kong identity project.

Cultural Security and the Right of Abode

To put it another way, once the historical problem was solved, a new set of problems quickly appeared. The return of Hong Kong to China was commonly viewed as the end of empire and the beginning of the "Pacific Century." But this century lasted only one day: the economic crisis that would soon envelop East Asia began the very next day in Bangkok, on 2 July 1997. The Hong Kong identity crisis quickly switched to an economic crisis. Rather than being concerned with "Will China try to control Hong Kong?" people were concerned about the general issues of globalization and localization and their immediate effect on personal socioeconomics (Abbas 1999, Interview; Pun Ngai 1999, Interview).

This configuration of power beyond "freedom" and "autonomy" in the Hong Kong/China relation raises a different set of issues— employment and family—and different forms of resistance—including oral history that gathers the stories of elderly, women, and workers for specific political purposes (Pun Ngai 1999, Interview). These issues were paramount in the first major challenge to the Central Government–Hong Kong relation; "when the two systems interact with each other, when should 'two systems' end and 'one country' begin[?]" (Chan, Johannes 2000, 61). The controversy of the Right of Abode in 1999 addressed issues of security, identity, borders, and transnational relations on a visceral level; it is a graphic example of the tension between territorial sovereignty and popular sovereignty.

It was often portrayed as a fight between David and Goliath, with the National People's Congress (NPC) in Beijing forcing its views on the principled judges of Hong Kong's Court of Final Appeal (CFA). But the controversy was not so simple, and actually it shows how anxieties have been reversed: before 1997, Hong Kong worried about Chinese intervention. But with the Right of Abode question, the Hong Kong Special Administrative Region (HKSAR) government begged a less than enthusiastic NPC to intervene to interpret the Basic Law, thus setting a precedent for Chinese intervention.

The issue concerned the definitions of "Hong Kongers" and "children." The controversy in 1999 thus is an example of a hands-on notion of how the frontiers of self and Other are negotiated in Hong Kong identity politics. The matter arose not in the abstract, but with specific relation to mainland China. Did children born on the mainland to Hong Kong parents have the Right of Abode in Hong Kong: are they Hong Kongers or mainlanders, citizens or immigrants, legal or illegal, moral or immoral? Is being a Hong Konger a right to be passed down in families, or is it a privilege to be determined according to social policy? Are mainlanders compatriots or competitors? (Pun Ngai 1999, 119).

Under the British colonial regime, children born on the mainland to Hong Kong parents were not automatically Hong Kong residents. Timing was important; if their parents became permanent residents of Hong Kong after the children were born, the children did not have automatic residence but had to apply as immigrants to enter Hong Kong. Children born out of wedlock also had to apply as immigrants. With the return of Hong Kong to Chinese sovereignty, the residency question was unclear under the Basic Law. A bill passed on 10 July 1997 stated that these children needed to obtain an exit permit from the PRC, like any other emigrant ("Legislative Council House Committees [Papers]" 2000). The technicalities of the rules and regulations are very confusing, combining the worst of British and Chinese bureaucratic culture (Lee, Jane 1997).[11]

Although both Hong Kong and mainland China were laboring to draw the clear distinctions that sovereignty demands—the Basic Law serves to separate Hong Kong from China (Ghai 1998)—the people on both sides of the border were mixing. This is part of the political economy of Greater China, where Hong Kong's economic success depends on a flow of capital and populations across borders (Hamilton 1999). Such a transnational economy took advantage of the Deng regime's economic reforms. But the statistics produced during the Right of Abode controversy show that, even before 1978 when China was "closed" to international relations, there were significant international affairs with Hong Kong, producing hundreds of thousands of children (Ching, Frank 1999c).

This transnational economy has specific class and gender features. It involves a flow of working-age men in both directions; many working-class mainland men go to Hong Kong for menial labor, while fewer middle-class Hong Kong men go to the mainland to manage factories. The mainland men come to Hong Kong alone because they cannot afford to bring their families—or, when they get married, they have to return to the mainland to find a suitable spouse because of the gendered population imbalance (Siu Yat-ming 1999). Because of migration restrictions under the colonial regime, most of the families had to stay long-term on the mainland. The Hong Kong political economy has taken advantage of the work of these "new immigrants." They were the key industrial laborers in the 1970s and 1980s, and now take work that born-and-raised Hong Kongers do not want, the "3Ds"—dirty, dangerous, and difficult jobs. Although they are an important part of Hong Kong's economic success, as second-class citizens they enjoy few of the benefits of Hong Kong society (Leung Hon-chu 1999).

Thus the Right of Abode controversy addresses not just a metaphor of family—as in the mainland's discourse of the return to the motherland and the Hong Kong counterdiscourse of abandoned children—but the actual workings of families across borders. Even though Hong Kong has returned to Chinese sovereignty, the borders still work as barriers. In addition to there being one country, two systems, there is a graduated sovereignty of one country, many borders (see Ong, Aihwa 1999, 214–29). Or as the protesters put it: "one country, two families separated by borders."

As the above description suggests, there were two sets of issues raised by the Right of Abode controversy: legal and social. The controversy itself erupted with the Court of Final Appeal's 29 January 1999 ruling that granted the Right of Abode to the new immigrants. This broad view of the law struck down the restrictions on timing and marriage, to state simply that children of Hong Kong residents enjoyed the Right of Abode. This decision was initially welcomed in Hong Kong by elites in government, political parties, and business (in Chan, Fu and Ghai 2000: 219–412).[12] The acting chief executive stated that "yesterday's ruling demonstrates that the rule of law is alive and well in Hong Kong" (in Chan, Fu, and Ghai 2000, 219).

Along with this celebration of the rule of law, there was a distinct Othering of mainland China's "Leninist" political use of law: "We in Hong Kong are given to some exaggeration of the virtues, and the prevalence, of the rule of law here, but as compared with practices on the mainland, the contrast is indeed striking" (Ghai 2000, 5). Thus "one country, two systems" entails not just a separation of two social systems, capitalist and socialist, but a separation of two legal systems (Ghai 2000, x). Although the elite groups were concerned about the impact of the new immigrants on social services, they were more impressed by how the CFA had upheld the sanctity of the law. The task, then, was the social issue of how the HKSAR government would implement the ruling.

Indeed, soon after the ruling, the legal victory was turned into a social problem. Rather than implementing the CFA ruling, Tung

Chee Hwa challenged the court's "interpretation." Part of Tung's change of heart can be explained as stemming from "pressure from the mainland."[13] But the main issue was whether Hong Kong could accommodate a rush of thousands of new immigrants. So the discourse first turned "children" from immigrants to residents, then turned them back into immigrants. Although some groups still supported the rule of law, and rights for new residents, public discussion was characterized by the rise of a particular "Yellow Peril." This "China threat" of millions of mainlanders overwhelming Hong Kong's job market and social services soon captivated both elite and public opinion. One judge said that the ruling risked "sinking Hong Kong" (SCMP 31 March 1999). Thus, rather than solve the social problem of accommodating the new residents, the HKSAR government decided to turn it back into a legal problem, and to ask the Standing Committee of the NPC in Beijing to interpret the CFA ruling in terms of the Basic Law.

The HKSAR government was able to make this radical move because it manufactured public opinion of a "mainland China threat" of new residents. It publicized survey research that suggested that 1.67 million people would enter Hong Kong under the CFA's ruling (see Chan, Fu, and Ghai 2000, 265–87). The research estimated a budgetary impact of HK$710 billion over ten years (while Hong Kong's total 1998–99 budget was HK$55 billion). This survey was roundly criticized on methodological grounds; the government also did not release another survey that calculated how many eligible people would actually come to Hong Kong (Leung Hon-chu 1999a, 7; Chan, Fu, and Ghai 2000, 291–92, 296; Ching, Frank 1999a; Ching, Frank 1999c). Indeed, previous surveys on the Right of Abode question—from the same government department—yielded far fewer eligible people. Thus the HKSAR government was criticized by human rights groups for inflating the numbers and exaggerating their impact: "All of this suggests that the government is manipulating the figures in order to instill in the public the perception that there is a huge and insoluble problem and that the only possible solution is to have the CFA judgment effectively overturned" (in Chan, Fu, and Ghai 2000, 296). Public opinion quickly responded—for understandable reasons—to this scaremongering (Pun Ngai 1999, 121). Surveys showed a large majority of Hong Kongers wanted to solve the problem legally, not socially—even though that meant going to Beijing, and thus sacrificing the sanctity of Hong Kong law.

This shift from legal to social, and back to legal again, is not just a legal-constitutional or a political-economic calculation but an issue of identity politics. While the CFA's judgment relied on Othering the PRC's "Leninist" legal system and institutions, the HKSAR government's response relied on Othering mainlanders as people. They were commonly portrayed as "burdens" on social services rather than productive members of society. Some groups claimed that the survey figures and the political-economic calculations were selectively exaggerated to discriminate against mainlanders. Hong Kong is an immigrant society and thus has made specific stereotypes to police identity boundaries: new vs. old immigrants. This is part of a long tradition of constructing the Hong Kong self against a mainland Other according to familiar categories: urban/rural, modern/backward, civilized/barbaric, rich/poor, and so on. The guiding Other in this discourse is the "new immigrant," the country bumpkin from the mainland who threatens the riches of Hong Kong's "old immigrants." As Leung explains:

> Many people say Hong Kong is an "immigrant society." But in the heart of most Hong Kongers, those who immigrated to Hong Kong in the 1940s, '50s and '60s are "old immigrants" and those who came after 1970 are "new immigrants," and they are not the same "kind" of people. "Old immigrants" are economic leaders, and part of the Hong Kong story, while "new immigrants" are bumpkins and barbarians who are Hong Kong's "burden"! (Leung Hon-chu 1999a, 8–9)

This sorting of immigrants into old and new is not an innovation from the late 1990s. It dates from the 1970s, when the newly prosperous Hong Kongers needed to differentiate themselves from their poorer cousins to the north to preserve their recent economic gains (Ma, Eric 1999, 69). This can be seen graphically in a popular 1980s television serial, *The Good, the Bad, and the Ugly*, which portrayed the brother from the mainland as not just as a bumpkin but a "naturally" violent criminal (Ma, Eric 1999, 64–65, 80). In this way, "The grievances of the mainlanders seldom catch the attention of the mainstream media because categorization blinds the Hongkongers to their own 'barbarity' to their fellow countrymen" (Ma, Eric 1999, 95).

Long after the controversy was over, the anti-mainlander "racism" that it encouraged—complete with police brutality—continued to be a problem in Hong Kong (Ching, Frank 2000a, 30). In fact, there is not much difference demographically between old and new immigrants (Ching, Frank 1999c; Ma, Eric 1999, 62). However, these "new immigrants" were not seen as Chinese compatriots, joined to the territory through family ties, so much as the opposite of people born and raised in Hong Kong.[14]

This class/gender distinction is further clarified when the emigrants in the opposite direction are considered. One response of middle- and upper-class Hong Kongers to the 1984 Joint Declaration, coupled with restrictions on Right of Abode in Britain, was to emigrate to safe havens in Australia, Canada, and (to a lesser extent) the United States. But these immigrants did not stay away long. Typically, they were abroad long enough to acquire a passport, and then would return to Hong Kong to continue making money (or, again in a gendered political economy, the "women and children" stayed abroad while the men returned to Hong Kong for economic reasons) (Ong, Aihwa 1999, 127–29; Wong Siu-Lin 1999, 145–46).

These returnees amount to a significant number: according to one survey, 700,000 people or 12 percent of Hong Kong's residents fit into this category; another gives the much higher figure of 30 percent (Lee 1997, 261; Wong Siu-Lin 1999, 145). If the same methodology used for the mainland constituency were employed (including projections of the second and third generation of potential residents), the final tally would be over 1.67 million people. Under the Basic Law, the people who had left Hong Kong and acquired foreign passports were no longer entitled to the Right of Abode (Lee, Jane 1997, 257); however, neither the Central Government in Beijing nor the HKSAR government has pursued these "illegals." Indeed, the NPC Standing Committee came to a different conclusion for these newer immigrants: "the statements of the NPC's standing committee . . . encouraged Hong Kong people to regard nationality as a matter of traveling convenience rather than a matter of national identity and political allegiance" (Lee, Jane 1997, 265).

Like the diasporic Chinese (described in chapter 2), these "Hong Kong" populations have an instrumental use of political identity: "Hong Kong migrants are keen collectors of passports and nationalities" (Wong Siu-Lun 1999, 137; Ong, Aihwa 1999, 1–2; Ching,

Frank 1999f, 243–47). Their cosmopolitanism functions in the service more of capital accumulation than of global democracy. The Chinese government supports this diasporic identity—again, for economic reasons—even though, as a "special style of overseas Chinese capitalism that is not dependent on any particular political order," such identity questions the discourse of national unity (Wong Siu-Lun 1999, 137).

Certain groups tried to fight the rising tides of public opinion against granting the Right of Abode that were bolstered by the rational discourses of law and social science, and fought via social movements and oral history (Leung Hon-chu 1999a, 1–2). The aim was to turn the displaced people from frightening statistics back into families made up of fellow human beings divided by bureaucracy (see Leung and Lam 1999, 66–102). As one father said: "My need is for my son to come home. All his relatives are in Hong Kong, and Hong Kong is his home. I spilled blood for Hong Kong, why can't my son come home?" (Leung Hon-chu 1999b, 126). The image of "family" was so powerful that the government felt the need to respond (Leung Hon-chu 1999a, 4–11; see Chan, Fu, and Ghai 2000, 300). Tung Chee Hwa began a press conference by noting, "All of us would like to see a family reunion" (in Chan, Fu, and Ghai 2000, 305).

In the end, the HKSAR government asked the National People's Congress to reinterpret the CFA ruling. The Standing Committee of the NPC's 26 June 1999 ruling severely restricted the Right of Abode in Hong Kong—and set the precedent for Beijing having the final say in Hong Kong justice (see Chan, Fu, and Ghai 2000, 478–86). Although this looks like Beijing compromising Hong Kong's autonomy, the Beijing leadership was also unhappy with the result. The leaders wanted Hong Kong to solve its own problems (see Xiao Weiyun 2000, 54; Chan, Fu, and Ghai, 305, 474–77; Ching, Frank 1999d; Interviews 1999). Frank Ching's prediction was spot-on: "The Court of Final Appeal will be undermined, China will be accused of interfering in Hong Kong's affairs, and the HKSAR government will be criticized for not defending judicial independence" (Ching, Frank 1999b).

The case was closed on 3 December 1999, when the CFA accepted the Standing Committee of the NPC's interpretation. Indeed, many drew the obvious conclusion that Hong Kong's sacred rule of law was compromised by this precedent. The social reaction included a mass protest that had to be dissolved by two hundred riot police. But the decision had more significant results. It was an interpretation of an interpretation of an interpretation: the bedrock of law was cast adrift, floating like the rest of Hong Kong. Once again, the quantitative methodology of surveys and law evaporated into qualitative judgments of values (Ghai 2000, iii). The relation of self and Other, one country and two systems, is either a negotiated harmony or an imposed hegemony.

As argued above, the Right of Abode controversy involved significant political reversals. The mainland relies heavily on Family metaphors to knit Hong Kong together with the rest of the PRC into One China, yet the NPC ruling did not reunite the country so much as split apart thousands of families. Although the PRC loudly proclaims its sovereignty over Hong Kong and encourages transnational socioeconomic flows in Greater China, this decision shows how the politics of "one country, two systems" is involved in dual containment. The Basic Law was written to contain Hong Kong, to separate the mainland from Hong Kong, as well as to contain mainland China from Hong Kong. As Deng Xiaoping said, Hong Kong and the mainland should be as separate as water in a well and water in a river.

Although the threat of China intervening in Hong Kong affairs was the main concern of Hong Kongers, it was the chief executive of Hong Kong who—with popular support—went to Beijing to beg an unwilling NPC to intervene. Thus, the HKSAR government was not defending the rule of law as a principle, but trading it for the convenience of social policy. Although it is common to see the "rule of law" as master narrative of the Hong Kong way of life, this controversy shows that the people themselves are more interested in the microeconomics of their lifestyle. And lastly, in this story, Hong Kong people are transformed, via an odd diasporic nativism, from victims into victimizers: their cosmopolitanism uses "racial" grounds to exclude their closest relatives and neighbors (Ching, Frank 2000a, 30).

CONCLUSION

This chapter has questioned the guiding binaries—East/West, China/Britain, parent/child, oppressor/victim—that cultural critics in Hong Kong have derided as guiding "conceptually misleading, academically futile, and socially oppressive identity 'constructs'" (Man and Lo

1998, 4). Although analyzing the discourse in terms of "British" and "Chinese" imaginaries risks reproducing these binaries, I have also highlighted how certain texts—the work of the CASS Hong Kong History Project and Yahuda's *Hong Kong: China's Challenge*—serve to critically examine such mainstream views. By deconstructing the master narratives of law, history, and family in British and Chinese discourse, I have aimed to leave space for the complicated dynamics of imagination and identity that produce Hong Kong.

Hong Kong is significant beyond the frontier of the Shenzhen River that divides it from the mainland. The strange circumstances of the handover, and the empirical problems these circumstances raised, served to foster theoretical innovation. The dynamics of Hong Kong as a post/imperial node can tell us much about the cultural economy of Greater China and global capitalism. Hong Kong also has a starring role in the narrative of the Century of National Humiliation. This narrative can tell us much about Chinese engagements with Otherness and modernity, both within and outside of China, especially given the important institutional links National Humiliation has that facilitate its reproduction and circulation.

But, as the last section showed, Hong Kong is more than a metaphor to describe something else, leading us away from the residents of the HKSAR (see Park, You-me 1996). It is important to resist the master narratives of Hong Kong, but not so as to "get it right" and define a new and proper Hong Kong identity: Hong Kong as the capital of Greater China, the center rather than the periphery, or the base of Confucian missionary activity for the mainland. Rather, the analysis must switch from the hegemony of master narratives to the recounting of stories to see how harmony produces "Hong Kong." In addition to appealing to film and fiction, with their stories of alienation and ambiguity, the chapter has more directly addressed the Hong Kong way of life through the issues of everyday life such as the Right of Abode.

Rather than providing an answer, harmony produces a new set of questions. It can be used to understand the negotiations taking place in the imaginaries in each of the three spaces, for each harmony involves a different set of elements and a different social grammar. The first harmonizing takes place in the British imaginary that sees Hong Kong as the harmony of East and West. Images like the centaur, which combines the familiar bodies of horse and man, are used to represent this new hybrid geobody (see Cheung, Dung Kai 1998b, 202). The best of the East and the West, the best of tradition and modernity, have been synthesized in Hong Kong to form social practices like Confucian capitalism and cosmopolitan capitalism (Hamilton 1999). While Max Weber and modernization theory saw a disjuncture between Confucianism and capitalism, the East-West harmony points to their synergy. This harmonizing actually entails reinforcing the notion that East and West are coherent, separate, and fundamentally different. Thus, "two systems" are more important than "one country" in this hegemony of dualisms.

The harmony of the Chinese nation-family works by bringing Hong Kong into the family as an important, albeit subordinate, part. This encounter works along the lines of the Chinese imperial harmony that integrates the unique particulars into a multicoded whole. An example of this hierarchical harmony can be seen in a small tourist guide, *Our Backyard: Hong Kong*. The guide is part of a series that describes the unique attractions of Hong Kong as a part of China just as it describes the unique attractions of other tourist destinations in China (He Delong 1998). In this hierarchical negotiation, the ultimate power to decide what is harmonious and what is not is located at the center in Beijing. Hong Kong cannot be unique in terms of democracy or human rights, and thus is limited to being unique in terms of authoritarian capitalism. Capitalism is integrated into the socialist state as an important part of China's "socialist market economy." In a sense, the unity of One China is merely symbolic; it did not aid the people involved in the Right of Abode controversy. Here harmony constructs Hong Kong and the mainland as distinct entities. It affirms the "two systems" within the guiding framework of "one country."

Harmony in the Hong Kong imaginary is more ambiguous. It uses both "one country" and "two systems," without either being hegemonic. As Xiao Si tells us, life in Hong Kong is multilayered and multicentered. Rather than appealing to the centaur, to synthesizing coherent bodies into a new whole, Cheung appeals to the fabulous geography of the *Shanhai jing* (Cheung, Dung Kai 1998b, 203). As we saw in chapter 2, this ancient text contains descriptions of new creatures that are neither completely new nor completely different. They combine features but are not bound to the goal of forming a whole body like the centaur's: rather, there are three heads and one body, three faces and one body, one face and three bodies, and so on (*Shanhai jing* 1996; *Shan Hai Ching* 1985).

This chapter has argued that the Hong Kong imaginary, rather than appealing to the hegemony of the epics of law or history, is characterized by a decentered harmony of stories. The discursive economy of such stories leads us away from master narratives of identity towards identity as the negotiation of multiple and conflicting stories. As the Right of Abode controversy shows, this negotiation is not a clean or easy process. Much as in Xiao Si's hazy story, Hong Kongers have "no way to explain ourselves clearly." Identity and difference are "stapled together with Hong Kong in a tangle of love and hate. . . . This contradiction is tangled into an unresolvable knot" (Xiao Si 1998, 4). But these tangles contain space for possibility, for a politics of possibility where power is invested in interpretation not just by elites but by common people.

The next chapter uses the situation in Taiwan to see how the sticky relation between culture and ethnicity, nation and state is negotiated differently than in Hong Kong. The text revisits debates over Confucianism and democracy in an effort to move from a diasporic to a democratic sense of popular sovereignty.

6

Recognizing Democracy:
Nationalism, Taiwan, and Friendship

Taiwan is often in the news as the major "flashpoint" in East Asia. With the Korean Peninsula, it is one of the few remaining outposts of Cold War/civil war conflict in the world. The dispute seems simple: either Taiwan is a successful democratic and capitalist state threatened by an autocratic irridentist regime in Beijing, or the People's Republic of China (PRC) is simply acting as a proper nation-state guarding its sovereignty against the renegade province of Taiwan. The potential violence of this contradiction came to a head with the 2000 presidential election in Taiwan: against the belligerent warnings of the PRC leadership, Taiwanese voters elected Chen Shui-bian from the Democratic Progressive Party (DPP), which had fought for Taiwanese independence from the mainland for decades. This was not an anomaly; Chen was reelected president in 2004.

Once in office, though, the DPP government was involved in bridging the Strait of Taiwan separating the mainland from the island, by further normalizing contacts between the two societies. For the first time in over fifty years, the Taipei regime allowed limited direct contact with the mainland, starting in January 2001. Likewise, Beijing continues to offer Taiwan an enhanced "one country, two systems" deal that would not only allow Taiwan to, like Hong Kong, keep its social system, but also choose its own government and maintain its own military. Although China is often criticized for pushing a blunt form of absolute sovereignty, this formula actually appeals to the traditional Chinese notion of shared sovereignty (examined in the analysis of the South China Sea disputes in chapter 3). All Taipei need do is recognize the symbolic sovereignty of the mainland, and then it could go about its business, Beijing tells us. Such a lowering of borders on both sides to economic, social, and cultural exchange is part of the general "Greater China" trend that we have been examining.

But beyond straightforward security issues, the "Taiwan problem" (as it is called on the mainland) presents theoretical questions. Taiwan still rankles analysts because it is hard to find on the world map. Taiwan is surely an international actor. It carries considerable economic power in terms of world trade and investment as the sixteenth largest economy in the world (see Chen Jie 2002, 105–73). But the Republic of China (ROC), Taiwan's official designation, is not recognized as a nation-state by the international community. Like the other spaces considered in this book—the South China Sea, South Korea, Hong Kong, the Chinese diaspora—Taiwan confounds the standard vocabulary of international relations. Once again, curious turns of phrase are necessary to place Taiwan in international affairs: Hughes calls Taiwan, as a de facto rather than a de jure nation-state, an "intermediate state" (Hughes 1997a, 127ff).

With only a handful of proper ambassadors and limited membership in international organizations, to be heard on the world stage Taiwan must engage in new forms of diplomacy: vacation diplomacy, pragmatic diplomacy, people-to-people diplomacy, and flexible diplomacy. Likewise, the PRC has to extend its own curious concepts to entice Taiwan; an even looser category of "one country, two systems" is on offer. The United States, meanwhile, has to cloud the clarity demanded by deterrence theorists in its policy of "strategic ambiguity" for Taiwan.[1]

Flexibility is necessary because of the contradiction between Taiwan's de facto presence and de jure absence. Certainly, ambiguity is not the first choice of the various regimes. It is fruitful mainly because clarity breeds violence: if Taiwan officially declares independence, the PRC will invade; if the United States directly interferes, the PRC will attack. This is part of regulatory logic of the "nation-state" that not only enables action—national liberation movements as well as cross-straits invasions—but dis-enables discussion of other forms of political community. Indeed, such identity politics can have deadly force. As Campbell points out, it was the obsession with categories like "nation-state" and "ethnicity" that constricted the realm of possibilities for the solution of the Bosnian war in the 1990s (Campbell 1998b).

In Taiwan there is the curious situation where "ethnicity" is used to forcibly unite rather than forcibly divide: an ethnic regeneration rather than an ethnic cleansing. As we shall see, the PRC asserts ethnic homogeneity, insisting that people on both sides of the straits are Chinese with "the same ancestors and the same culture"; in Taiwan, on the other hand, mainstream and critical views do not deny ethnic or cultural difference but celebrate it; hence ethnicity is not the main criterion for dividing groups there, either. Rather than a clear self/Other relation between China and Taiwan, Taiwan is both the self and the Other: the self (China) insists that the Other (Taiwan) is actually the self. The Taiwan problem is a question of Chineseness. Hence, though the regulatory logic of the category of "nation-state" works in opposite directions in Bosnia and Greater China, it still threatens the same violence.

In Taiwan and the United States, as we saw in chapter 1, many people are looking to "democracy" as the new regulatory logic for cross-straits relations. Rather than agree that Taiwan is a "renegade province" that the PRC has a duty to recover under international law, they point to "democratic peace" theory. Since Taiwan democratized in the 1990s, such analysts argue, the key to unification is a similar democratization in the PRC. Rather than democracy being a "problem" for Chinese identity, it is the key to reunification. Instead of Taiwan having to measure up to a nation-state standard, the PRC now has to conform to the regulatory logic of democratization (Bernstein and Munro 1998, 204).

Such a deployment of "democracy" in international space often leads to charges of American cultural imperialism. The United States certainly has been involved in the Taiwan Straits crisis since its inception, in more traditionally imperialist ways—i.e., exerting political-military and political-economic power and influence. But what is interesting about the cross-straits struggle is that—as in the South China Sea, Korea, and Hong Kong—the United States is receding from view. Its most important role in the conflict is to restrain Taiwan from independence overtures, while at the same time persuading the PRC to use peaceful methods. The main threat to the PRC in this context is no longer American imperialism; Taiwan is now the key source of the democratic challenge to the Chinese Communist Party (CCP) (CND 23 April 2000).

The Taiwan Straits crisis, then, is not just a political-military struggle, part of the Cold War/civil war logic. The struggle is also over different notions of Chineseness, and how they are realized, recognized, and institutionalized in political space in much more direct ways than in Hong Kong. This debate not only takes place in cultural studies programs in the academy; it also produces the diplomatic performances of the Chinese State Council's White Papers on Taiwan, and more popular performances such as the "Taiwan Problem Picture Exhibit" in the Revolutionary History Museum (Guowuyuan 2001).

In other words, the crisis has produced not just dangers but opportunities. Political ambiguity and flexibility are not the preference of the ROC government. Diplomatic and military pressures from outside Taiwan, and the demographic pressures from inside Taiwan, have pushed both the regime and the populace to craft flexible identities. Politics has expanded from an absolute notion of state sovereignty to nuanced expressions of popular sovereignty. Taiwan's parliament, for example, debated identity in terms of five options: Taiwanese, citizen of the ROC, citizen of China, ethnic Chinese, and "all of the above" (in Klintworth 2001, 50).[2] According to institutions of power in Taipei, Other is an inclusive and constitutive part of the self.

Here, Charles Taylor's "politics of recognition" is useful. He argues that democratic politics, as part of a general ethic of self/Other relations in multicultural society, involves a shift from hierarchical to egalitarian images of society. But this egalitarian society is not reduced to a collection of atomized autonomous individuals. Taylor quotes Hegel to argue that "we flourish to the extent that we are recognized" in intersubjective relations (Taylor 1994, 50). A politics of difference grows out of this horizontal notion of shared human dignity (Taylor 1994, 39). What is interesting about Taylor's arguments is that they can apply in various social spaces: among individuals in face-to-face relations, among communities in a multicultural society, and among nation-states in multilateral international society. The social interaction of recognition is so important, Taylor points out, that even the most "closed societies" are tremendously sensitive to world opinion, and demand to be recognized on their own terms in the international community (Taylor 1994, 64). North Korea is a case in point: the key demand of the "Hermit Kingdom" is to be diplomatically recognized by the United States.

Recognition, then, is not simply an ethical relation of self and Other but an institutional relationship in diplomacy (Biersteker and Weber 1996b). One of the great battles and achievements of the PRC has been to gain recognition from the international community (Chinese Ministry of Foreign Affairs 1999). Since the watershed of its entry into the United Nations in 1971, the PRC has been winning the game of diplomatic recognition against the Republic of China.[3] On the other hand, Taiwan has been winning the game of democratic recognition as a prominent East Asian member of the "family of democracies" (Ling and Shih 1999, 223). Both these games underline the performative nature of politics and foreign policy, state sovereignty and popular sovereignty. Chineseness only exists to the extent that it is recognized by Others. These diplomatic performances are certainly directed at domestic audiences for national legitimacy, but they are also directed at the United States and the world community, for international legitimacy.

Still, Chinese sources argue that state sovereignty and democracy not only are separate issues but are in conflict. As Li Peng famously declared after the NATO bombing of China's Belgrade embassy in 1999, international relations is now a battle between nationalist state sovereignty and interventionist human rights:

> Facts have enabled people to see more clearly the true nature of the fallacy of "human rights above sovereignty," and be more vigilant against the forces of hegemonism. There is also the issue over attempts to interfere in and invade other countries under the pretext of human rights and we need to be more aware of the necessity and urgency of the establishment of a just and reasonable new international order. (Li Peng in RMRB 12 June 1999; also see Ching, Frank 1999e)

One of the premier international relations theorists in China, Liang Shoude, agrees with Li Peng's formulation of world politics: the rights and interests of the state trump human rights (Liang Shoude 1996, 302; Liang and Hong 2000).

Although the state sovereignty of diplomatic recognition and the popular sovereignty of democracy are seen as a contradiction in cross-straits relations and international politics, Taylor's politics of recognition can bring them together. Both nationalism and democracy are horizontal and antihierarchical relations of recognition. Actually, the Chinese terms—*zhuquan* for sovereignty and *renquan* for human rights—also show how the concepts are not separate but interlinked. They are different sorts of *quan*-rights, referring to different modes of power and legitimacy (see chapter 3).

Most considerations of the cross-straits crisis frame their analysis in terms of the struggle between Beijing and Taiwan on opposite sides of geographical, ideological, and cultural boundaries. This boundary is not just physical but figurative. In Cold War discourse, China and Taiwan were not just on opposite sides of the strait but were ontological opposites as well. Post–Cold War discussions of cross-straits relations are also organized in this way: you are on either one side or the other.

Rather than choosing sides to argue the case for either the PRC's national sovereignty or Taiwan's democracy, I wish to examine how *renquan* and *zhuquan* are not opposites but are related in a tension that both joins and divides people across the Taiwan Strait. This involves a shift from questions of unification and independence, to examine the dynamic between state sovereignty and popular sovereignty. Hence in this chapter I examine how "Greater China" in its various forms is constructed and resisted, and how the Taiwan crisis not only presents new dangers but yields different opportunities for political community.

The chapter is divided into four sections. In the first section, I examine how Beijing understands the Taiwan issue in terms of the "One China Principle"—and the ontological questions such an understanding raises. Not surprisingly, Beijing employs the logic of the nation-state to argue that Taiwan has been part of China "since ancient times." An analysis of White Papers, museum exhibitions, and recent academic writings will show how Greater China is constructed to include Taiwan by looking to shared cultures, even drafting Confucius to solve the nationalist crisis.

The second section examines the development of democracy and identity on Taiwan, to argue that the discourse of legitimacy increasingly looks away from state sovereignty towards popular sovereignty. The main division of nativism and flexibility is not *between* the nationalist Guomindang (KMT) and the pro-independence DPP, but within each of them. While the PRC seeks to conclude its nationalist project through unification, Taiwan has moved beyond the regulatory logic of the nation-state to a looser and more productive notion of nation/state that fits into a cosmopolitan construction of Greater China.

Rather than taking the "democratic peace" theory for granted, section three explores a more nuanced notion of democracy, identity, and violence to trace how violence can be produced in electoral democracy. The section reframes the focus from East/West analyses of Confucianism vs. liberal democracy to differentiate between two different practices of democracy, institutional electoralism and a democratic ethos. The section looks not only to Taiwan's top-down political reforms that have produced elected leaders, but to Taiwan's vibrant social movements as examples of a democratic ethos in Greater China.

Since Confucius is deployed to argue for authoritarianism, unification, and state sovereignty, section four considers how Confucianism manages human relationships not only through the hierarchical institutions of the patriarchy and the state, but through more horizontal encounters with friends. The recognition of friendship, thus, is part of Taylor's transition from hierarchical to egalitarian views of society—not just in domestic politics, but in international society. Rather than a shared ancestry in One China, we have shared friendships in a transnational community.

In this way, chapter 6 explores how Chineseness is constructed in transnational ways that both reinforce and confound borders of identity, sovereignty, and political-economy. Taiwan is a prime example of the Greater China dynamic, because the tension is not only between governments in Beijing and Taipei, but between institutional structures and popular movements, between state sovereignty and popular sovereignty, in both places. Rather than relying on vertical notions of institutional power, this chapter explores more horizontal notions of ethical encounters: face-to-face encounters and people-to-people diplomacy. Network power can work in democratic friendship as well as in family-based business.

PRC: ONE CHINA, NATIVISM, AND CONQUEST

Beijing's discourse on Taiwan should be familiar. It deploys many of the same images and grammar that we have already seen in the

PRC's claims to the South China Sea and Hong Kong. Like Hong Kong, the "Taiwan problem" is seen as part of the nationalist struggle against imperialism that continued into and past the Cold War. But Taiwan is a special case because it is not simply a "lost territory" under foreign control; Taiwan not only has a rival government but constitutes a rival Chinese state. Unlike the South China Sea archipelagoes, Taiwan not only has a population, but has one that is democratically represented in political institutions. In this sense, Taiwan is more like South Korea than like Hong Kong or the Spratlys, because it is caught up in the Cold War/civil war logic of rival claims of sovereignty and identity.

Indeed, China uses the regulatory logic of the nation-state, on the one hand, to draw in Taiwan and, on the other hand, to keep out foreign governments like the United States. The PRC seeks to nationalize Taiwan, rather than to internationalize the issue. To achieve unification, the PRC has pursued a policy that combines a peaceful offensive with coercive diplomacy (Zhao Suisheng 1999). The official formula is "peaceful unification and one country, two systems."

As in the South China Sea disputes and the Koreanization of Confucianism, Beijing expends much effort discussing sovereignty to make the nation coterminous with the state (Taiwan Affairs Office 2000; Taiwan Affairs Office 1993; Zhonggong 1998; Guowuyuan et al. 2000).[4] Sovereignty here is defined by territory more than by populations: one of Beijing's arguments is that the popular sovereignty of elections and referenda cannot legitimately be used to fragment the nation-state (Taiwan Affairs Office 2000; Interviews 1999). The Chinese government goes to great lengths to argue that this view is not peculiar to China; this notion of sovereignty is respected by other states, including the United States.

Here, the PRC's sovereignty becomes performative. Such arguments are written into official White Papers from the Taiwan Affairs Office, whose audiences include not just mainlanders or Taiwanese but the international community. The first Taiwan Affairs Office White Paper was published in 1993 as a reaction to Taiwanese attempts to join the United Nations; the second White Paper was published not only to warn Taiwanese against voting for the pro-independence party in the 2000 presidential election, but also to instruct foreigners in the naturalness of the Chinese nation-state, thus the artifice of Taiwanese independence.

Diplomatic performances that confirm the One China policy are more formal. Whenever the PRC is recognized, it insists that the Republic of China is derecognized; each time the PRC normalizes relations, Taiwan is represented as abnormal. Thus when China was admitted to the United Nations in 1971, Taiwan had to be expelled. This process was repeated with each specific normalization event: the treaty that normalized relations between the United States and China stated that the United States "recognizes the government of the People's Republic of China as the sole legal government of China" (in Zhonggong 1998, 271). This genre of treaty, normalizing relations with China, is known as a "friendship treaty," for example the Sino-Japanese Peace and Friendship Treaty (1978). China has been winning the recognition game against Taiwan, with 162 countries recognizing the PRC at last count. Chinese officials can declare that "the One China Policy is accepted by the world, including the United States" (Zhonggong 1998, 118; Guowuyuan et al. 2000: 16-8). Thus the One China policy is often not really focused on Taiwan, but is "meant only for foreign consumption" in diplomatic practice (Ching, Frank 2000b).

The One China policy is curious because, though it sounds like common sense, it raises ontological questions. On the one hand, it is very legalistic, as the normalization treaties attest, in demanding that there be only one legitimate Chinese government in the world. The government of the PRC now constitutes the Chinese regime, after winning the civil war against the ROC in 1949. Since one state (the ROC) passed out of legal existence when the other (the PRC) was born, according to international law, the issue is succession, not secession (see Campbell 1998b, 18).

But on the other hand, One China is a transcendental assertion: the One China *Principle*. The 1993 White Paper concludes "there is only one China in the world, of which Taiwan is an unalienable part" (Taiwan Affairs Office 1993). The 2000 White Paper has a whole section on the subject of "One China Principle," but it has a rather tautological definition: there is one China because there is One China. As the government repeatedly announces, any question can be discussed under the One China Principle—except the One China Principle (Taiwan Affairs Office 2000; also see Guowuyuan et al. 2000, 13-20).

Legality: The Clarity of the Nation-State

Unlike with Hong Kong, the PRC government appeals to *law* in its arguments for unification with Taiwan. While it does not recognize the legality of the Treaty of Shimonoseki (1895) that started the Japanese occupation of Taiwan, the PRC does recognize the ROC's World War II diplomacy to recover it. In the Cairo Agreement (1943), Chiang Kai-shek insisted that the postwar settlement return all Chinese territories occupied by Japan since 1894, not simply those taken in World War I and World War II. The PRC government always notes that the Potsdam Agreement (1945) pledged to carry out the provisions of the Cairo Agreement (Taiwan Affairs Office 1993). Since the government of the PRC legally succeeded the government of the ROC in 1949, Taiwan is Chinese property. Likewise, China's agreements with the United States acknowledge the PRC's claims to Taiwan.

Yet official Chinese sources also state that Taiwan only became a "problem" because of the United States. By the end of the 1940s, the U.S. government had given up on the KMT because it was so corrupt. It stated that it would not impede the resolution of the Chinese civil war. But after the Korean War began in 1950, Truman decided to defend Taiwan against PRC. Since the KMT could only resist the CCP with the support of the United States, Chinese feel that the United States stole Taiwan: "the US government is responsible for holding up the settlement of the Taiwan question" (Taiwan Affairs Office 1993; Ming Zhang 1999, 147). The Taiwan independence movement is likewise seen as a product of the anti-China policies of the United States and Japan (Guowuyuan 2001, panels 3.7–3.8).

The United States continues to impede unification both symbolically and materially: it granted a visa to the ROC president in 1995, continues to sell arms to Taiwan, and plans to include Taiwan as a node in a Theater Missile Defense network aimed at containing the PRC (see Taiwan Security Enhancement Act 2000). Rather being clear about "recognizing" Chinese claims to Taiwan, in all of the Sino–United States agreements the United States actually uses weaker language, "acknowledging" Chinese claims (in Zhonggong 1998, 269; Hughes 1997a, 18): thus the "strategic ambiguity" of acknowledging, but not recognizing, Chinese sovereignty, while supporting Taiwan's defense. Taiwan therefore is seen as the most sensitive issue in Sino–U.S. relations. When the 1999 Chinese university entrance exam asked what was the core issue in Sino–United States relations, the correct answer was the "Taiwan problem" (CND 13 July 2000). When American China threat theorists want a war scenario, they look to Taiwan (Bernstein and Munro 1998, 149–65; Gertz 2000, 171–98).

Culture and History: Ontological Anchors

"One China" is not just a policy, but a principle. Here the nation-state is naturalized as the sole legitimate political community. The unity of the Chinese nation is taken for granted as its natural state. As a Beijing University student said after Taiwan's 2000 presidential election: "The idea of unity is very important to the Chinese people, and we treasure the idea. These ideas have sunken deeply into people's minds, and we just accept them and wouldn't think of changing them" (IHT 20 March 2000). Since there is only One China in the world, multiple and less state-centric notions of Chineseness are dismissed as heinous separatist projects (He and Guo 2000, 108–9; Wang Fei-Ling 2001, 93–95).

The One China Principle is taken literally in descriptions of Taiwanese life. In a "Reader for [Communist] Party Cadres," the section on Taiwanese culture starts by underlining homogeneity: "The two sides have the same nationality, the same ancestors, and the same culture" (Zhonggong 1998, 33). The Taiwan Problem Picture Exhibit has many panels showing Taiwanese people doing obviously "Chinese" things (Guowuyuan 2001, panels 2.1–2.15). Taiwanese culture has its peculiarities but, as in Hong Kong, is simply a variant of greater Chinese culture. As an academic in Beijing put it, "Taiwanese authorities have to recognize not just the One China Principle, but the fact that they are Chinese" (RMRB 27 April 2000).

According to this nativist logic, the Taiwanese independence movement cannot be characterized as an alternative Chinese community. Rather it is dismissed as a "fundamental negation of Chinese culture" (Lou Jie 1998, 98). Unification is thus transformed from a political issue that has room for negotiation, into an ontological declaration either affirming or denying essential Chinese culture. Beijing demands that Taipei unconditionally agree to the One China Principle.

As with the Spratlys and Hong Kong, the PRC bases its claim to

Taiwan on the historical evidence of Chinese civilization. Taiwan has its own specific history, but only as a part of Chinese history (Zhonggong 1998, 33). The White Papers and the exhibition duly tell us that Taiwan "has belonged to China since ancient times." It has been settled and developed by the Chinese people since China was unified under the Qin dynasty, and became a province in 1885 (Taiwan Affairs Office 1993). Even though Taiwan was colonized by the Dutch and Spanish in the seventeenth century, and the Japanese from 1895 to 1945, Taiwanese people, because they are fundamentally Chinese, according to this argument, did not become culturally Dutch or Japanese (Lou Jie 1998, 278). Indeed, "Japanese occupation" is an experience that Taiwan shared with mainland China during World War II. Occupation makes Taiwan even more Chinese—and thus it is more even important to recover the island.

Peaceful Offensive

Although this narrative could be described as conquest rather than nativist, the problems of "two Chinas" and "one China, one Taiwan" are relatively new. Up until the 1980s, the ROC and the PRC had not just a shared culture, but a shared imaginary of a unified China. Thus, the 2000 White Paper concludes that for nearly forty years after 1949, there was a "common understanding" between the KMT and the CCP that there was only one China; both opposed "two Chinas" and "Taiwan independence" (Taiwan Affairs Office 2000). The One China policy was shared by the two Leninist parties, the KMT and the CCP, who merely differed on their ideological definition of "China": communist or nationalist.

In Beijing, the Taiwan problem is understood as the outgrowth less of international relations than of interparty relations. The battle for unification was between the KMT and the CCP. Statements by Mao (1958), Deng Xiaoping (1983), and the 2000 White Paper very clearly define the issues in terms of KMT/CCP relations; their appeals blur the distinction between "Taiwanese friends" and "KMT friends" (in Zhonggong 1998, 221, 222, 224; Taiwan Affairs Office 2000; Zhao Suisheng 1999, 212). Even more than "the return of Hong Kong," the "Taiwan problem" is best studied in terms of party history and at the Central Party School (see Lou Jie 1998). The "Reader for Party Cadres" is authored first by the CCP's Taiwan Office, and only second by the PRC State Council's Taiwan Office

(Zhonggong 1998). Even after the 2000 election challenged the basis of Beijing's Taiwan policy, party history figurations persisted: the Taiwan Problem Picture Exhibition was held at the headquarters of party history propaganda, the Revolutionary History Museum.

As part of its economic reforms after 1978, the PRC shifted from vowing to militarily liberate Taiwan to wooing Taiwan through increased social and economic contact. Rather than being a political-military problem, unification became an economic-cultural issue, as part of Beijing's "peaceful offensive." While politics have separated Taiwan and the mainland for merely fifty years, civilization has joined them for millennia: "Confucianism has influenced Taiwan very much . . . and Confucianism is rooted in the motherland on the mainland" (Lou Jie 1998, 1–2).[5] Like South Korea, which looked to shared civilization to bridge the gap of the Korean War, here Beijing appeals to a shared Confucian heritage to bridge seventy years of interparty war.

Chinese civilization, then, can solve political problems. Culture is not just a common tradition, but a common resource for modernization; it is a "foundation of shared heritage that cannot be denied, which helps economic development and social progress on both sides of the Strait, and aids the realization of the rapid rise of the Chinese nation" (Lou Jie 1998, 280). The key to unification is increased contact via economic and cultural exchange. Such free trade is not just for economic profit but for political benefit (Lou Jie 1998, 3; Guowuyuan 2001).

This move from politics to culture characterizes official statements, and is the mainland version of "Greater China" discourse. Indeed, the economic draw of the mainland continues to exert considerable influence on cross-straits relations with President Chen Shui-bian (Hughes 2001). Beijing considers itself generous in what it offers Taiwan. Indeed, the deal has been called "one country, three systems," since Beijing would allow Taiwan much more autonomy than Hong Kong or Macao (Wang Fei-Ling 2000, 96). Specifically, in addition to continuing to choose its own government, Taiwan could maintain its own independent military force. Hence, it is easy to see how leaders in Beijing are frustrated with the "prevarication" of both the KMT and the DPP.

Even so, because political developments in Taiwan since the early 1980s led to a more open society and a more democratic politics,

192 · RECOGNIZING DEMOCRACY

Beijing has been losing control of its Taiwan policy. While in the 1970s there was little structural difference between the KMT regime and the CCP regime—both were led by Leninist party-states—new challenges developed in the 1980s and 1990s. As a result of reforms instituted by Republic of China Presidents Chiang Ching-kuo and Lee Teng-hui, the One China consensus has been challenged by new groups pushing for either two Chinas or Taiwanese independence. Even the KMT has been changing, becoming less of a "nationalist" party as it "nativized" to Taiwan.

Thus ways of understanding the Taiwan problem also have had to change. Starting in 1988, there was a shift in the research agenda in Beijing from straight party history and interparty relations to a territorial notion of the problem, "two sides relations." But rather than being a complete shift, this "new approach to the problem" pledged to "research not just the KMT, or the CCP, but use history to research the more than seventy years of party relations . . . [and] not just research Taiwan or the mainland, but the more than forty years of cross-straits relations" (Wang and Mao 1998, 2). This special series has produced many popular books on cross-straits relations, since 1993.

The view presented in documents since 1990, where unification was transformed from a political struggle with the KMT into an ontological declaration of Chineseness, comes from this shift in the research agenda. While nationalism and One China are taken to be "natural," Taiwanese independence is dismissed as a fallacy (Taiwan Affairs Office 1993). All of the political titles and institutions in Taiwan are put in quotation marks to highlight their dubious status: "president," "parliament," "constitution," "elections," "inauguration," and "pragmatic diplomacy." Taiwanese nationalism is not real, either; it is dismissed as a dangerous and divisive "ethno-nationalism" (He and Guo 2000, 108; Zheng, Yongnian 1999, 35). Worse than a fallacy or a misunderstanding, it is a disease: "'Taiwan independence' is a tumor on [Chinese] political culture, which clashes with the benefits of national existence and national security" (Lou Jie 1998, 2; Zhonggong 1998, 17).

Rather than looking for friends in the KMT, this argument frames DPP leaders as enemies (BR 17 April 2000). Because they are said to "fundamentally negate Chinese culture" (Lou Jie 1998, 98), independence activists must be "vilely rely[ing] on foreign patronage to detach Taiwan from China" (Taiwan Affairs Office 1993; Guowuyuan 2001, panel 3-8). Both the United States and Japan are criticized for nurturing independence dissidents in exile, and encouraging a Western-style political system, parliamentary democracy, in Taiwan. Lee Teng-hui is held personally responsible; he "betrayed the One China Principle" with his Taiwanization of the KMT that "connived and supported the separatists" (Taiwan Affairs Office 2000; Guowuyuan 2001, panel 3-8; Zhonggong 1998, 13, 33; He and Guo 2000, 113; Zhao Suisheng 1999, 221–23).

Coercive Diplomacy

This new challenge necessitated a new response: Beijing appealed to coercive diplomacy to complement its peaceful offensive. The best examples of coercive diplomacy are Beijing's reactions to independence overtures in Taiwan's 1996 and 2000 presidential election campaigns: war games off Taiwan in 1995–96 (see Zhonggong 1998, 115–17) and the propaganda war of 1999–2000. The war games and missile attacks in 1995–96 shocked people around the world, and disrupted the Taiwanese economy. They provoked a visit by two aircraft carrier battle groups from the U.S. Navy. There were no war games in 1999–2000, but the statements from Beijing were bellicose. The 2000 White Paper threatened to use force for unification, while Premier Zhu Rongji threatened to invade Taiwan if people voted for the independence party: "Taiwan independence forces' victory will spark a cross-strait war and hamper cross-strait peace" (BBC/SWB 15 March 2000).

After the presidential election in 2000, there was no war. But the military's role in Beijing's Taiwan policy was strengthened (CND 23 November 2000; *White Paper on China's National Defense* 2002; Zhongguo guofangbao 2001). Rather than encouraging all Taiwanese to invest in the mainland, as it had with the peaceful offensive, Beijing targeted pro-independence businesspeople with economic sanctions for the first time (Hughes 2001; Wright 2001). It also stepped up its propaganda on independence "extremists" in Taiwan: the DPP vice president, Annette Lu, was called "scum" and a "traitor" (CND 11 April 2000; BR 17 April 2000; Wright 2001).

Although the peaceful offensive and coercive diplomacy seem to be going in opposite directions, they are actually two sides of the same coin in Beijing's quest to assert state sovereignty over Taiwan (Zhao

Suisheng 1999, 211). But in its effort to contain Taiwan, Beijing treats the island as simply real estate. As with Hong Kong, Beijing does not devote much time or energy to understanding Taiwan (see Zhonggong 1998; Wagner 1991, 121). The Revolutionary History Museum exhibition, as well as numerous documents, show that even after the shocks of 2000 the PRC still uses a romanticized concept of Taiwan as a lost territory that needs to be reclaimed, rather than seeking to convince the Taiwanese people themselves.

The rhetoric of the PRC's argument privileges state sovereignty over popular sovereignty: it is more interested in talking to representatives of institutions in the United Nations and the United States than with the people on Taiwan. By appealing to shared essential culture rather than interparty debate, the PRC's nativism naturalizes the discourse in a way that impoverishes discussion. The PRC's appeal to "culture" rather than "politics" in understanding Taiwan did not loosen up the categories and provide space for negotiation—quite the opposite: because they rely on essentialized notions of national identity, cultural arguments limit the possibility of compromise.

The "Taiwan problem" discourse is similar to South Korean nativist discourses that frame unification with North Korea as a "sacred goal," thus beyond critical examination. Both official and popular discourses see the North/South division as the foreign-engineered disruption of a homogeneous Korean community. As in China, the problem is seen as the division, and unification as the solution. But Grinker points out that Korea was never homogeneous in the past and never will be in the future. As with Hong Kong, the real politics would actually begin with unification: "Arrivals, like borders, are not only endpoints but beginnings. They shatter preconceived images and point to new directions, sometimes forward and sometimes backward." Reunification politics, Grinker argues, involves "not a military or political process, but a cultural one" that is attentive to difference as well as homogeneity (Grinker 2000, xii, 268, 269). Or more to the point, the crucial issue is whether politics and culture should be framed in terms of nativist appeals to homogeneity, or whether cultural encounters can encourage difference.

In its nativist appeal to essential Chineseness, the PRC has restricted debate about how Taiwan fits in. Actually, Chinese nativism has difficulties because it encounters not a counter-Chinese nationalism in Taiwan so much as a counter-nativism. Taiwanese nativism is fascinating not just because it appeals to difference but because it uses some of Beijing's most treasured discursive tactics. In his 2000 inauguration address, President Chen Shui-bian echoed Mao's famous foundational phrase when he declared, "Taiwan stands up!"

TAIWAN: FROM UNIFICATION/INDEPENDENCE TO NATIVISM/FLEXIBILITY

While the PRC insists that the "Taiwan problem" is an issue of state sovereignty, important changes in Taiwan since the early 1980s have introduced popular sovereignty into the calculus. This shift is part of a move from the nativism of Chiang Kai-shek's own One China policy to a flexible notion of sovereignty and identity, not just in the opposition DPP but in the KMT itself. Or to put it another way, one thing the KMT and the DPP share is internal debate over the merits of nativism and flexibility, state sovereignty and popular sovereignty.

Nationalizing Taiwan

The PRC's post-1988 Taiwan policy of appealing to shared Chinese tradition closely mirrors the policy of the KMT after Chiang Kai-shek retreated to Taiwan and lost the Civil War in 1949. When the KMT accepted the Japanese surrender and took control of Taiwan in 1945, it singled out the island for special treatment. At that time, Taiwan was the only province seen as not ready for its own local government. Because of the fifty-year Japanese occupation, the KMT's military governor was suspicious of the Taiwanese, seeing them as at best backward provincials and at worst traitorous collaborators. Taiwanese thus were treated as second-class citizens. When they protested against such treatment in the 2-28 Movement in 1947, the KMT responded with a massacre that targeted local leaders and intellectuals (Hughes 1997a, 24–26; Kuo, Liangwen 1997, 4).

After losing the Civil War in 1949, the KMT regime enforced martial law that restricted all political activity. In addition to such political control, the KMT also instituted a far-reaching cultural policy to create and promote Chinese national identity in Taiwan. This was deemed necessary since the Japanese had enforced their own vigorous cultural policy on Taiwan—to such an extent that "Chineseness" was a dim memory limited to elderly Taiwanese, few of whom had ever been to the mainland (Hughes 1997a, 24). Hence, the KMT worked to "nationalize" Chinese culture in distinction not only to the mainland's new communist Chinese identity but also to a local Taiwanese identity and a colonial Japanese identity. This was done by enforcing the use of the "national language" *(guoyu)* of Mandarin, as opposed to Taiwanese or Japanese.

The KMT's political domination, as in most countries, proceeded less via the use of coercion than through the construction and management of knowledge practices (Chun 1996, 136). Like the rulers in South Korea, the KMT deployed "tradition" to legitimize its sovereignty. It appointed itself the "guardian of traditional Chinese culture" as part of its own One China Principle. This activity was often reactive to activities on the mainland. When Mao declared the Cultural Revolution in 1966, Chiang Kai-shek countered with the Cultural Renaissance movement; while Confucius was criticized in the PRC, he was praised in the ROC.

This activity went far beyond anticommunist rhetoric, for the KMT in a top-down Leninist management of society built a sophisticated cultural infrastructure to disseminate Chinese identity at the local level (Chun 1996, 134). There were large publication programs, as well as awards for model citizens, including filial piety awards. As under the current PRC policy, Taiwanese culture could not exist as an autonomous discourse but only as "local folkways within the larger cultural stream of Chinese history" (Chun 1996, 144). In this way, the KMT not only countered mainland propaganda but, in its assertion of a pure, unitary, and continuous Chinese history, worked to "anchor Taiwan to the Chinese nation-state as a whole" (Chun 1996, 133). Thus, until the 1980s, the One China Principle was intact on both sides of the strait. Strangely, just when China began to present itself as the guardian of Chinese culture, the debate in Taiwan moved on to other subjects.

Taiwan Independence Movement

Although the KMT's cultural policy was very thorough, the persistent activities of the Taiwanese independence movement show it was unable to "eradicate local cultures of resistance" (Chun 1996, 146; Hughes 1997a, 35).[6] More to the point, the mainland serves not just as the Other for the KMT's Chinese nationalism but as the Other against which a Taiwanese counternationalism was constructed (Tu

Weiming 1998, 82). Resistance to the One China principles of both the CCP and the KMT, like resistance to Japanese colonialism, produced Taiwanese identity as a counternationalism. Independence activists used a primordial notion of nationalism—which looked to soil, blood, and history—to promote Taiwan as an autonomous culture rather than as an adjunct or derivative of Chinese culture.

DPP leaders, including Chen Shui-bian, declared that Taiwan was a New Country, populated by a New People, who needed a New Constitution to guide a New Body Politic (Hughes 1997a, 43; Wei Hung-Chin 1999, 20; Chang, Mau-Kuei 1997, 20). Yet Taiwanese nationalism was largely an inversion of Chinese nationalism, using the CCP/KMT's nationalist categories against both (see Gold 1998). Taiwanese history was written as a counternationalist history. Rather than being part of a continuous flow of five thousand years of Chinese history, Taiwan was refigured as a space of disruption, the site of frequent rebellions (Hughes 1997a, 36). Rather than mainland rule of Taiwan being the norm, it was now represented as the exception, enduring for only four years in the twentieth century, 1945–49. Rather than the KMT liberating Taiwan from Japan, "it represented a kind of colonialism which was no less 'foreign' than the Japanese interregnum that preceded it" (Chun 1996, 133).

Rather than speaking Mandarin, the counternationalists have promoted Taiwanese. Rather than looking to common ancestry, they maintain the KMT's "ethnic" categories of "islander" and "mainlander," but reverse their moral valence. Nor do they promote Confucius; one mainland philosopher reported after a visit to Taiwan that the sage was on the ropes (Interviews 1999). Yet, as a reversal of Chinese nationalism, this Taiwanese nativism still runs into many of its fundamentalist conceptual problems. Rather than "unmask[ing] the hegemonic fictions of traditional Chineseness" of KMT (and now PRC) propaganda, it reproduces the discourse of origins when it tries to deny Chineseness (Chun 1996, 146–47).

Taiwan as a Shared Community

This exclusive nativist notion of Taiwan-ness is *counter-Chinese*, but other groups in the Taiwanese independence movement have been creatively addressing the status of the hyphen between nation and state. Rather than looking to a discourse of essentials, the *Dangwai* ("outside the ruling party") dissident movement has, since the 1960s, been crafting a more open view of Taiwan-ness and Chineseness. Rather than appeal to ethnicity or language to distinguish between mainlanders and islanders, in 1964 Dangwai intellectual Peng Mingmin wrote that he sees Taiwan identity as something shared by all who live there in a "community of shared destiny." While the history of National Humiliation links Taiwan's status to the issue of China's crisis at the hands of imperialism, Peng argues that China ceased to be a victim with the founding of "New China" in 1949. Thus, with no National Humiliation, no national salvation of Taiwan is necessary. Patriotism does not look to the abstract concept of the "nation," but to the political community of "the people" (Peng Mingmin 1972, 241–46; Hughes 1997a, 38–40; Wei Hung-Chin 1999).

Hence, while both the KMT and the radical independence groups looked to the mainland as the Other, the Dangwai group did "not want to be [exclusively] defined by this Otherness" (Tu Weiming 1998, 73). Foreign-ness is not a problem that needs to be controlled, they stated, whether it comes from the mainland, the United States, or Japan; people might criticize Lee Teng-hui for speaking Japanese better than Mandarin, and DPP leaders for their Americanization, but colonization and exile were the key experience of that generation.

While Taiwanese nativism uses ethnicity to separate people, in Peng's discourse ethnicity is used to bring them together. Rather than there being "only One China in the world," as the PRC claims, Peng feels, "Chinese" should be an ethnic category attachable to many distinct and autonomous states: Taiwanese and mainlanders should be like Americans, Australians, and British (Hughes 1997a, 37). They are linked in cultural, social, and ethnic community rather than by (legal) citizenship. In this way, people can acknowledge being Chinese without signing up to any One China Principle.

This appeal was more to a diasporic Chinese discourse of flexibility than a nativist notion of citizenship. For example, when Chen Shui-bian said that he was proud to be Chinese, he was acknowledging shared Chinese ethnicity *(Huaren)* rather than a single Chinese citizenship *(Zhongguo ren)* (CND 19 October 2000; Chen Shuibian 2000). The regulatory functions of "nation-state" were thus questioned. The state sovereignty of the KMT/CCP was countered with the popular sovereignty of Taiwanese/Chinese people rather than by a counter-state sovereignty of the Republic of Taiwan.

Nativism and Flexibility in the DPP

Examining the "China Policy" of the DPP is helpful because it shows how both a Taiwanese self and a Chinese Other are constructed in relation to state and popular sovereignty. The DPP was formed out a loose confederation of dissident groups. Hence, the debate between nativist and flexible conceptions of Taiwanese identity has continued in its two main factions. The New Tide faction argued that it was necessary to first achieve independence from mainland China; only then could Taiwan gain full security and democracy (Wei Hung-Chin 1999; Hughes 1997a, 40). Thus it was necessary to win state sovereignty before struggling for popular sovereignty. Taking a lesson from the People Power movements in the Philippines (1986) and South Korea (1987), the New Tide reasoned that the battle must be fought via the direct action of mass demonstrations to topple the KMT party-state. Indeed, after martial law was lifted in 1987, there were over one thousand strikes in 1988 alone (Tu Weiming 1998, 86; Hughes 1997a, 41; Wei Hung-Chin 1999, 77–78). Once power was seized, a Republic of Taiwan would seek international recognition, especially diplomatic recognition and U.N. membership.

The Formosa faction, on the other hand, argued that Taiwan was already independent in practice. Thus a DPP-led government would not need to formally declare independence immediately—and thus risk provoking a military response from the PRC. To achieve independence, Taiwan first needed to obtain a working democratic system: popular sovereignty was necessary for state sovereignty. Popular sovereignty was to be won through political reform within the system; thus the DPP needed to work as a formal political party struggling to get elected (Wei Hung-Chin 1999, 29, 78; Hughes 1997a, 40).

While the New Tide faction appeals to the Taiwanese nativists, the Formosa faction appeals to the more flexible pragmatists. The DPP's hard-core secessionist platform alienated voters in the 1991 and 1996 elections, so the Formosa faction reasoned that the DPP must first get elected—on a more flexible platform—before it could pursue independence. Members of the New Tide faction also have moderated their revolutionary views for better electoral success (Hughes 1998, 11; Hughes 1997a, 44, 93; Wei Hung-Chin 1999, 90).

The distinctive nativistic and flexible approaches to sovereignty were mirrored in each faction's mainland policy, presented at the

DPP's first China policy conference in February 1998 (DPP 1998). Formosa's China policy followed its open view of Chineseness (Hsu and Chen 1998). According to its "advance West boldly" strategy, the Formosa faction suggested that Taiwan "normalize" relations with the PRC. Starting from the principle that all policies would foreground the security and prosperity of Taiwan, the Formosa faction outlined a policy of expanding trade and investment links with China for the benefit of Taiwanese business interests. Although Hsu and Chen were wary of any "Greater Chinese Economic Sphere," "Southern Chinese Economic Community," or "Greater China Framework," they still outlined a general "Greater China" policy, albeit under the protection of the internationalized liberal trade regime of interdependence. Thus Taiwan could use its knowledge of Chinese "history, culture, and language," on the one hand, and capitalist experience, on the other, to be an intermediary between China and the world. Taiwan thus would help China's liberalization, while acting as a guide for Euro-American business in China (Hsu and Chen 1998; Wei Hung-Chin 1999, 79). In this way, Taiwan could counter increasingly common views that the island was a regional troublemaker and a thorn in Sino-U.S. relations. Otherwise, the proposal reasoned, time was not on Taiwan's side. The island was becoming more and more isolated (Hughes 1998, 14; Wei Hung-Chin 1999, 64).

While the Formosa faction wanted to "advance West boldly" to engage China, the New Tide argued for building a "strong base" with merely a "gradual advance" toward China. Rather than an appeal to a neoliberal view of world politics, the New Tide proposal was inspired by a realist understanding of Taiwan's national interest. As the West was still anticommunist, Taiwan was not so isolated as the Formosa faction feared. New Tide was thus suspicious of expanding business ties with China, fearing that the Taiwanese economy could be held hostage to the mainland's political interests; rather than being the solution, Greater China was a major problem for national security (Lin Cho-shui 1998). After the DPP's presidential victory in 2000, this concern was realized when the PRC sanctioned pro-independence business people from Taiwan (Hughes 2001; CND 6 June 2000). The New Tide faction thus proposed that Taiwan deal with China from a position of strength: a strong base of Taiwanese "civic consciousness" (Hughes 1998, 15–16; Wei Hung-Chin 1999, 66–68).

The DPP's 1998 Mainland Affairs Conference concluded by looking to the common ground between the two main policy proposals. Both a "Westward advance" and a "strong base" were necessary, and both sides acknowledged the need to talk with Beijing (Hughes 1998; Wei Hung-Chin 1999, 68). This was a major step for the New Tide faction, which previously had followed more of a containment strategy of limiting contacts with the mainland (Wei Hung-Chin 1999, 63).

Meanwhile, similar nativist and flexibility arguments were going on in the KMT. Hence in the 1990s, the real issue in Taiwanese politics was less the choice between unification or independence than identity formation according to narratives of nativism or of flexibility.

Political Reform and Democratic Recognition

After the United Nations recognized the PRC in 1971, the ROC was thrown into a diplomatic crisis. Over the next three decades, most countries shifted their diplomatic recognition from Taipei to Beijing. As of 2002, only twenty-eight countries recognized Taipei, while 162 recognized Beijing. Thus Taiwan had to be more flexible in its diplomacy, cultivating the ties of "low diplomacy"—that is, economic and cultural ties—rather than those of the "high diplomacy" of political and military representation. Taiwan thus was obliged to enter GATT in 1982 as a "customs area"—like Hong Kong—rather than as a sovereign state. It had to enter the WTO just after the PRC, in 2001. Most countries followed Japan's model, which substituted an unofficial Japan Interchange Association for the Japanese embassy in Taibei, and the Nationalist China's Association of East Asian Relations in Japan for the ROC embassy in Tokyo; the unofficial American "embassy" is called the American Institute in Taiwan (Hughes 1997a, 130). Like the PRC before 1971, Taipei has to rely on flexible diplomacy, pragmatic diplomacy, and people-to-people diplomacy (see Chen Jie 2002, 223–72).

This diplomatic crisis was accompanied by an identity crisis. The world was telling the ROC that it did not represent "China," but just what did it represent? Constitutionally, the political institutions of the ROC represented not just the mainland and Taiwan province, but overseas Chinese as well. Practically, this led to a political crisis. Like the CCP, the KMT's nationalism represented the idea of "China" rather than the people of Taiwan; thus, the KMT was forced to recognize the demographic reality of a constituency dominated by ethnic Taiwanese voters (Chun 1996, 146; Hughes 1997a, 70).

To maintain its legitimacy, the KMT instituted a number of political reforms, starting in the early 1980s under Chiang Ching-kuo, and after 1988 under Lee Teng-hui. Since this process has been well analyzed elsewhere, I will only summarize it (Hughes 1997a, 70–94; Tien and Chu 1998). In 1986, the loose Dangwai group was allowed to establish the Democratic Progressive Party (DPP). Once martial law was lifted, in 1987, political activity exploded. While the government was adjusting to its new international isolation, it reorganized political institutions to better represent the Taiwanese electorate. Thus in the 1990s, Lee Teng-hui, working with the DPP, instituted constitutional reforms that rationalized the government structure, thus "finishing the absurdity of provincial and national government over the same jurisdiction" (Hughes 1998, 6).

Most dramatically, constitutional reforms in 1991 changed the way the president was chosen. Rather than being picked by the National Assembly, which still represented both the mainland and overseas Chinese, the president of the ROC as a result of the reform would be directly elected. Thus political reform shifted the notion of "the people" from the "Chinese nation" to Taiwanese voters. When Lee Teng-hui declared that "sovereignty resided in the people," he meant the people of Taiwan. (Mainland arguments respond by saying that popular sovereignty has to come from the whole people— the 1.3 billion citizens of the PRC, not the 23 million of the ROC.) Thus under Chiang Ching-kuo and Lee Teng-hui, Taiwan was transformed from a Leninist party-state to a democratic polity via the "quiet revolution" of an election-led, gradual, and peaceful process (Tien and Chu 1998; Lee Teng-hui 1995; Lee Teng-hui 2002). Both democracy and identity were further consolidated in 2000 with the election of the opposition party candidate as president.

Political reform was accompanied by cultural reform. Under Lee Teng-hui, the first native Taiwanese leader of the ROC, the KMT was nativized and Taiwanized to save the KMT from failure at the polls. Appropriating Taiwanese consciousness from the DPP, Lee "fundamentally deconstructed Taiwan's political ecology" (Tu Weiming 1998, 85). Following the Dangwai group, Lee spoke of a "community of shared destiny" whose membership was defined on inclusive civic rather than exclusive ethnic grounds. Taiwanese identity and citizenship was based on affiliation—those who lived in Taiwan—rather than essence—those who had Taiwanese origins (Hughes 1997a, 97–98; Chang, Han-pi 1997).

Rather than continuing the nationalization cultural policy, state resources were used to foster a "pluralistic and creative national identity" (Hughes 1997a, 99; Hsiao Hsin-huang 1995). Recall the parliamentary debate with five options for identity. Thus social integration was promoted by both the KMT and DPP. Against this convergence, the nativists of each main party splintered off: KMT nationalists formed the New Party (originally called the China New Party) in 1993, and the radical independence wing of the DPP formed the Taiwan Independence Party in 1996.

The basis of sovereignty and legitimacy shifted from nationalism to democracy not just in domestic politics but in international politics. Rather than basing its legitimacy on being the one true representative of China, Taipei now appeals to its democratic reform and economic success for international recognition. Democratic performances replace diplomatic performances (see Hwang 2001). The focus is not so much on the U.S. State Department as on Euro-American public opinion: Taiwan is a "democratic friend" in East Asia with considerable economic power (Ling and Shih 1999, 223; Chen Jie 2002, 223ff; Taiwan Security Enhancement Act 2000; Hughes 1997a, 144; Tu Weiming 1998, 82).

This focus on economic and friendship diplomacy rather than on political and military diplomacy is nothing peculiar to Taiwan. It is the general trend with the neoliberal regime of the post–Cold War to focus on geoeconomics rather than on geopolitics. Of course, Taiwan has flexible identity and diplomacy not out of choice but out of necessity. The curious contradiction of Taiwan's international nonstatus pushed both the KMT regime and the people to think creatively about the relation of nation, state, and democracy.

IDENTITY, NATIONALISM, AND DEMOCRACY

The "Taiwan model"' of democratization for the mainland is often trumpeted in Taipei and Washington as the solution to cross-straits tensions. As we saw in chapter 1, many Western international relations analysts look to "democratic peace" theory to argue that both unification and regional peace would best be guaranteed by the democratization of the PRC (see Friedman and McCormick 2000; Bernstein and Munro 1998).

The democratic peace argument is part of a post–Cold War trend that sees new challenges in international relations, and new forms of violence, coming from intrastate ethnic and nationalist conflict rather than from interstate war. Yet rather than trying to determine whether nationalism is civic (i.e., good) or ethnic (bad), it is important to see how democracy forms identity in different ways: institutional forms of electoral democracy, or ethical forms of a democratic ethos. Democracy is not unambiguously hitched to peace; at certain times and in certain forms, democracy itself fosters violence. Indeed, because the structures of electoral democracy divided its multinational community into pure ethnic constituencies, the Bosnian experience serves as a cautionary tale of how democracy is sometimes linked not to peace but to violence (see Campbell 1998b).[7]

Beijing: Structural Problems and Solutions

In Beijing, leaders are suspicious of democratic peace arguments. But their structural view of the Taiwan problem also limits their political imagination to certain structural solutions. In other words, democratization is not seen as the solution but as the problem. This follows from an instrumental view of party history: "In short, the KMT promoted democratization as a strategy to regain legitimacy, while the CCP resisted democratization as a strategy to avoid disintegration" (He and Guo 2000, 118; CND 23 April 2000; Wang Fei-Ling 2000, 95–96).[8]

While the relation of nation and state has been deconstructed in Taiwan to allow for more fluid identity practices, according to PRC sources nationalization is the primary objective. Like neorealists in Euro-America, Beijing uses the regulatory logic of the national state to promote unity rather than plurality. If democracy can help nationalization, then it is useful. Hence, to fight corruption and increase efficiency, many village councils in the PRC have been elected since 1988 (Diamond and Myers 2000, 382; O'Brien and Li, Lianjiang 2000; Pastor and Tan 2000; Pei, Minxin 2000, 87–89). Other activists and scholars point to federalism as a strategy to include numerous constituencies in a united Chinese nation (Yan Jiaqi 1992, 269–70; Friedman 1995; Duara 1995; He and Guo 2000, 123). Indeed, the "one country, two systems" formula is already a successful constitutional answer to reunification politics in Hong Kong and Macao; Taiwan could be democratic within such a federal system.

But if democracy does not aid nationalization, then it is a problem. In Hong Kong, for example, Beijing was hostile to Governor Chris Patten's 1992 democratization proposals because they became enmeshed in the rivalry between the United Kingdom and the PRC. Democracy in Hong Kong thus was seen as an imperialist trick, divisive of Chinese nationalism (He and Guo 2000, 176). The structural imperatives of democracy are seen as, as in Bosnia, dividing the nation; an elected Hong Kong leader structurally would be pushed to represent Hong Kong's interests against the central government in Beijing (see Zhonggong 1998, 119).

Democracy became a major issue in cross-straits relations in 1999–2000. In its 2000 White Paper, Beijing repeatedly declared that Taipei should not use democratic demands to delay unification; under the "one country, two systems" formula, Taipei should respect the social system (i.e., Communist Party rule) of the mainland (Taiwan Affairs Office 2000). The issue according to the White Papers is not democratization but unification. Indeed, democracy became an issue again with the 2004 presidential elections in Taiwan: to mobilize the otherwise waning vote for his re-election, President Chen Shui-bian concurrently held a referendum on whether Taiwanese were threatened by the PRC's ballistic missiles that targeted the island.

Many international relations experts in China point out that the world should be happy that China is not democratic, because Chinese public opinion is overwhelmingly in favor of using force to retake Taiwan (Interviews 1999). This populist sentiment was confirmed in the comment book at the Taiwan Problem Picture Exhibit; quite a few people wrote that they wished to "use military force to resolve the Taiwan problem" (Guowuyuan 2001). According to Beijing, the election of a DPP president proved that democracy divides a people. The upshot of this is dire: "Democratization threatens the very existence of the Chinese nation-state" (He and Guo 2000, 201). Democracy is not the key to peace, but a security threat: "Taiwanese nationalist votes cannot stop Chinese bullets if they come" (He and Guo 2000, 119; Bachman 2000).

The problem with this logic, of course, is that it is not working. In addition to begging the question of the difference between populism and popular sovereignty, events in both 1996 and 2000 showed that, the more aggressively nationalistic the PRC became, the more it alienated Taiwan's electorate and fostered the legitimacy of Beijing's targets, Lee Teng-hui in 1996 and Chen Shui-bian in 2000 and 2004. Beijing "has not yet learned that propaganda war is not the best way to influence the outcome of elections" (Hughes 2001, 137).

Taiwan: From Institutions to Ethos

Although there is a more open view of the relation between democracy and nationalism in Taiwan, political reform is still figured more as a structural problem than as an ethical question. As the above description confirms, in Taiwan democracy was seen as a technical issue: Taiwan was democratized through a series of government-instituted top-down political and constitutional reforms. This technical understanding of politics follows mainstream democratization theory, which defines political development in terms of regular, free, and fair elections to produce leaders whose power, in turn, is limited by constitutional structures (Diamond and Myers 2000, 366). Democracy in Greater China is regulated by the electoral institutions of states: the PRC, Hong Kong, and the ROC (Diamond and Myers 2000, 365).

Analyses of the democratization of Taiwan thus focus on elites, Chiang Ching-kuo and in particular Lee Teng-hui, known as the "Father of Taiwan's democratization" (Wang Fei-Ling 2000, 96). Even civic notions of democracy have been instituted from above: Lee Teng-hui changed the ROC's cultural policy to encourage more openness. (For example, Lee Teng-hui told Taiwanese that the foreign idea of *Gemeinschaft*, the community of shared destiny, had to be grafted onto traditional Chinese family ethics [in Hughes 1997a, 97]). In the late 1980s, therefore, the examples of political reform in South Korea and Taiwan led democratic advocates in the PRC to talk in terms of a "new authoritarianism" whereby elites imposed political reform from above in a gradual and orderly fashion (Ma, Shu-Yun 1994, 172, 175; Link 1992, 283–89). Yet, while these reforms were democratic in the sense of broadening the use of elections to choose leaders, they were not democratic in the sense of limiting executive power; reforms in Taiwan actually extended presidential powers.

Democracy and Chinese Culture

The top-down institutional view of democratization leads into two of the mainstream arguments about political culture in East Asia:

first, that East Asian culture is antidemocratic; second, that, since the natural unit of politics is the family, the state follows a patriarchal logic.

In the early 1990s Tu Weiming declared, "If Taiwan (the Republic of China) becomes truly democratic, the question of Taiwan's Chineseness will inevitably become a matter of public debate" (Tu Weiming 1994a, 10). Huntington took a clear position in this debate when he declared that "Confucian democracy is an oxymoron" (Huntington 1991, 300). Likewise, the PRC government sees democracy in Taiwan as a foreign commodity imported by exiles returning from the United States and Japan (Zhonggong 1998, 13–15, 33; Tu Weiming 1998, 82; Guowuyuan 2001, panel 3-8).

Once democracy is taken as foreign, it is either imported in the name of political development or restricted in the name of Asian values (see Callahan 2002b; Callahan 2002a; Rodan 1996; Callahan 1996a; Callahan 1996b). Lee Teng-hui chose to graft civil society onto Confucian family values, but Singapore's Lee Kuan Yew and leaders in the PRC choose to limit democratization because it is foreign (see Zakaria 1994; Bauer and Bell 1999). Others have been searching for democratic roots in China's past, trying to carve civil society out of ancient Chinese institutions—with limited success.[9] Chinese political culture is thus seen as a problem, an obstacle to be overcome for political reform (see Shi, Tianjian 2000, 540–42).

This leads to the second issue: Chinese political culture necessitates that politics in Confucian society uses a hierarchical, top-down family structure (Ling and Shih 1999, 213–14). Although many democratic reformers point to classical Chinese concepts such as "people-based government" and the "right to rebel" against autocratic rule (Kim Dae Jung 1994, 191), others feel that such liberal views misrepresent tradition. Such arguments lead to a compromise between Western democratic institutions and Confucian ethics. This "illiberal democracy," like Lee Teng-hui's cultural policy, "grafts" democratic institutions onto Asian political culture (Ling and Shih 1999, 217; Jones et al. 1995). Thus, as we saw in chapter 4's discussion of Confucian social science, such scholars argue that the best that China and Taiwan can get is an illiberal democracy of free and fair elections in a restricted and hierarchical civil society. These scholars keep "democracy" by subtracting "liberal" and end up with electoralism (Callahan 1996, 129–37; Chan Heng Chee 1994; Bauer and Bell 1999; Fukuyama 1995).

There are theoretical problems with this democratic arithmetic. It assumes that Western democracy and Confucian tradition are coherent, one representing individual rights and the other community obligations—then uses a liberal logic of balancing to split the difference (Fukuyama 1995, 33; Callahan 1996b, 130). Both Confucianism and democracy are reduced to clichés, so that one coherent system can be grafted onto the other in synthesis.

The emergence of popular democracy in Taiwan and South Korea also presents empirical problems to culturalist arguments that compromise civil society for electoralism (Weller 1999, 6; Callahan 2002a; White et al. 1996, 217). Rather than be preoccupied with the comparative study of utopian ideals of liberalism and Confucianism, we should examine the struggle of people in social movements (Rorty 1996; Rorty 1991). It turns out that the state did not create civil society and popular politics through top-down reform. As the explosion of activity in 1987–88 just after martial law was lifted in Taiwan and the military government stepped down in South Korea shows, social movements existed before they were technically legal (Weller 1999, 136); before Chiang Ching-kuo and Lee Teng-hui liberalized society, there were very active informal community-based social movements organized to represent women, the environment, labor, consumers, nonhomeowners, peasants, new religions, minority groups, and democratic students (Weller 1999, 6–7; Chang, Mau-Kuei 1997, 9; Kuo Liangwen 1997b, 4; Callahan 1998b; Hughes 1997a, 42; White et al. 1996). More to the point, we should remember that Lee Teng-hui took his reform ideas from social movements in Taiwan's informal opposition.

These informal community organizations look to a social notion of democracy more than an electoral one; they are "communities of memory" more than interest groups (Madsen 1993, 192). While formal associations in both Taiwan and the PRC are more "easily coopted or simply repressed," informal community groups in villages and urban neighborhoods are often much bolder, and more difficult for the state to manage (Weller 1999, 110, 126, 129; Callahan 2002a; White et al. 1996, 215). By cultivating community relations via horizontal ties of trust, these social movements are political in a wider sense of "quality of life" issues, and need not have specific "party political" goals (Weller 1999, 13, 110; Chang, Mau-Kuei 1997, 14). Weller explains that, contrary to stereotypes of Confucian patriarchy, many of the most militant grassroots social movements in Taiwan are led by women (Weller 1999, 140–42).

Rather than being a top-down technical problem of reforming institutions, democracy thus is an ethos that fosters nonviolent political conflict: "it is precisely the uneven, unwieldy nature of politics in Taiwan that, conversely, offers a ray of hope: in destabilizing the political environment, it pushes society to consider more (and possibly alternative) understandings of the common good" (Ling and Shih 1999, 229; Chang, Mau-Kuei 1997). The informal community-based social movements suggest that democracy is an ethical question that requires ongoing negotiation; the discussion would continue even after any democratic unification with the PRC.

Democratic change in both Taiwan and Greater China can appeal to Otherness in face-to-face cultural encounters rather than in institutional arrangements. Instead of seeing democracy in terms of "a substance, a fixed set of values, a particular kind of community, or a strict institutional form," Campbell uses Derrida and Levinas to think of democracy as "a particular attitude or spirit, an ethos, that constantly has to be fostered" (Campbell 1998b, 196). We have seen this ethos of democracy in the community of shared destiny and the informal community-based social movements. Like Ling and Shih, Campbell argues that it is an ethos of disturbance that "embodies productive ambiguity" and allows for difference.

The promise of democratic ethos does not demand that everyone agree. Rather, it would "actively nourish and nurture antagonism, conflict, plurality, and multiplicity, not at the expense of security or identity but in terms of security's and identity's contamination by and indebtedness to its other(s)" (Campbell 1998b, 219). Although "Antagonism and conflict are democracy's life blood," such political encounters need to be negotiated via nonviolent face-to-face relationships (Campbell 1998b, 202). Derrida's "democratic promise" thus coincides more with the local Taiwan experience of participatory organizations than with Lee Teng-hui's top-down institutional reforms.

In this way, Chinese culture has not been an obstacle to democracy; it has enabled democratic change: "Taiwan has not abandoned Chinese culture. . . . In fact there is something of a cultural renaissance going on, with everything from a religious revival to tea houses to a new Confucianism developing in opposition to Lee

Kuan Yew's conservative understanding of Confucianism" (Weller 1999, 7, xii). Confucian culture and Chinese society thus are not monolithic but are multifaceted and adaptable:

> democratization in a postcolonial context encompasses multiple practices, ideals, and institutions that shade into, clash against, and spill over conventional boundaries between "liberalism" and "Confucianism," "dissent" and "loyalty," "representation" and "reality," "democracy" and "authoritarianism." (Ling and Shih 1999, 219)

Politics in Taiwan is not derivative of Chinese tradition, Western democracy, or the European Enlightenment, but represents an "alternative civility" (Weller 1999; Ling and Shih 1999, 229).

FRIENDSHIP AND THE POLITICS OF RECOGNITION

Since Confucius has been enlisted, once again, into Greater Chinese politics, it is helpful to reexamine the classical texts to explore this alternative civility. Certainly, democratic civility is not found in mainstream readings of Chinese tradition, where Confucianism is seen as the opposite of liberalism. Yet, instead of locating difference between Eastern and Western civilizations, this section deals with difference *within* Confucian culture. Hence I must look to the margins of tradition to challenge the hegemonic interpretation that sees Confucianism only in terms of hierarchical ordering (see Madsen 1993, 192). Rather than searching the texts for democratic political institutions or nascent human rights (Bauer and Bell 1999; Kim Dae Jung 1994), I recover the workings of the concept of Confucian friendship. Here I expand from chapter 4, where Han Sang-jin argued that "Confucianism has not just legitimized authoritarian regimes, but criticized them" (Han 1997b, 10), to see how Confucianism not just criticizes the state but provides models of alternative social relations.

"Friendship" is not an obvious place to look. It seems a lightweight concept. But, as we have seen, friendship can be a technical term: for instance, "friendship treaties" are an important part of the PRC's diplomatic strategy. Indeed, in addition to the One China policy, the PRC has a one-child policy, under which the scope of kinship relations is rapidly shrinking. With this new demography, soon there will not be any siblings, and few cousins, but only friends. In recent years, friendship has been taken much more seriously in the analysis of the contradictions and ambiguities of social relations (Derrida 1997; Farrands 2001; Rouner 1994; Badhwar 1993); here, I use Confucian friendship to see more egalitarian images of Chinese society—friends who are joined by sharing trust, will, and virtue. Rather than an appeal to common ancestors, we have a flexible sharing of friends.

Confucian Friendship

Confucianism is not metaphysical so much as ethical. It is a guide to human relationships: father-son, ruler-subject, husband-wife, elder brother-younger brother, and friend-friend. Mencius clarifies the social grammar of these relationships: "love between father and son, duty between ruler and subject, distinction between husband and wife, precedence of old over the young, and trust between friends" (Mencius 1970, 3A/4).[10] These three social spaces in Confucian society—family, friends, and the state—are not separate, as in the division between public and private spheres, but are integrally interrelated (Mencius 1970, 4A/13).

Although friendship comes last on this list, it is not least in either quality or quantity. We should recall that the opening lines of the Confucian *Analects* address neither the ruler nor the father, but the friend: "Isn't it a joy to acquire knowledge and be able to put it to use? Isn't it a great pleasure to have a friend visiting from afar?" (Confucius 1979, 1/1). Friendship is also quantitatively important in the two main Confucian classics, the *Analects* and the *Mencius*.[11] But just what does friendship entail in classical China?

One way to understand friendship is to see it as an extension of the hierarchical relationships of the family, where "being a good friend" is like "being a good son" or "being a good brother." Classical sources, modern dictionaries, and recent scholarship all confirm this understanding of friendship as the practice of brotherly relations and filial piety (Xu Shen 1981, 116; *Cihai* 1979, 354; Hall and Ames 1994). But the economy of classical Chinese language can also lead to the opposite conclusion: friendship and family are put together in parallel passages just because they are *different*: "Fathers and sons are at odds for taxing each other over moral issues. It is for friends to demand goodness from each other. For fathers and sons to do so seriously undermines the love between them" (Mencius 1970, 4B/30).

The *Analects* and the *Mencius* are both very explicit in stating that the relations between family and friends are quite different. Family relations emphasize solidarity and the avoidance of controversy; because of potential conflict, brotherly relations should be "genial and happy." On the other hand, friendship provides a different space, characterized by active demands for goodness in keen and earnest discussion (Confucius 1979: 13/28). Like Derrida's democratic ethos, it involves a critical stance: "The asking of questions itself is the correct rite" (Confucius 1979, 3/15).

Friendship here echoes the notion of harmony (examined in the previous chapter), which values difference and debate over homogeneity and uncritical agreement: "a single opinion about things does not make a conversation" (*Guoyu* 1978, SPTK 16/Zhengyu). In a community, "Each person pursues different goals: having what is deviant, they have what is correct" (*Zhuangzi* 1985, 72/25/59).

Similar parallels are drawn between the relationship between ruler/subject and relations between friends. Again, mainstream views point to the similarities between these two sets of social relationships: "Bo Yi would serve only the right prince and befriend only the right man" (Mencius 1970, 2A/9). But more importantly, the parallels highlight quite different reactions to friendship:

> Duke Mu went to see [the sage] Zi Si and asked: "In antiquity how did kings of large states make friends with scholar-officials."
>
> Zi Si was displeased. He said: "What the ancients talked about was serving kings, not making friends with them."
>
> The reason for Zi Si's displeasure was surely this: "According to social position, you are the ruler and I am your subject. How dare I be friends with a ruler? According to virtue, it is you who ought to serve me. How can you presume to be friends with me?"
>
> If the ruler of a large state cannot even hope to be friends with Zi Si, how much less can he hope to summon such a man. (Mencius 1970, 5B/7)

The relations cannot be mixed, according to Zi Si, because they work in different ways. The ruler/subject relation is based on position and works through a hierarchical economy of authority and service. Friendship relations, on the other hand, work according to virtue, and are open to anyone to perfect (see Derrida 1997, 1–24). The *Analects* and the *Mencius* both confirm that the sage must make friends with the ruler outside of his position (Confucius 1979, 4/26). While friendship challenges family hierarchies with more egalitarian relations, here it uses meritocracy to question the aristocratic state.

Making Friends: Social Recognition

The *Analects* and the *Mencius* organize social life in terms of three interconnected spaces: family, friends, and the state. People fulfill themselves not just through family and the state, but also through friendship. These passages suggest that, while state and family relations are hierarchical, friendship leads to a third space of more egalitarian social relations (Mencius 1970, 5B/3). The first Chinese lexicon, the *Shuowen*, defines friendship outside the hierarchical relations of family and state: "Friends share will. Friendship follows from two hands [shaking] making a mutual connection" (Xu Shen 1981, 116; Karlgren 1957, 261). While you "serve" your parents and your ruler, you recognize and communicate with friends (Confucius 1979, 1/7).

Hence, friendship is not passive but flexible. While the four relationships of family and state are formed according to fate, the texts show that friendship is a very active concept, often verbal—"making friends" through careful consideration (Confucius 1979, 16/4). The mutual connection of making friends is a negotiated relationship based not on the "honor" of blood or service, but on the "dignity" of affinity and mutual respect (see Taylor 1994, 39). It is an equality not so much of sameness, but of the sharing of will and virtue. The sharing of friendship is an active negotiation of contingent relations: people are continually making and unmaking friends. According to Confucius, it is the duty of an exemplary person to make friends with humane people (Confucius 1979, 15/9). People are judged by the company they keep; the choices taken in making friends are indicative of character (Confucius 1979, 16/5).

Because friendship relations are contingent, trust is very important (Confucius 1979, 1/3, 1/7, 5/25). Etymologically, trust *(xin)* relates the sharing of virtue to the sharing of language: "Make it your guiding principle to do your best for others and to be trustworthy in what you say. Do not accept as friend anyone who is not as good as you. When you make a mistake do not be afraid of mending your ways" (Confucius 1979, 9/24, 1/8). Friendship is contingent because if you make a mistake, you can unmake it (see Confucius 1979, 12/23).

The passages above have shown how friendship constitutes a social space separate from and different than the hierarchical relations of family and state, yet friendship is also intimately engaged in politics—not so much in formal service as via an alternative civility. Politics is not limited to the election of elites: Confucian friendship constructs a politics of recognition that grows out of people-to-people dynamics:

> Someone asked Confucius: Why don't you take part in government? The Master said: The *Book of History* says: "Simply by being filial and friendly with his brothers a man can exert influence on government." In so doing, a man is in fact taking part in government. How can there be any question of his having actively to "take part in government"? (Confucius 1979, 2/21)

For Confucius, proper behavior in all social relationships is good politics; democracy would not be limited to state institutions, but would look to biopolitical activities with family, work, and friends. Mencius connects friendship with politics in a way more suggestive of social movements. He instructs that in a good system, "If those who own land within each neighborhood befriend each other both at home and abroad, help each other to keep watch, and succor each other in times of illness, they will live in love and harmony" (Mencius 1970, 3A/3). Political community here is not formed on the basis of a social contract between citizens, but of the sharing of friendship. Thus, alongside the relations between ruler and subject, father and son, there is another space of political activity where people act according to mutuality and friendship to "live in love and harmony."

Friendships, then, are a source of participation and equality in the Confucian classics for democratic civility (see Wang et al. 1994, 600). Certainly, neither Confucius nor Mencius now seem revolutionary. But they were a part of a fundamental shift in Chinese thought away from hierarchical status to more active and egalitarian friendship (Graham 1989, 19; Callahan 1996b). Friendship and trust, in the community-based social movements examined above, are constituted as a set of largely informal relations that run alongside family and state, sometimes supporting them but also serving as a space apart providing other images of society and political community (Weller 1999). Rather than inscribing a new set of norms, friendship affords a new set of possibilities.

From Friendship Diplomacy to Democratic Friendship

Confucian friendship works both parallel to and directly opposite from the PRC's friendship diplomacy. The friendship treaties recognize difference in international society. Before China achieved widespread diplomatic recognition, the PRC's foreign policy utilized international friendship associations (e.g., the Sino-British Friendship Association) to pursue informal people-to-people diplomacy. The Chinese People's Association for Friendship with Foreign Countries, which coordinated these activities, was part of the Foreign Ministry. Within the PRC, "Friend of China" was a semiofficial title for foreigners—usually Westerners—who supported the Chinese Revolution and the PRC state when it was isolated in the 1950s–1970s (Brady 1997, 614–18).

But this was not a friendship of engaged discussion. Quite the opposite: "To be a Friend in this era entailed complete adherence to whatever the current political line was in Beijing" (Brady 1997, 615). The job of Friends of China was to promote the PRC to the Euro-American world. This parallels China's friendship treaties: one of the conditions of normalizing relations has been to recognize the PRC as the one and only China. Friendship here requires unequivocal agreement with the Chinese government. Rather than harmony, in this friendship, there is sameness. Recall that the patriotic "Spratly Spirit" examined in chapter 3 called for "unity in friendship" (Ling Xingzheng 1998).

Since most countries have switched diplomatic recognition to the PRC, Taiwan now has to cultivate friendship diplomacy, people-to-people diplomacy, flexible diplomacy, and pragmatic diplomacy. President Lee Teng-hui conducted "vacation diplomacy" whereby he met with world leaders unofficially. But even flexible diplomacy has its risks: Lee's 1995 visit to Cornell University led to a crisis in Sino-American, Taiwan-American, and cross-straits relations, and set the stage for the PLA's war games off Taiwan in 1995–96.

More important, some groups in Taiwan want to reorganize their foreign relations from interstate relations to the people-to-people relations of an expanded community of shared destiny. Hence, rather than merely to reconcile relations between mainlanders and locals on Taiwan, the community of shared destiny can be used to join the PRC and the ROC in social, cultural, and economic relations (Tu Weiming 1998). Taiwanese elites have argued that "China" was distinct from two states that claimed it, while Lee Teng-hui said he wished to "improve the lives of the whole body of the people of the Chinese race" (in Hughes 1997a, 75–76).

Going beyond ethnic and cultural China, Lee Teng-hui proposed that the community of shared destiny would work not just for a new moral order in Taiwan or Greater China, but for East Asian regional politics and world order in general. This shared community would "foster the consensus that joys and sorrows are to be shared and problems jointly tackled in the global village" (in Hughes 1997a, 142, 128; Lee Teng-hui 2002, 40; Tu Weiming 1998).

Chen Shui-bian's cultural politics also joins intra-Taiwanese relations with extra-Taiwanese relations. Chinese culture and ethnicity is not singular but plural; it appeals to diasporic Chinese as well as the mainland (Chen Shui-bian 2000; Simon 2000). By loosening Chineseness from any state, this non-Sinocentric identity affords an inclusive conceptualization of Chineseness in the world community (Tu Weiming 1998, 77). Rather than seeing this Chineseness in terms of a top-down cultural policy, this non-state-centric understanding of identity recognizes how grassroots community organizations construct the transnational community of shared destiny through people-to-people relations. In such transnational friendship relations, the ambiguity of identity needs to be maintained: as we saw earlier, clarity in cross-straits relations will likely generate violence.

CONCLUSION

The Taiwan Straits define the greatest threat of violence in East Asia. On the one hand, the PRC refuses to give up its right as a sovereign nation to use force to resolve this internal affair. In this sense, the PRC is still engaged in completing its nationalist project; this is not simply a policy of the elite in Beijing, but an ardently held sentiment in popular opinion. Whoever loses Taiwan would be seen as a "historical criminal" similar to Li Hongzhang, the official who signed away many Chinese territories during the Century of National Humiliation—including Taiwan in 1895 (Deng Xiaoping 1993, 1).

The democratization of Taiwan, on the other hand, threatens to provoke violence. As electoral democracy consolidates on the island, constituencies that question unification are solidifying. But as this chapter has shown, though the PRC campaigns for a unified One China nation-state, Taiwan is not necessarily moving toward establishing its own counter-nation-state. The issues have moved beyond unification/independence to more flexible notions of identity. The problems go beyond Beijing's and Taipei's arguments over state structures and national boundaries to concern how people can recognize each other in face-to-face encounters: the ethos of Confucian friendship. In this way, the real issue is not "who will win in struggles of war and peace"—nationalist China or democratic Taiwan—but what form cosmopolitics will take in Greater China.

Conclusion
Contingent Peoples

In his weekly column "On Language," William Safire proudly declared that "Chinese prefer their own language to gloss over differences but turn to English to introduce degrees of difference. Our language is as subtle as their minds" (Safire 1999, 27–28). Safire was discussing the multiple meanings of the Chinese word *guojia*—state, country, nation—which are better differentiated in English. But in declaring that "Chinese are forced to argue in English," Safire misses the point. Since the social, political, and economic vocabulary in modern Chinese language comes from European languages, Chinese leaders are already speaking "English." More to the point, Safire forgets that Euro-American scholars have their own problems with the English language, and are forced to use an unwieldy phrase, *nation-state*.

By questioning the relation between state sovereignty and popular sovereignty, this book has examined the ambiguities of the nation-state, especially the elusive hyphen that joins the two seeming stable nouns "nation" and "state." In the same realist epistemological spirit as Safire, many seek to nail down this hyphen to stabilize both the concept of nation-state in general and specific nation-states in particular—the People's Republic of China (PRC), Taiwan, South Korea, and so on. Against this scientific view of international politics, I have appealed to a political aesthetic that highlights the ambiguity and negotiation of meaning. Instead of analyzing international law and diplomacy, I have looked to the cultural epistemology of knowledge practices to see how they produce "Greater China." The aim of this book thus has not been precision, definition, and prediction so much as to show how East and West, mainland China and Taiwan/Hong Kong, nation and diaspora, power and knowledge, are all joined in contingent relationships.

The hyphens joining these concepts are much like the waves and shore in Seamus Heaney's "Lovers on Aran." The last stanza of the epigraph asks, "Did sea define the land or land the sea? Each drew new meaning from the waves' collision. Sea broke on land to full identity." Land and sea do not exist as essential autonomous objects, but define each other in a contingent state; they take on meaning according to the shifting boundaries of waves as they crash onto the shore. Heaney's poem is helpful for international politics because it explores perspectives—the land and the sea: China, Taiwan, Hong Kong, and South Korea—without naturalizing them into any stable national culture, civilization, or other identity enclave. The crash of the waves in "Lovers on Aran" highlights how identity and politics are invested with both intimacy and violence in the struggle for meaning.

"Lovers on Aran" tells of struggles between Europe and America in the North Atlantic, Catholic and Protestant in Northern Ireland. The land and the sea also point to more productive consideration of the defining features of Greater China—the Strait of Taiwan, the South China Sea, and the Shenzhen River (in Hong Kong). The narrow band of sea that forms the Strait of Taiwan is exemplary, because it is not just a physical barrier. In the Cold War it also constituted a metaphysical barrier, a straight line that divided the mutually exclusive binary oppositions not just of capitalism/communism but of inside/outside, self/Other, and good/evil. Yet, as this book has shown, in the 1980s this clear ideological, geopolitical, and metaphysical border began to blur. The concept of Greater China emerged with the explosion of trade, investment, and travel across the Strait of Taiwan after both sides relaxed restrictions. The two territories were involved in overcoming Cold War hostilities, weaving themselves together according to the informal workings of the market and family ties rather than through formal state-to-state diplomacy. Such face-to-face encounters were reproduced along the Shenzhen River that divided the British Crown Colony of Hong Kong from the PRC, as well as in the Yellow Sea between the PRC and South Korea.

But Greater China has also produced much hype, including dreams of fabulous economic opportunities and nightmares of threatening political dangers, which has tended to essentialize politics and identity. Questioning such fantasies, my analysis has pointed to the intimacy and violence of the struggles for meaning in Greater China that have produced not just identities but theoretical innovations: the waves breaking on the shores that join nation and state, foreign and domestic, culture and ethnicity, state sovereignty and popular sovereignty, and race, nation, and ethnicity. To chart out these theoretical innovations, I have appealed to Foucault's concept of heterotopia, which describes a decentered space/time. Rather than follow many who seek to define Chinese nationalism as either utopic or dystopic, I have addressed the contingency of Greater China and East Asian international relations through an analysis of the discursive economies of four overlapping narratives of civilization/barbarism—nativism, conquest, conversion, diaspora—to say something, but not to claim to say everything. As the book has shown, the point is not to find one *true answer,* but to examine how politics is produced in the interplay between narrative modes. Greater China is not a place; it is a bundle of concepts.

Although many in Asia agree with Huntington that "culture" and "Confucianism" are conservative forces, my aesthetic view of politics does not seek to define a culture, but to provide a mode of analysis and interpretation. In line with Campbell, I see foreign policy as the ethical relation of self and Other as it defines domestic and foreign politics. Following Shapiro, I look to ethnography to engage in both criticism of the present and recovery of alternative modes of being. Like Walker, I see theory not as a repository of principles awaiting application but as an ongoing practice that emerges in response not only to historical conditions but to historical contradictions and reversals in Europe.

"Greater China" has likewise been the product of a series of reversals—in the PRC from communism to capitalism, revolutionary state to conservative state; from civil war to new nation-state, low-wage site of foreign investment to promoter of globalization in South Korea and the PRC as well. Thus Greater China emerged as a set of crises that spurred theoretical innovations. Elites and common people alike recycled tradition on a grand scale to relaunch Confucianism and the Chinese World Order, and on a smaller scale "one country, two systems" for Hong Kong, Macao, and Taiwan and "indisputable sovereignty/joint development" in the South China Sea. The book concludes that the struggles are actually not geopolitical, not between the PRC and a host of Others. Rather, the struggles are theoretical, between institutional structures and popular movements, between state sovereignty and popular sovereignty—on both sides of the Strait of Taiwan and throughout the world.

To be sure, Greater China is not a new locus of liberation. Popular sovereignty has been examined in this book largely in terms of diasporic movements of people and ideas across borders. In this way, it showed how the idea of Greater China is used to construct and discipline subjects: Chineseness and filial piety have been deployed to discipline workers and citizens, and Confucian shared civilization has been invoked to facilitate East Asian trade and investment. As we have seen, "Greater China" most often has been used, like Confucianism before it, as part of the state's management of populations in a characteristically top-down style: nationalization, regionalization, and globalization from above. Civilization not only guides an active cultural life, but produces a disciplined industrial labor force. The cosmopolitics of the diaspora, as we saw in Southeast Asia, South Korea, and especially Hong Kong, often preyed on the weaker members of society, defining them as the Other.

Although Taiwan has experienced institutional and ethical democratization since the early 1990s, democracy is not limited by the borders of Taiwan. It involves new notions of community (in relations of friendship) that problematize both top-down and bottom-up notions of power and influence. Rather than relying on vertical notions of institutional power, the book ended with an exploration of more horizontal notions of ethical encounters. Network power can work in democratic friendship as well as in family-based business when it emerges out of face-to-face encounters and people-to-people diplomacy.

NORMALCY AND VIOLENCE

Greater China is an exemplary contingent state because it does not exist as a legal or an institutional body. There is no seat for Greater China in the United Nations; it is not recognized by international law. Greater China, thus, is not normal. The strategy of criticism and recovery has also led to odd and unexpected places: traditional Chinese cartography, Confucian social science, filial piety awards, the Party History Department, and a community of shared destiny. Against this backdrop of the strange, there has been a persistent search for normalcy and legitimacy in East Asia. But which norms attract states in East Asia? And what does this tell us about "normal" international politics? In other words, what can Safire's interest in the Chinese word for nation-state tell us about the commonsense understanding of international relations not just in realism, but also in sociological constructivism.

Recall that since joining the United Nations in 1971, the goal of the PRC has been to normalize relations with every other state. Beijing has joined institutions of international society ranging from U.N. organizations to the WTO, and will host the 2008 Olympics. Academic discourse in China likewise promotes the PRC as a normal and responsible power, rather than a revolutionary threat (Xia Liping 2001). Indeed, Deng and Gray suggest that this policy is not just pragmatic but also theoretical: to narrow the normative gap between Western international relations theory and Chinese international relations theory (Deng and Gray 2001, 6–7). On the other hand, until 1971, Taiwan (as the Republic of China [ROC]) was normal; but as the PRC has gained normalcy, the ROC has become more and more deviant. It is a de facto state that now lacks de jure legitimacy.

Other states in the region have also taken "normalcy" as the focus of their diplomatic desires. After four decades of civil war, in 1991 North Korea and South Korea decided to sideline their Cold War/civil war predicament; they opted for shared recognition by international society via a simultaneous entry into the U.N. General Assembly. Soon after normalizing relations with the Soviet Union and the PRC, South Korea pursued a globalization policy that looked to normal international politics beyond the Korean Peninsula. Most prominently, Japanese politicians have stated that they want Japan to become a "normal nation" that is not only an economic superpower but can also take up its global security and political "responsibilities" (Ozawa 1994, 93–112). While Taiwan is a de facto state seeking de jure status, Japan is a de jure state seeking de facto power and influence.

But how is such normalcy achieved? Certainly, these countries are acting as model nation-states in such diplomatic performances. But most notions of normalcy in international politics involve violence; (the word *normalcy* was coined in 1920 by Warren G. Harding to campaign for happier days after World War I). To answer the question "What is normal?" a character in Taiwanese director Edward Yang's *A Confucian Confusion* lists a series of violent and xenophobic events, "the Boxer Rebellion, the Great Proletarian Cultural Revolution, Tian'anmen, a unified China, all are normal" (Yang, Edward 1994). In his *Blueprint for a New Japan*, Ozawa clarifies that normalcy necessitates amending Japan's peace constitution (Ozawa 1994, 109–12), which states that "the Japanese people forever renounce war as a sovereign right of the nation and the threat or use of force as means of settling international disputes." Whenever there is an international crisis, the Japanese elite has repeated this call to re-arm in order to take up Japan's peace and security "responsibilities." Much like the violence of structural notions of democracy (examined in chapter 6), normalcy comes at a price. As Enloe points out for gendered states, it takes an enormous amount of effort, of structural and physical violence, to keep the norms of international society in place (Enloe 1993, 51).

CONTINGENT POPULATIONS

Rather than taking the nation-state, diplomacy, and international law as the norm, this book has considered how they are deviant. Like globalization discourse, which examines transnational flows of capital and the barriers of nation-states, most studies of Greater China look to how borders are crossed—in three territories—the PRC, Hong Kong, and Taiwan—especially by overseas Chinese from Southeast Asia. This book questions the state-ness and territoriality of these places (as well as of South Korea and the Spratly Islands), to see how states, territory, and history are produced by border crossings. Rather than positing a withering away of the state from globalization, the previous chapters showed how the state was produced via border crossings. For example, in 1997 Hong Kong did not join the PRC so much as become separated from it; since the return of Hong Kong, it has become more difficult for mainland Chinese citizens to visit Hong Kong. "One country, two systems" has been implemented as a method to contain and regulate Hong Kong's influence on China. Hence the policy aim was not just to "protect" Hong Kong from the mainland. As chapter 5 showed, this policy has served to keep out the Chinese underclass.

This is not just a political-economic concern. Racial anxieties over the bastardization of native populations are an enduring and shared concern in East Asia. In the 1910s a Thai nationalist poet worried about Chinese and Thai "[u]navoidably mixing, clashing with one another./Jek [Chinese] mix with Thai beyond recognition,/Who is who, one can't help but wonder" (Nai Busya in Kasian 1992, 115). Since the 1970s, the Hong Kong elite has used a racial/ethnic logic to differentiate "old" and "new" immigrants. Ethnic categories are likewise used in Taiwan to differentiate between islander and main-lander populations. The distinction between ethnic Chinese on either side of the Hong Kong border or the Taiwan Strait is similar to the anxieties raised in Seoul over the encounter between ethnic Koreans who are Chinese citizens and those who are South Korean citizens (Moon, Katherine 2000).

But rather than take mixing as a problem for stability, this book has looked to contingency as the norm. One conclusion is that inter-national politics needs to be understood in terms of contingent peoples as well as contingent states. Given its messy history of imperialism and war, East Asia is a prominent site of such contingent peoples, who have multiple identities. As one prominent "Taiwanese" explains: "I grew up as a Japanese during the colonial period [1895–1945], be-came Chinese under the KMT dictatorship, may die as a naturalized American, but in heart and soul I have always been a Taiwanese" (in Tu Weiming 1998, 80). A 72-year-old Korean man told of his differ-ent names during different regimes: "I have three names: Ch Yon-sup [Korean], Tamakawa Yensho [Japanese], and the Chinese called me Nojo" (in Kim Ji-soo 1999).

Although these seem like exceptions that prove the normative rule of the nation-state, I think they provide an aesthetic framework for better understanding international politics. "We are all demo-crats today," John Dunn declared in 1979; I suggest that we are all diasporic today, regardless of family history and national fate. Certainly, diaspora is a popular topic in critical cultural studies, anthropology, and international relations theory, where diaspora are seen as the heroes in the (anti-)globalization era. They are hailed as postnational groups, nomadic heroes, modern cosmopolitans, and transnational yuppies whose mobile and autonomous "third culture" challenges both state sovereignty and global capitalism (Appadurai 1996, 19–21; Hardt and Negri 2000, 361; Cheah and Robbins 1998; Ong 1999; Nonini and Ong 1997).

Diaspora exemplify a contingent politics that loosens up the boundaries of nation and state. But such understandings of diaspora and cosmopolitics have their limits. As we saw in chapter 2, diasporic Chinese are not simply a cosmopolitian community of free-floating transnational yuppies. The analysis of Greater China has shown how borders were not simply transgressed and effaced by diasporic flows; diaspora are intimately involved in the production of borders in local, national, regional, and transnational space (see Callahan 2003a). They are engaged in making distinctions, and being made by distinctions. Who is diasporic in Hong Kong: the poor from the mainland, the rich who also live in Vancouver, or the born-and-raised Hong Kongers themselves? How do we code the "Taiwanese" and "Korean" wanderers: Japanese-Chinese-Korean-Taiwanese-American? Rather than the expected cosmopolitan "third culture," these contingent people seem more like the fabulous creatures from the *Shanhai jing*'s heterotopia: five heads and one body, or five bodies and one head.

If diaspora is considered in terms of political poetics rather than ethnic identity, it is clear that we are all diaspora today. Diaspora almost by definition lack formal political status. Since they have little or no legal purchase on the powers of the state, diasporic activities are not best understood according to the popular sovereignty of representative government and civil society. Rather, the politics of these "essential outsiders" (Chirot and Reid 1997) is best understood as part of a governmentality active in cultural, social, and economic spaces: the office, family, factory, and school in addition to the familiar state institutions. Indeed, this does not just describe the exception of diasporic populations. In a neoliberal network global political-economy, the political sovereignty of representative government is increasingly transferred to transnational capital and quasi-governmental organizations such as the WTO, the European Commission, the IMF, and the World Bank. We are all diasporic now in the sense that power is located outside and alongside the regulatory state. Rather than working through civil society as "citizens," resistance is increasingly productive in economic and cultural spheres for all populations.

BASTARDS AND OUTLAWS

The film *Beijing Bastards* begins with an illegitimate pregnancy, and ends with either an abortion or a birth—it is unclear. Punctuated by long interludes of rock music played at rehearsals and gigs, the film follows the drunken and violent exploits of a local band in Beijing. The characters proudly describe themselves as bastards (*zazhong*—mixing species/race/seed) and hooligans (*liumang*—fluid commoners/outsiders). Such impurity and fluidity is seen by both rebels and authorities alike as a problem for the normality and stability of the nation-state (see Dutton 1998, 62–69; Barmé 1999, 62–98; Bakken 2000, 329–30). In this Chinese version of "sex 'n booze 'n rock-n-roll," the young men jam Beijing's economic reform policy by refusing to work at "normal" jobs; the title of Wang Shuo's novel *Playing for Thrills* cogently describes their modus vivendi. This is a popular rebellion: the characters of *Beijing Bastards* are played by prominent rock stars; Wang Shuo is China's most famous contemporary novelist (Zhang Yuan 1993; Chen Baoliang in Dutton 1998, 63–65; Wang Shuo 1997).

Beijing Bastards, like *A Confucian Confusion* and East Asian anxieties over racial purity, questions legitimacy and normalcy. Although many see the diaspora as yuppies and heroes, these petty criminals are bastards. The Chinese word for bastard is very broad, and involves the impurity of mixing species, races, and seed. Being a bastard in Greater China thus is not just a question of legitimate paternity; it involves a jamming of social and theoretical norms in many spaces. Bastards are people who do not just fall through the cracks of social categories but often flourish in the fertile manure of the interstices. Beijing bastards are part of a heterodox rebellion against orthodoxy among the youth and the underclass, who have no sense of political or economic sovereignty and little purchase on society. In this sense they are part of an unlionized diaspora, the floating population of China's internal migration who seek fortune and/or freedom in the cities. The floating population exceeds 120 million people—five times the 25 million diasporic Chinese. This domestic movement of "overseas Chinese" wanderers, vagrants, and hooligans shows the underside of Confucian capitalism's wealthy urban elites in the PRC and diasporic Chinese. Hence hooligans are not the heroic partisans of any democratic revolution or antiglobalization mass movement; these bastards are anti-heroes exploiting and resisting modernity at the micro-level of everyday life, in a rebellion against the biopolitics of social control and economic production.

In analogous ways to the slacker culture of hooligan Beijing, overachievers in hypercapitalist Taiwan also question middle-class morality and the norms of fidelity and family demanded by the state and capital. By the end of *A Confucian Confusion,* everyone has been unfaithful to lovers and bosses—and feels strangely happy about the possibilities of this new *Age of Independence* (the Chinese title of the film). Yet, true to their nature, these bastards produce mixed feelings: rather than heroes in utopia (Hardt and Negri 2000), they are anti-heroes in heterotopia. In this way they are all "outlaws" (Bakken 2000, 330), a diaspora from below pushing an antipolitics of counter-norms.

While the popular hooligan narrative challenges the norms of Chinese society at a micro level of social order, Taiwan challenges international society at the macro level of diplomacy. Both question unified notions of identity, and the tight fit between nation and state that both international relations theory and the PRC demand. Recalling chapter 6, we can see that what the hooligans and Taiwan both present is not a nationalist or a diplomatic challenge so much as a conceptual challenge to the regulatory logic of the nation-state, not only for cross-straits relations but for Greater China and international politics at large.

Taiwan challenges the logic of the nation-state on a macro scale, not to *Play for Thrills* but because it has been forced to. The political crisis of the ROC's sovereignty produced conceptual opportunities as well as dangers. When Taiwan was ejected from international society in 1971, it became an outlaw, like the infamous Dao Zhi discussed in chapter 1. Zhi was the bandit whom Confucius tried to convert back into the bosom of civilization. Zhi responded by saying that he was not a robber but an outlaw who operated outside and alongside the hegemonic code of civilization; rather than being the opposite of civilization—a barbarian—Zhi and his band of thieves had their own heterotopic society. In a twist on the extant "civilization," they performed their own versions of the "five virtues" of humanity, sageliness, justice, wisdom, and courage—as counter-norms. Indeed, this illusory civilization made us question other codes of civilization (*Zhuangzi* 1985; Graham 1981, 207–10, 233–42; Foucault 1986, 27).

Since it is no longer under the protection of international law, Taiwan is such an outlaw. With no duly recognized sovereign status, it cannot argue its case via high diplomacy in embassies, international organizations, or the United Nations. Hence, Taiwan has been forced, like Dao Zhi, to take the norms of (inter)national society—sovereignty, nation-state, democracy—and twist them. Taiwan's heterotopic re-writing of the codes, however, is not a simple "illegality," for Taiwan is recognized in international society, through, e.g., pragmatic diploma-cy, the American Institute in Taiwan, Nationalist China's Association of East Asian Relations in Japan, the community of shared destiny, the Greater Chinese Common Market, vacation diplomacy, Cultural China, *Huaren*, "democratic friend in East Asia." Such odd codes of the nation-state, "create a space of illusion that exposes every real space, all the sites inside of which human life is partitioned," including the nation-state, "as still more illusory" (Foucault 1986, 27).

With these concepts, Taiwan moves in the shadows; but the island actually casts a long shadow with its economic power and demo-cratic achievements. It is a thorn in the legalistic side of international society. Chapter 6 showed that the push from the regulatory logic of the nation-state to that of democracy was not simply a top-down strategy to keep the KMT in power, but a Taiwanization/Sinicization of popular democracy. Rather than appeal to common ancestors in a unified nation-state, Taiwanese activists promote a flexible sharing of friends in a community of shared destiny. In this way, Taiwanese politics is involved in cosmopolitics, where the hyphen between na-tion and state is loosened not just for Chinese identity but for global politics. This is an exemplary transition from a search for normalcy via state sovereignty to legitimacy according to popular sovereignty.

Rather than the problem lying between the ROC and the PRC, China and Taiwan, the debate is about different notions of Chinese-ness and political community. The most interesting politics is nei-ther pro-China nor anti-China, is neither about empires nor about nation-states, but is created in the tension between essential nativism and flexible diaspora, foreign and domestic, state sovereignty and popular sovereignty. The struggle here is among different produc-tions of Chineseness along the Taiwan Strait, the Shenzhen River, the South China Sea, and among overseas Chinese, Korean Confucians, and hooligans in China's floating population. Rather than a clash of civilizations, we have the contingent politics of identity production.

We are all democrats today, we are all diasporic today, we are all outlaws today. We are all bastards today.

Appendix
Chinese Character List

ba, bawang	霸 ，霸王	hegemon
bentuhua	本土化	nativism
Da Zhongguo	大中国	Greater China
Da Zhonghua	大中华	greater Chinese
daguo	大国	great powers
datong	大同	Great Harmony
de	德	virtue
guanxi	关系	connections, network
guo	国	country
guochi	国耻	national humiliation
guojia	国家	country, country-family
guoxue	国学	traditional Chinese studies

haiwai huaren	海外华人	overseas Chinese
he	和	harmony
huaqiao	华侨	overseas Chinese
huaren	华人	Chinese people
huayi	华夷	civilization/barbarian
hyo [Korean]	孝	filial piety
junzi	君子	cultivated person
liumang	流氓	hooligan
Nanhai	南海	South Sea, South China Sea
Nansha	南沙	Spratly Islands
ren	仁	benevolence
renquan	人权	human rights
Shanhai jing	山海经	Classic of Mountains and Seas
tianming	天命	Mandate of Heaven, legitimacy
tianxia	天下	All-under-Heaven, the world, the empire
tianzi	天子	emperor
ti-yong	体用	Chinese essence, Western technology
tongwen	同文	shared civilization, shared writing
wangdao	王道	benevolent governance, the kingly way
weiji	危机	crisis

Wenhua Zhongguo	文化中国	cultural China
wen	文	culture, civilization
wenming	文明	civilization
xiao	孝	filial piety
xin	信	trust
you	友	friend
zazhong	杂种	bastard
Zhongguo	中国	China, Middle Kingdom
Zhongguo ren	中国人	Chinese person, Chinese citizen
Zhonghua minzu	中国民族	Chinese race/nation
zhuquan	主权	sovereignty

Notes

1. DEFINING GREATER CHINA

1. Initially the East Asian economic miracle was proposed as a development model for the Third World (Tu Weiming 1996; Berger 1987; Hsiao 1988). The discussions compared East Asia's Confucian capitalism with dependency theory and Latin America (Hsiao, Hsin-Huang 1988, 12; Clegg et al. 1990). Soon, the East Asian miracle was considered a model for the industrialized West.

2. Actually, economic culture was not a new idea. It had been elaborated in the early twentieth century by Max Weber to explain how capitalism arose in Europe as part of the spirit of Protestantism. Here lies a major problem for the notion of Confucian capitalism: in another seminal work, Weber argued that Confucianism was a barrier to capitalist development; Puritan rationalism meant rational mastery of the world, but Confucian rationalism meant rational adjustment to the world (Weber 1951, 248). Development theory, drawing from Rostow, argued that tradition needed to be overcome to modernize society for liberal democracy and capitalist prosperity. Hence, much of the argumentation for Confucian capitalism seeks to show how Weber was right about economic culture but wrong about Confucianism, to show how East Asia can have capitalism, but in a different way, for a different form of modernity (Tu Weiming 1996; Redding 1993; Berger 1987; Ong 1999; Hamilton 1999; Callahan 2003a).

3. Many people still argue that Japan is the center of the East Asian economy (Katzenstein and Shiraishi 1997; Cumings 1999).

4. The "China threat" is posed as a debate between two articles, both

of which were abstracted from books (Bernstein and Munro 1997; Ross 1997). I will be looking to the books in my arguments (Bernstein and Munro 1998; Nathan and Ross 1997). Five years later, these two articles were still seen as important enough to be republished as the opening volleys of "The Rise of China" (*Foreign Affairs* 2002). For a more measured view of China's military and political power see Pumphrey 2002; Yee and Storey 2002.

5. It is easy to take for granted that Chinese civilization is singular, with five thousand years of cultural history being reduced to short-hand terms like "Confucian tradition," "Confucian capitalism," and "Confucian democracy." But even for the historical figure we now call Confucius, genealogies are not clear—"Confucius" and "Confucianism" were invented by Jesuit missionaries out of the materials of Kongzi and *Rujia,* and now have been re-exported back into China (Jensen 1997; Rule 1986). Even before the Jesuit excursion, Kongzi himself was a disputed figure in the classical Chinese texts: he appears more often in the heterodox *Zhuangzi* than in orthodox "Confucian" texts (Callahan 1994).

2. QUESTIONING CIVILIZATION

1. Figuring Chinese civilization in terms of these four narratives owes much to Todorov's conquest/conversion explanation of self/Other relations (Todorov 1984; also see Eco 1998, 53–54; Connolly 1991). The nativist narrative is helped by Dikötter's analysis of race in China (Dikötter 1992). Arif Dirlik suggested that I use the notion of repertoire to relate the narratives (Dirlik, correspondence, 7 April 1999).

2. The passages quoted below from the *Analects* and the *Mencius* use D. C. Lau's standard translations, with my own emendations. Rather than list a page number, I list the chapter and verse according to traditional organizations of the text.

3. The enthusiastic reception of the television documentary *River Elegy* is a case in point. It was critical of the icons of Chinese civilization—the Yellow River, the Great Wall, the dragon, etc.—and urged Chinese people to look to the West for modernity (Su and Wang 1991; Su Xiaokang et al. 1988).

4. The reasons for the flowering of *Guoxue* in the 1990s are not just cultural but also political and political-economic. After 1989, scholars rediscovered Chinese studies in part because they were restricted from the heated discussion about the West that animated the 1980s: "conservatives arose simply because radicals were stifled after 1989.... The only legal topic left for academics was to uphold national culture" (Chen Shaoming 1998, 64). The publishing industry also expanded rapidly, on the one hand,

while international copyright laws were beginning to be enforced, on the other. Hence, there was much space but it could not be filled, as before, with translations of Western books. The result was the republication of many Chinese classics and commentaries (Chen Lai 1998, 45–46).

5. This is the caption to a photograph of a naval vessel on the high seas, part of a Defense Ministry exhibit in October 1999.

6. A 1996 article from *Guofang* [National Defense], *"Haiyang, hai-yang guan, haishang changcheng" [The Ocean, the Maritime Perspective, and the Great Wall on the Seas]*, states: "The South China Sea is China's Great Wall at our Southern gate. It is important to defend this part of our territory" (in Stenseth 1999, 54).

7. While *wenren*, civilized person, used to refer to someone who had cultivated Confucian practices, now awards are given to "civilized enter-prises" *[wenming danwei]* and "civilized households" *[wenming hu]* ac-cording to more mundane standards: "national models and defined criteria in terms of sanitation and social order" (Anagnost 1997, 86).

8. In addition to such academic and popular business books, other books look to Confucianism more directly: *How Would Confucius Ask for a Raise?* (Osborn 1994), *Confucius in the Boardroom: Ancient Wisdom, Modern Lessons for Business* (Rudnicki 1998), and *Confucius Lives Next Door: What Living in the East Teaches Us about Living in the West* (Reid 1999). Chinese civilization in general, and Confucianism in particular, are therefore the "answer" to explain the crisis question: the answer to under-stand both danger and opportunity at home and abroad.

9. Also see the *Overseas Chinese Historical Studies,* a journal linked to the Overseas Chinese Office of the State Council; Zhao Wenlie's 1995 article, showing a flexible understanding of Chineseness, serves as the exception to prove the rule of stiff essentialism in the other articles. Con-versely, Southeast Asian Studies in China focuses disproportionately on overseas Chinese topics. This can be seen in how a Chinese bibliography covers both Southeast Asian studies and diasporic Chinese studies (Yu and Zhang 2002).

10. Part of the Thai community obliged such an image of the Sino-Thai: Bangkok's Chinese language newspapers were full of full-page ads wel-coming President Jiang. Of course, this could also show there is no unified Chineseness in Thailand: the ads were not signed by a single national orga-nization, but by the various local and clan associations: the Teichow Asso-ciation, Hainan Association, etc. (*Sing sian yit pao* [Mandarin: Xingxian ribao] 1 September 1999; Callahan 2003a; Interviews 2000).

11. *Jek* is a derogatory term for Chinese in Thailand; a more neutral word is *Jin.*

12. Wang Gungwu, the doyen of overseas Chinese studies, runs into

such problems, as soon as he initiates discourse. The first substantive foot-notes in many of his essays mourn the impossibility of defining Chineseness or naming the overseas Chinese (Wang Gungwu 1991, 216, 236, 253).

13. Though *Huaqiao* was the common way of saying overseas Chinese in the twentieth century, before 1858 *qiao* was used to describe migration within China (Wang Gungwu 1991, 238; also see Callahan 2003a).

14. It is not a coincidence that the *Shanhai jing* is the most referenced classic in the Hong Kong identity literature, like *Hong Kong Collage: Contemporary Stories and Writing* (Cheung, Martha P. Y. 1998). The *Shanhai jing* addresses the ambivalent and multiple identities of that strange place.

15. Although Singapore is an interesting case of a small power gaining a global voice (primarily because people there speak English) it is not a good case from which to discuss what is going on in Greater China. Hence I have deliberately resisted using Singapore to frame my analysis. I have commented on Singapore in other spaces (Callahan 2002b; Callahan 1996a; Callahan 1996b).

16. Typically it is antidemocratic, in the parliamentary sense, since the overseas Chinese do not see themselves primarily as citizens of a nation-state. But Kasian argues that Sino-Thai were a key part of the 1992 democratic movement in Thailand, fighting against a state which they saw as "an impediment on economic prosperity and political freedom" (Kasian 1997, 87; also see Callahan 1998a). He goes on to map out how Chinese-ness will add to Thai civil, economic, and political society.

17. For example, the pamphlet from the People's Liberation Army's political education department takes a very hard line toward the situation in Hong Kong. It divides up the populace into pro- and anti-China groups, and talks about "social diseases." Since distribution of this publication was restricted to the PLA, it can give a better sense of how the military understands such matters (Zongzheng 1997).

3. SHARING SOVEREIGNTY

1. Disputes with Vietnam over the Gulf of Tonkin are specifically framed in these terms: it was taken by the French Empire in the "unequal treaty" of 1887 (Valencia 1995, 24; *Jindai Zhongguo* 1997, 35; He Yu 1997, 481).

2. All countries use force to arrest fishermen, and the Philippines Navy exerted influence over Scarborough Shoal in 1997 (Zha, Daojiong 2001; Sherry 1997, 17, 20).

3. It is serendipitous that the Chinese court was convinced of the use of international law by its utility in solving a sea dispute in 1864 (Hsu 1960, 133). But not everyone was pleased with this project, and with the emer-

gence of sovereignty in China. The French charge d'affaires complained that it would cause endless trouble, and a Euro-American newspaper in Shanghai editorialized in terms that seem to have come true in the 1990s: "Whether we are supplying weapons which may at some future period be directed against ourselves, or which will only be turned to the acquisition of new conquests, cannot at present be decided. To stem the stream while it is still near its source, and guide it into proper channels should now be our aim" (in Hsu 1960, 138).

4. There is nothing peculiarly Chinese or cosmological about this. Modern Chinese maps put China at the center, with Eurasia to the left and the Americas to the right. European maps put Europe at the center, with the Americas to the left and Asia to the right. The United States puts itself at the center and puts Asia to the left and Europe to the right.

5. Many of the administrative maps of the empire mark centers of government to show the spread of populations (see Yee 1994d, 168; Yan Ping et al. 1998, 152; Cao Wanru et al. 1994, plate 1). CASS's *Simple Historical Atlas of China,* which creates clear boundaries between China and the barbarians, also shows the thinning of populations at the frontier: it records county seats, which become less frequent at the frontier (Tan Qixiang 1996).

6. *Tian* is not a transcendent deity in Chinese cosmology, but is immanent and interrelated with human society (Hall and Ames 1987, 209).

7. The main sources for this are the "Foreign Affairs Briefings" published in the *Renmin ribao [People's Daily],* for example on 16 January 1999 and 3 March 1999. (Also see Austin 1998, 84, 89, 316; Valencia 1995, 16; Lee Lai To 1999, 109).

8. *Nanhai changcheng* (Li and Hao 1976) is based on an opera by the same name that was produced in the late 1950s. Also see films such as "Stormy South China Sea" *[Nanhai fengyun]* (Bai Chen 1955), which describes fisherfolk militias defending the islands against the Japanese during World War II, and "Dawn in the South China Sea" *[Nanhai de zaochen]* (1964), where patriotic peasants defend the Southern Chinese coast in Guangdong against infiltration from Nationalist and American spies. Also see "Children of the Paracels" *[Xisha ernu]* [n.d.] (in Li Yangguo 1998, 11).

9. A *li* is equal to one third of a mile.

10. Even the most mathematical maps are artistic. The notes on the "Coastal Map of Guangdong" (1561–62) state: "In the maps sea is placed above with land below. This is also the case with Chinese painting which puts the distant view above and the close view below" (Cao Wanru et al. 1994, plate 195–p. 42).

11. It is worth noting the way Austin argues the Chinese case for the Spratlys in terms of international law: he discards ancient claims from

China and Vietnam in favor of those of European imperialists. The British Empire has the first legal claim in 1877, and the main claim under dispute is the French imperial claim of 1933. According to Austin, South Vietnam inherited this claim, but the Socialist Republic of Vietnam did not, because of North Vietnamese recognition of Chinese sovereignty (Austin 1998, 132–34, 146, 149). Thus empires can claim sovereignty but decolonized successor states cannot. Even the precedent in international law, the Island of Palmas case (1928), concerned how three empires—the Dutch, Spanish, and American—could divide up the Philippines (Austin 1998; Pan Shiying 1996).

12. China, Taiwan, Vietnam each claim all the islands, reefs, and rocks, arguing that these have been part of their territory "since ancient times." The Philippines claims that the islands are vital to state security and economic survival. Malaysia claims seven features because they fall within its continental shelf boundary. Brunei uses the Law of the Sea's Exclusive Economic Zone of 200 nautical miles as the basis of its claim (Valencia 1995, 8).

13. This is curious because, in its maritime disputes in the Yellow Sea and the East China Sea, China appeals to a scientific measure: the continental shelf (Whiting 1998, 293; Austin 1998; Interviews 1999). China actually uses "science" in the South China Sea, but not to evidence sovereignty claims. Rather "science" is utilized for fieldwork activities—for example, meteorological research stations—which in turn demonstrate Chinese sovereignty (Si Tuxiang 1996; Sun and Ding 1998).

14. Diplomats in both Bangkok and Beijing remarked how China strongly urges neighboring states to sign up to its view of the world—One China Principle, human rights, Falun Gong, and Tibet—as part of joint declarations (Interviews 1999; Interviews 2000). For example, the Chinese ambassador to Seoul was roundly criticized when he forcefully told the South Korean government not to give a visa to the Dalai Lama in 2000 ("Inappropriate Remarks by Chinese Ambassador (Editorial)" 2000). According to the diplomats, this is not standard diplomatic practice.

4. MODERNIZING CONFUCIANISM

1. Typically, defectors from North Korea declare themselves in the PRC. Before 1997, Hong Kong served as a neutral conduit through which defectors from North Korea could travel to South Korea without embarrassing Beijing. There were worries that once Hong Kong became part of the PRC, it would be more difficult to transfer such defectors.

2. There was much controversy over the deconstruction. This seemingly nationalist project actually destroyed the National Museum, which was located in the Japanese headquarters building. It was removed to temporary

accommodations on the palace grounds that have now become permanent—thus endangering the collection of Korean artifacts. The museum itself has entered the discussion of its territorial base; its brochure seems to imply that the Korean National Museum is nomadic, being located in nine places since its founding in 1908—five of which are on the Kyongbok Palace grounds. Other public intellectuals thought that the past could not be buried by pulling down a building; the colonial headquarters should be left standing as a reminder of the past (Kwon Tai-Joon 1997, Interview; Han Sang-Jin 1997, Interview; Shin Young-ha 1997, Interview).

3. Kim Young-sam and Kim Dae-Jung use Confucianism in different ways; one for globalization, the other for democracy (see Kim, Samuel 2000a; Kim Dae-Jung in BBC/SWB 10 December 2000).

4. Since I am using English-language texts, authenticity becomes an issue. How can we be sure that what is written for a foreign audience is what Koreans tell each other? Actually, much like the cultural border between China and Korea, the border between foreign and domestic in these texts is blurred. Although the Korean Foundation texts were originally written in Korean for translation into English, French, Spanish, Japanese, and Chinese (there is no Korean edition), the internal discussions often slip through. The common nationalist use of "we Koreans" in both sets of texts appears as a reflection of the national self: it is when national identity comes into contact with the Other that what seems to be "common sense" needs to be clarified (Kim Cheol-Hyeon 1997, Interview).

More to the point, the authors are not always entirely clear just who their audience is; though the Korea Foundation tells its authors to write for a foreign audience, the peculiarly nationalist discourse of Korean uniqueness slips through: "most of the authors are professors, and deep in their hearts they feel it is their duty to instruct the Korean people. This is because many Koreans don't know their own culture." When the articles are translated from the original Korean into English, the nationalist rhetoric is generally toned down to make it more general and objective (Yoon Keumjin 1997, Interview).

5. The framing of cultural discourses of Korean nationalism with the scientific objectivity of satellite photos is persistent. The same satellite photo begins *The Koreans*, published by the Korea Overseas Information Service. It also graces a wall at the entrance to the National Folk Museum in Seoul. The museum's satellite photo uses the technical possibilities and problems of photography for seemingly naked political aims. The photo is not an "objective" reflection of the geographic reality of the Korean Peninsula. Rather it is more artistic, much like a map from the eighteenth century that is on display at the Central National Museum (see Ledyard 1994). The orientation of the photo in the Folk Museum has been rotated 90 degrees:

north is not up; east is up. North Korea is to the left and South Korea is to the right, in a wonderful replay of ideological categorization. Further, because of the angle of the satellite photograph—it was taken from south of the peninsula—the image is distorted. The north is smaller, thinner, while the south is larger and fatter, again replaying the images of poverty vs. plenty, and the very real juxtaposition of famine vs. prosperity. This first image in the National Folk Museum is uncaptioned, so its meaning needs to be constructed (see Shapiro 1988, 124–78).

6. Just as all Chinese are said to be "Sons of the Yellow Emperor," Koreans see themselves as "descendents of Tan'gun" (Jeong Young-hun 2001, 54). Tan'gun's "birthday" is celebrated as National Foundation Day in South Korea. North Korea dedicated a Tan'gun mausoleum in 1994. Although it alienates China, Tan'gun here is used to bridge the gap between North and South Korea (see Choe Yong-shik 2000).

7. The head of the religious affairs section of the Ministry of Culture and Sport states that the government does not regulate Confucianism or any other religion. He pointed out that the Confucian Foundation actually had previously proclaimed Confucianism a religion in the 1960s (Kim Cheol-Hyeon 1997, Interview).

8. For example, Kim Jung Il waited three years before becoming the leader of North Korea—the traditional mourning period, for Confucians. Much of the rhetoric of post–Kim Il Song North Korea uses metaphors of family and *hyo* (filial piety)—for example, the 1995 expression "respect for revolutionary elders" (Armstrong 1998, 44–45).

9. There are a number of possible explanations for this curious state of affairs: (1) Confucian scholars are not interested in modernizing Confucianism, being content with their philological studies, and are more interested in the text than the context. Rightly or wrongly, the Sung Kyun Kwan is seen by many political and social theorists as too parochial, and is marginalized from most discussions about Confucianism and modernity; (2) Scholars from Sung Kyun Kwan are interested, but do not have the theoretical tools of "scientific analysis" and cannot speak the "international language" of English. Although the Confucian Foundation has been active in the 1990s in public events to popularize the new orthodoxy, it has not encouraged critical academic research. As mentioned above, although one would expect the Sung Kyun Kwan to be prominent in the various international conferences held about Confucianism and Korean philosophy, its attendance has been negligible. (3) Those few younger scholars who are skilled in both classical Chinese language and modern social theory are suspicious of the recent "Confucian fad" (Kim Hong-kyung 1997, Interview; Cho Soon-Kyoung 1997, Interview).

5. HARMONIZING BOUNDARIES

1. Although many Euro-American scholars talk at length about democratization in Hong Kong, this was never a major issue (see Hook 1997, 556–58; Chan, Ming 1997, 577–79). I discuss democracy and Greater China in chapter 6.

2. Mortgages in Hong Kong typically last for fifteen years, and people wanted to know if they would still be valid after 1997. Thus real estate issues, according to the key British negotiator, led to the initial talks between Beijing and London in 1982 that produced the Joint Declaration in 1984 (Cradock 1999, 164–65).

3. In a "Valedictory," Patten gets misty-eyed at the thought of the handover of Hong Kong. But he consoles himself with the fact that "it will not literally end the British Empire. There are other colonies scattered across the seas, other plumed hats and Letters Patent, other dependencies where the common law rules and where many Hong Kong firms have now made their legal home" (Patten 1997, 127).

4. In 1841, the British foreign secretary called Hong Kong a "barren island"; this is repeated ad nauseum in British writings about Hong Kong (Mathews 1997, 5).

5. This view of race/class ordering in Hong Kong society is shared by grassroots organizers of women's groups in Hong Kong and postcolonial historians (Choi Po-King 1998; Ngo 1999; Chow, Rey 1998). For a discussion of how racial discrimination affected the Chinese elite in Hong Kong, see Ching, Frank 1999f; for a criticism of racial bias in the civil service, see Chan, Ming 1997, 570–73.

6. When an elite Hong Kong banker suggested that she negotiate with China in 1982, Thatcher responded: "You want us to negotiate a deal with China? They are barbarians" (in Ching, Frank 1999f, 166).

7. In November 1999, the British Foreign Office Minister "described the rule of law as the 'keystone' of Hong Kong's success" (Foreign and Commonwealth Office 2000, 4). As Munn argues, this impartial "rule of law" by a benevolent colonial regime is a myth. The law was used as a tool of governance by early Hong Kong governors in a very unequal way which "demanded heavy punishments and intrusive control for the Chinese but urged consideration and leniency towards Europeans" (Munn 1999, 66). For a similar criticism of post–World War II Hong Kong, see Chan, Ming 1997, 567–70.

8. The permanent exhibition of the Museum of Revolutionary History closed in January 2002 and will not reopen until 2008. It is likely that the revolutionary exhibition is being reformed to greet the visitors to Beijing's 2008 Summer Olympics.

9. Luk's article was first published in Chinese in Elizabeth Sinn's *Culture and Society in Hong Kong*. Sinn tells us this book is the product of the

first conference on Hong Kong culture and society (in 1991), and thus is an artifact of the *very late* formation of the field of Hong Kong Studies (Sinn 1995, iii).

10. Xiao Si's haziness works itself out in two editions of the same book, but with slightly different organization and chapter titles. I use the Ji'nan edition (Xiao Si 1998), in consultation with the Hong Kong edition (Xiao Si 1996).

11. The Right of Abode issue actually was initiated during the British colonial regime. Parliament passed nationality laws in 1971 and 1981 to deny the Right of Abode in the United Kingdom to people from Hong Kong, although it was afforded to the "white" colonies (Tambling 1997, 358–59; Cradock 1999, 233–34).

12. Chan, Fu, and Ghai have gathered most of the relevant documents in one book, *Hong Kong's Constitutional Debate: Conflict over Interpretation*. It is an excellent collection from a legal point of view, but is sadly lacking in sources on the social issues involved. Rather than list each of the documents separately, I list the authors and cite the collection.

13. Legal scholars from Beijing criticized the CFA's ruling in two areas: they thought that the CFA was challenging PRC sovereignty in Hong Kong, and they thought that the ruling would cause social problems. The Central Government soon made these views official. It is interesting that these critics employ "history" in their criticism: the CFA made a mistake and "should bear the historical responsibility for its own folly." They also used Confucian language to demand that the CFA decision be "rectified" (Xiao Weiyun et al. 2000, 53–59).

14. This phrase is a common way of distinguishing between authentic and inauthentic Hong Kongers. It appears in much of the Hong Kong literature mentioned above. Xiao Si mentions "born-and-raised" four times in the preface to her *Hong Kong Stories*. P. K. Leung mentions it in his "The Story of Hong Kong." Feng declares in a subheading that "People born and raised in Hong Kong are Hong Kongers!" (Feng Renzhao 1998, 41).

6. RECOGNIZING DEMOCRACY

1. When George W. Bush suddenly clarified U.S. military support for Taiwan in 2001, this was seen by editorialists as a problem: "Foreigners are concerned that President George W. Bush's language is sometimes fuzzy. Maybe they should worry more when he tries to make himself clear." In regard to U.S. Taiwan policy, the *Financial Times* thus declared that "Ambiguity sometimes has its purposes" (FT 26 April 2001). At any rate, Bush changed the policy back to strategic ambiguity a few hours later.

2. Klintworth's article is illustrated by a picture of Taiwan's parliament chamber, which has these five options projected on a screen. In Chinese they are *Taiwan ren, Zhonghua minguo ren, Zhongguo ren, Huaren,* and *yi shang jie shi*. Citizen of the PRC is not one of the options.

3. A scorecard of diplomatic recognition was a prominent part of the State Council's "Taiwan Problem Picture Exhibition." The PRC started with only 17 states recognizing it in 1950. By 1971, 75 countries recognized the PRC; this figure jumped to 120 in 1979, 157 in 1992. But the trend is not unidirectional. In 1999, the PRC went from 162 embassies to 161 (Guowuyuan 2001: panel 1.14). Then in 2002 the figure gained another country, making its total 162 again.

4. For example, discussions of sovereignty argue that China cannot be a divided country with two sovereign states, like Germany or Korea. These nations were split due to external factors—World War II—while China was split because of a civil war. (Zhonggong 1998, 14; Taiwan Affairs Office 2000; Zhao Suisheng 1999). Yet the PRC uses World War II documents from Cairo and Potsdam to claim Taiwan.

5. Also see the international conference on "Confucian Thought and the Great Task of Chinese Unification" held in Hong Kong in September 2000. The opening speech addressed cross-straits relations ("Kongzi sixiang" 2000, 7–8).

6. For example, the suppression of the 2–28 Movement in 1947 was "the most significant formative experience preventing the consolidating of a Chinese national identity for decades" (Hughes 1997a, 24–26; Kuo, Liangwen 1997, 4).

7. Rather than elections liberating Bosnia, Campbell notes, the "1990 elections marked the beginning of the end for Bosnian identity and its hybridity" (Campbell 1998b, 220). As a result of the end of the Cold War, successful political parties in Bosnia campaigned with nationalist platforms against the ancien régime of communism. The war grew out of this enthnicization of Bosnia—and then so did the peace. Since the international community saw world politics as an anarchical assembly of nation-states, the solution to the "Bosnian problem" was a partitioning of the country into pure ethnic constituencies (Campbell 1998b, 14). The U.N. regime in postwar Bosnia followed this logic, and the 1996 elections further entrenched ethno-nationalist divisions (Campbell 1998b, 221–22). As Campbell concludes: "the international community's structural solutions for Bosnia produced the very ethnicization of politics they later criticized, furthered the nationalist project they ostensibly wanted to contest, and provided no space for the nonnationalist formations they professed to support" (Campbell 1998b, 225).

8. Another lesson that the CCP learned was that democratic elections

could bring down the richest Leninist Party in the world, the KMT (CND 23 April 2000).

9. The debate on civil society in China is vast. I analyze it (in Callahan 2002a), and good sources of the debate can be found (in Kuo, Liangwen 1997; Chang, Mau-Kuei 1997; Wang Miaoyang et al. 1997; Brook and Frolic 1997; White et al. 1996; Ma, Shu-Yun 1994; Chamberlain 1993; Wang Hui et al. 1994; Chan, Adrian 1997; Madsen 1993; Rowe 1993). The weakness of such approaches is that, rather than looking at social movements close by in South Korea and Taiwan, they largely examine civil society in terms of postcommunism and comparisons with Eastern Europe. They try to find a suitable tea shop in China to match the coffee shop that Habermas said was an integral part of the formation of civil society in early modern Europe (Rowe 1993, 145; Madsen 1993, 190). One of the other main problems with such analysis is that its conceptual use of "civil society" does not contest state power so much as reify it in terms of limiting politics to the state/civil society dynamic (see Chang, Mau-Kuei 1997, 14–16).

10. The passages quoted below use D. C. Lau's standard translations, with my own emendations. Rather than listing a page number, I list the chapter and verse according to traditional organizations of the text.

11. The concept of friendship appears twenty-seven times in seventeen passages in the *Analects,* and thirty times in eleven passages in the *Mencius,* as *you, peng,* or *pengyou.*

Bibliography

1997: 5000 Years ago, Hong Kong Was Already Chinese. 1997. Beijing: PLA Press.

Abbas, Ackbar. 1997a. *Hong Kong: Culture and the Politics of Disappearance.* Minneapolis: University of Minnesota Press.

———. 1997b. "Hong Kong: Other Histories, Other Politics." In Ackbar Abbas and Wu Hung, eds., 293–313.

Abbas, Ackbar, and Wu Hung, eds. 1997. "Hong Kong 1997: The Place and the Formula." *Public Culture* 9 (special issue): 3.

Abelman, Nancy. 1993. "Minjung Theory and Practice." In Harumi Befu, ed., *Cultural Nationalism in East Asia: Representation and Identity* 139–68. Berkeley: Institute of East Asian Studies, University of California.

Acharya, Amitav. 1997. "Ideas, Identity, and Institutions: Asean-Way to Asian-Pacific Way?" *Pacific Review* 10:319–46.

Agnew, John. 1998. *Geopolitics: Re-visioning World Politics.* London: Routledge.

Almond, Gabriel A., and Sidney Verba. 1963. *The Civic Culture: Political Attitudes and Democracy in Five Nations.* Princeton: Princeton University Press.

Ames, Roger T. 1998. "Rites as Rights." In Leroy S. Rouner, ed., *Human Rights.* Notre Dame, Ind.: University of Notre Dame Press.

An Byung-ju. 1996. "Songgyun'gwan: Sanctuary of Korean Confucianism." In Korea Foundation, ed., 132–37.

An Jinglin and Xiong Zengyan. 1994. "Pillboxes Are Linked with the Motherland." *FBIS–China Daily Report*, 21 June: 9–10.

Anagnost, Ann. 1997. *National Past-Times: Narrative, Representation, and Power in Modern China.* Durham, N.C.: Duke University Press.

Anderson, Benedict. 1991. *Imagined Communities.* Rev. ed. London: Verso.

———. 1998. *The Spectre of Comparisons: Nationalism, Southeast Asia, and the World.* London: Verso.

Appadurai, Arjun. 1996. *Modernity at Large: Cultural Dimensions of Globalization.* Minneapolis: University of Minnesota Press.

Armstrong, Charles K. 1998. "'A Socialism Our Style': North Korean Ideology in a Post-Communist Era." In Samuel Kim, ed., *North Korean Foreign Relations in the Post-Cold War Era,* 32–53. New York: Oxford University Press.

Armstrong, David. 1993. *Revolution and World Order: The Revolutionary State in International Society.* Oxford: Clarendon Press.

Arnold, Wayne. 1998. "Chinese Diaspora Using Internet to Aid Plight of Brethren Abroad." *Wall Street Journal,* 23 July.

Art Space. 1996. "Korean Rites." In Korea Foundation, ed., 146–53.

Asan Foundation. 1997a. *Proceedings of "The Challenge of the Twenty-First Century, The Response of Eastern Ethics" Conference.* Seoul: Asan Foundation.

——— 1997b. *Asan chaedan uiryowon nyonbo [Asan Foundation Annual Report].* Seoul: Asan Foundation.

Ash, Robert, and Y. Y. Kueh. 1995. "Economic Integration within Greater China: Trade and Investment Flows between China, Hong Kong, and Taiwan." In Shambaugh, ed., 59–93.

Austin, Greg. 1998. *China's Ocean Frontier: International Law, Military Force, and National Development.* Sydney: Allen and Unwin.

Bachelard, Gaston. 1994. *The Poetics of Space.* Boston: Beacon Press.

Bachman, David. 2000. "China's Democratization: What Difference Would It Make for U.S.–China Relations?" In Friedman and McCormick, eds., 195–223.

Badhwar, Neera Kapur, ed. 1993. *Friendship: A Philosophical Reader.* Ithaca, N.Y.: Cornell University Press.

Bai Chen. 1955. *Nanhai fengyun [Stormy South China Sea].* Shanghai: Shanghai dianying zhipianchang.

Baker, Hugh D. R. 1995. "Social Change in Hong Kong." In Shambaugh, ed., 212–25.

Bakken, Børge. 2000. *The Exemplary Society: Human Improvement, Social Control, and the Dangers of Modernity in China.* Oxford: Oxford University Press.

Banning, Garrett, and Bonnie Glaser. 1995. "Looking across the Yalu: Chinese Assessments of North Korea." *Asian Survey* 35 (6): 528–45.

Barmé, Geremie. 1997. "Hong Kong the Floating City." *Index on Censorship* 1:154–60.

———. 1999. *In the Red: On Contemporary Chinese Culture.* New York: Columbia University Press.

Barnett, Michael N. 1996. "Identity and Alliances in the Middle East." In Katzenstein, ed., 400–447.

Bartelson, Jens. 1995. *A Genealogy of Sovereignty.* Cambridge: Cambridge University Press.

Barthes, Roland. 1979. "From Work to Text." In Josue V. Harari, ed., *Textual Strategies,* 73–81. Ithaca, N.Y.: Cornell University Press.

Basic Law of the Hong Kong Special Administration Region of the People's Republic of China. 1991. Hong Kong: Joint Publishing Co.

Bauer, Joanne R., and Daniel A. Bell, eds. 1999. *The East Asian Challenge for Human Rights.* Cambridge: Cambridge University Press.

Beck, B. J. Mansvelt. 1986. "The Fall of the Han." In Denis Twitchett and Michael Loewe, eds., *The Cambridge History of China.* Vol. 1., 357–76. Cambridge: Cambridge University Press.

Benewick, Robert, and Stephanie Donald. 1999. *The State of China Atlas.* London: Penguin Reference.

Berger, Peter L. 1987. *The Capitalist Revolution: Fifty Propositions about Prosperity,* Equality, and Liberty. Aldershot, U.K.: Wildwood House.

———. 1988. "An East Asian Development Model?" In Berger and Hsiao, eds., 3–11.

Berger, Peter L., and Michael Hsin-Huang Hsiao, eds. 1988. *In Search of an East Asian Development Model.* Oxford: Transaction Books.

Bernstein, Richard, and Ross H. Munro. 1997. "The Coming Conflict with America." *Foreign Affairs* 76 (2): 18–32.

———. 1998. *The Coming Conflict with China.* Vintage Books.

Bessho, Koro. 1999. *Identities and Security in East Asia.* Adelphi Paper 325. Oxford: Oxford University Press.

Bhabha, Homi, ed. 1990. *Nation and Narration.* London: Routledge.

Bickford, T. J. 1993. "The Chinese Military and Its Business Operations: PLA as Entrepreneur." *Asian Survey* 34 (5): 46–74.

Biersteker, Thomas J., and Cynthia Weber, eds. 1996a. *State Sovereignty as Social Construct.* Cambridge: Cambridge University Press.

Biersteker, Thomas J., and Cynthia Weber. 1996b. "The Social Construction of State Sovereignty." In Bierstecker and Weber, eds., 1–21.

Bist, Captain D. S. 1998. "Misadventure on the High Seas." *Financial Times,* 17–18 January: 4.

Blanden, Edmund. 1959. Foreword. In Luff, 1–2.

Blyth, Sally, and Ian Wotherspoon. 1996. *Hong Kong Remembers.* Hong Kong: Oxford University Press.

Bøckman, Harald. 1998. "China Deconstructs? The Future of the Chinese Empire-State in a Historical Perspective." In Kjeld Erik Brødsgaard and David Strand, eds., *Reconstructing Twentieth-Century China: State*

Control, Civil Society, and National Identity, 310–46. Oxford: Clarendon Press.

Bolt, Paul J. 2000. *China and Southeast Asia's Ethnic Chinese: State and Diaspora in Contemporary Asia.* Westport, Conn.: Praeger.

Bong Shik Park. 1983. Foreword. In Korean National Commission for UNESCO, ed., v–x.

Bontekoe, Ron, and Marietta Stepaniants, eds. 1997. *Justice and Democracy: Cross-Cultural Perspectives.* Honolulu: University of Hawaii Press.

Booth, Ken, and Russell Trood, eds. 1999. *Strategic Cultures in the Asia-Pacific Region.* London: Macmillan.

Brady, Anne-Marie. 1997. "Who Friend, Who Enemy? Rewi Alley and the Friends of China." *China Quarterly,* no. 151: 614–32.

Brook, Timothy, and B. Michael Frolic, eds. 1997. *Civil Society in China.* Armonk, N.Y.: M. E. Sharpe.

Brown, Judith M., and Rosemary Foot, eds. 1997. *Hong Kong's Transitions, 1842–1997.* London: Macmillan.

Cai Zhizhong. 1987. *Renzhede dingning: Kongzi shuo [Message of the Benevolent: Sayings of Confucius].* Taipei: Shibao manhua yeshu.

Callahan, William A. 1994. "Resisting the Norm: Ironic Images of Marx and Confucius." *Philosophy East and West* 44 (2): 279–302.

———. 1996a. "Rescripting East/West Relations, Rethinking Asian Democracy," *Pacifica Review* 8:1–25.

———. 1996b. "Confucianism/Democracy." In Rah Jong-Yil, ed., *Democratization and Regional Cooperation in Asia,* 113–64. Seoul: Asia-Pacific Peace Press.

———. 1998a. *Imagining Democracy: Reading the Events of May 1992 in Thailand.* Singapore/London: Institute of Southeast Asian Studies Press.

———. 1998b. "Challenging the Order: Social Movements." In Richard Maidment, Jeremy Mitchell, and David Goldblatt, eds., *Governance in the Asia Pacific,* 150–71. London: Routledge.

———. 2001. "China and the Globalization of IR Theory: Discussion of 'Building International Relations with Chinese Characteristics.'" *Journal of Contemporary China* 10 (26): 75–88.

———. 2002a. "Comparing the Discourse of Popular Politics in Korea and China: From Civil Society to Social Movements." In Korean National Commission for UNESCO, ed., 283–321.

———. 2002b. "Gender, Democracy, and Representation: Asian Revolutionary Images." In Louiza Odysseos and Hakan Seckinelgin, eds., *Gendering the International,* 140–73. London: Palgrave.

———. 2003a. "Beyond Cosmopolitanism and Nationalism: Diasporic Chinese and Neo-Nationalism in China and Thailand." *International Organization* 57 (3): 481–517.

————. 2003b. "Great Harmony: The Next Big Idea in Chinese International Relations Theory." Presented at the Association of Asian Studies annual conference, New York (March) and the Fairbank Center, Harvard University (April).

————. 2004a. "National Humiliation, Cultural Governance, and Chinese Foreign Relations." *Alternatives* 29: 1.

————, ed. 2004b. "The Limits of Chinese Nationalism." *Journal of Contemporary China* (special issue).

———— and Steven Olive. 1995. "Chemical Weapons Disposal in the South Pacific." In Rob Wilson and Arif Dirlik, eds., *Asia/Pacific as Space of Cultural Production*, 57–79. Durham, N.C.: Duke University Press.

Campbell, David. 1992. *Writing Security: United States Foreign Policy and the Politics of Identity*. Minneapolis: University of Minnesota Press.

————. 1996. "Political Prosaics, Transversal Politics, and the Anarchical World." In Shapiro and Alker, eds., 7–32.

————. 1998a. *Writing Security: United States Foreign Policy and the Politics of Identity*. Rev. ed. Minneapolis: University of Minnesota Press.

————. 1998b. *National Deconstruction: Violence, Identity, and Justice in Bosnia*. Minneapolis: University of Minnesota Press.

————. 1998c. "The Deterritorialization of Responsibility: Levinas, Derrida, and Ethics after the End of Philosophy." In Campbell and Shapiro, eds., 29–56.

———— and Michael J. Shapiro, eds. 1998. *Moral Spaces: Rethinking Ethics and World Politics*. Minneapolis: University of Minnesota Press.

Cao Deben. 1998. *Zhongguo chuantong wenhua yu Zhongguo xiandaihua [Chinese Traditional Culture and Chinese Modernization]*. Liaoning: Liaoning daxue chubanshe.

Cao Wanru, Zheng Xihuang, Huang Shengzhang, Niu Zhongxun, Ren Jincheng, Qin Guojing, and Wang Qianjin, eds. 1997. *Zhongguo gudai dituji (Qing) [An Atlas of Ancient Maps in China (Qing Dynasty)]*. Beijing: Wenwu chubanshe.

Cao Wanru, Zheng Xihuang, Huang Shengzhang, Niu Zhongxun, Ren Jincheng, Qin Guojing, Hu Bangbo, eds. 1994. *Zhongguo gudai dituji (Ming) [An Atlas of Ancient Maps in China (Ming Dynasty)]*. Beijing: Wenwu chubanshe.

Cao Wanru, Zheng Xihuang, Huang Shengzhang, Niu Zhongxun, Ren Jincheng, Ju Deyuan, eds. 1990. *Zhongguo gudai dituji (Zhanguo–Yuan) [An Atlas of Ancient Maps in China (From Warring States Period to the Yuan Dynasty {476 BC–AD 1368})]*. Beijing: Wenwu chubanshe.

Cao Zengmei and Huang Xiaoxian, eds. 1932. *Xinbian guochi xiaoshi [A Short History of National Humiliation: New Edition]*. Shanghai: Shangwu chubanshe.

Castells, Manuel. 2000. *End of Millennium.* 2d ed. Oxford: Blackwell.

Central Television Overseas Center, ed. 1998. *Huigui de shunjian: CCTV Xianggang huigui 41 xiaoshi de yingyu baodao jinian [Returning Live: Reflections on CCTV's "Hong Kong Returns" 41 Hours of Reporting].* Beijing: Central Compilation and Translation Press.

Ch'en, Ta-tuan. 1968. "The Investiture of Liu Ch'iu Kings in the Ch'ing Period." In Fairbank, ed., 135–64.

Cha, Victor. 1997. "Engagement Strategies in East Asia: The China-Korea Case." Presented at the International Political Science Association Seventeenth World Congress. Seoul, Korea.

Chaiwat Satha-Anand. 1992. "Towards a Peace Culture in Asia." In A. Eide and K. Rupesinghe, eds., *Peace and Conflict Issues after the Cold War,* 135–59. Tokyo: United Nations University Press.

Chaliand, Gérard, and Jean-Pierre Rageau. 1995. *The Penguin Atlas of Diasporas.* New York: Penguin.

Chamberlain, Heath B. 1993. "On the Search for Civil Society in China." *Modern China* 19 (2): 199–215.

Chan, Adrian. 1997. "In Search of Civil Society in China." *Journal of Contemporary Asia* 27 (2): 242–51.

Chan Goh. 1997. *Made in Hong Kong.* Hong Kong: Asian Video Publishing.

Chan, Johannes M. M. 2000. "Judicial Independence: A Reply to the Comments of the Mainland Legal Experts on the Constitutional Jurisdiction of the Court of Final Appeal." In Chan, Fu, and Ghai, eds., 61–72.

———, H. L. Fu, and Yash Ghai, eds. 2000. *Hong Kong's Constitutional Debate: Conflict over Interpretation.* Hong Kong: University of Hong Kong Press.

Chan, Ming K. 1997. "The Legacy of British Administration of Hong Kong: A View from Hong Kong." *China Quarterly,* no. 151: 567–82.

Chan, Steve. 1993. *East Asian Dynamism.* 2d ed. Boulder, Colo.: Westview.

Chang, Han-pi. 1997. *Taiwan: Community of Fate and Cultural Globalization.* Munich: Lit Verlag.

Chang Hsien-chao. 2000. "Political View of Why the 'One China' Principle Should Be an Issue, Not a Precondition." *Peace Forum,* 15 July. www.dsis.org.tw/peaceforum.

Chang, Maria Hsia. 1995. "Greater China and the Chinese 'Global Tribe.'" *Asian Survey* 35 (10): 955–67.

———. 2001. *Return of the Dragon: China's Wounded Nationalism.* Boulder: Westview.

Chang, Mau-Kuei. 1997. "Civil Society, Resource Mobilization, and New Social Movements: Theoretical Implications for the Study of Social Movements in Taiwan." In Kuo, ed., 7–41.

Chao, Linda, and Ramon H. Myers. 2000. "How Elections Promoted Democracy in Taiwan under Marital Law." *China Quarterly* (special issue: "Elections and Democracy in Greater China"), no. 162: 387–409.

Che Zhenhua, Cui Minxuan et al. 1999. *Zhongguo zhoubian jingji quan [The Economic Circle of China and Its Periphery]*. Beijing: Zhongguo jingji chubanshe.

Cheah, Pheng. 1998. "The Cosmopolitical–Today." In Cheah and Robbins, eds., 20–38.

Cheah, Pheng, and Bruce Robbins, eds. 1998. *Cosmopolitics: Thinking and Feeling Beyond the Nation*. Minneapolis: University of Minnesota Press.

Chee, Chan Heng. 1994. "Democracy: Evolution and Implementation, An Asian Perspective." In Robert Bartley et al., *Democracy and Capitalism: Asian and American Perspectives*, 1–28. Singapore: Institute of Southeast Asian Studies.

Chemillier-Gendreau, Monique. 1996. *La Souveraineté sur les Archipels Paracels et Spratleys*. Paris: Editions L'Harmattan.

Chen Chengxiang, Jiang Yihao, and Jiang Jian, eds. 1993. *Jianming guochi cidian [A Simple Dictionary of National Humiliation]*. Beijing: Changchun chubanshe.

Chen Hurng-yu. 1993. "A Comparison between Taipei and Peking in Their Policies and Concepts Regarding the South China Sea." *Issues and Studies* 29:22–57.

Chen Lai. 1998. "Research in Chinese Traditional Studies: Hard-Pressed in the 1990s." *Contemporary Chinese Thought* 29 (4): 35–49.

Chen Shaoming. 1998. "Tone Down a Little: Advice to Cultural Conservativism," *Contemporary Chinese Thought* 29 (4): 63–72.

Chen Shui-bian. 2000. "Taiwan Stands Up: Toward the Dawn of a Rising Era [inaugural speech]." 20 May. www.taipei.org/current/chen.htm.

Chen Wanjun and Zhang Zhao. 1998. "Luoshi Jiang zhuxi '5 juhua' zongyaoqiu haijun quanmian jianshe zaishang xintaijia" [Fulfill Chairman Jiang [Zemin]'s "5 Instructions" to Completely Develop the Navy to a New Level]. *Renmin ribao*, 29 October.

Chen, Gerald. 1998. "Toward an International Relations Theory with Chinese Characteristics?" *Issues & Studies* 34 (6): 1–28.

———. 1999. *Chinese Perspectives on International Relations: A Framework for Analysis*. London: Palgrave.

Chen Jie. 2002. *Foreign Policy of the New Taiwan*. Cheltenham, U.K.: Edward Elgar.

Chen, Kathy. 1996. "Chinese Say 'Yes' to 'China Can Say No.'" *Asian Wall Street Journal*, 25 June.

Chen, Xiaomei. 1995. *Occidentalism: A Theory of Counter-Discourse in Post-Mao China*. Oxford: Oxford University Press.

Cheng Gang and Cao Li. 1998. "Wenhua minzuzhuyi yu wenhua shijiezhuyi:

jiushi niandai 'Guoxue' yu 'Hanxue' de huayu qianyi" [Cultural Nationalism and Cultural Cosmopolitanism: The Discursive Migration of Guoxue and Sinology in the 1990s]. In Wang and Xue, eds., 301–21.

Cheung, Dung Kai. 1998a. "The Atlas: Archeology of an Imaginary City." In Martha Cheung, ed., 40–52.

———. 1998b. "The Centaur of the East." In Martha Cheung, ed., 202–4.

Cheung, Martha P. Y., ed. 1998. *Hong Kong Collage: Contemporary Stories and Writing.* Oxford: Oxford University Press.

Chiang Kai Shek. 1947. *China's Destiny and Economic Theory.* New York: Roy Publishers.

"China: Friend or Foe?" 1996. *Newsweek,* 1 April.

Chinese Ministry of Foreign Affairs. 1980. "China's Indisputable Sovereignty over the Xisha and Nansha Islands." *Beijing Review* 7 (18 February): 15–24.

———. 1999. *Guanghui 50 licheng: Xin Zhongguo waijiao wushinian [Glorious Course: New China's Diplomacy in Five Decades].* Beijing: n.p.

Ching, Frank. 1997. "Misreading Hong Kong." *Foreign Affairs* 76 (3): 53–66.

———. 1998. "Have Asian Values Finished?" *Far Eastern Economic Review,* 22 January.

———. 1999a. "Inviting Trouble." *Far Eastern Economic Review,* 21 January.

———. 1999b. "Judgment Call." *Far Eastern Economic Review,* 18 February.

———. 1999c. "Scare Tactics." *Far Eastern Economic Review,* 13 May.

———. 1999d. "A Shadow over Hong Kong." *Far Eastern Economic Review,* 15 July: 30.

———. 1999e. "Sovereignty vs. Human Rights." *Far Eastern Economic Review,* 22 July: 33.

———. 1999f. *The Li Dynasty: Hong Kong Aristocrats.* Oxford University Press.

———. 2000a. "Race Bias: Hong Kong Must Act." *Far Eastern Economic Review,* 24 February: 30.

———. 2000b. "What Does 'One China' Mean?" *Far Eastern Economic Review,* 11 May.

Chirot, Daniel. 1997. "Conflicting Identities and the Dangers of Communalism." In Chirot and Reid, eds., 3–32.

Chirot, Daniel, and Anthony Reid, eds. 1997. *Essential Outsiders: Chinese and Jews in the Modern Transformation of Southeast Asia and Central Europe.* Seattle: University of Washington Press.

Cho Hein. 1997. "The Historical Origin of Civil Society in Korea." *Korea Journal* 37 (2): 24–41.

Choe Yong-shik. 2000. "Progenitor Tangun Abused in Both Koreas." *Korea Herald,* 3 October.

Choi Kun Duk [Chinese: Cui Gendu]. 1998. *Hanguo ruxue sixiang yanjiu [Confucian Thought in Korea]*. Beijing: Xueyuan chubanshe.

Choi Po-King. "The Politics of Identity: The Women's Movement in Hong Kong." In Man and Lo, eds., 65–74.

Chon Shi-yong. 1998. "President Kim Dae-jung Urges Chinese Intellectuals to Endorse Security System in Asia." *Korea Herald,* 13 November.

Choung Haechang and Han Hyong-jo, eds. 1996. *Confucian Philosophy in Korea*. Seoul: The Academy of Korean Studies.

Chow, Larry Chuen-ho, and Yiu-Kwan Fan. 1999a. "Introduction: The First Year of Hong Kong as a Chinese Special Administrative Region." In Chow and Fan, eds., xxvii–xxxix.

———, eds. 1999b. *The Other Hong Kong Report 1998*. Hong Kong: Chinese University of Hong Kong Press.

Chow, Rey. 1993. *Writing Diaspora: Tactics of Intervention in Contemporary Cultural Studies*. Bloomington: Indiana University Press.

———. 1998. "King Kong in Hong Kong: Watching the 'Handover' from the U.S.A." *Social Text* 55: 93–108.

Christensen, Thomas J. 1996. "Chinese Realpolitick." *Foreign Affairs* 75 (5): 37–52.

———. 1999. "Pride, Pressure, and Politics: The Roots of China's Worldview." In Deng and Wang, eds., 239–56.

———. 2002. "Beijing's Views of Taiwan and the United States in Early 2002: The Renaissance of Pessimism." *China Leadership Monitor,* no. 3: 1–12.

Chua Beng-Huat. 1995. *Communitarianism and Democracy in Singapore*. London: Routledge.

Chun, Allen. 1996. "From Nationalism to Nationalizing: Cultural Imagination and State Formation in Postwar Taiwan." In Unger, ed., 126–47.

Chung Chin-hong. 1996. "Adapting to Historical Circumstances." In Korea Foundation, ed., 221–27.

Chung Yang-mo. 1997. "Round Table: Commemorating the Year of Cultural Heritage." *Koreana* 11 (1): 4–13.

Cihai. 1979. Shanghai: Shanghai cishu chubanshe.

CIA. 2002. *The World Factbook 2000*. www.cia.gov/cia/publications/factbook/geos/pg.html.

Clarke, David. 1998. "Found in Transit: Hong Kong Art in a Time of Change." In Gao Minglu, ed., 175–81.

Clegg, Stewart R., Winton Higgins, and Tony Spybey. 1990. "'Post-Confucianism,' Social Democracy, and Economic Culture." In Clegg, Redding, and Cartner, eds., 31–77.

Clegg, Stewart R., S. Gordon Redding, and Monica Cartner, eds. 1990. *Capitalism in Contrasting Cultures*. New York: Walter de Gruyter.

Clifford, James. 1998. "Mixed Feelings." In Cheah and Robbins, eds., 362–69.

CND (China News Digest) Global Editors. cnd-editor@cnd.org.

Coaldrake, William H. 1996. *Architecture and Authority in Japan.* London: Routledge.

Cohen, Jean L., and Andrew Arato. 1992. *Civil Society and Political Theory.* Cambridge, Mass.: MIT Press.

Cohen, Paul A. 2002. "Remembering and Forgetting: National Humiliation in Twentieth-Century China." *Twentieth-Century China* 27 (2): 1–39.

Cole, Bernard D. 2001. *The Great Wall at Sea: China's Navy Enters the Twenty-First Century.* Annapolis, Md.: Naval Institute Press.

Confucian Thought and the Twenty-First Century International Conference Volume. 1997. Hong Kong: Confucian Academy.

Confucius. 1979. *The Analects.* D. C. Lau, trans. London: Penguin.

Connolly, William. 1991. *Identity\Difference: Democratic Negotiations of Political Paradox.* Ithaca, N.Y.: Cornell University Press. Reprint; Minneapolis: University of Minnesota Press, 2002.

Constantinou, Costas M. 1996. *On the Way to Diplomacy.* Minneapolis: University of Minnesota Press.

Courtauld, Caroline, et al. 1997. *The Hong Kong Story.* Oxford: Oxford University Press.

Cowhig, David. 1999. "Beijing Sanlian Bookstore Bestseller List on June 4, 1999." H-Net List for Asian History and Culture, 5 June.

Cox, Christopher. 1999. *U.S. National Security and Military/Commercial Concerns with the People's Republic of China.* Washington: The United States House of Representatives Select Committee. www.house.gov/coxreport/.

Cradock, Percy. 1997. "Losing the Plot in Hong Kong." *Prospect,* April.

———. 1999. *Experiences in China.* New ed. London: John Murray.

Cronenberg, David. 1993. *M. Butterfly.* Los Angeles: Warner Entertainment.

Cumings, Bruce. 1996. *South Korea's Academic Lobby.* Cardiff, CA: Japan Policy Research Institute, Occasional Paper no. 7.

———. 1999. *Parallax Visions: Making Sense of American-East Asian Relations at the End of the Century.* Durham, N.C.: Duke University Press.

Dai Xiudian. 2000a. *The Digital Revolution and Governance.* Aldershot, U.K.: Ashgate.

———. 2000b. "Chinese Politics of the Internet: Control and Anti-control," *Cambridge Review of International Affairs* 13 (2): 181–94.

Dallmayr, Fred, ed. 1999. *Border Crossings: Toward a Comparative Political Theory.* Lanham, Md.: Lexington Books.

de Bary, W. T., ed. 1960. *Sources of Chinese Tradition,* vol. 1. New York: Columbia University Press.

——— and JaHyun Kim Haboush, eds. 1985. *The Rise of Neo-Confucianism in Korea.* New York: Columbia University Press.

"Declaration on the Conduct of Parties in the South China Sea." 2002. Jakarta: ASEAN Secretariat, 4 November. www.aseansec.org/13163.htm.

de Lauretis, Teresa. 1987. *Technologies of Gender: Essays on Film, Theory, and Fiction.* Bloomington: Indiana University Press.

"Demolition of Old Colonial Headquarters [Editorial]." 1996. *Dong-A Ilbo,* 16 November, translated in *Korea Focus* 4 (6): 160.

Deng Xiaojun. 1998. "Guoxue yanjiu de taidu yu yiyi" [The Attitude and Ideas of Guoxue Research]. *Zhongguo wenhua yanjiu [Chinese Culture Research],* no. 20: 20–3.

Deng Xiaoping. 1987. *Jianshe you Zhongguo tesede shehuizhuyi [Building Socialism with Chinese Characteristics].* Rev. ed. Beijing: Renmin chubanshe.

———. 1993. *Lun Xianggang wenti [On the Hong Kong Problem].* Hong Kong: Sanlian chubanshe.

———. 1994. *Selected Works of Deng Xiaoping.* Vol. 3 (1982–1992). Beijing: Foreign Languages Press.

Deng, Yong. 1999. "Conception of National Interests: Realpolitick, Liberal Dilemma, and the Possibility of Change." In Deng and Wang, eds., 47–72.

——— and Sherry Gray. 2001. "Introduction: Growing Pains—China debates its international future." *Journal of Contemporary China* 10 (26): 5–16.

Deng, Yong, and Fei-Ling Wang, eds. 1999. *In the Eyes of the Dragon: China Views the World.* Oxford: Rowman and Littlefield Publishers.

Der Derian, James, and Michael J. Shapiro, eds. 1989. *International/ Intertextual Relations: Postmodern Readings of World Politics.* Lexington, Mass.: Lexington Books.

Derrida, Jacques. 1997. *Politics of Friendship.* George Collins, trans. London: Verso.

Deuchler, Martina. 1992. *The Confucian Transformation of Korea: A Study of Society and Ideology.* Cambridge, Mass.: Harvard University Press.

Deudney, Daniel. 1996. "Binding Sovereigns: Authorities, Structures, and Geopolitics in Philadelphian Systems." In Biersteker and Weber, eds., 190–239.

Diamond, Larry, and Raymond H. Myers. 2000. "Introduction: Elections and Democracy in Greater China." *China Quarterly* (special issue: Elections and Democracy in Greater China), no. 162: 365–86.

Diamond, Larry, and Marc F. Plattner, eds. 1998. *Democracy in East Asia*. Baltimore: The Johns Hopkins University Press.

Diaoyutai: Zhongguo de lingtu! [Diaoyu Islands: China's Sovereign Territory!]. 1996. Hong Kong: Mingbao chubanshe.

Dikötter, Frank. 1992. *The Discourse of Race in Modern China*. Palo Alto: Stanford University Press.

Dirlik, Arif. 1995. "Confucius in the Borderlands: Global Capitalism and the Reinvention of Confucianism." *boundary 2* 22 (3): 229–73.

———. 1997. *The Postcolonial Aura: Third World Criticism in the Age of Global Capitalism*. Boulder, Colo.: Westview.

———. 1998a. "Introduction: Pacific Contradictions." In Dirlik, ed., 3–14.

———, ed. 1998b. *What Is in a Rim? Critical Perspectives on the Pacific Rim Idea*. 2d ed. Oxford: Rowman and Littlefield.

———, and Zhang Xudong, eds. 2000. *Postmodernism and China*. Durham, N.C.: Duke University Press.

Dittmer, Lowell, and Samuel S. Kim, eds. 1993. *China's Quest for National Identity*. Ithaca, N.Y.: Cornell University Press.

DPP. 1998. "Democratic Progressive Party China Policy Symposium." February. taiwan.yam.org.tw/china_policy/e_bg.htm.

"Duanpo" ["Ripples"]. 1998. *Renmin ribao*, 22 October.

Duara, Pasenjit. 1995. *Rescuing History from the Nation: Questioning Narratives of Modern China*. Chicago: University of Chicago Press.

Dutton, Michael. 1998. *Streetlife China*. Cambridge: Cambridge University Press.

Eckert, Carter. 1991. *Offspring of Empire, The Koch'ang Kims and the Colonial Origins of Korean Capitalism, 1876–1945*. Seattle: University of Washington Press.

Eco, Umberto. 1998. *Serendipities: Language and Lunacy*. New York: Columbia University Press.

Edmonds, Richard Louis. 1995. "Macau and Greater China." In Shambaugh, ed., 226–54.

"Elections and Democracy in Greater China." 2000. *China Quarterly* (special issue), no. 162.

Elias, Norbert. 1978. *The Civilizing Process: The History of Manners*. New York: Pantheon.

Elman, Benjamin A., John B. Duncan, and Herman Ooms, eds. 2002. *Rethinking Confucianism: Past and Present in China, Japan, Korea, and Vietnam*. Los Angeles: UCLA Asian Pacific Monograph Series.

Em, Henry H. 1999. "Minjok as a Modern and Democratic Construct: Sin Ch'aeho's Historiography." In Gi-Wook Shin and Michael Robinson, eds., *Colonial Modernity in Korea*, 336–61. Cambridge, Mass.: Harvard University Press.

Enloe, Cynthia. 1993. *The Morning After: Sexual Politics at the End of the Cold War.* Berkeley: University of California Press.

Fairbank, John King. 1968a. "A Preliminary Framework." In Fairbank, ed., 1–19.

———, ed. 1968b. *The Chinese World Order: Traditional China's Foreign Relations.* Cambridge, Mass.: Harvard University Press.

Farrands, Chris. 2001. "Touching Friendship beyond Friendship: Friendship and Citizenship in Global Politics." *Alternatives* 26 (2): 143–73.

Fei Xiaotong. 2001. "Chuangjian yige he er bu tong de quanqiu shehui–zai guoji renleixue yu minzuxue lianhehui zhong qi huiyishang de zhuzhi fayan" [Creating a Harmonious but Different World Community: A Speech at the International Conference of Anthropology and Ethnology]. *Sixiang zhanxian [Ideological Front].* No. 6: 1–5, 16.

Feng Renzhao. 1998. "The Hongkongnese: Who Are the Hongkongese?" In Man and Lo, eds., 37–44.

Filial Piety and Future Society. 1995. (In Korean and English). Seoul: Academy of Korean Studies.

Fok, K. C. 1990. *Lectures on Hong Kong: Hong Kong's Role in Modern Chinese History.* Hong Kong: The Commercial Press.

Foreign and Commonwealth Office. 1997–. *Six-Monthly Reports on Hong Kong.* www.fco.gov.uk/news/keythemepage.asp?PageId=56.

Foreign Affairs, ed. 2002. *The Rise of China.* New York: Council on Foreign Relations.

Foucault, Michel. 1970. *The Order of Things.* New York: Vintage.

———. 1972. *The Archaeology of Knowledge.* New York: Pantheon Books.

———. 1979. "What Is an Author?" In Josue V. Harari, ed., *Textual Strategies,* 141–60. Ithaca, N.Y.: Cornell University Press.

———. 1980a. *The History of Sexuality.* Vol. 1. New York: Vintage.

———. 1980b. *Power/Knowledge: Selected Interviews and Writings, 1972–1977.* Colin Gordon, ed. New York: Pantheon.

———. 1982. "Afterword: The Subject and Power." In Hubert L. Dreyfus and Paul Rabinow, eds., *Michel Foucault: Beyond Structuralism and Hermeneutics,* 208–26. New York: The Harvester Press.

———. 1984. "Nietzsche, Genealogy, and History." In Paul Rabinow, ed., *The Foucault Reader,* 76–100. New York: Pantheon.

———. 1986. "Of Other Spaces." *Diacritics* 16: 22–27.

———. 1991. "Governmentality." In Graham Burchell, Colin Gordon, and Peter Miller, eds., *The Foucault Effect: Studies in Governmentality,* 87–104. London: Harvester Wheatsheaf.

Fracasso, Riccardo. 1993. "Shan hai ching." In Michael Lowe, ed., *Early Chinese Texts: A Bibliographical Guide,* 357–67. Berkeley: Society for the Study of Early China and Institute of East Asian Studies, University of California, Berkeley.

Frank, André Gunder. 1998. *ReOrient: Global Economy in the Asian Age.* Berkeley and Los Angeles: University of California Press.

Friedman, Edward. 1995. *National Identity and Democratic Prospects in Socialist China.* Armonk, N.Y.: M. E. Sharpe.

———. 2000. "Immanuel Kant's Relevance to an Enduring Asia-Pacific Peace." In Friedman and McCormick, eds., 224–35.

———, and Barrett L. McCormick, eds. 2000. *What If China Doesn't Democratize? Implications for War and Peace.* Armonk, NY: M. E. Sharpe.

Frye, Northrop. 1957. *Anatomy of Criticism: Four Essays.* Princeton: Princeton University Press.

Fukuyama, Francis. 1995. "Confucianism and Democracy." *Journal of Democracy* 6 (1): 20–33.

———. 1998. "Asian Values and the Asian Crisis." *Commentary* 105: 23–27.

Gao Minglu, ed. 1998. *Inside Out: New Chinese Art* [exhibition catalog]. Berkeley and Los Angeles: University of California Press.

Gao Weinong. 1999. *Guoji haiyangfa yu taipingyang diqu haiyang guanxiaquan [The Law of the Sea and Maritime Jurisdiction in the Pacific Region].* Guangdong: Guangdong gaodeng jiaoyu chubanshe.

Garver, John W. 1998. "Sino-Russian Relations." In Samuel Kim, ed., 114–32.

Geaney, Jane. 2000. "Shame and Sensory Excess in Chinese Thought." Presented at the Eighth East-West Philosophers' Conference, Honolulu, January.

Geertz, Clifford. 1980. *Negara: The Theater State in Nineteenth Century Bali.* Princeton: Princeton University Press.

Gertz, Bill. 2000. *The China Threat: How the People's Republic Targets America.* Washington, D.C.: Regnery Publishing.

Ghai, Yash. 1998. "Autonomy with Chinese Characteristics: The Case of Hong Kong," *Pacifica Review* 10 (1): 7–22.

———. 2000. "Litigating the Basic Law: Jurisdiction, Interpretation, and Procedure." In Chan, Fu, and Ghai, eds., 3–52.

Giddens, Anthony. 1990. *The Consequences of Modernity.* Palo Alto: Stanford University Press.

Gills, Barry K., and Dongsook S. Gills. 2000. "Globalization and Strategic Choice in South Korea: Economic Reform and Labor." In Samuel Kim, ed., 29–53.

Glaser, Bonnie. 2001. "Discussion of 'Four Contradictions Constraining China's Foreign Policy Behavior.'" *Journal of Contemporary China* 10 (27): 303–8.

Godement, Francois. 1996. "Nationalism on the Rocks in the China Sea." *Asia Times* [Bangkok], 14 October.

Gold, Thomas B. 1998. "Taiwan Society at the Fin de Siecle." In Shambaugh, ed., 47–70.

Gong, Gerrit W. 1984. *The Standard of "Civilization" in International Society.* Oxford: Clarendon Press.

Goodman, David S. G., and Gerald Segal, eds. 1997. *China Rising: Nationalism and Interdependence.* London: Routledge.

Graham, A. C. 1989. *Disputers of the Tao: Philosophical Argument in Ancient China.* La Salle, Ill.: Open Court.

———, trans. 1981. *Chuang-tzu.* London: George Allen and Unwin.

Grewal, Inderpal, Akhil Gupta, and Aihwa Ong. 1999. "Guest Editors' Introduction [for special issue on Asian transnationalities]." *positions: east asia cultural critique* 7 (3): 653–66.

Grinker, Roy Richard. 2000. *Korea and Its Futures: Unification and the Unfinished War.* London: Macmillan.

Gui Hanbiao, ed. 2001. *Nansha shiji meng [Spratly Century Dreams].* Beijing: Zhongguo wenlian chubanshe.

Guo Qifu. 1996. *Wuwang guochi: zaichuang huihuang [Never Forget National Humiliation: Glorious Renaissance].* Wuhan: Wuhan daxue chubanshe.

Guoyu. 1978. Shanghai: Shanghai guji chubanshe.

Guochi [National Humiliation]. 1915, no. 1 (June).

Guowuyuan Taiwan shiwu bangongshe. 2001. *Taiwan wenti tupianzhan [Taiwan Problem Picture Exhibit].* Beijing: Museum of Revolutionary History, 23 April–7 May.

Guowuyuan Taiwan shiwu bangongshe xuanchuanju, Zhongguo shehui kexueyuan Taiwan yanjiusuo, zhongyang dianshitai haiwai zhongxin xinwenbu [State Council Taiwan Affairs Office Propaganda Section, Chinese Academy of Social Sciences Taiwan Institute, Central Television Foreign News Section]. 2000. *Taiwan baiwen [100 Questions about Taiwan].* Beijing: Zhongguo guangbao dianshi chubanshe.

Hahm Chaibong. 1997a. "Confucian Tradition and Economic Reform in Korea." *Chontonggwa hyondae* 1 (1): 26–49 [translated in *Korea Focus* 5 (3): 76–92].

———. 1997b. "The Order of the Tao: The Confucian Understanding of Order." Presented at the International Political Science Association Seventeenth World Congress. Seoul, Korea.

———. 1997c. "Reconsidering Former-President Park Chung-hee." *Chuntonggwa hyondae* 1 (2): 159–93.

Hall, David, and Roger Ames. 1987. *Thinking Through Confucius.* Albany, N.Y.: SUNY Press.

————. 1994. "Confucian Friendship: The Road to Religiousness." In Rouner, ed., 77–94.

Halloran, Richard. 1999. "Reading Beijing: U.S. Strategist Turns to History to Understand China." *Far Eastern Economic Review*, 25 February: 28.

Hamilton, Gary G. 1996. "Overseas Chinese Capitalism." In Tu, ed., 328–42.

————, ed. 1999. *Cosmopolitan Capitalists: Hong Kong and the Chinese Diaspora at the End of the Twentieth Century*. Seattle: University of Washington Press.

Han Sang-Jin. 1997a. "The Public Sphere and Democracy in Korea: A Debate on Civil Society." *Korea Journal* 37 (4): 78–97.

————. 1997b. "Globalization and Postcolonialism: Confucianism and East Asian Development." Presented at the 1997 Kwangju Biennale International Symposium on Globalization and Postcolonialism, 30–31 October.

————. 1998. "The Korean Path to Development and Risk Society." *Korea Journal* 39 (1): 5–27.

Haraway, Donna. 1985. "A Manifesto for Cyborgs: Science, Technology, and Socialist Feminism in the 1980s." *Socialist Review* 15 (2): 65–107.

Harding, Harry. 1994. *The Evolution of Greater China and What It Means for America*. New York: National Committee China Policy Series, no. 10 (December).

————. 1995. "The Concept of 'Greater China': Themes, Variations, and Reservations." In Shambaugh, ed., 8–34.

Hardt, Michael, and Antonio Negri. 2000. *Empire*. Cambridge, Mass.: Harvard University Press.

Harley, J. B., and David Woodward. 1994. *The History of Cartography*. Vol. 2, Book 2, *Cartography in the Traditional East and Southeast Asian Societies*. Chicago: University of Chicago Press.

Harris, Michael, and Geert Hofstede. 1990. "The Cash Value of Confucian Values." In Clegg, Redding, and Cartner, eds., 383–90.

H-Asia. 1999. H-Net list for Asian History and Culture. H-ASIA@H-NET .MSU.EDU.

Hawksely, Humphrey, and Simon Holberton. 1997. *Dragonstrike: The Millennium War*. London: Macmillan.

Hay, John. 1994a. "Introduction." In Hay, ed., 1–55.

————, ed. 1994b. *Boundaries in China*. London: Reaktion Books.

He Baogang. 1997. *The Democratic Implications of Civil Society in China*. London: Macmillan.

————, and Yingjie Guo. 2000. *Nationalism, National Identity, and Democratization in China*. Aldershot, U.K.: Ashgate.

He Beilin. 1996. "*Qianyan*" [Foreword]. In Song Qiang et al., 1–3.

He Degong, Pu Weizhong, and Jin Yong. 1997. *Qingting Zhongguo: xin-*

lengzhan yu weilai moulue [Listen Carefully to China: The New Cold War and Future Strategy]. Guangdong renmin chubanshe.

He Delong. 1998. *Women de jiayuan: Xianggang [Our Backyard: Hong Kong]*. Ji'nan: Shandong renmin chubanshe.

He Xin. 1996. *Zhonghua fuxing yu shijie weilai [The Renaissance of China and the Future of the World]*. Vols. 1 and 2. Chengdu: Sichuan renmin chubanshe.

He Yu. 1997. *Bainian guochi jiyao [A Summary of the Century of National Humiliation]*. Beijing: Beijing yanshan chubanshe.

———. 1999. *Shiji huishuo: bainian guochi lu [Looking Back on the Century: A Record of a Century of National Humiliation]*. Beijing: Zhongguo shudian.

HEFCE. 1999. *Review of Chinese Studies: Report 99/09*. Bristol: HEFCE. www.niss.ac.uk/education/hefce/pub99/ 99_09.html#summ.

Henderson, John B. 1994. "Chinese Cosmographical Thought: The High Intellecutal Tradition." In Harley and Woodward, eds., 203–27.

Heryanto, Ariel. 1997. "Silence in Indonesian Literary Discourse: The Case of the Indonesian Chinese." *Sojourn* 12:26–45.

Hevia, James. 1995. *Cherishing Men from Afar: Qing Guest Ritual and the Macartney Embassy of 1793*. Durham, N.C.: Duke University Press.

Hicks, George, and J. A. C. Mackie. 1994. "Overseas Chinese—A Question of Identity: Despite Media Hype, They Are Firmly Settled in Southeast Asia." *Far Eastern Economic Review*, 14 July: 46–51.

Higgins, Andrew. 1996. "Gold of the Tigers." *Guardian: The Week*, 2 November: 1–2.

Higgott, Richard. 2000. "The International Relations of the Asian Economic Crisis: A Study in the Politics of Resentment." In Robison et al., eds., 261–82.

Hofheinz, Roy, Jr., and Kent E. Calder. 1982. *The Eastasia Edge*. New York: Basic Books.

Holloway, Nigel, Julian Baum, Charles S. Lee, and Sachiko Sakamaki. 1997. "Learned Puppets: U.S. Academics Take Asian Funding—and the Strings Attached." *Far Eastern Economic Review*, 22 May: 29–30, 32.

Holsti, K. J. 1995. *International Politics: A Framework for Analysis*. 7th ed. Englewood Cliffs: Prentice-Hall International.

Hong Doo Pyo. 1995. "Opening Speech by the KBS President." In *Filial Piety and Future Society*, v–x.

Hong Kong Society and Culture Section, Hong Kong and Macao Affairs Office, State Council. 1997. *Xianggang wenti duben [Hong Kong Problem Reader]*. Beijing: Communist Party Central Committee Press.

Hong Sun-hee. 1997. "Ban on Same-Surname Marriage Lifted: Court's Ruling Puts End to Centuries-Old Taboo." *The Korea Times*, 17 July: 3.

Hook, Brian. 1995. "Political Change in Hong Kong." In Shambaugh, ed., 188–211.

———. 1997. "British Views of the Legacy of the Colonial Administration in Hong Kong: A Preliminary Assessment." *China Quarterly*, no. 151: 553–66.

Howland, D. R. 1996. *Borders of Chinese Civilization: Geography and History at Empire's End*. Durham, N.C.: Duke University Press.

Hsiao, Hsin-Huang Michael. 1988. "An East Asian Development Model: Empirical Explorations." In Berger and Hsiao, eds., 12–23.

———. 1995. "The Development and Organization of Foundations in Taiwan: An Expression of Cultural Vigor in a Newly Born Society." In Jason C. Hu, ed., 386–420.

Hsu Hsin-liang and Chen Chong-hsin. 1998. "Zai guoji xinzhixu geju xia zhongqi liang'an guanxi xin juyuan" [The New World Order Opens Up a New Era of Cross-Straits Relations]. Paper presented at The Democratic Progressive Party China Policy Conference, February. taiwan.yam.org.tw/China_Policy/C_Shu-c.htm.

Hsu, Immaneul C. 1960. *China's Entrance into the Family of Nations*. Cambridge, Mass.: Harvard University Press.

Hu Huiqiang et al. 1998. *Bainian fengyun shou yandi: Zhongguo geming bowuguan [A Century of Turbulence Displayed before Our Eyes: The Museum of the Chinese Revolution]*. Beijing: Zhongguo dabaikequanshu chubanshe.

Hu, Jason C., ed. 1995. *Quiet Revolutions on Taiwan, the Republic of China*. Taipei: Kwang Hwa Publishing Company.

Hu Weixing. 1995. "China's Security Agenda after the Cold War." *Pacific Review* 8 (1): 117–35.

Hu Zhanfan. 1994. "Dedication on the Nansha Islands." *FBIS–China Daily Report*, 21 June: 10–11.

Huang Kunzhang. 1998. "Lun Huaren wenhuade shiying, chuancheng yu gaizao" [The Adaptation, Success, and Innovation of Chinese Culture Abroad]. *Huaqiao Huaren lishi yanjiu* [Historical Studies of Overseas Chinese] 44 (Winter): 28–33.

Hughes, Christopher R. 1995. "China and Liberalism Globalized." *Millennium* 24 (3): 425–45.

———. 1997a. *Taiwan and Chinese Nationalism*. London: Routledge.

———. 1997b. "Globalization and Nationalism: Squaring the Circle in Chinese IR Theory." *Millennium* 26 (1): 103–24.

———. 1998. "Taiwan's Political Changes and Challenges." Taipei: Chinese Council for Advanced Policy Studies, paper no. 28.

———. 2000. "Nationalism in Chinese Cyberspace." *Cambridge Review of International Affairs* 13 (2): 195–209.

———. 2001. "Living with 'One Country, Two Systems'?" *Cambridge Review of International Affairs* 14 (2) (April): 125–38.

Hung, Eva, ed. 1999. *Hong Kong Stories: Old Themes New Voices.* Hong Kong: Renditions Paperbacks.

Huntington, Samuel P. 1991. *The Third Wave: Democratization in the Late Twentieth Century.* Norman: Oklahoma University Press.

———. 1993. "The Clash of Civilizations?" *Foreign Affairs* 72 (3): 22–49.

———. 1996. *The Clash of Civilizations and the Remaking of World Order.* New York: Simon and Schuster.

Hwang Sun-myung. 1996. "The Origins of Korean Religious Beliefs." In Korea Foundation, ed., 20–27.

Hwang, David Henry. 1988. *M. Butterfly.* London: Penguin.

Hwang, Ginger Ching-Chane. 2001. "Still the Superior Man? Changing Notions of the Mandarin in Taiwan's Contemporary Confucian Context." Presented at the Forty-Second Annual International Studies Association Convention, Chicago, February.

"Inappropriate Remarks by Chinese Ambassador [Editorial]." 2000. *Dong-A Ilbo,* 16 November. In *Korea Focus* 8 (6): 10–20.

Inoue, Yasushi. 1992. *Confucius.* Tokyo: Tuttle.

Ip Iam-Chong. 1998. "The Spectres of Marginality and Hybridity: 'Hong Kong Identity' in Cultural Criticism." In Man and Lo, eds., 45–64.

Jagchid, Sechin, and Van Jay Simons. 1989. *Peace, War, and Trade along the Great Wall.* Bloomington: Indiana University Press.

Janelli, Robert L., with Dawnhee Yim. 1993. *Making Capitalism: The Social and Cultural Construction of a South Korean Conglomerate.* Palo Alto: Stanford University Press.

Jensen, Lionel M. 1997. *Manufacturing Confucianism: Chinese Traditions and Universal Civilization.* Durham, N.C.: Duke University Press.

Jeong Young-hun. 2001. "Myth of Dangun and 'Dangun Nationalism.'" *Korea Focus* 9 (4): 53–68.

Ji Guoxing. 1998. "China versus the South China Seas Disputes." *Security Dialogue* 29 (1): 101–12.

———. 2001. "Rough Waters in the South China Sea: Navigation Issues and Confidence Building Measures." *Asia Pacific Issues,* no. 53. Honolulu: East West Center.

Jia Shenda, Ma Yong, and Wang Shilu. 1998. *Zouxiang 21 shijide dongnanya yu Zhongguo [Twenty-First Century Trends for Southeast Asia and China].* Kunming: Yunnan daxue chubanshe.

Jiang Gongsheng. 1927. *Guochi shi [A History of National Humiliation].* Shanghai: Xinhua shuju.

Jiang Linxiang and Tang Minggui. 2000. "Ruxue yu Yazhou jinrong weiji" [Confucianism and the Asian Financial Crisis]. *Guoji ruxue yanjiu*

[International Confucian Studies] 10, 293–315. Beijing: Guoji wenhua chubanshe.

Jiang Zemin. 1997. "Speech Commemorating Hong Kong's Return." In Xinhua News Agency Hong Kong Office, ed., *Xianggang huigui diyitian [The First Day of the Return of Hong Kong]*. Beijing: Xinhua.

Jiang Zemin. 1999. *Jiang Zemin lun shehuizhuyi jingshen wenming jianshe [Jiang Zemin on the Construction of Socialist Spiritual Civilization]*. Beijing: Central Committee Documents Press.

Jindai Zhongguo: bainian guochi ditu [An Atlas of the Century of National Humiliation in Contemporary China]. 1997. Beijing: Renmin chubanshe.

Johnson, Paul. 1997. "A Contrarian View of Colonialism: Hong Kong Wasn't Just the Case of Exploiter and Exploited." *Far Eastern Economic Review* (special 1997 issue, *Hong Kong: A New Beginning*): 8–16.

Johnston, Alastair Iain. 1995. *Cultural Realism: Strategic Culture and Grand Strategy in Chinese History*. Princeton: Princeton University Press.

———. 1996. "Cultural Realism and Strategy in Maoist China." In Katzenstein, ed., 216–70.

———, and Robert S. Ross, eds. 1999. *Engaging China: The Management of an Emerging Power*. New York: Routledge.

Jones, D. M., K. Jayasuriya, D. A. Bell, and D. Brown. 1995. *Towards Illiberal Democracy*. London: Macmillan.

Junn Sung-chull. 1998. "Economic Crisis and Asian Values." *Korea Focus* 6 (2): 126–28.

Kalton, Michael C., ed. 1994. *The Four-Seven Debate: An Annotated Translation of the Most Famous Controversy in Korean Neo-Confucian Thought*. Albany, N.Y.: SUNY Press.

Kang, David C. 2002. *Crony Capitalism: Corruption and Development in South Korea and the Philippines*. Cambridge: Cambridge University Press.

Kao, Charng. 1992. "A 'Greater China Economic Sphere': Reality and Prospects." *Issues and Studies* 28 (11): 49–64.

Kao, John. 1993. "The World Wide Web of Chinese Business." *Harvard Business Review* 71 (March–April): 24–34.

Karlgren, Bernard. 1957. *Grammatica Serica Recensa*. Stockholm: Museum of Far Eastern Antiquities.

Kasian Tejapira. 1992. "Pigtail: A Pre-History of Chineseness in Siam." *Sojourn* 7 (1): 95–122.

———. 1997. "Imagined Uncommunity: The Lookjin Middle Class and Thai Official Nationalism." In Chirot and Reid, eds., 75–98.

———. 1999. *Chaosivilai: Kanmuang wattanatham Thai tai ngoa IMF*

[Civilized People: Thai Political Culture under the Shadow of the IMF]. Bangkok: Komolkeemthong Foundation Publishing.

Katzenstein, Peter J. 1996a. "Introduction: Alternative Perspectives on National Security." In Katzenstein, ed., 1–32.

Katzenstein, Peter J. 1997. "Introduction: Asian Regionalism in Comparative Perspective." In Katzenstein and Shiraishi, eds., 1–44.

Katzenstein, Peter J, ed. 1996b. *The Culture of National Security: Norms and Identity in World Politics*. New York: Columbia University Press.

Katzenstein, Peter J., and Takashi Shiraishi, eds. 1997. *Network Power: Japan and Asia*. Ithaca, N.Y.: Cornell University Press.

Kavi Chongkittavorn. 1996. "ASEAN-China Ties are Maturing." *The Nation* [Bangkok], 31 May: 4.

Keene, Edward. 2001. *Beyond the Anarchical Society: Grotius, Colonialism, and Order in World Politics*. Cambridge: Cambridge University Press.

Kennedy, Paul M. 1989. *The Rise and Fall of Great Powers*. New York: Vintage.

Khagram, Sanjeev, James V. Riker, and Kathryn Sikkink. 2002a. "From Santiago to Seattle: Transnational Advocacy Groups Restructuring World Politics." In Khagram et al., eds., 3–33.

Khagram, Sanjeev, James V. Riker, and Kathryn Sikkink, ed. 2002b. *Restructuring World Politics: Transnational Social Movements, Networks, and Norms*, Minneapolis: University of Minnesota Press.

Kim Byung-Kook. 1997. "Anti-Confucian Confucian Politics: Contradiction and Political Argument in Korea." *Chontonggwa hyondae* 1 (1): 50–73.

Kim Dae Jung. 1994. "Is Culture Destiny? The Myth of Asia's Anti-Democratic Values." *Foreign Affairs* 73 (6): 189–94.

Kim Ji-ho. 1999. "Disputed North Korea–China Border Confirmed by South Korean Expert." *Korea Herald*, 21 October.

Kim Ji-soo. 1999. "Ethnic Korean Chinese Take Issue with New Bill They Say Unfairly Excludes Them." *Korea Herald*, 2 September.

Kim Key-Hiuk. 1980. *The Last Phase of the East Asian World Order: Korea, Japan, and the Chinese Empire, 1860–1882*. Berkeley and Los Angeles: University of California Press.

Kim Kwang-Ok. 1996. "The Reproduction of Confucian Culture in Contemporary Korea: An Anthropological Study." In Tu Weiming, ed., 202–27.

———. 1997. "The Role of *Madangguk* in Contemporary Korea's Popular Culture Movement." *Korea Journal* 37 (3): 5–21.

Kim Kyong-Dong. 1994. "Confucianism and Capitalist Development in East Asia." In Leslie Sklair, ed., *Capitalism and Development*, 87–106. London: Routledge.

———. 1997. "Business and Culture for the Future." *Korea Focus* 5 (5): 85–88.

Kim Kyung Hyun. 1996. "The Fractured Cinema of North Korea, The Discourse of the Nation in Sea of Blood." In Xiaobing Tang and Stephen Snyder, eds., *In Pursuit of Contemporary East Asian Culture*, 85–106. Boulder, Colo.: Westview.

Kim Myong-ha. 1997. "The Mandate of Heaven and the Election." *Chuntonggwa hyondae* 1 (2): 54–73.

Kim Young Hie. 1998. "Debate on Asian Values: Truths and Falsehoods." *Korea Focus* 6 (2): 121–23.

Kim Young Sam. [n.d.]. *Korea's Reform and Globalization: President Kim Young Sam Prepares the Nation for the Challenges of the Twenty-First Century*. Seoul: Korea Overseas Information Service.

Kim Yung Myung. 1997. "'Asian Style Democracy': A Critique from East Asia." *Asian Survey* 37 (12): 1119–34.

Kim, Dalchoong, et al., eds. 1996. *UN Convention on the Law of the Sea and East Asia*. Seoul: Institute of East and West Studies, Yonsei University.

Kim, Eun Mee. 2000. "Globalization of the South Korean *Chaebol*." In Samuel S. Kim, ed., 2000b, 102–25.

Kim, Samuel S. 1994a. "China and the World in Theory and Practice." In Samuel S. Kim, ed., 1994c, 3–41.

———. 1994b. "China and the Third World in the Changing World Order." In Samuel S. Kim, ed., 1994c, 128–68.

———. 1998a. "Chinese Foreign Policy in Theory and Practice." In Samuel S. Kim, ed., 1994c, 3–33.

———. 2000a. "Korea's Segyehwa Drive: Promise versus Performance." In Samuel S. Kim, ed., 2000b, 242–81.

———, ed. 1994c. *China and the World: Chinese Foreign Relations in the Post–Cold War Era*. 3d ed. Boulder, Colo.: Westview.

———, ed. 1998b. *China and the World: Chinese Foreign Policy Faces the New Millennium*. 4th ed. Boulder, Colo.: Westview.

———, ed. 2000b. *Korea's Globalization*. Cambridge: Cambridge University Press.

Klintworth, Gary. 2001. "China and Taiwan—From Flashpoint to Redefining One China." *Taipei Review* 51 (3): 46–53.

Knight, Alan, and Yoshiko Nakano, eds. 1999. *Reporting Hong Kong: Foreign Media and the Handover*. London: Curzon.

Köllner, Patrick. 1998. "Going Regional: South Korea's Growing Economic Links with Asia Pacific." Presented at the Tenth Biennal Meeting of the British Association for Korean Studies, Oxford University, 7–8 April.

"Kongzi sixiang." 2000. "'Kongzi sixiang yu Zhongguo tongyi daye' Guoji Xueshu taolunhui zai Xianggang zhaokai" ['Confucian Thought and the Great Task of Chinese Unification' Held in Hong Kong]. *Guoji ruxue lianhehui jianbao* [International Confucian Association Bulletin], no. 24: 7–9.

Koo, Hagen. 1993. "The State, *Minjung*, and the Working Class in South Korea." In Hagen Koo, ed., *State and Society in Contemporary Korea,* 131–62. Ithaca, N.Y.: Cornell University Press.

Korea Foundation, ed. 1996. *Thought and Religion, Korean Cultural Heritage.* Vol. 2. Seoul: Korea Foundation.

Korea-China Joint Statement. 1998. *Korea Focus* 6 (6): 152–55.

Korean National Commission for UNESCO, ed. 1983. *Main Currents of Korean Thought.* Seoul: Si-sa-yong-o-sa Publishers.

Korean National Commission for UNESCO, ed. 2002. *Anthology of Korean Studies. Vol. 2: Korean Politics: Striving for Democracy and Unification.* Elizabeth, N.J., and Seoul: Hollym.

Korean Overseas Information Service. 1997. *The Koreans.* Seoul: Ministry of Culture and Sports.

Krause, Keith, and Michael C. Williams, eds. 1997. *Critical Security Studies.* Minneapolis: University of Minnesota Press.

Krishna, Sankaran. 1996. "Cartographic Anxiety: Mapping the Body Politic in India." In Shapiro and Alker, eds., 193–214.

Kuo, Liangwen (Wayne). 1997. "Guest Editor's Introduction." In Liangwen (Wayne) Kuo, ed. and trans., "Taiwan's Social Movements: A Discussion of the State and Civil Society." *Chinese Sociology and Anthropology* 29 (4): 3–6.

Kurth, James. 1993. "Mitteleuropa and East Asia: The Return of History and the Redefinition of Security." In Meredith Woo-Cumings and Michael Loriaux, eds., *Past as Prelude: History in the Making of a New World Order,* 35–58. Boulder, Colo.: Westview.

Lampton, David M., et al. 1992. *The Emergence of "Greater China": Implications for the United States.* New York: National Committee on United States–China Relations, China Policy Series, no. 5.

Lapid, Yosef, and Friedrich Kratochwil, eds. 1996. *The Return of Culture and Identity in International Relations Theory.* Boulder: Lynne Rienner Publishers.

Lattimore, Owen. 1951. *Inner Asian Frontiers of China,* 2d ed. New York: American Geographical Society.

Ledyard, Gari. 1983. "Yin and Yang in the China-Manchuria-Korea Triangle." In Rossabi, ed., 313–53.

———. 1994. "Cartography in Korea." In J. B. Hartley and David Woodward, eds., 235–345.

Lee Kun-hee. 1997a. "Globalization Strategies." *Korea Times,* 3 September.

———. 1997b. "Great Changes Engulf World as New Epoch About to Dawn." *Korea Times*, 28 August.

———. 1997c. "The Spirit of Rugby." *Korea Times*, 14 September.

Lee Kyong-hee. 2000. "Tangun's Place in History." *Korea Herald*, 24 April.

Lee Lai To. 1999. *China and the South China Sea Dialogues*. London: Praeger.

Lee Seung-Hwan. 1997. "Who Dares Bring Disgrace on Tradition?" *Chontonggwa hyondae* 1 (1): 176–97.

Lee Su Hoon. 1998. "Social Science from an East Asian Perspective: With a Focus on Sociology." *Asian Perspective* 22 (1): 187–207.

Lee Teng-hui. 1995. "The Beginning of a New Era." In Jason C. Hu, ed., 3–6.

———. 2002. "Understanding Taiwan: Bridging the Perception Gap." In *Foreign Affairs*, ed., 40–46.

Lee, Chae-Jin. 1996. *China and Korea: Dynamic Relations*. Palo Alto: Hoover Institution Press.

———. 2000. "South Korean Foreign Relations Face the Globalization Challenges." In Samuel Kim, ed., 170–95.

Lee, Jane C. Y. 1997. "Nationality and the Right of Abode." In Joseph C. Y. Cheng, ed., *The Other Hong Kong Report, 1997*, 253–65. Hong Kong: Chinese University of Hong Kong Press.

Lee, Peter H., ed. 1996. *Sourcebook of Korean Civilization*. Vol. 2. New York: Columbia University Press.

"Legislative Council House Commmittees (Papers)." 2000. In Chan, Fu, and Ghai, eds., 259–64.

Leng Shao-Chuan and Cheng-yi Lin. 1995. "Political Change in Taiwan: Transition to Democracy?" In Shambaugh, ed., 153–87.

Leung Hon-chu. 1999a. "Tuanjie zenmeyang chengwei tequan: lishi, jiegou yu wenming shijiao" [How Unity Became a Special Right: Historical, Structural and Cultural Perspectives]. In Leung and Lam, eds., 4–8.

———. 1999b. "Shui de Xianggang? shui de jia? kongjiande zhengzhi yu juliu quan" [Whose Hong Kong? Whose family? Between Politics and the Right of Abode]. In Leung and Lam, eds., 124–26.

Leung Hon-chu and Lam Hoi-wan, eds. 1999. *79.97.167: Luohuguanwaide gangren ernu [1979, 1997, 1.67 million: Hong Kong Children outside the Lo Wu border]*. Hong Kong: Coalition Fighting for Hong Kong Peoples' Right of Abode.

Leung, P. K. 1998. "The Story of Hong Kong." In Martha Cheung, ed., 3–13.

Levenson, Joseph R. 1966. *Confucian China and Its Modern Fate*. Berkeley and Los Angeles: University of California Press.

Lew Seok-Choon. 1997. "Confucian Capitalism: Possibilities and Limits."

Chontonggwa hyondae 1 (1): 74–93; translated in *Korea Focus* 5 (4): 80–93.

Li Changdao. 1999. "Datong xiaoyi, geju tese–Xianggang jibenfa yu Ao'men jibenfa bijiao" [Great Harmony with Small Differences, Each Having Its Special Characteristics—A comparison of the Basic Laws of Hong Kong and Macau]. *Fudan xuebao*, no. 6: 86–91.

Li Hongyan. 1997. "Developments in the Study of Confucianism on the Mainland China in Recent Years." *Social Sciences in China* 18 (1): 17–30.

Li Hou. 1997. *Bainian qurushide zongjie: Xianggang wenti shimou [Conclusion of the Century of Humiliating History: The Hong Kong Problem from Beginning to End]*. Beijing: Zhongyang wenxian chubanshe.

Li Jun and Hao Guang. 1976. *Nanhai changcheng [Great Wall of the South China Sea]*. Beijing: Ba-yi dianying zhipianchang.

Li Shaojun. 1999. "Lun Zhongguo wenmingde heping neihan: cong chuantong dao xianshi: dui 'Zhongguo weixie' lun de huida" [The Peaceful Orientation of Chinese Civilization: From Tradition to Reality: A Response to "China Threat" Theory]. *Guoji jingji pinglun* [Review of International Economy], no. 19: 30–33.

———. 2002. *Guoji zhengzhixue gailun [An Introduction to International Politics]*. Shanghai: Renmin chubanshe.

Li Tianchen. 1997. "Harmony—A Prescription to Build a Better World in the Twenty-First Century." In *Confucian Thought and the Twenty-First Century*, 147–50.

Li Xiangdong and Xiong Zengyang. 1994. "Cherish the Reefs with Deep Feelings." *FBIS–China Daily Report*, 21 June: 10.

Li Xiguang. 1998. *Zhongguo you duo huai? [How Bad Is China?]*. Nanjing: Jiangsu renmin chubanshe.

Li Yang and Hu Weiping, eds. 1997. *Huashuo Xianggang [Hong Kong Stories]*. Tianjin: Tianjin renmin chubanshe.

Li Yangguo. 1998. *Hainan: womende jiayuan [Hainan: Our Backyard]*. Ji'nan: Shandong huabao chubanshe.

Liang Fengyi. 1997. *Lanpo wanli feng [Ten Thousand Miles of Struggle]*. Beijing: Renmin wenxue.

Liang Shoude. 1996. "Guoji zhengzhixue zai Zhongguo: lun guoji zhengzhixue lilun de 'Zhongguo tese'" [International Politics Studies in China: On International Politics Studies' Theory of "Chinese Characteristics"]. In Liang Shoude, ed., *Guoji shehui yu wenhua [International Society and Culture]*, 291–305. Beijing: Beijing daxue chubanshe.

———. 1997. "Constructing an International Relations Theory with 'Chinese Characteristics.'" *Political Science* 49 (1): 23–49.

Liang Shoude and Hong Yinxian. 2000. *Guoji zhengzhixue lilun [International Politics Theory]*. Beijing: Beijing daxue chubanshe.

Lii Ding-Tzann. 1998. "A Colonized Empire: Reflections on the Expansion of Hong Kong Films in Asian Countries." In Kuan-Hsing Chen, ed., *Trajectories: Inter-Asian Cultural Studies*, 122–41. London: Routledge.

Liji jijie [The Book of Rites, Critical Edition]. 1998. Beijing: Zhonghua shuju.

Lin Cho-shui. 1998. "Qiangben jianjin de Zhongguo zhengce" [Strong Base and Gradual Advance China Policy]. Paper Presented at the Democratic Progressive Party China Policy Conference, February. taiwan.yam.org.tw/China_Policy/L_Lin.htm.

Lin Jinzhi and Wu Fengbin. 1988. *Zhuguo de nanjiang–nanhai zhudao [The Southern Border of the Motherland–Islands in South (China) Sea]*. Shanghai: Shanghai renmin chubanshe.

Lin Tongqi, Henry Rosemont Jr., and Roger T. Ames. 1995. "Chinese Philosophy: A Philosophical Chapter on the 'State-of-the-Art.'" *Journal of Asian Studies* 54 (3): 727–58.

Lin, Chong-pin. 1995. "Beijing and Taiwan: Post-Tiananmen Interactions." In Shambaugh, ed., 118–52.

Ling Xingzheng. 1998. "Haiyi" [Ocean memories]. *Renmin ribao*, 7 August.

Ling, L. H. M, and Chih-yu Shih. 1999. "Confucianism with a Liberal Face: Democratic Politics in Postcolonial Taiwan." In Dallmayr, ed., 213–35.

Link, Perry. 1992. *Evening Chats in Beijing: Probing China's Predicament*. New York: W. W. Norton.

Liu Jinzhi, Zhang Meiqiu, and Zhang Xiaoming. 1998. *Dangdai Zhong-Han guanxi [Contemporary Sino-Korean Relations]*. Beijing: Zhongguo shehui kexue chubanshe.

Liu Shengjun. 2000. *Nansha zai huhuan [Calling Out the Spratlys]*. Beijing: Huanghe chubanshe.

Liu Shuyong. 1996. "Xianggangshi yanjiu gaikuang" [A Survey of Hong Kong Historical Research]. *Beijing ribao [Beijing Daily]*: 2.

———. 1997a. *An Outline History of Hong Kong*. Beijing: Foreign Languages Press.

———. 1997b. "Hong Kong: A Survey of Its Political and Economic Development over the Past 150 Years." *China Quarterly*, no. 151: 583–92.

———. 1998. *Jianming Xianggang shi [A Simple History of Hong Kong]*. Hong Kong: Joint Publishing Co.

Liu Zhen. 1974. *Guochi shigang [Outline History of National Humiliation]*. Taipei: Zhengzhong shuju.

Liu Zhiguang. 1992. *Dongfang hepingzhuyi: yuanqi, liubian ji zouxiang [Oriental Pacificism: Its Origins, Development, and Future]*. Changsha, Hunan: Hunan chubanshe.

Long, Simon. 1998. "Special Report: The Overseas Chinese." *Prospect*, April: 60–65.

Lou Jie. 1998. *Zhonghua wenhua yu zuguo heping tongyi [Chinese Culture and the Peaceful Unification of the Motherland]*. Wuhan: Wuhan chubanshe.

Lüshi chunqiu. 1996. Shanghai: Shanghai guji chubanshe.

Luff, John. 1959. *The Hong Kong Story*. Hong Kong: South China Morning Post.

Luk Hung-Kay. 1998. "Hong Kong History and Culture." In Man and Lo, eds., 12–24.

Luo Chenglie. 1997. "Harmony but Not Uniformity" and "One Country, Two Systems." In *Confucian Thought and the Twenty-First Century*, 130–33.

Luo Rongqu, ed. 1990. *Cong "xihua" dao xiandaihua [From "Westernization" to Modernization]*. Beijing: Beijing daxue chubanshe.

Luo Zhitian. 1993. "National Humiliation and National Assertion: The Chinese Response to the Twenty-one Demands." *Modern Asian Studies* 27 (2): 297–319.

Ma, Eric Kit-Wai. 1999. *Culture, Politics, and Television in Hong Kong*. London: Routledge.

Ma, Shu-Yun. 1994. "The Chinese Discourse of Civil Society." *China Quarterly*, no. 147: 180–93.

MacFarquhar, Roderick. 1980. "The Post-Confucian Challenge." *Economist*, 9 February: 67–72.

Machetzki, Rudiger. 1998. "China—Great Power or 'Greater China'?" In Wolfgang Pape, ed., *East Asia by the Year 2000 and Beyond: Shaping Factors: A Study for the European Commission*, 115–74. London: Curzon.

Madsen, Richard. 1993. "The Public Sphere, Civil Society, and Moral Community: A Research Agenda for Contemporary Chinese Studies." *Modern China* 19 (2): 183–98.

Man Si-wai and Lo Sze-ping. 1998. "Guest Editor's Introduction." In Man Si-wai and Lo Sze-ping, eds., "Cultural Identities and Cultural Politics: Colonial and Postcolonial Imaginations in Hong Kong." *Chinese Sociology and Anthropology* 30 (3): 3–12.

Mancall, Mark. 1968. "The Ch'ing Tribute System: An Interpretative Essay." In Fairbank, ed., 63–89.

———. 1984. *China at the Center: Three Hundred Years of Foreign Policy*. New York: Free Press.

Mathews, Gordon. 1997. "Heunggongyahn: On the Past, Present, and Future of Hong Kong Identity." *Bulletin of Concerned Asian Scholars* 29 (3): 3–13.

McCormick, Barret L., Su Shaozhi, and Xiao Xiaoming. 1992. "The 1989 Democracy Movement: A Review of the Prospects for Civil Society in China." *Pacific Affairs* 62 (2): 182–202.

McCormick, Barrett L. 2000. "U.S.–PRC Relations and the 'Democratic Peace.'" In Friedman and McCormick, eds., 305–28.

Mearsheimer, John J. 2001. *The Tragedy of Great Power Politics.* New York: W. W. Norton.

Mencius. 1970. *Mencius.* Trans. D. C. Lau. London: Penguin.

Metzger, Thomas A., and Ramon Hawley Myers, eds. 1996. *Greater China and U.S. Foreign Policy: The Choice between Confrontation and Mutual Respect.* Palo Alto: Hoover Press Publication.

Meyer, Jeffrey E. 1991. *The Dragons of Tiananmen: Beijing as a Sacred City.* Columbia: University of South Carolina Press.

Miao Junjie. 1993. "Introduction." In Yang Shu'an, 3–17.

Ming Wan. 1999. "Human Rights and Democracy." In Deng and Wang, eds., 97–117

Ming Zhang. 1999. "Public Images of the United States." In Deng and Wang, eds., 141–57.

Ministry of Culture and Sports, ed. 1996. *Religious Culture in Korea.* Seoul: Holly M.

Mirsky, Jonathan. 1997. "The Way We Live Now." *Index on Censorship* 1, 140–44.

Mitter, Rana. 2000. "Behind the Scenes at the Museum: Nationalism, History, and Memory in the Beijing War of Resistance Museum, 1987–1997." *China Quarterly,* no. 161: 279–93.

Moon Myung-ho. 1998. "Status of Ethnic Koreans Abroad, and Diplomatic Friction." *The Munhwa Ilbo,* 5 September; translated in *Korea Focus* 6 (5): 120–22.

Moon, Katherine H. S. 2000. "Strangers in the Midst of Globalization: Migrant Workers and Korean Nationalism." In Samuel Kim, ed., 147–69.

Morris, Jan. 1990. *Hong Kong: Epilogue of an Empire.* London: Penguin.

Munn, Christopher. 1999. "The Criminal Trial under Early Colonial Rule." In Ngo, ed., 46–73.

Nah Seoung. 1996. "Confucianism." In Ministry of Culture and Sports, ed., 56–67.

Naisbitt, John. 1996. *Megatrends Asia: The Eight Asian Megatrends That Are Changing the World.* London: Nicolas Brealey.

Nanhai de zaochen [Dawn in the South China Sea]. 1964. [n.p.].

Narine, Shaun. 1997. "ASEAN and the ARF: The Limits of the 'ASEAN Way.'" *Asian Survey* 37 (10): 961–79.

Nathan, Andrew J., and Robert S. Ross. 1997. *The Great Wall and the Empty Fortress.* New York: Norton.

"Nationality Law of the People's Republic of China." 1980. *Beijing Review*, no. 40 (6 October): 17–18.

Ngo Tak-wing, ed. 1999. *Hong Kong's History: State and Society under Colonial Rule*. London: Routledge.

Ni Jianmin and Song Yichang, eds. 1997. *Haiyang Zhongguo: wenming zhongxin dongyi yu guojia liyi kongjian [Maritime China: The Eastern Migration of the Core of Civilization and the Space of National Interest]*. Beijing: Zhongguo guoji guangbao chubanshe.

Nonini, Donald M., and Aihwa Ong. 1997. "Chinese Transnationalism as an Alternative Modernity." In Ong and Nonini, eds., 3–33.

Northeast Asian Women's Studies Association. 1994. *Korean/Chinese Women: Past and Present*. Beijing: Proceedings of the Second Northeast Asian Women's Studies Association Conference.

O'Brien, Kevin J., and Lianjiang Li. 2000. "Accommodating 'Democracy' in a One-Party State: Introducing Village Elections in China." *China Quarterly* [special issue: Elections and Democracy in Greater China], no. 162: 465–89.

Odgaard, Liselotte. 2002. *Maritime Security between China and Southeast Asia: Conflict and Cooperation in the Making of a Regional Order*. Aldershot, U.K.: Ashgate.

————. 2003. "The South China Sea: ASEAN's Security Concerns about China." *Security Dialogue* 34 (1): 11–24.

Oi, Jean C., and Scott Rozelle. 2000. "Elections and Power: The Locus of Decision-Making in Chinese Villages." *China Quarterly* [Special Issue: Elections and Democracy in Greater China], no. 162: 513–39.

Ong, Aihwa. 1998. "Flexible Citizenship among Chinese Cosmopolitans." In Cheah and Robbins, eds., 134–62.

————. 1999. *Flexible Citizenship: The Cultural Logics of Transnationalism*. Durham, N.C.: Duke University Press.

———— and Donald Nonini, eds. 1997. *Ungrounded Empires: The Cultural Politics of Modern Chinese Transnationalism*. New York: Routledge.

Osborn, Carol. 1994. *How Would Confucius Ask for a Raise? One Hundred Enlightened Solutions for Tough Business Problems*. New York: Morrow.

Osius, Ted. 2001. "Discussion of 'The Rise of China in Chinese Eyes.'" *Journal of Contemporary China* 10 (26): 41–45.

OSS [Office of Strategic Services]. 1944. "Greater China," map no. 3448 (3 August).

Ozawa, Ichiro. 1994. *Blueprint for a New Japan: The Rethinking of a Nation*. New York: Kodansha International.

Paik Nak-chung. 1996. "Habermas on National Unification in Germany and Korea." *New Left Review*, no. 219: 14–21.

Pan Shiying. 1996. *Nansha qundao, shiyou zhengzhi, guojifa: Wan'anbei–21 shiyou hetongqu liyu Zhongguo guanxia haiyu wutong zhiyi [The Petropolitics of the Nansha Islands—China's Indisputable Legal Case]*. Hong Kong: Xianggang jingji daobaoshe.

Park Sung-bong. 1996. "The Spiritual Potential of the Korean People." In Korea Foundation, ed., 14–19.

Park Sun-yong. 1996. "Confucian Influences on Education." In Korea Foundation, ed., 138–45.

Park Tae-Kyu. 1995. "Corporate Foundations in Korea." In Tadashi Yamamoto, ed., *Emerging Civil Society in the Asia Pacific Community*, 583–90. Singapore: Institute for Southeast Asian Studies Press.

Park, You-me. 1996. "Against Metaphor: Gender, Violence, and Decolonization in Korean Nationalist Literature." In Tang and Snyder, eds., 33–47.

Pastor, Robert A., and Qingshan Tan. 2000. "The Meaning of China's Village Elections." *China Quarterly* [special issue: Elections and Democracy in Greater China], no. 162: 490–512.

Patten, Chris. 1997. "Valedictory." In Courtauld, 117–27.

Patten, Christopher. 1998. *East and West: China, Power, and the Future of Asia*. New York: Times Books.

Pei, Minxin. 2000. "China's Evolution toward Soft Authoritarianism." In Friedman and McCormick, eds., 74–98.

Peng Mingmin. 1972. *A Taste of Freedom: Memoirs of a Formosan Independence Leader*. New York: Holt, Rinehart, and Winston.

Pieterse, Jan, and B. Parekh. 1995. "Shifting Imaginaries: Decolonisation, Internal Decolonisation, and Postcoloniality." In Jan Pieterse and B. Parekh, eds., *The Decolonisation of the Imagination: Culture, Knowledge, and Power*, 1–19. London: Zed Press.

"Preface." 1996. In *Religious Culture in Korea*, 3–4. Seoul: Holly M.

Proceedings of "Oriental Thought and Social Development." 1996. Coorganized by the *Dong-A Ilbo* and the *People's Daily*. Seoul: Dong-A Ilbo.

Pun Ngai. 1999. "Yige shijiwei mengxiang de daijia" [The Cost of a Fin de Siecle Dream]. In Leung and Lam, eds., 116–23.

Pumphrey, Carolyn W., ed. 2002. *The Rise of China in Asia: Security Implications*. Carlisle, Penn.: Strategic Studies Institute, U.S. Army War College.

Pye, Lucian W. 1990. "China: Erratic State, Frustrated Society." *Foreign Affairs* 69 (4): 56–74.

———. 1992. *The Spirit of Chinese Politics*. New ed. Cambridge, Mass.: Harvard University Press.

———, with Mary Pye. 1985. *Asian Power and Politics: The Cultural Dimensions of Authority*. Cambridge, Mass.: Harvard University Press.

————, and Sidney Verba, eds. 1965. *Political Culture and Political Development*. Princeton: Princeton University Press.

Qi Luo and Christopher Howe. 1995. "Direct Investment and Economic Integration in the Asia Pacific." In Shambaugh, ed., 94–117.

Qi Mei. 1998. *Zhong-Han rujia wenhua bijiao [A Comparison of Chinese and Korean Confucianism]*. Beijing: Wenjin chubanshe.

Qi Pengfei. 1997. *Richu riluo: Xianggang wenti 156 nian (1841–1997) [The Sun Rises, The Sun Sets: 156 Years of the Hong Kong Problem (1841–1997)]*. Beijing: Xinhua chubanshe.

Redding, S. Gordon. 1993. *The Spirit of Chinese Capitalism*. New York: Walter de Gruyter.

————. 1996. "The Distinct Nature of Chinese Capitalism." *Pacific Review* 9 (3): 426–40.

Reid, Anthony. 1997. "Entrepreneurial Minorities, Nationalism, and the State." In Chirot and Reid, eds., 33–71.

Reid, T. R. 1999. *Confucius Lives Next Door: What Living in the East Teaches Us about Living in the West*. New York: Random House.

Renan, Ernest. 1990. "What is a Nation?" In Bhabha, ed., 8–22.

"Rise of Modern China (Exhibition)." 1999. Hong Kong Museum of History, 16 September–21 November.

Robbins, Bruce. 1998. "Actually Existing Cosmopolitanism." in Cheah and Robbins, eds., 1–19.

Robinson, Michael. 1991. "Perceptions of Confucianism in Twentieth-Century Korea." In Rozman, ed., 204–26.

———— 1996, "Narrative Politics, Nationalism and Korean History." In Alan J. K. Sanders, (ed.), *Nationality and Nationalism in East Asia (Papers of the British Association for Korean Studies)* 6:26–40.

Robison, Richard, et al., eds. 2000. *Politics and Markets in the Wake of the Asian Crisis*. London: Routledge.

Rodan, Garry. 1996. "The Internationalisation of Ideological Conflict: Asia's New Significance." *Pacific Review* 9 (3): 328–51.

Rorty, Richard. 1991. "Philosophy, Literature, and Inter-cultural Comparison." In Eliot Deutsch, ed., *Culture and Modernity: East/West Philosophic Perspectives,* Honolulu: University of Hawaii Press.

————. 1996. "Idealizations, Foundations, and Social Practices." In Seyla Benhabib, ed., *Democracy and Difference: Contesting the Boundaries of the Political,* 333–36. Princeton: Princeton University Press.

Ross, Robert S. 1997. "Beijing as a Conservative Power." *Foreign Affairs* 76 (2): 33–44.

Rossabi, Morris. 1983a. "Introduction." In Rossabi, ed., 1–13.

————, ed. 1983b. *China among Equals: The Middle Kingdom and Its*

Neighbors, Tenth–Fourteenth Centuries, Berkeley and Los Angeles: University of California Press.

Rouner, Leroy S., ed. 1994. *The Changing Face of Friendship.* Bloomington, Ind.: University of Notre Dame Press.

Rowe, William T. 1993. "The Problem of 'Civil Society' in Late Imperial China." *Modern China* 19 (2): 139–57.

Rowley, Chris, and Mark Lewis, eds. 1996. *Greater China: Political Economy, Inward Investment, and Business Culture.* London: Frank Cass.

Roy, Denny. 1996. "The China Threat Issue." *Asian Survey* 36 (8): 758–71.

Rozman, Gilbert. 1991a. "Introduction: The East Asian Region in Comparative Perspective." In Gilbert Rozman, ed., *The East Asian Region: Confucian Heritage and Its Modern Adaptation,* 3–42. Princeton: Princeton University Press.

———. 1999. "China as a Great Power." *Orbis* 43:383–402.

———, ed. 1991b. *The East Asian Region: Confucian Heritage and Its Modern Adaptation.* Princeton: Princeton University Press.

Rubin, Amy Magaro. 1997. "South Korean Support for U.S. Scholars Raises Fears of Undue Influence." *The Chronicle of Higher Education,* October 6: A10–A11.

Rudnicki, Stefan, ed. 1998. *Confucius in the Boardroom: Ancient Wisdom, Modern Lessons for Business.* Los Angeles: Dove Press.

Rule, Paul A. 1986. *K'ung-tzu or Confucius? The Jesuit Interpretation of Confucianism.* Sydney: Allen and Unwin.

Ruxue yu ershiyishiji. 1996. [*Confucianism and the Twenty-first Century: Proceedings of the International Confucian Studies Conference to Commemorate the 2545th Anniversary of Confucius.* Vols. 1 and 2.] Beijing: Huaxia chubanshe.

Safire, William. 1999. "On Language: One Guojia? Why Chinese Are Forced to Argue in English." *New York Times Sunday Magazine,* 15 August: 27–28.

Said, Edward. 1978. *Orientalism.* New York: Vintage.

Sakai, Robert K. 1968. "The Ryuku Islands as a Fief of Satsuma." In Fairbank, ed., 112–34.

Schein, Louisa. 1998. "Importing Miao Brethren to Hmong America: A Not-So-Stateless Transnationalism." In Cheah and Robbins, eds., 163–91.

Schell, Orville. 1999. "Prisoner of Its Past." www.Salon.com, 8 June.

Schmid, André. 1997. "Rediscovering Manchuria: Sin Ch'aeho and the Politics of Territorial History in Korea." *Journal of Asian Studies* 56 (1): 26–46.

———. 2002. *Korea between Two Empires.* New York: Columbia University Press.

Seagrave, Sterling. 1995. *Lords of the Rim: The Invisible Empire of the Overseas Chinese.* London: Bantam Press.

Second International Confucian Studies Association Conference Volume. 1999. Beijing (October 7–12).

Segal, Gerald. 1997. "'Enlitening' China?" In Goodman and Segal, eds., 172–91.

———. 1999. "Does China Matter?" *Foreign Affairs* 78 (5): 24–36.

Shambaugh, David. 1991. "Foreword by the Editor," *China Quarterly,* no. 128: 687–90.

———. 1995a. "Introduction: The Emergence of Greater China." In Shambaugh, ed., 1–7.

———. 1996. "Containment or Engagement of China? Calculating Beijing's Responses." *International Security* 21 (2): 180–209.

———. 2002. "Sino-American Relations Since September 11: Can the New Stability Last?" *Current History,* September: 243–49.

———, ed. 1995b. *Greater China: The Next Superpower?* Oxford: Oxford University Press.

———, ed. 1998. *Contemporary Taiwan.* Oxford: Clarendon Paperbacks.

Shan Hai Ching: Legendary Geography and Wonders of Ancient China. 1985. Kuo P'o (commentary), Hao Yi-shing (explanatory notes, Qing dynasty), Hsiao-Chieh Cheng, Hui-Chen Pai Cheng and Kenneth Lawrence Thern (trans.). Taipei: The Committee for Compilation and Examination of the Series of Chinese Classics.

Shanhai jing. 1996. *Xinhui shenyi quantu Shanhai jing.* Beijing: Kunlun chubanshe.

Shapiro, Michael J. 1988. *The Politics of Representation: Writing Practices in Biography, Photography, and Policy Analysis.* Madison: University of Wisconsin Press.

———. 1997. *Violent Cartographies: Mapping the Cultures of War.* Minneapolis: University of Minnesota Press.

———. 1998. "The Ethics of Encounter: Unreading, Unmapping the Imperium." In Campbell and Shapiro, eds., 57–91.

———, and Hayward R. Alker, eds. 1996. *Challenging Boundaries: Global Flows, Territorial Identities.* Minneapolis: University of Minnesota Press.

Sherry, Andrew. 1997. "Law of the Seize." *Far Eastern Economic Review,* 12 June: 17, 20–1.

Shi, Tianjian. 2000. "Cultural Values and Democracy in the People's Republic of China." *China Quarterly* [special issue: Elections and Democracy in Greater China], no. 162: 540–59.

Shih Ti-tsu. 1975. "South China Sea Islands, Chinese Territory since Ancient Times." *Peking Review,* no. 50 (12 December): 10–15.

Shih, Chih-yu. 1993. *China's Just World: The Morality of Chinese Foreign Policy.* Boulder: Lynne Rienner Publishers.

Shin Hye-son. 1998. "Sungkyunkwan to Host North Korean Scholars at 600th Anniversary." *Korea Herald,* 27 May.

Shin Yoo-Keun. 1992. *Business Management in Korea: Its Phenomena and Prospects.* [In Korean]. Seoul: Parkyoung Publishing Co.

———, and Kim Heung-Gook. 1994. "Individualism and Collectivism in Korean Industry." In Gene Yoon and Choi Sang-Chin, eds., *Psychology of the Korean People: Collectivism and Individualism,* 185–206. Seoul: Tong-A Publishing and Printing Co.

Si Tuxiang, ed. 1996. *Lingnan haiyang guotu [The Maritime Territory South of the Five Ridges].* Guangzhou: Guangdong renmin chubanshe.

Sikkink, Kathryn. 2002. "Restructuring World Power: The Limits and Asymmetries of Soft Power." In Khagram et al., eds., 301–17.

Simon, Scott. 2000. "Formosa Diary #22, May 20: A Great Proletarian Cultural Revolution." H-Asia: dokuhebi@hotmail.com, (25 May).

Sinn, Elizabeth, ed. 1995. *Xianggangde wenhua yu shehui [Culture and Society in Hong Kong].* Hong Kong: Center for Asian Studies, University of Hong Kong.

Siu Yat-ming. 1999. "New Arrivals: A New Problem and an Old Problem." In Chow and Fan, eds., 201–28.

Smith, Richard J. 1996. *Chinese Maps: Images of "All Under Heaven."* Hong Kong: Oxford University Press.

———. 1998. "Mapping China's World: Cultural Cartography in Late Imperial Times." In Wen-hin Yeh, ed., *Landscape, Culture, and Power in Chinese Society,* 52–105. Berkeley: Institute of East Asian Studies, University of California at Berkeley.

Snyder, Scott. 2001. "Consummating 'Full-Scale Cooperative Partnership.'" *Comparative Connections* 2 (4). www.csis.org/pacfor/cc/004Qchina_skorea.html, (January).

———. 2003. "Regime Change and Another Nuclear Crisis," *Comparative Connections* 5 (1). www.csis.org/pacfor/cc/0301Qchina_skorea.html, (April).

Son Moon-ho. 1997. "The Press and the Imperial Censor," *Chuntonggwa hyondae* 1 (2): 92–111.

Song Qiang. 1996. "Cangtian dangsi, huangtian danli [Blue Sky Is Falling, Yellow Sky Is Rising]." In Song et al., *Zhonggou keyi shuo bu [China Can Say No],* 3–51. Beijing: Zhonghua gongshang lianhe chubanshe.

Song Qiang, Zhang Zangzang, and Qiao Bian. 1996. *Zhonggou keyi shuo bu [China Can Say No].* Beijing: Zhonghua gongshang lianhe chubanshe.

Song Xinning. 2001. "Building International Relations Theory with Chinese Characteristics." *Journal of Contemporary China* 10 (26): 61–74.

South China Sea Informal Working Group. 2001. Vancouver: University of British Columbia, School of Law. http://faculty.law.ubc.ca/scs.

Spottiswoode, Roger. 1997. *Tomorrow Never Dies*. Hollywood: MGM/ UA Video.

Stenseth, Leni. 1999. *Nationalism and Foreign Policy: The Case of China's Nansha Rhetoric*. Oslo: Centre for Development and the Environment (SUM), Dissertations and Theses, no. 1/99.

Su Shaozhi and Michael J. Sullivan. 2000. "Aggressive Engagement, Not Containment: Political Repression's Role in Sino-American Relations." In Friedman and McCormick, eds., 284–304.

Su Xiaokang and Wang Luxiang. 1991. *Deathsong of the River: A Reader's Guide to the Chinese TV Series "Heshang."* Richard W. Bodman and Pin P. Wan, trans. Ithaca, N.Y.: East Asia Program, Cornell University.

Su Xiaokang et al. 1988. *Heshang [River Elegy]*. Beijing: CCTV (Chinese Central Television).

"Subic Memories." 1995. *Asian Wall Street Journal*, 17–18 February: 6.

Suh Kyoung-yo. 1996. "Loyalty, Filial Piety, and the Sonbi Spirit." In Korea Foundation, ed., 30–35.

Sun Dejian and Ding Haitao. 1998. *Laizi dahaide yiwen [Questions from the Great Sea]*. Qingdao: Qingdao haiyang daxue chubanshe.

Sunzi. 1994. *Sun-Tzu: The Art of War*. Ralph D. Sawyer, trans. Boulder, Colo.: Westview.

Swaine, Michael D., and Ashely J. Tellis. 2000. *Interpreting China's Grand Strategy: Past, Present, and Future*. Santa Monica: Rand.

Tai Hung-chao, ed. 1989. *Confucianism and Economic Development: An Oriental Alternative?* Washington, D.C.: The Washington Institute Press.

Taiguo Puji qiao lianhehui [Overseas Chinese Association of Phuket, Thailand]. 1999. *Puji Taihua xuexiao xinxiao sheluo chengjie muji jianxiao jiushi zhounian jiniankan, 17/02/1999 [The Commemorative Volume to Celebrate the Opening of the New School Building of the Thai-Hua School of Phuket on the Ninetieth Anniversary of Phuket Thai-Hua School, 17 February 1999 (in Thai and Chinese)]*. Phuket: Gongtong yinshuashe.

Taiwan Affairs Office. 1993. *The Taiwan Question and Reunification of China*. (August). Beijing: Information Office of the State Council. english .peopledaily.com.cn/whitepaper/7.html.

———. 2000. *The One-China Principle and the Taiwan Issue*. Beijing: Information Office of the State Council. (February 22). http://www .ChinaDaily.com.cn/highlights/Taiwan/WhitePaper.html.

Taiwan Security Enhancement Act (H.R.1838). 2000. (1 February). www .taiwanstudies.org/on_record/view_story.php3?159.

Tambling, Jeremy. 1997. "The History Man: The Last Governor of Hong Kong." In Abbas and Wu, eds., 355–75.

Tanaka, Stefan. 1993. *Japan's Orient: Rendering Pasts into History.* Berkeley and Los Angeles: University of California Press.

Tang Weilun. 1997. "Kongzi sixiang yu Xianggang heping huigui" [Confucian Thought and Hong Kong's Peaceful Return]. In *Confucian Thought and the Twenty-First Century,* 525–29.

Tanzer, Andrew. 1994. "Overseas China: The Giant Economy That Knows No Borders; The Bamboo Network." *Forbes,* 18 July: 138 ff.

Taylor, Charles. 1994. "The Politics of Recognition." In Amy Gutman, ed., *Multiculturalism and the Politics of Recognition,* 25–73. Princeton: Princeton University Press.

Taylor, Robert. 1996. *Greater China and Japan.* London: Routledge.

Theroux, Paul. 1997. *Kowloon Tong.* New York: Houghton Mifflin.

Thongchai Winichakul. 1994. *Siam Mapped: A History of the Geo-body of a Nation.* Honolulu: University of Hawaii Press.

Thorsten, Marie. 2004. "They Lost the War, But. . . . The Grand Cliché of the Japanese Superstate." *Alternatives* 29 (2).

Tian Guangqing. 1998. *Hexian lun: Rujia wenming yu dangdai shehui [On Harmony: Confucian civilization and contemporary society].* Beijing: Zhongguo Huaqiao chubanshe.

Tien, Hung-mao, and Yun-han Chu. 1998. "Building Democracy in Taiwan." In Shambaugh, ed., 97–126.

"To Put Rightly What This Era Requires." 1997. *Chontonggwa hyondae* 1 (1): 13–23.

Todorov, Tzvetan. 1984. *The Conquest of America: The Question of the Other.* New York: Harper Collins.

Tomlinson, Jonathan. 1991. *Cultural Imperialism.* Cambridge: Polity.

Tong Yun Kai. 1999. "Ruxue zai shiji zhi jiaode huigui yu zhanwang" [Confucianism at the Turn of the Century: Returning and Looking to the Future]. In *The Second International Confucian Studies Association Conference Volume,* Beijing (October 7–12), 3–8.

"Treacherous Shoals." 1992. *Far Eastern Economic Review.* 13 August: 14.

Tsai, Jing-fang. 1993. *Hong Kong in Chinese History.* New York: Columbia University Press.

Tsang Shu-ki. 1996. "The Political Economy of Greater China." In Rowley and Lewis, eds., 23–43.

Tu Weiming. 1990. "Wenhua Zhongguo: chutan" [Cultural China: Preliminary Explorations]. *Jiushi niandai yuekan,* no. 6: 60–61.

———. 1994a. "Cultural China: The Periphery as the Center." In Tu, ed., 1–34.

———. 1998. "Cultural Identity and the Politics of Recognition in Contemporary Taiwan." In Shambaugh, ed., 71–96.

———, ed. 1994b. *The Living Tree*. Palo Alto: Stanford University Press.

———, ed. 1996. *Confucian Traditions in East Asian Modernity: Moral Education and Economic Culture in Japan and the Four Mini-Dragons*. Cambridge, Mass.: Harvard University Press

Tung Chee Hwa. 2000. *The 2000 Policy Address: Serving the Community, Sharing Common Goals*. Hong Kong: Hong Kong Special Administrative Region of the People's Republic of China.

Twitchett, Denis. 1992. *The Writing of Official History Under The T'ang*. Cambridge: Cambridge University Press.

Uhalley, Stephen. 1994. "'Greater China': The Content of a Term." *positions: east asia cultural critique* 2 (2): 274–93.

Unger, Jonathan, ed. 1993. *Using the Past to Serve the Present: Historiography and Politics in Contemporary China*. Armonk, N.Y.: M. E. Sharpe.

———, ed. 1996. *Chinese Nationalism*. Armonk, N.Y.: M. E. Sharpe.

Universal and Particular Natures of Confucianism. 1994. Proceedings of the Eighth International Conference on Korean Studies, 22–24 June. Seoul: Academy of Korean Studies.

"Upgrading of Ties [editorial]." 1998. *Korea Herald,* 14 November.

Valencia, Mark J. 1995. *China and the South China Sea Disputes: Conflicting Claims and Potential Solutions in the South China Sea*. Oxford: Adelphi Paper no. 298.

———. 2002. "The Rights of Spy Vessels." *Far Eastern Economic Review,* April 11.

———, et al. 1999. *Sharing the Resources of the South China Seas*. London: Martinus Nijhoff Publishers.

Van Kemenade, Willem. 1999. *China, Hong Kong, Taiwan, Inc.* London: Abacus.

Vatikiotis, Michael, et al. 1994, "Gunboat Diplomacy." *Far Eastern Economic Review,* 16 June: 22–28.

———. 1998. "Compatriot Games: China Changes Tack on Atrocities in Indonesia." *Far Eastern Economic Review,* 20 August.

"Vietnam Rejects China's Claim to Archipelagos." 1996. *The Nation* [Bangkok], 11 May.

Vogel, Ezra F. 1979. *Japan as Number One: Lessons for America*. New York: Replica Books.

———. 1991. *The Four Little Dragons: The Spread of Industrialization in East Asia*. Cambridge, Mass.: Harvard University Press.

Wade, Robert. 1996. "Japan, the World Bank, and the Art of Paradigm Maintainence: *The East Asian Miracle* in Political Perspective." *New Left Review,* no. 217: 3–34.

———. 1998. "From 'Miracle' to 'Cronyism': Explaining the Great Asian Slump." *Cambridge Journal of Economics* 22: 693–706.

Wagner, Rudolf. 1991. "Political Institutions, Discourse, and Imagination in China at Tiananmen." In James Manor, ed., *Rethinking Third World Politics,* 121–44. London: Longman.

Waldron, Arthur. 1990. *The Great Wall of China: From History to Myth.* Cambridge: Cambridge University Press.

Walker, R. B. J. 1993. *Inside/Outside: International Relations as Political Theory.* Cambridge: Cambridge University Press.

———. 1997. "The Subject of Security." In Krause and Williams, eds., 61–81.

Wan Lifeng. 2000. "Deng Xiaoping 'yiguo liangzhi' gouxiang shi tongyi zhanxian quitong caiyi yuanzede shengdong tixian" [Deng Xiaoping's "One Country, Two Systems" Idea Is the Lively Embodiment of the Unification Strategy of Seeking Common Ground While Reserving Differences], *Nanchang jiaoyu xueyuan xuebao* 15 (3): 16–20.

Wang, Fei-ling. 1999. "Self-image and Strategic Intentions: National Confidence and Political Insecurity." In Deng and Wang, eds., 21–45.

———. 2000. "Hai'an liang'an de minzu zhuyi jiqi qianjing" [Nationalism on Both Sides of the Straits, and Its Prospects]. *Zhanlüe yu guanli [Strategy and Management],* no. 41: 93–104.

Wang Gong'an and Mao Lei. 1998. "Zongxu" [Preface]. In Lou Jie, 1–4.

Wang Gungwu. 1968. "Early Ming Relations with Southeast Asia: A Background Essay." In Fairbank, ed., 34–62.

———. 1991. *China and the Chinese Overseas.* Singapore: Times Academic Press.

———. 1994. "Among Non-Chinese." In Tu, ed., 127–47.

Wang Hongqi. 1996. "*Shanhai jing* dianzhu" [Comments on the *Shanhai jing*]. In *Shanhai jing,* 371–79.

Wang Hui, Leo Du-fan Lee, with Michael M. J. Fischer. 1994. "Is the Public Sphere Unspeakable in Chinese? Can Public Spaces *(gonggong kongjian)* Lead to Public Spheres?" *Public Culture* 6: 598–605.

Wang Jisi. 1995. "'Wenming chongtu' Lunzhan Pingshu" [Comments on the "Clash of Civilizations" Debate]. In Wang Jisi, ed., *Wenming yu guojizhengzhi: Zhongguo xuezhe ping Huntingdunde wenming chongtulun [Civilization and International Politics: Chinese Scholars Comment on Huntington's Clash of Civilizations Thesis],* 18–56. Shanghai: Shanghai renmin chubanshe.

Wang Miaoyang, Yu Xuanmeng, and Manuel B. Dy, eds. 1997. *Civil Society in a Chinese Context.* Washington, D.C.: The Council for Research in Values and Philosophy.

Wang Ning. 1998. "Bianzhe de hua" [Editors Preface]. In Wang and Xue, eds., 1–10.

Wang Ning and Xue Shaoyuan, eds. 1998. *Quanqiuhua yu houzhimin piping [Globalization and Post-Colonial Criticism].* Beijing: Central Translation and Documentation Press.

Wang Pujun. 1997. *Wo de 1997 [My 1997].* Beijing: Jiefangjun wenyi chubanshe.

Wang Shuo. 1997. *Playing for Thrills.* Howard Goldblatt, trans. London: No Exit Press.

———. 2000. *Please Don't Call Me Human.* Howard Goldblatt, trans. London: No Exit Press.

Wang, Qingxin Ken. 2001. "Cultural Idealism and Chinese Foreign Policy." *Asian Thought and Society* 27 (77): 126–47.

Wang Yizhou. 1999. *Huanqiu guandian [Global Perspective].* Beijing: Zhongguo fazhan chubanshe.

Wang Yuechan. 1997. "The Craze for National Learning: Causes, Significance, and Deviations." *Social Sciences in China* 18 (1): 31–33.

Wasserstrom, Jeffrey N. 1994. "Afterword: History, Myth, and the Tales of Tiananmen." In Jeffrey N. Wasserstrom and Elizabeth J. Perry, eds., *Popular Protest and Popular Culture in Modern China,* 2d ed., 279–89. Boulder, Colo.: Westview.

———, and Perry, Elizabeth J., eds. 1994. *Popular Protest and Popular Culture in Modern China.* 2d ed. Boulder, Colo.: Westview.

Watson, Adam. 1992. *The Evolution of International Society: A Comparative Historical Analysis.* London: Routledge.

Watson, Burton. 1963. *Hsun tzu: Basic Writings.* New York: Columbia University Press.

Watts, William. 1999. "Americans Look at Asia," October. www.hluce.org.

Weber, Cynthia. 1995. *Simulating Sovereignty: Intervention, the State, and Symbolic Exchange.* Cambridge: Cambridge University Press.

———. 2001. *International Relations Theory: A Critical Approach.* London: Routledge.

Weber, Max. 1951. *The Religion of China.* New York: The Free Press.

Wei Hung-Chin. 1999. *Taiwan's Democratic Progressive Party and Its Mainland China Policy.* M.A. thesis, University of Durham, England.

Weigelin-Schewiedrzik, Susanne. 1993. "Party Historiography." In Unger, ed., 151–73.

Weldes, Jutta, Mark Laffey, Hugh Gusterson, and Raymond Duval. 1999. "Introduction: Constructing Insecurity." In *Cultures of Insecurity: States, Communities and the Production of Danger,* ed. Jutta Weldes, Mark Laffey, Hugh Gusterson, and Raymond Duval, 1–33. Minneapolis: University of Minnesota Press.

Weller, Robert P. 1999. *Alternative Civilities: Democracy and Culture in China and Taiwan.* Boulder, Colo.: Westview.

Wendt, Alexander. 1999. *The Social Theory of International Politics*. Cambridge: Cambridge University Press.

White Paper on China's National Defense. 1998. Information Office of the State Council, Beijing: Xinhua. (27 July), www.china.org.cn/English/WhitePapers/NationalDefense/NationalDefense-3.html.

White Paper on China's National Defense in 2000. 2000. Beijing: Information Office of the State Council of the People's Republic of China. (October 16). www.chinadaily.com.cn/highlights/paper/ndefence.html.

White Paper on China's National Defense in 2002. 2002. Information Office of the State Council of the People's Republic of China, Beijing: Xinhua. (9 December). http://english.peopledaily.com.cn/features/ndpaper2002/nd.html

White, Geoffrey M. 1997. "Museum/Memorial/Shrine: National Narrative in National Spaces." *Museum Anthropology* 21 (1): 8–27.

White, Gordon, Jude Howell, and Shang Xiaoyuan. 1996. *In Search of Civil Society: Market Reform and Social Change in Contemporary China*. Oxford: Clarendon Press.

Whiting, Allen. 1995. "Chinese Nationalism and Foreign Policy after Deng." *China Quarterly*, no. 142: 295–316.

———. 1998. "Chinese Foreign Policy, Retrospect and Prospect." In Samuel Kim, ed., 287–308.

Wilson, Rob. 1998. "A New Cosmopolitanism Is in the Air: Some Dialectical Twists and Turns." In Cheah and Robbins, eds., 351–61.

"Wired China: The Flies Swarm In." 2000. *Economist*, 22 July: 23–25.

Wolf, Charles, Jr. 1998. "Too Much Government Control." *Wall Street Journal*, 4 February.

Wong Siu-Lin. 1999. "Deciding to Stay, Deciding to Move, Deciding Not to Decide." In Hamilton, ed., 135–51.

World Bank [The International Bank for Reconstruction and Development]. 1993. *The East Asian Miracle: Economic Growth and Public Policy*. New York: Oxford University Press.

Wright, Teresa. 2001. "The Trials and Tribulations of China's First Democracy: The ROC One Year after the Victory of Chen Shui-bian." *Foreign Policy in Focus*. fpif.org/commentary/0102taiwan.html.

Wu Chunguang. 1998. *Taipingyangshangde jiaoli: dangdai Zhongguo de haiyang zhanlue wenti [Pacific Disputes: Contemporary China's Maritime Strategy]*. Beijing: Jinri Zhongguo chubanshe.

Wu Hung. 1997. "The Hong Kong Clock—Public Time-Telling and Political Time/Space." In Abbas and Wu, eds., 329–54.

Xi Mi. 1999. "Opportunity Offered to Look Back and Ahead." *China Daily*, 18 September: 4.

Xi Xi. 1997. *Marvels of a Floating City, and Other Stories*. Eva Hung, ed. Hong Kong: Renditions Paperbacks.

———. 1998. "The Case of Mary." In Martha Cheung, ed., 199–201.

Xia Liping. 2001. "China: A Responsible Great Power." *Journal of Contemporary China* 10 (26): 17–26.

Xianggang zhishi: 500 wenti [Knowledge about Hong Kong: 500 Questions]. 1996. Beijing: Kexue jishu chubanshe.

Xiao Si. 1996. *Xianggang gushi [Hong Kong Stories].* Hong Kong: Oxford University Press.

———. 1998. *Xianggang gushi [Hong Kong Stories].* Ji'nan: Shandong youyi chubanshe.

Xiao Weiyun et al. 2000. "Why the Court of Final Appeal Was Wrong: Comments of the Mainland Scholars on the Judgment of the Court of Final Appeal." In Chan, Fu, and Ghai, eds., 53–59.

Xie Jin. 1997. *Yapian zhanzheng [The Opium War].* Beijing: Yapian zhanzheng yingshi.

Xie Qian. 1998. *Guoxue cidian [Dictionary of Guoxue].* Chengdu: Sichuan renmin chubanshe.

Xu Shen, compiler, and Duan Yucai, commentator. 1981. *Shuowen jiezizhu.* Shanghai: Shanghai guji chubanshe.

Xu, Ben. 1998. "'From Modernity to Chineseness': The Rise of Nativist Cultural Theory in Post-1989 China." *positions: east asia cultural critique* 6 (1): 203–37.

Yahuda, Michael. 1995. *The International Politics of the Asia-Pacific, 1945–1995.* London: Routledge.

———. 1996. *Hong Kong: China's Challenge.* London: Routledge.

———. 1997. "Hong Kong: A New Beginning for China?" In Brown and Foot, eds., 192–210.

Yamazaki, Masakazu. 1996. "Asia, a Civilisation in the Making." *Foreign Affairs* 75 (4): 106–18.

Yan Jiaqi. 1992. *Toward a Democratic China: The Intellectual Autobiography of Yan Jiaqi.* Trans. D. S. K. Hong and D. C. Mair. Honolulu: University of Hawaii Press.

Yan Ping, Jin Yingchun, Zhou Rong, Sun Guoging, Yin Junke, Qiu Fuke, Han Beisha. 1998. *Treasures of Maps—A Collection of Maps in Ancient China.* Harbin: Harbin Cartographic Publishing House.

Yan Xuetong. 1995. *Zhongguo guojia liyi fenxi [An Analysis of China's National Interest].* Tianjin: Renmin chubanshe.

———. 2001. "The Rise of China in Chinese Eyes." *Journal of Contemporary China* 10 (26): 33–40.

———, et al. 1998. *Zhongguo jueqi: guoji huanjing pingzhan [The Rise of China: Analysis of the International Environment].* Tianjin: Renmin chubanshe.

———, et al. 1999. *Zhongguo yu Yatai anquan [China and Asia-Pacific Security].* Beijing: Shishi chubanshe.

Yang Lien-sheng. 1968. "Historical Notes on the Chinese World Order." In Fairbank, ed., 20–33.

Yang Shu'an. 1993. *Confucius*. Beijing: Panda Press.

Yang, Edward. 1994. *Duli shidai [Era of independence*. English title: *A Confucian Confusion]*. Taipei: Good Friends Productions.

Yao Youzhi, Senior Colonel, and Colonel Liu Hongsong. 1998. "Future Security Trends in the Asia-Pacific Region." In Michael Pillsbury, ed., *Chinese Views of Future Warfare*, rev. ed., Washington, D.C.: National Defense University Press. http://www.ndu.edu/inss/books/chinview/chinapt2.html#4.

Yates, Robin D. S. 1994. "Body, Space, Time, and Bureaucracy: Boundary Creation and Control Mechanisms in Early China." In Hay, ed., 56–80.

Yee, Cordell D. K. 1994a. "Reinterpreting Traditional Chinese Geographical Maps." In Harley and Woodward, eds., 35–70.

———. 1994b. "Chinese Maps in Political Culture." In Harley and Woodward, eds., 71–95.

———. 1994c. "Taking the World's Measure: Chinese Maps between Observation and Text." In Harley and Woodward, eds., 96–127.

———. 1994d. "Chinese Cartography among the Arts: Objectivity, Subjectivity, Representation." In Harley and Woodward, eds., 128–69.

———. 1994e. "Traditional Chinese Cartography and the Myth of Westernization." In Harley and Woodward, eds., 170–202.

———. 1994f. "Concluding Remarks: Foundations for a Future History of Chinese Mapping." In Harley and Woodward, eds., 228–30.

———. 1996. "Space and Place: Ways of World-making." In *Space and Place: Mapmaking East and West, Four Hundred Years of Western and Chinese Cartography* (Exhibition Catalogue for the Library of Congress), 7–65. Annapolis, Md.: St. John's College Press.

Yee, Herbert, and Ian Storey, eds. 2002. *The China Threat: Perceptions, Myths, and Reality*. London: RoutledgeCurzon.

Yi Sang-un. 1983. "On the Criticism of Confucianism in Korea." In Korean National Commission for UNESCO, ed., 112–46.

Yoon Yeong-il. 1997. "Silent Workers Doomed to Fail." *Korea Times,* 30 August: 8.

Yu Shengwu and Liu Cunkuan, eds. 1993. *Shijiu shijide Xianggang [Hong Kong in the Nineteenth Century]*. Beijing: Zhonghua shuju.

Yu Shengwu and Liu Shuyong, eds. 1995. *Ershi shijide Xianggang [Hong Kong in the Twentieth Century]*. Beijing: Zhongguo baike quanshu.

Yu Wu and Zhang Changhong, eds. 2002. *Dongnanya yu Huaqiao Huaren yanjiu lunwen suoyin (1996–2000) [Bibliography of Southeast Asian Studies and Diasporic Chinese Studies (1996–2000)]*. Xiamen: Xiamen daxue chubanshe.

Yuan Qishan. 1999. *Sunzi bingfa yu shangzhan [Sunzi's Art of War and Trade Wars]*. Shanghai: Cishu chubanshe.

Yun Sa-soon. 1996. "Confucian Thought and Korean Culture." In Korea Foundation, ed., 108–13.

Yun Seoung-yong. 1996. "Outline of Religious Culture." In *Religious Culture in Korea*, 7–38. Seoul: Holly M.

Yung Dug Hee. 1995. "Publication Note (by the President of the Academy of Korean Studies)." In *Filial Piety and Future Society*, iii–iv.

Zakaria, Fareed. 1994. "Culture Is Destiny: A Conversation with Lee Kuan Yew." *Foreign Affairs* 73 (2): 109–26.

Zha Daojiong. 1995. "A Political Economy of Contemporary U.S.–China Relations." Ph.D. dissertation. University of Hawaii at Manoa.

———. 2001. "Security in the South China Sea." *Alternatives* 26 (1): 33–52.

Zhang Guolong et al. 1998. *Wenming yu yeman [Civilization and Barbarism]*. Beijing: Shehui kexue wenlian chubanshe.

Zhang, Tiejun. 2002. "Chinese Strategic Culture: Traditional and Present Features." *Comparative Strategy* 21 (2): 73–80.

Zhang Xiaobo and Song Qiang. 1996. "A China That Can Say No to America." *New Perspectives Quarterly*; reprinted in *Bangkok Post*, 1 September: 7.

Zhang Xudong, ed. 1998. *Intellectual Politics in Post-Tiananmen China* [special issue]. Social Text 55 16 (2).

Zhang, Yongjin. 1998. *China in International Society Since 1949*. London: Macmillan.

———. 2001. "System, Empire, and State in Chinese International Relations." *Review of International Studies* 27 (December): 43–63.

Zhang Yuan. 1993. *Beijing zazhong [Beijing Bastards]*. Beijing/Hong Kong: Beijing Bastards Group.

Zhang Zangzang. 1996. "Zhongguoren: lengzhanhou shidaide qingganji zhengzhi xuanchi" [Chinese People: Emotional and Political Choices for the Post–Cold War Era]. In Song Qiang et al., 55–156.

Zhao Guanglan. 1996. "Kongzi xueshuo zai 21 shiji" [Confucian doctrine in the Twenty-First Century], *Rujia yu ershiyi shiji jinian Kongzi yanchang 2545 zhounian guoji ruxue taolunhui huiyi wenji [Confucian Studies and the Twenty-First Century: Proceedings of the International Confucian Studies Association's Conference to Commemorate the 2545th Birthday of Confucius]*. Vol. 1, 120–25. Beijing: Huaxia chubanshe.

Zhao Suisheng. 1997. "Chinese Intellectuals' Quest for National Greatness and Nationalistic Writing in the 1990s." *China Quarterly*, no. 152: 725–45.

290 · BIBLIOGRAPHY

———. 1998a. *Power Competition in East Asia*. New York: St. Martin's Press.

———. 1998b. "A State-led Nationalism: The Patriotic Education Campaign in Post-Tiananmen China." *Communist and Post-Communist Studies* 31 (3): 287–302.

———. 1999. "Taiwan: From Peaceful Offensive to Coercive Strategy." In Deng and Wang, eds., 211–38.

———. 2000. "Chinese Nationalism and Its International Orientations." *Political Science Quarterly* 115 (1): 1–33.

Zhao Wenlie. 1995. "Dui 'Zhongguo jingjiquan' gezhong yilunde pingshu" [Comments on the various discourses of the "Chinese Economic Sphere"]. *Huaqiao Huaren lishi yanjiu [Historical Studies of Overseas Chinese]*, no. 1: 63–70.

Zheng Degang. 1999. "Weile napian lansede gutu—Nansha qundao xing (Xia)" [This Ancient Piece of Blue Territory—Traveling in the Spratly Archipelago (part 2)]. *Renmin ribao*, 22 June.

Zheng, Yongnian. 1999. *Discovering Chinese Nationalism in China: Modernization, Identity, and International Relations*. Cambridge: Cambridge University Press.

Zheng Ziyue. 1947. *Nanhai qundao dili zhilue [The Geography of the Archepelagoes of the South China Sea]*. Shanghai: Shangwu yinshuguan.

Zhonggong yongyang Taiwan gongzuo bangongshi [and] Gouwuyuan Taiwan shiwu bangongshi [Chinese Communist Party Taiwan Office and State Council Taiwan Affairs Office]. 1998. *Zhongguo Taiwan wenti (ganbu duben) [China's Taiwan Problem (a Reader for Party Cadres)]*. Beijing: Jiuzhou tushu chubanshe.

Zhongguo geming bowuguan [Chinese Revolutionary History Museum], ed. 1997. *Zhongguo: cong churu zou dao huihuang, 1840–1997* [China: From Shame to Glory, 1984–1997]. 4 vols. Beijing: Zhongguo minzu sheying yishu chubanshe.

Zhongguo gemingshi chenlie zilao [Chinese Revolutionary History Exhibition Materials]. 1990. Beijing: Zhongguo geming bowuguan.

Zhongguo guofangbao [Chinese National Defense Newspaper], ed. 2001. *Taiwan junli xiezhen [The Truth about Taiwan's Military Power]*. Beijing: Changzheng chubanshe.

Zhongguo renmin kangri zhanzheng jinianguan [Museum of the War of Chinese People's Resistance against Japan (Catalogue)]. 1998. Beijing: Zhongguo heping chubanshe.

Zhou Shan and Zhang Chunbo, eds. 1997. *Tushuo Zhonghua bainian guochi lu [A Record of Pictures and Stories of China's Century of National Humiliation]*. Lanzhou: Gansu qingnian chubanshe.

Zhou Yizhi. 1996. *Xianggang de wenhua [Hong Kong Culture]*. Beijing: Xinhua.

Zhuangzi jinzhu jinyi. 1985. Chen Guying, ed. Beijing: Zhonghua shuju.
Zongzheng lianluobu bian [General Political Liason Department, eds.].
1997. *Xianggang jiben qingkuang: budui zhengzhi jiaoyu cancao cailiao*
[Hong Kong's Basic Situation: Reference Materials for the Political Edu-
cation of the Troops]. Beijing: Huayi chubanshe (restricted distribution).

INTERVIEWS

Abbas, Ackbar, Professor of Comparative Literature, University of Hong
Kong: 28 October 1999.
Cho Soon-Kyoung, Professor of Women's Studies, Ewha Women's Univer-
sity, Seoul: 29 July 1997.
Fok Kai Cheong, Professor of History, University of Macau (interviewed in
Hong Kong): 30 October 1999.
Hahm Chaibong, Professor of Political Science, Yonsei University, Seoul:
3 September 1997.
Han Sang-Jin, Professor of Sociology, Seoul National University, Seoul:
6 August 1997.
Hwang Kyung-Sig, Professor of Philosophy, Seoul National University, Seoul:
1 September 1997 and 5 September 1997.
Interviews 1999, in Beijing and Shanghai: September–November.
Interviews 2000, in Bangkok and Phuket: December.
Interviews 2001, in Beijing: April.
Interviews 2002, in Xiamen, China: May.
Interviews 2003, in Durham, England: March.
Jang Dong-Jin, Professor of Political Science, Yonsei University, Seoul:
3 September 1997.
Kim Cheol-Hyeon, Director of the Religious Affairs Division, Ministry of
Culture and Sports, Seoul: 13 August 1997.
Kim Hong-kyung, Professor of Philosophy, Sung Kyun Kwan University,
Seoul: 30 August 1997.
Kwon Tai-Joon, Secretary-General, Korean National Commission for
UNESCO, Seoul: 6 August 1997.
Lee Chong-Suk, Adviser, the *Dong-A Ilbo,* Seoul: 7 August 1997.
Lee Seung-hwan, Professor of Philosophy, Korea University, Seoul: 30 July
1997.
Ng, Louis, Curator, Hong Kong Museum of History, Hong Kong: 4 Novem-
ber 1999.
Park, Myoung-kyu, Professor of Sociology, Seoul National University, Seoul:
8 August 1997.
Pun Ngai, Research Assistant Professor, Centre for Asian Studies, Univer-
sity of Hong Kong, Hong Kong: 30 October 1999.

Shin Yoo-Keun, Professor of Management, Seoul National University, Seoul: 4 September 1997.

Shin Young-ha, Professor of Sociology, Seoul National University, Seoul: 12 August 1997.

Suwanna Satha-Anand, Professor of Philosophy, Chulalongkorn University, Bangkok: 27 August 1999 and 29 December 2000.

Valencia, Mark, Senior Fellow, East-West Center, Honolulu: 26 November 1999.

Yoon Keum-jin, Director of Publications Department, Korea Foundation, Seoul: 4 September 1997.

Index

WILLIAM A. CALLAHAN is senior lecturer of international politics and director of the Centre for Contemporary Chinese Studies at the University of Durham, England. He has been a visiting scholar at Harvard University, Renmin University of China, Chulalongkorn University (Thailand), Seoul National University (South Korea), the University of Hawaiokino'i, and the University of Hong Kong. He is the author of *Imagining Democracy: Reading "The Events of May" in Thailand*; *Poll Watching, Elections, and Civil Society in Southeast Asia*; and articles in journals such as *International Organization, Millennium, Alternatives, Asia Survey,* and the *Journal of Contemporary China.*